(UN)BELIEVING IN MODERN SOCIETY

(Un)Believing in Modern Society

Religion, Spirituality, and Religious-Secular Competition

JÖRG STOLZ
University of Lausanne, Switzerland

JUDITH KÖNEMANN
University of Münster, Germany

MALLORY SCHNEUWLY PURDIE
University of Lausanne, Switzerland

THOMAS ENGLBERGER
University of Lausanne, Switzerland

MICHAEL KRÜGGELER
University of Münster, Germany

ASHGATE

Published by
Ashgate Publishing Limited
Wey Court East
Union Road
Farnham
Surrey, GU9 7PT
England

Ashgate Publishing Company
110 Cherry Street
Suite 3-1
Burlington, VT 05401-3818
USA

www.ashgate.com

British Library Cataloguing in Publication Data
A catalogue record for this book is available from the British Library

The Library of Congress has cataloged the printed edition as follows:
Stolz, Jörg.
   (Un)believing in Modern Society: Religion, Spirituality, and Religious-Secular
   Competition / by Jörg Stolz, Judith Könemann, Mallory Schneuwly Purdie,
   Thomas Englberger, Michael Krüggeler.
      pages   cm
   Includes bibliographical references and index.
   1. Switzerland – Religion. 2. Religion. 3. Spirituality. I. Title.
   BL980.S9S76 2015
   306.609494–dc23   2015017489

ISBN: 9781472461285 (hbk)
ISBN: 9781472461292 (ebk – PDF)
ISBN: 9781472461308 (ebk – ePUB)

Printed in the United Kingdom by Henry Ling Limited,
at the Dorset Press, Dorchester, DT1 1HD

Contents

Figures

List of Tables

Contributors

Jörg Stolz is professor of the Sociology of Religion at the University of Lausanne. Substantively, he works on the description and explanation of different forms of religiosity, evangelicalism, secularization, and comparison of religious groups across religious traditions. Methodologically, he uses quantitative, qualitative and mixed-method approaches. Theoretically, he stands in a tradition of comprehensive and explanatory sociology. He has written *Die Zukunft der Reformierten: Gesellschaftliche Megatrends – kirchliche Reaktionen* (together with Edmée Ballif), has edited an issue of *Social Compass* on 'Salvation goods and religious markets', and has edited *Religions as Brands: New Perspectives on the Marketization of Religion and Spirituality* (with Jean-Claude Usunier). He is the author of many articles in leading sociology journals, among which 'Explaining religiosity: towards a unified theoretical framework' in the *British Journal of Sociology*. Currently, he is the president of the International Society for the Sociology of Religion.

Judith Könemann is professor of practical theology in the Faculty of Catholic Theology at the University of Münster, Germany. She works on the description and explanation of various forms of individual religiosity, and religion in the public sphere. Methodologically she works with qualitative and mixed-method approaches. She has written: '*Ich wünschte, ich wäre gläubig, glaub ich*': *Zugänge zu Religion und Religiosität in der Lebensführung der späten Moderne*, has edited several books, such as *Bildung und Gerechtigkeit: Warum religiöse Bildung politisch sein muss* (co-authored with Norbert Mette) and is the author of many articles in leading peer-reviewed (theological) journals, including 'Religion and All-Day Schools', in *Journal of Empirical Theology*, and 'Religious reasons in the public sphere: an empirical study of religious actors' argumentative patterns in Swiss direct democratic campaigns', in *European Political Science Review* (co-authored with A. Bächtiger and A. Jödicke). She is a member of the Cluster of Excellence on Religion and Politics in Pre-Modern and Modern Cultures, at the University of Münster and a board member of the Centre for Religion and Modernity at the University of Münster.

Mallory Schneuwly Purdie holds a PhD in Sociology of Religion and Applied Study of Religion. She is a researcher at the Institute for the Social Sciences of Religions at the University of Lausanne. Among other research interests, she studies the impact of religious and ethnic pluralisation in institutions (such as hospitals and prisons), minority Islamic movements in Europe (such as the Muslim Brotherhood and Salafi movements) as well as Islamic mobilizations in public spheres. She is the president of the Research Group on Islam in Switzerland. She is the author of many articles and book chapters. Among her recent publications: with co-author Andrea Rota (2014) 'Religion, education and the State: Rescaling confessional boundaries in Switzerland' in Stan Brunn (ed.) *The Changing World Religion Map*, New York, Springer (2013); and 'Formatting Islam versus mobilizing Islam in prison: Evidence from the Swiss case'.

Thomas Englberger, MA, has worked on the description of religiosity in Switzerland, especially on Roman Catholicism, and on the pluralization of values and religiosity. Following a qualitative approach, he has written (together with M. Krueggeler et al.) *Solidarität und Religion: Was bewegt Menschen in Solidaritätsgruppen?* Analysing and comparing different quantitative surveys about religiosity, he has written (together with A. Dubach et al.) *Lebenswerte: Religion und Lebensführung in der Schweiz*. He is author (together with M. Jakobs et al.) of *Konfessioneller Religionsunterricht in multireligiöser Gesellschaft* focusing on attitudes of religious education teachers in Switzerland.

Michael Krüggeler, PhD, is a sociologist of religion who has worked both quantitatively and qualitatively on the secularization and individualization of religion. He is a co-author of the books *Jede/r ein Sonderfall? Religion in der Schweiz – Ergebnisse einer Repräsentativbefragung* and *Solidarität und Religion: Was bewegt Menschen in Solidaritätsgruppen?*. He has published many articles in both sociology and (practical) theology journals, for example, 'Religion, Individualisierung und Moderne: Empirische religionssoziologische Studien aus der Schweiz' in *Internationale Katholische Zeitschrift* Communio 31 (2003). Currently, he works as a scientific collaborator at the chair of Sociology of Religion and the Centre for Religion and Modernity at the University of Münster, Westphalia. At present, he is working on the issue of the development of the two major Christian churches in Germany after World War II.

Preface

While Grace Davie famously asked if 'believing without belonging' was the future of religion, our study shows that 'unbelieving' may well be a more probable outcome in the long run. However, not everyone will start unbelieving, and certainly not immediately – hence our book that proposes a new theory of religious-secular competition, a typology of 'four types of (un-)belief' and a historical account, grounded both qualitatively and quantitatively, of how and why religion and spirituality have changed in Switzerland since the 1960s.

The present book appeared in 2014 in German under the title 'Religion und Spiritualität in der Ich-Gesellschaft. Vier Gestalten des (Un-)Glaubens'. (TVZ/NZN) and in 2015 in French under the title 'Religion et spiritualité à l'ère de l'ego. Profils de l'institutionnel, de l'alternatif, du distancié et du séculier'. The results have led to much publicity in Switzerland and have been reviewed (sometimes on the front pages) of the *Neue Zürcher Zeitung*, the *Neue Zürcher Zeitung am Sonntag*, *24heures*, *Le Temps* and other newspapers.

Our typology has especially met with much success among journalists, church leaders, and the general public and is often cited when religion in Switzerland in general is discussed.

While the results of our study evidently concern the Swiss case, we believe that most general – theoretical and empirical – points we make about (un-) believing in modern society can be generalized to almost all western countries. For example, the four types we identify (institutional, alternative, distanced, secular) can be found in most western countries and have been described by various researchers in national and international studies. However, in our study one can for the first time see a representative yet in-depth description and explanation of the types with both quantitative and qualitative data. We also believe that our way of linking quantitative and qualitative data may encourage other researchers to conduct similar studies in other countries. This is why we have decided to publish this English version of our book.

Apart from writing a new foreword, we have also slightly rewritten the introduction, chapter 9, as well as the conclusion, for greater clarity. Furthermore, we have added some information to the appendix concerning the 'mixed methods' approach and our explanatory Chapter 9.

The data that our book is based on were taken from the project "Religiosity in the modern world: construction, conditions and social change: a qualitative and quantitative study of individual religiosity in Switzerland", a project which was supported by the Swiss National Science Foundation (SNF) as part of National

Research Programme 58. From this emerged a publicly accessible final report,[1] and a special issue published by the SNF.[2]

This book would not have been possible without the support of many people, and we would like to thank the following for their support, assistance and cooperation. First, the 1302 interviewees, who reported, sometimes in qualitative and sometimes in quantitative surveys, how they felt in relation to questions of religiosity and spirituality.

Bettina Combet, Eva Marzi, Emilie Fleury and Julie Montandon carried out excellent additional interviews and transcriptions for our project. Ingrid Storm participated in the project for three months as a post-doctoral researcher at the Observatoire des Religione en Suisse, and had a decisive influence on the typology that we ultimately chose. Her brilliant objections forced us (reluctantly) to throw everything overboard and to start all over again!

The Swiss National Science Foundation was a source of great support. We would especially like to thank the members of the steering committee of SNF 58, and in particular Christoph Bochinger and Christian Mottas. It was very satisfying to be able to count on the efficient and judicious management of the overall programme for a project that was far from easy.

For the development of the additional quantitative questionnaire and the evaluation of the ISSP data, we worked very fruitfully with FORS and especially with Dominique Joye, Marlène Sapin and Alexandre Pollien.

In the recruitment of the qualitative interview partners, we worked with the survey institute LINK and wish to thank Isabelle Kaspar and Ermelinda Lopez for their excellent support.

For the announcement of the results of the project, we worked very well with Almut Bonhage, Célia Francillon, Xavier Pilloud and Urs Hafner.

A number of people read and critically commented on parts of the manuscript at various stages of its formation, and their (sometimes) persistent objections allowed us to avoid many mistakes and pitfalls. We would like to mention here Christoph Bochinger, Olivier Favre, Denise Hafner Stolz, Stefan Huber, Daniel Kosch, Gert Pickel, Detlef Pollack, Ingrid Storm and Monika Wohlrab-Sahr. Stefan Rademacher read through the final manuscript once more and commented carefully on it. Our discussions with Urs Altermatt, Mark Chaves, Philippe Portier, David Voas and Jean-Paul Willaime were also very important to us at critical moments of the project.

The results of the project were presented and discussed at the ISSR conferences in Aix-en-Provence and Turku, and at the ISSRC conference on "Religions as Brands" in Lausanne, as well as in lectures at the GSRL (Paris),

---

[1]   Available at http://www.nfp58.ch/files/downloads/Schlussbericht__Stolz.pdf.
[2]   Available   at   http://www.nfp58.ch/files/downloads/NFP58_Themenheft04_DE.pdf.

at the CSRES (Strasbourg), at the Institute of Sociology of the University of Zurich, at the Institute of Religious Studies at the University of Bayreuth, at the graduate class "Secularity" at the University of Leipzig. These discussions greatly enriched the project. David West has translated the text from German to English in an exemplary fashion. Christine Rhone and Bryan Campbell have proofread the book and helped us to add some final details. Sarah Lloyd and David Shervington from Ashgate were very professional in their editorial support. The photography used on the cover of the book was provided by Jean-Charles Rochat, while the layout was carried out by Kirsten Weissenberg. We dedicate our book to Roland J. Campiche and Alfred Dubach.

Lausanne, 2 January 2015

JÖRG STOLZ,
JUDITH KÖNEMANN,
MALLORY SCHNEUWLY PURDIE,
THOMAS ENGLBERGER,
MICHAEL KRÜGGELER

Chapter 1
Introduction: Religion and Spirituality in the Me-Society

Jörg Stolz, Judith Könemann

The way to God is by our selves. (Phineas Fletcher)

Introduction

However we characterize today's society, no sociological description can avoid assigning a prominent place to the individual person, to the *individual*. Never before has the individual been able to make such a wide variety of decisions on his or her own, whether educational, political, economic, lifestyle-related, sexual – or religious. Never before has the individual been solely responsible for so much, or has had so much to cope and deal with alone when things in life do not go to plan. And never before have individuals had to draw the meaning of experiences and actions so much from within themselves and from the consequences of their own decisions. It is in this sense that we truly are living in a me-society.

Central Questions

Formulated as briefly as possible, our study analyses the influence that this me-society has had on religiosity, spirituality and secularity. More precisely, we are concerned with exploring:

- which central religious and social types we can identify in society. By *types*, we mean large groups of people who characterize themselves through common perceptions, values and social-structural features, as well as through the social boundaries that they create;[1]
- which religious and spiritual beliefs, practices, values, relationships to religious suppliers, and perceptions these religious and social types have;

---

[1]   Altermatt (1981), Mayer (2007), Schulze (1995).

- how the religiosity, spirituality and secularity of these types have changed in the last few decades, and how this change can be explained.

Each chapter of our book provides part of the answer to these questions.

Answers So Far

There is of course already a large literature which attempts to describe and explain the religious and social changes of the last few decades in Western European countries. The best-known theories today are secularization theory, individualization theory, and market theory.[2] According to *secularization theory*, elements of modernization have led to the declining significance of religion in both public and private life.[3] According to *individualization theory*, what we are witnessing is not so much a decline in religiosity, but a situation in which religiosity is becoming ever more individual and multiform.[4] Finally, *market theory* draws on economic insights to explain changes in the domain of religion. According to this theory, we are increasingly living in a religious market with religious suppliers (churches) and religious customers (believers). Since the religious market in European countries is heavily regulated (i.e., there is no free market), people are increasingly distancing themselves from religiosity. For proponents of this theory, it is only when the market is liberalized and new suppliers can enter the market that a religious revival might be possible again.[5] However, all three theories are, as we will show in this book, only convincing in part. Above all, they each fail to explain satisfactorily the phenomena in their *entirety* – the fact, that is, that we can see not only religious decline but also religious revival, more religious individualization but also more fundamentalism, and more religious freedom but also more religious indifference. It is precisely here that the importance of our own contribution lies, for we attempt to give a more satisfactory answer to the central set of questions posed above, and we do so by providing a typology, a theory, and a thesis.

A New Typology

A first part of our answer to the question of how people in the me-society experience religiosity, spirituality and secularity lies in a new typology. We

---

[2]   See the edited volume Pollack & Olson (2008).
[3]   Dobbelaere (2002), Wilson (1982).
[4]   Luckmann (1967).
[5]   Iannaccone (1991), Stark & Bainbridge (1985).

distinguish on an abstract level among four types: the institutional, the alternative, the distanced, and the secular. Each of these types can then be further distinguished into subtypes. The purpose of the typology is first of all to simplify the complex world in which we live. If we listen carefully to how people in Switzerland and other Western European countries talk about their religiosity, spirituality or irreligiosity, we are immediately confronted by a huge diversity of opinion. Here we give just a few examples. The 50-year-old widow Mima has distanced herself from the Catholic Church as a result of various deaths in her family. For reasons not entirely clear to Mima herself, she was angry at fate, God and the Church. Quite different is Barnabé, a 58-year-old farmer who converted to Christianity as a young man, joined a free church with his wife, and now holds the office of elder in this community. No such stability can be found in the comparatively short life story of the 24-year-old student Julie, who was brought up as a Catholic, went through an atheist phase, was then attracted by esotericism and Buddhism, and has become interested in Christianity again (this time Orthodox, though) since the sudden death of her father. The 39-year-old engineer Siegfried tells a different story again. When he and his wife asked themselves whether they wanted to have their two children baptized, the answer was, *no*. And so the couple came to the logical conclusion – and left the church.

If we consider the forms of religiosity mentioned here in their biographical contexts, what we notice first of all is the uniqueness of each person. But, if we then multiply the examples, it soon becomes clear that, behind the individual life stories, we can identify perpetually recurring social forms which can be described as types and milieus. In this book, we try to show that Mima, Barnabé, Julie and Siegfried belong to different and easily distinguishable religious and social types and milieus, and that these types and milieus can help us to come to a better understanding of the religious changes that Switzerland has undergone in recent decades. What is important to stress here is that we can find the central properties created by the *me-society* identified at the beginning of this chapter in all groups. In all types, for example, people tell us how they rely completely on themselves with regard to their beliefs and practices. Nonetheless, the contents, forms of practice, and beliefs of each of the separate types differ drastically from those of the other types.

A New Theory

We are concerned here, though, not only with *describing* the types, but also with *explaining* them. To that end, we present in Chapter 2 a new theory of religious-secular competition. According to this theory, we find in all societies religious and secular (collective) actors who compete for three things: power in society, power within groups/organizations/milieus, and individual demand.

To be able to survive in this competition, the collective actors employ different strategies. They try, for example, to mobilize their members, to begin political campaigns, to provoke scandals, to enter coalitions, to offer attractive goods, etc. They are influenced by four external factors: by scientific and technical innovations (e.g., the invention of television), by social innovations (e.g., the invention of democracy), by major events (e.g., wars), and by socio-demographic forces (e.g., differing birth rates). The struggles lead in effect to diverse results, and it is the goal of the theory to explain these results. In addition to the victories and defeats of the various competitors, there are also stalemates and agreements, as well as situations of differentiation and de-differentiation, of individualization and collectivization, of secularization and re-sacralization. The theory can only provide satisfactory explanations, though, if it is adapted to the particular historical development of the society concerned, which is why we outline in Chapter 2 the events in the story of secular-religious competition in Switzerland since about 1800. From the theory thereby made concrete by historical constraints, we can derive a series of hypotheses that we then test in the course of our work.

The Thesis of Regime Change of Religious-Secular Competition

The third part of our response to the question outlined above is the forwarding of our central thesis; namely, that in the 1960s there occurred a regime change of the religious-secular competition. According to our thesis, there was a cultural revolution in this period which we will denote as a change from a 'regime of industrial society' to a 'regime of the me-society'.[6] Against the backdrop of an unprecedented economic boom from 1945 to 1973 (the 'economic miracle'), a cultural revolution occurred in the 1960s in which authorities of all kinds were attacked, and the individual as an autonomous entity was given centre stage. The ideas of subjectivity, freedom and self-determination which had increasingly caught on since the Enlightenment became the shaping forces in people's lives. The individual thereby became the ultimate authority on decisions of all kinds, whether political, familial, economic, consumerist, sexual – or even also religious. It is true that we find religious-secular competition on all three levels – for power in society, for power within groups/organizations/milieus, and for individual demand – in both the old as well as the new regime. But what has changed is that the central point around which competition revolves is now completely different. In the old regime of industrial society, religion and denomination were a central and collective characteristic of identity for society,

---

[6]   We see our theory as complementary to the important historical studies of McLeod (2007) and Altermatt (2009).

while Christianity was regarded as a fundamental feature that unified society. In the new regime of the me-society, however, this is no longer the case. Instead, religion and denomination are now seen as a private and optional characteristic of identity, while Christianity is being increasingly viewed as just one religion among others. In the collectivist regime of industrial society, the sovereignty of Christianity was taken as given, and the most important religious-secular struggles revolved around the question of how much space could be taken by Protestants or Catholics, or how strongly Christianity was besieged by alternative value systems. In the individualistic regime of the me-society, though, the most important religious-secular struggle is that which relates to individual demand. Religious practice is now no longer a social expectation; it is no longer something that belongs to the public person. Rather, it has been relegated to the domain of leisure time, where it faces stiff competition from other forms of 'leisure activity' and 'self-development'.[7]

The new regime of the me-society has led in the last few decades to different *effects* on both an individual as well as a collective level. On the *individual level*, there are tendencies of 'secular drift' and of advancing religious-secular individualization and consumerization. In many areas of the competition between the secular and the religious, individuals are choosing the secular rather than the religious options. Other ways to spend time (such as sleeping in or playing football) are displacing going to church on Sunday morning; secular professions (such as psychologists and personal coaches) are taking the place of the church minister; secular explanations (such as the Big Bang and the theory of evolution) are increasingly seen as being more plausible than religious explanations (e.g., creation). In terms of upbringing in particular, the religious-secular competition and the new freedoms granted to children have led to a situation in which religious options are now no longer chosen at all. In effect, each new generation is now more secular than the previous. In addition, religious individualization and consumerization have now prevailed to such an extent that people usually see themselves as the 'final authority' in religious matters, and believe that they do not have the right to impose religious ideas on anyone, and not even on their own children. Individuals should choose for themselves, and should 'consume' whatever they consider to be the most important thing for them.

On the *collective level*, the effects of the new regime of the me-society can be seen in the fact that religious types or subtypes can succeed primarily either by waging battle on the secular competition or by trying to outdo this competition on its own field. This is best achieved either through withdrawal, that is, excluding competing secular opportunities, as is practised by the free churches; or, through completely adopting the market form, by presenting everything on offer as a good to be bought and sold, as is practised by suppliers

---

[7]   Luhmann (1982).

to the alternative type. And various mixtures of the two are also tried out – with varying degrees of success.

Method[8]

In some ways, the scientific study of religious and social change resembles detective work. Just like a detective, the social researcher must rely on existing facts and circumstantial evidence from which he or she must draw – always with a degree of uncertainty – conclusions (inferences). The more independent evidence there is that points in the same direction, the more certain the detective will be that his or her conclusions are sound. This technique is often called 'triangulation' by researchers, and it is of the greatest importance for our study.[9] To make our findings as reliable as possible, we rely on a variety of very different types of data. Our most important source of data is a 'mixed methods' survey which was conducted in 2008–09. In this survey, 1229 randomly selected people living in Switzerland were given standardized questionnaires on religiosity and spirituality.[10] This quantitative part of the study can be considered representative for the Swiss population. In addition, 73 people (again selected randomly, but this time chosen according to quotas) were interviewed in semi-open interviews on the same issues. These interview partners told us in detail in interviews lasting around 60–90 minutes about how they grew up, what they think now about religiosity and spirituality, what is important to them in life, and how they bring up their children. This combination of the two parts of the study has allowed us to triangulate quantitative and qualitative data: statistical correlations can be linked to individual narratives and modes of action, so that what we thereby obtain is a coherent overall picture of religiosity, spirituality and irreligiosity in Switzerland.[11] Besides this main study, we also drew on census data, and on 22 representative surveys of religiosity in Switzerland.[12] Among these surveys, the two previous studies from 1989 and 1999 are particularly important

---

[8]   For more details on the method used, see the Appendix.

[9]   Hammersley (2008).

[10]   This in the framework of MOSAiCH, which stands for Mesures et Observation Sociologiques des Attitudes en Suisse. This is a survey which is financed by the Swiss National Science Foundation and which is carried out every two years. MOSAiCH systematically records a number of sociodemographic variables, two modules of the International Social Survey Programme (ISSP), and a specific module for Switzerland. In 2009, MOSAiCH included the ISSP modules Religion III and Social Inequality IV. In 2009, the sample comprised 1229 people.

[11]   Kelle (2007), Tashakkori & Teddlie (1998).

[12]   The earliest survey was from 1961. See Thomas Englberger's internal research report 3, 'Further data sets for Switzerland'.

because our study directly replicates many of their questions.[13] Finally, for the purposes of comparison, we have also consulted the data from a representative and mixed-methods study of Protestant free churches in Switzerland.[14] Let us add a word on statistics. When trying to analyse the beliefs and practices of hundreds of individuals at different points in time, the use of complex statistical procedures such as cluster analysis, multiple regressions, factor analysis etc. are of great help and we have used them extensively. Nevertheless, we have tried to minimize the presence of complex statistics in our text in order to make our story as easily comprehensible as possible. The differences we report are all statistically significant,[15] and we have always analysed our data in multivariate models, 'controlling' for all kinds of background variables.[16] Again, though, in our presentation we have opted for graphs and tables that show the important points of our story in as simple and striking a way as possible.[17]

What is New?

Although in many ways we build on previous work, we nonetheless seek to make a new contribution in various respects. Firstly, we provide a new *description* of the religious and spiritual landscape of society. We hope that our typology of the institutional, alternative, distanced and secular, together with their subtypes, can help future research and will prove to be a useful resource by which practitioners can orientate themselves. In contrast to previous studies, we have made especially sure not only to investigate the highly (and, above all, institutionally) religious, but also to give due and proper attention to alternative spirituality, to secular thinkers, and to the very large, but so far rather neglected, group of people who are distanced from the church. Secondly, we provide a new *explanation* of religious change, one which we call the theory of religious-secular competition. For us, this theory explains the existing phenomena better than competing theories, and it can also be dovetailed better with historical analyses. Finally, we are also entering new territory with our *method*, in that we use both

---

[13]   Campiche (2010, 2004), Dubach & Campiche (1993).

[14]   Stolz, Favre, Gachet & Buchard (2013).

[15]   At least with $p < .05$, but mostly with $p < .01$.

[16]   Our standard control variables were age, sex, education, urban-rural, nationality, language region, and confession/religion. Depending on the specific research questions, additional control or intervening variables were used. In the analyses using the typologies, we routinely analysed the data with both levels of the typology. For more information on data analysis, see the Appendix.

[17]   Note, also, that additional tables for every empirical chapter are available in the Appendix. Many figures noted in passing in the main text can be inspected more closely in these tables.

qualitative and quantitative data, and represent the phenomena both in statistics and in their subjectively perceived reality.

Limitations and Our Own Position

Scientific statements are characterized by the fact that their range has to be reflected with care. A first limitation of our study is that our results relate only to the individual level. Communities and organizations – such as churches – appear only from the perspective of individual people. A second important limitation is that our typology and explanation are limited to Christian, alternative and non-denominational religiosity or irreligiosity. For simple methodological and organizational reasons, we therefore exclude from our analysis members of non-Christian religions and of minority religions in Switzerland (such as Islam, Buddhism, Hinduism, Judaism, and new religious movements). To include all these would have exceeded the framework of our study and have required a very different (and much more complex) research design. Besides, a number of research projects on these different religions have already been carried out as part of the National Research Programme (NFP 58) on 'Religious communities, the state and society' (which has also supported this study).[18] A third limitation concerns the range of validity of our findings: although we believe very strongly that our main results are applicable in many ways to what is happening in other Western European countries, they are still, strictly speaking, only valid for Switzerland since about 1930.

Finally, let us give a word on our position as scientists. We take here a decidedly *sociological* position with regard to religion, one which considers religious and secular phenomena 'from the outside'. This is simply to allow us to understand and explain the phenomena as accurately as possible, and we do try, as best we can, to keep our own values out of the analysis. We therefore refrain from commenting on whether the shrinkage or growth of a certain milieu is to be welcomed or regarded with concern, and we do not represent a particular religious, spiritual or secular position.[19] A further feature of our study

---

[18]   See http://www.nfp58.ch/d_index.cfm. Baumann & Stolz (2007a) provide an overview of the religious diversity of Switzerland.

[19]   We therefore strive for what Max Weber called *Wertfreiheit* (freedom from values). The discussions of the past few decades have made it clear that neutrality of values can never be fully achieved, but only represents an ideal which we can aspire to in a greater or lesser degree. In the research question, the methodology, and the interpretation of the data, the value judgments of the researcher are always already present. Yet, freedom from values is more than just a pious hope, and in concrete practice it can usually be seen quite quickly whether researchers are guided by what 'is' or by what 'should be'. To control personal value judgments as far as possible, explanatory social science also relies on the reflexivity of the

is therefore its so-called 'methodological agnosticism',[20] by which is meant that we exclude, for methodological reasons, the question of the truth of specific religious, spiritual or secular positions.[21]

Presentation and Plan of the Book

Sociologists, so the saying goes, merely say what everyone already knows, only in a language that no one understands. In this book, we have all made every effort to prove the opposite and to present our statements in a language which is easy to understand. Although we could not abandon scientific terminology completely, we have tried to explain difficult concepts as simply as possible. More complex methodological considerations and statistical analyses can be found in the Appendix.

A note on how we quote our respondents. Longer quotations are positioned separately from the main text, and are accompanied by the (anonymized) identity, age and denomination of the person quoted. Chapter 3 and the Appendix provide brief descriptions of the respondents, so that interested readers can reconstruct a further personal context (again, anonymized) for the individual respondents. Short quotations in the text are enclosed in quotation marks, and we do not always indicate who said what is quoted. We are concerned here with showing how the same situation can often be formulated in the most diverse ways.

In Chapter 2, we present previous theories, our own theory of competition, and hypotheses derived from this theory. Chapter 3 presents an overview of the four types or 'forms of (un)belief'. In Chapter 4, we describe the socio-structural characteristics and self-descriptions of the types, while in Chapter 5 we explore their religiosity (beliefs, practices, experiences) and in Chapter 6 we discuss their relationships to values. Thereafter, we show how the types differ from each other in terms of how they relate to religious suppliers (Chapter 7) and how they perceive the multi-religious society (Chapter 8). Finally, in Chapter 9, we return to our explanatory model by testing empirically the hypotheses from Chapter 2. Chapter 10 then combines the results and concludes with an outlook on the future of religion and spirituality in the me-society.

---

researcher, on methodology which is independent of the researcher, and on the criticism of other researchers. See Adorno (1989), Albert (1984), Weber (1988 (1922)).

[20]   Hamilton (2001).

[21]   Such issues may well be interesting – and they are often the issues which are primarily responsible for moving religious, spiritual or secular people. But, in our view, the sociology of religion should be content here also with neutrality in order to devote itself entirely to the task of description and explanation. For discussion of this, see Berger (1990 (1967)), Bocking (2005), Cox (2003), Porpora (2006), Smart (1973), Stark (1999a).

Chapter 2

A Theory of Religious-Secular Competition

Jörg Stolz, Judith Könemann

Instead of praying pilgrims, what we see are singers, gymnasts, firemen,
soldiers, year-goers, Sunday defilers in company with modern ladies
overflowing hill and valley, chasing in impetuous haste and irrepressible
lust free breath and the pleasures of life. (The Annals of Pius, 1875)

In this chapter, we present a new theory of religious-secular competition, one
attempting to explain the observable changes that religion has undergone in
society. Although previous attempts at explanation have contributed important
insights, they also have several shortcomings. In particular, they are sometimes too
descriptive and too unhistorical. In contrast, the theory presented here should be
in a position to explain the phenomena in clear proximity to specific historical
circumstances. We first discuss in this chapter the most important theses and
theories in existence today: secularization theory, individualization theory, and
market theory. We then outline our own theoretical position, which is what we
have called *the competition theory of religious and social change*. From this theory, we
then draw several hypotheses, which we test empirically in the course of our book.[1]

2.1 Theories of Religion and Modernity

Secularization Theory[2]

The most important classics of sociology – Auguste Comte, Herbert Spencer,
Max Weber, Emile Durkheim and Karl Marx – were all convinced that the
consequences of the Enlightenment, the advance of industrialization, and the

---

[1]   As might be expected from research which uses a mixed-methods approach, this theory
was already present at the outset in the foundations of our study, but it was nonetheless adjusted
through the formulation of bridging hypotheses in the course of research and in particular through
analysis of the qualitative material. On this approach, see Kelle (2007). It is important for us to
present a theory that seeks to connect with general sociological theory. On this problematic, see
Beckford (2000).

[2]   For a good summary of the three models in the sociology of religion, see Pollack
(2009). See also Pickel (2011) for a recent introduction to the state of research.

growing division of labour would lead eventually and inevitably to the decline of the religious. It was they who established the tradition which we are referring to here as 'secularization theory'. Comte,[3] for example, thought that human society develops in its entirety from the theological stage to the metaphysical stage, and finally to the fully scientific stage. According to Comte, science (and especially sociology) would therefore come to replace religion. For Weber,[4] Protestantism in particular had (inadvertently) led to the development of modern capitalism. Once created, though, modern capitalist society now increasingly rejects the religious as a 'sphere of values' foreign to it.[5] Finally, Durkheim[6] argued that modern society is characterized by an ever-growing division of labour, and that this division made religion, which could once encompass everything, ever weaker.[7]

Various scholars in the sociology of religion have taken up and developed secularization theory in the second half of the twentieth century,[8] with each highlighting different key elements of the modernization process. For Wilson,[9] Luhmann[10] and Casanova,[11] for example, the element of the *differentiation of society* already observed by Durkheim and Weber is particularly important.[12] According to these theorists, society differentiates itself, which leads to the emergence of various systems (e.g., business, education, law, politics, medicine), each of which works according to its own laws and 'logic'. Different positions are taken here with regard to the importance of religious references in society. Wilson and Luhmann, for example, argue that differentiation will push religious references more and more into the background. For them, religion as an autonomous system finds itself in a state of structural tension with regard to modernization, and, what is more, is comparatively weak. In contrast, Casanova argues for the hypothesis of structural compatibility between religion and modernity, according to which differentiation does not necessarily lead to a decline in religious beliefs – even if this is empirically often the case in

---

3   Comte (1995 (1844)).

4   Weber (1984 (1920)).

5   Weber (1988 (1920)).

6   Durkheim (1985, 7th edition).

7   For Durkheim, though, no society can exist without integration, and it is therefore to be expected that future societies will have to develop new forms of religion: Durkheim (1985, 7th edition, pp. 609–10).

8   See Dobbelaere (2002), Tschannen (1991), Wallis & Bruce (1995). See also the important contributions of Yamane (1997), Chaves (1994), Pollack (2003), Bruce (1990, 1996, 2002). For empirical work in the German context, see Wolf (2008).

9   Wilson (1966).

10   Luhmann (1982). On Luhmann, see Krech (2011).

11   Casanova (1992).

12   Differentiation theory as a whole is much broader than the version of secularization theory which is based on it.

Europe. From this, Casanova then builds a model of 'public religion', whose organizational forms can be powerful actors in civil society.[13]

A second form of secularization theory is represented by Pippa Norris and Ronald Inglehart. This variant foregrounds the fact that, in the course of modernization, there has been a significant *increase in living standards and a reduction in central risks to life.*[14] Compared with other regions of the world, the highly modernized countries of Western Europe, for example, are characterized by great wealth, a welfare state, high-quality medical care, insurances, etc. Since religion is centrally concerned with helping people to overcome difficult life situations, and since modernization either has made such situations disappear (e.g., the plague, infant mortality) or has provided technical and secular means better to deal with them, the demand for religion is falling in modernized countries.

In a third variant of secularization theory, the sociologist of religion Steve Bruce draws particular attention to the fact that, up until and into the period of modernity, religion and religiosity were not personal matters, but were actually *socially expected.*[15] A deviation from the true faith could have had serious consequences, as was made abundantly clear by the inquisitions, witch hunts, and the many wars waged over religion. Through modernization and the accompanying laws encouraging tolerance and protecting religious freedom, the norms that declared religion as binding for people are being increasingly dissolved. It used to be *unbelief* that was a private matter; today, it is *belief.*[16]

A fourth and final variant foregrounds the link between increasing modernization and the decreasing *plausibility* of religion. For Peter Berger,[17] the modern consciousness is finding it increasingly difficult to believe in 'transcendental powers' such as gods, angels and devils. One reason lies, again, in the modern society around us, which can give routinely scientific explanations (geological, medical, physical, etc.) for unexpected events. Another reason can be that modern societies are plural: the individual is confronted by many different religions and non-religious worldviews, each of which makes its own (sometimes absolute) claim to truth.[18] This leads in the modern consciousness to a self-relativization and to a distancing by people from their own religious

---

[13]   Casanova (1994, 1996, p. 187). See for a critical assessment of Casanova's claims Beckford (2010).

[14]   Gill & Lundsgaarede (2004), Norris & Inglehart (2004).

[15]   Bruce (2002). Tönnies (1963 (1887)) can be regarded as a classic of this variant.

[16]   We have slightly reformulated the Luhmann quotation (1982, p. 239).

[17]   Berger (1980).

[18]   There is now a huge literature on the concepts of religious plurality, pluralism and pluralization. For an overview for Switzerland, see Baumann & Stolz (2007a), Bochinger (2012). In general, see Giordan & Pace (2014), Baumann & Behloul (2005).

point of view.[19] All religion thereby loses its certainty; and there is a 'compulsion to heresy'.[20]

Many of these arguments are plausible and, empirically, we cannot dismiss out of hand that modernization (democratization, the development of the welfare state, literacy, industrialization) and the decline in religiosity worldwide go hand in hand.[21] Nevertheless, secularization theory has been heavily criticized from various sides as being too general, unilinear, ethnocentric, gender-blind, etc.[22] As Detlef Pollack has shown, though, many of these criticisms are justified only in part and are often based on exaggerations and false assumptions.[23] Nevertheless, we believe that three points of secularization theory can indeed be criticized.

First, many approaches in modernization theory lack an *actor perspective*.[24] Individuals and collective actors (such as groups and organizations) are simply not present in such approaches; instead, discussion centres on abstract processes, such as 'differentiation', 'societalization' and 'pluralization', which are supposed to influence each other in ways never made clear. As Dobbelaere writes: 'Too little attention has been paid to the question of just which people in just which social positions became the "sacralizers" or the "secularizers" in given situations. (...) Laicization is not a mechanical process to be imputed to impersonal and abstract forces'.[25]

Second (and related to the first point), modernization theory lacks a clear idea of the *precise causal mechanisms* which its explanation presupposes. Such mechanisms would need to specify exactly how social conditions influence the situation of (collective) actors, the interests, resources, beliefs, etc. which underlie how these actors then act, and the intended and unintended effects which thereby arise. Only a theory which connects macro-, meso- and micro-phenomena through causal mechanisms in this way is really explanatory. Instead, we find in most approaches in modernization theory relatively general statements about relationships between macro-processes. Smith formulates this criticism as follows: 'A (...) problem with secularization theory is that scholars in this tradition often under-specify the causal mechanisms that are presumed to

---

[19]   Berger (1990 (1967)).

[20]   But religious plurality can also lead to secularization independently of its influence on consciousness – namely, by forcing the state to construct religiously neutral regulations and institutions to ensure religious peace. On this, see, for example, Bruce (2002, 2006), Stolz & Baumann (2007).

[21]   Barro & Mcleary (2003); Norris & Inglehart (2004).

[22]   See, for example, Smith (2003b), Casanova (1992), Gorski (2000), Stark (1999b), Woodhead (2008), Berger (1999).

[23]   For a good compilation and reconstruction of the criticisms, see Pollack (2011a).

[24]   On this criticism, see also Chaves (1994), Smith (2003a).

[25]   Dobbelaere (1981, pp. 61 and 67).

link the social factors that are claimed to have transformed the role of religion in public life with the secularization outcome'.[26]

Third, these two points lead finally to the fact that modernization theory often remains relatively abstract, that it can *be dovetailed with concrete historical events only with difficulty*, and, in particular, that it is not in a position to explain great historical, regional and national differences. The historian Mark E. Ruff criticizes the sociological secularization theories as follows:

> (.) these debates have operated with a host of weaknesses. They have consistently lacked a sound empirical basis and have frequently bordered on the ahistorical. (...) Most importantly most of the theorists of secularization from the 1960s and 1970s applied these processes indiscriminately to almost all European nations, regardless of differing national and religious traditions.[27]

We will soon be introducing our own theory, one which attempts to solve these problems in a more satisfactory way. First, though, we shall discuss Thomas Luckmann's criticism of secularization theory.

Theory of Individualization and Spiritual Revolution

In the late 1960s, Thomas Luckmann sharply criticized secularization theory in his book *The Invisible Religion*.[28] According to Luckmann, the real error made by all the classics, but especially by the sociology of the church which was strong at the time, lay in a definition of the facts too narrow to be explained.

> What is usually believed to be merely a symptom of the decline in traditional Christianity could actually be a sign of a much more revolutionary change: the replacement of institutionally specialized religion by a new social form of religion. One thing at least can be said with certainty: the norms of traditional religious institutions solidified into an 'official' or once 'official' model of religion can no longer serve as a yardstick for the assessment of religion in modern society.[29]

According to Luckmann, then, the error of secularization theory is that it defines religion too narrowly. In doing so, says Luckmann, modernization theorists only see a decline in religion and are blind to other religious forms that have replaced the old forms. If historians, for example, were to define 'political organization' too

---

[26] Smith (2003a, p. 20).

[27] Ruff (2005, p. 9).

[28] Luckmann (1967). See on Luckmann's concept of invisible religion Knoblauch (1991). See also the interesting debate between Pollack & Pickel (1999) and Wohrab-Sahr & Krüggeler (2000).

[29] Luckmann (1991, p. 132).

narrowly as 'kingdom', then what would have been observable in the course of the last few centuries would have been a steady decline in 'political organization' – without the rise of the totalitarian regimes and of the democracies ever coming into view as new forms of political organisation.[30] For Luckmann, then, we are dealing here in reality not with a decline, but with a *change*, in religion and religiosity in modern societies. The 'official' model with its 'solidified' norms – that is, traditional churchliness – has of course shrunk. But this form has been replaced by individualized, freely choosable and new forms of spirituality. What exactly constitutes this new spirituality is not made entirely clear by Luckmann, though. At one point, he says that advice pages, positive thinking in *Playboy*, and pop-music lyrics contain elements of ultimate meaning.[31] And, elsewhere, he says that issues related to the individual and his or her autonomy (such as self-realization, familialism, sexuality) are religiously charged.[32]

Luckmann's argument, along with the memorable title of his book, inspired whole generations of sociologists and scientists of religion to look in various (sometimes counter-intuitive) places for 'invisible' religion (which would then be made visible through the act of research).[33] Here, we can distinguish three major variants. A first group of researchers see invisible religion in diverse phenomena which common sense would not necessarily associate with religion, but which, according to these researchers, also satisfy a 'need for ultimate meaning' or for 'ritual'. According to Hans-Joachim Höhn's thesis of religious dispersion, for example, religion has shifted into various cultural props of modern society such as football, advertising and television.[34] Hubert Knoblauch, who was strongly influenced by Luckmann, speaks in this context in terms of popular religion.[35] A second variant sees invisible religion in elements of traditional religiosity which had previously received little attention. It may be true, according to these theorists, that observable religious practice and people's connection to the churches are falling. But people still hold fast to their beliefs. This is Grace Davie's well-known thesis of 'believing without belonging'.[36] Another form of this thesis can be seen in Roland Campiche's idea of a 'dualization of religion'.[37] Although

---

[30]   This is our example.

[31]   Luckmann (1991, p. 147).

[32]   Luckmann (1991, pp. 153 ff.)

[33]   The special case study by Dubach & Campiche (1993) also begins from (among others) a paradigm of individualization.

[34]   Höhn (2007, pp. 33–50).

[35]   Knoblauch (2009).

[36]   Davie (1990). A variant of *believing without belonging* formulated by Davie herself (2006) is the concept of 'vicarious religion', according to which many people in Western societies may in fact not be very religious, but they nevertheless want others to be religious and see these others to a certain extent as being their own representatives with regard to God.

[37]   Campiche (2010, 2004).

institutional religiosity is declining, argues Campiche, a universal religiosity (which, above all, contains general values) still exists. A third variant, meanwhile, sees 'invisible religion' in phenomena that are often today called 'New Age' or 'alternative spirituality'. Paul Heelas and Linda Woodhead have even spoken of a 'spiritual revolution' here.[38] For these theorists, church religiosity will be replaced in the long term by phenomena such as astrology, yoga, channelling, belief in angels, crystal healings, or will transform itself imperceptibly into some such thing.[39]

Individualization theory has been sharply criticized, too, however. Although it is undoubtedly the case that in recent decades some such thing as an 'individualization' has taken place in Western European countries,[40] the question remains as to how this influences religion exactly. Criticism of individualization theory has been made on both an empirical and a theoretical level. *Empirically*, several studies have shown that there is no sharp separation between believing and belonging,[41] and that the rise of so-called alternative spirituality nowhere nearly outweighs the decline in institutional churchliness. There can therefore be no question of a 'spiritual revolution'.[42] *Theoretically*, critics have complained that Luckmann and his followers define religion too widely, the result of which is that virtually anything can be religion and the concept loses all of its sharpness. Purely due to the definition, it is therefore no longer possible to observe either a 'decrease' or an 'increase' in religion.

For us, it is also important that individualization theory can be criticized in exactly the same way as secularization theory. Here, again, what is missing is an actor perspective. Although individualization theory claims that individuals are becoming ever more individual, in many versions of the theory this is presented as an abstract process which sees individuals in terms of objects. So here it remains unclear, too, how the changes in situation, and individual and collective actions resulting from these changes, are supposed to have led to individualization, and how the theory can be brought into connection with concrete historical events. Strictly speaking, individualization theorists have ultimately proposed no new explanation for an existing phenomenon. Their main contribution consists mainly in two things. First, they point out that individual freedom of choice in religious and spiritual matters arises through modernization, this freedom of choice having very important effects on religion and religiosity. Second, they also call for a new definition of the phenomenon to be explained; in other

---

[38]   Heelas & Woodhead (2004).

[39]   Bochinger, Engelbrecht & Gebhart (2009). For important literature on this, see also Bloch (1998), Bochinger (1995), Gebhart et al. (2005), Hanegraaf (1998). For Switzerland, see Mayer (1993, 2007), Stolz (2009a), Stolz & Sanchez (2000), Rademacher (2009).

[40]   Beck (1986), Buchmann & Eisner (1997), Putnam (2000).

[41]   Voas & Crockett (2005).

[42]   Pollack (2006), Voas & Bruce (2007).

words, for religiosity to be understood more broadly than a focus on Christian-church religiosity can achieve. In our opinion, these two points must be taken up by every future theory of religious change.

Market Theory

Since the 1980s in particular, representatives of market theory have strongly questioned secularization theory. A group of mainly US researchers – Rodney Stark, Roger Finke, William Bainbridge and Laurence Iannaccone – have claimed what is in many ways the exact opposite of what modernization theorists had accepted for many decades as being reliable knowledge.[43] The market theorists vigorously deny that the modernization of Western societies has led to a decline in religion and religiosity. This is a self-deception that should be buried once and for all.[44] Rather, according to the market theorists, religious decline in Europe is a myth; religious beliefs in Europe are still very strong; people used to be much less religious than is often claimed; and, generally, developments in the US, in the Arab countries and in Eastern Europe all testify against the thesis of advancing secularization.[45] If not through modernization theory, then how can we explain the major differences in religiosity between, for example, different countries?

For the market theorists, the solution is deceptively simple: it is enough, they argue, to understand religion as a market with suppliers (churches and religious groups) and customers (believers), and to apply the general economic market laws of supply and demand.[46] A crucial assumption which underlies this approach is that there exists a constant and steady religious demand – that is, that people all over the world have in principle the same religious needs, the same thirst for 'transcendental goods'. That means, though, that differences between different countries can be explained solely by differences in religious supply, which in turn depends centrally on state regulation of the religious market.

According to market theory, in regulated markets (in which we find a monopoly or oligopoly, for example), people are provided with religious products which are too expensive and poor in quality. Religion is therefore unattractive and there is consequently little demand for it, which would explain the low level of religiosity in Western Europe. In contrast, in countries without regulation (those with free competition, that is), religious communities compete with each other, vie for the attention of believers, and produce precisely those religious goods which most appeal to people, the consequence of which is a high overall

---

[43] Iannaccone (1998), Warner (1993), De Graaf (2012).

[44] Stark (1999b).

[45] Stark & Iannaccone (1994); for the religious market in Latin America, see Bastian (2007).

[46] Iannaccone (1991), Stark & Bainbridge (1989).

religiosity, as can be seen, for example, in the US. Indeed, for the market theorists, the history of the US shows precisely how industrialization and modernization are accompanied not by a decrease, but by an increase, in religiosity.[47]

Market theory has completely different strengths and weaknesses to both modernization and individualization theory. On the positive side, it includes the actor perspective, and talks in terms not only of abstract processes, but also of individuals and collective actors (churches, organizations, etc.) which are not only passively exposed to the events described, but which can also actively shape them. Also, in contrast to the two previous theories, market theory presents a clear causal mechanism. For proponents of the theory, it is clear how different social macro-conditions change the situation for individuals and collective actors, how they react to the new situation, and how new situations then emerge from this interaction.

The weakness of the theory, though, lies not in its lack of concreteness, but in just the reverse: in the fact that it excessively generalizes a very specific mechanism across all possible times and societies. It is obvious, for example, that churches in very many countries do *not* understand themselves as businesses, and that believers do *not* behave like customers.[48] Empirically, it can also be shown that the mechanism postulated by market theory often plays no role, with increased pluralism, a freer market and less regulation often *not* leading to more religiosity.[49] Also, religious demand cannot be viewed simply as a constant, but is something which is subject to changes and influences from particular regions and environmental conditions.

Although the ideas of the market theorists have not proved themselves as a whole, there are various elements of the theory which are certainly useful. For our own theory, for example, what is particularly useful is the idea of competition for people's attention, time and energy.

2.2 The General Theory of Religious-Secular Competition

We wish now to put forward a new theory, one which attempts to avoid the pitfalls of the previous approaches. Our theory sees religious change as the result of religious-secular and intra-religious competition at different levels. Different internal and external factors (e.g., wars or discoveries) have an effect on who prevails in this competition. We also postulate a *change of religious competition*

---

[47] Finke & Stark (1992).

[48] Bruce (1999), Bryant (2000).

[49] Chaves & Gorski (2001), Lechner (1996), Voas, Olson & Crockett (2002), Beyer (1997). On regulation in the Swiss context, see Becci (2001); and, for a review of market theory, see Stolz (2009a).

regime in the 1960s, by which we mean that the social rules governing religious-
secular and intra-religious competition underwent a profound change in
direction during this period. We first outline the general theory and then apply
it in a 'socio-historical concretization' to the case of Switzerland which interests
us here.[50]

A terminological observation: our theory relates to both religious-secular
and intra-religious competition. It is important that the area of competition can
include both religious and secular suppliers. In what follows, we often use for
the sake of readability the term 'religious-secular competition' inclusively, that
is, intra-religious competition is also meant. Where we deal exclusively with one
or the other, we make this explicit.

Preliminary Observations

Precursors of the theory

Other researchers have already highlighted religious-secular and intra-religious
competition. We can discover such findings and observations, for example, in
disciplines as diverse as sociology, economics, marketing and history. However,
these insights have never been presented as a whole and combined into a unified
theory. Let us consider briefly the most important of these insights.[51]

A number of authors have drawn attention to religious-secular or
intra-religious *competition for power and prestige* on a social level or within
organizations. For example, both Max Weber and Pierre Bourdieu have
analysed competition between priests, prophets and magicians in a 'religious
field'.[52] In his excellent *Systems of professions*, Andrew Abbott has shown how
the clergy and other professions are in permanent competition with each other
for the monopoly on certain production opportunities and jurisdictions.[53]
Christian Smith has explained the secularization of institutions in the United
States between 1870 and 1930 as being the result of competition between the
Protestant establishment and the new, secular elites. Similarly, Mark Chaves has
suggested explaining secularization as arising on three levels from competition
for religious or secular authority.[54] Finally, a research group led by Monika
Wohlrab-Sahr has for some years been analysing competition and conflict
between religious and secular worldviews (and the elites behind them).[55]

---

[50]   In the general part, we give several examples from the most diverse historical periods
and geographical provenances to show that the theory has a general claim to validity.

[51]   For an overview, see Stolz (2013).

[52]   Weber (1988 (1920)), Bourdieu (1971, 1987a).

[53]   Abbott (1988). See also Abbott (1980).

[54]   Chaves (1994).

[55]   See, for example, Wohlrab-Sahr & Burchardt (2012), Wohlrab-Sahr, Schmidt-Lux
& Karstein (2008), Wohlrab-Sahr (2011).

Other authors have placed *competition for individual demand* at the forefront of their analyses.[56] The economists Corry Azzi and Ronald Ehrenberg, as well as Laurence Iannaccone, have developed a model in which individuals can choose between religious and secular ways to spend their time, so that churches, employers and suppliers of leisure activities are in competition with each other for the time of individuals. In another economic study, Jonathan Gruber and Daniel M. Hungerman have shown that opening supermarkets on Sunday leads to a decrease in church attendance.[57] The sociologists Tony Gill and Erik Lundsgaarde have shown in an important study that the modern welfare state in Western countries competes with religious suppliers by offering similar goods.[58] Jochen Hirschle, who is also a sociologist, has shown with the example of the secularization of Ireland and in other works how modern consumer culture became an important competitor to religion.[59] And historians such as Urs Altermatt, Hugh McLeod and Mark Edward Ruff have shown how the youth work of the churches in the Western world gained an unassailable adversary after 1945 in the form of rock 'n' roll, James Dean, teen magazines, the cinema and dance houses.[60] In order to turn all these analyses and insights into a unified concept, though, we need a theoretical framework. This is provided by analytical sociology.

Analytical sociology
Analytical sociology is an approach going back largely to the research programme of Max Weber which assumes that sociology should explain puzzling social phenomena *causally with the help of interpretive understanding*. This means on the one hand reconstructing in a hermeneutic manner the subjective view of

---

[56] Also important in this context are publications from the science of marketing: Mara Einstein (2008, 2011) and Sandra Mottner (2007) have analysed the struggle between the religious and secular book and film industries. See also a growing literature that analyses market-like religious phenomena not from a rational choice perspective, but from other (e.g. bourdieusian, weberian, exchange) perspectives: for example, Pace (2008), Bastian (2007), see in general the contributions in Stolz (2007).

[57] Gruber & Hungerman (2008).

[58] Gill & Lundsgaarde (2004).

[59] Hirschle (2010, 2011, 2012).

[60] Altermatt (2009), McLeod (2007), Ruff (2005). Luhmann (1982, p. 239) also points to this phenomenon: 'Through privatization, religion falls into the area of leisure time demarcated from work and determined by it. (....) Today, it seems to be decided that the church in leisure time has to compete against strong, structurally privileged tendencies – a problem which repeats itself within 'churchly leisure times' in the marginalization of 'Bible work'.

actors, and, on the other, working out the exact causal mechanisms leading to a specific phenomenon.[61]

The explanations thereby resulting build on the principle of *methodological individualism*, by which is meant that the social world consists of different 'levels' which are linked to each other by causal mechanisms: a macro-level of cultural and social constraints, a meso-level (groups, organizations, milieus), and a micro-level of individual perceptions and actions. Sociological explanations always seek to account for phenomena at the meso- or macro-level – something that is only possible, however, if these phenomena are seen as being the result of the behaviour of individuals at the *micro*-level.[62]

From the perspective of analytical sociology, individuals usually act in a *(restrictedly) rational* manner. They usually have 'good reasons' for their behaviour, and the choices that they make are in accordance with their resources, preferences, beliefs, as well as with the perceived current norms and the goods that are on offer. If an action appears from the outside to be incomprehensible or irrational, it makes sense to examine with qualitative methods the situation of the individual concerned, for this often leads to a satisfactory explanation of the behaviour.[63] Since many (restrictedly) rational individuals in changing social environments make similar choices, social trends emerge, for example, phenomena of secularization or resacralization. Only the sum of the many individual decisions leads to what our model wishes ultimately to explain.

From the perspective of analytical sociology, good explanations are ultimately only possible when they are *placed in the historical context*, that is, when they show under what typical initial conditions (resources, preferences, beliefs, options) typical actors have acted.[64] Particularly suitable here are therefore not only quantitative but also qualitative and historical methods.

---

[61]　See classic Weber (1985 (1922b)). On analytical or explanatory sociology, see Boudon (1983), Esser (1999), Hedström (2005). There is a debate as to whether analytic sociology is basically similar to explanatory sociology or not. We take the former position. See for the debate Manzo (2007, 2010), Kalter/Kroneberg (2014).

[62]　On the macro-micro-macro structure, see Coleman (1990), Schelling (2006 (1978)).

[63]　On the basis of this assumption of rationality, we can then formulate hypotheses, such as: If, say, the secular options increase or are made more attractive, so individuals will increasingly decide on these – and against religious options (or *vice versa*). See Boudon (2003). On the concept of restricted rationality, see Simon (1983). Experimental research has shown that individuals very often act intentionally and with subjectively 'good grounds', but that their behaviour differs from the model of *homo oeconomicus* in the most diverse ways. For a collection of 'anomalies' (from the perspective of *homo oeconomicus*), see Esser (1996). Also well worth reading here is Kahneman (2011).

[64]　In the language of analytical sociology, it is a matter of determining 'bridge hypotheses'. On this, see Popper (1960). On the concept of constraints and bridge hypotheses, see Esser (1999, p. 15), Lindenberg (1996), Kelle & Lüdemann (1998).

Overall, this framework of analytical sociology can help us to avoid the pitfalls of modernization and individualization theory outlined above. In particular, it will force us to think in an actor-oriented way and to identify the precise causal mechanisms which have brought forth the phenomena which we wish to explain.

Religion, Religious Organizations, Religiosity

Definitions
It is clear that a theory of religious-secular competition only makes sense if we can separate religious from secular phenomena. For our purposes, then, we distinguish religion, religious groups and religiosity in the following way:[65]

- *Religion* is the totality of *cultural* symbol systems that respond to problems of meaning and contingency by pointing to a transcendental reality. This transcendental reality influences daily life in accordance with these symbol systems, but cannot be brought completely under control. Religious symbol systems include mythical, ethical and ritual elements, as well as notions of salvation goods.[66] The use of a transcendental level (with gods, spirits, etc.) allows us nevertheless to understand the inexplicable, and to process the uncontrollable, in a symbolic manner.[67] Examples of such religions are Judaism, Islam, Christianity, Hinduism and Raelianism.
- *Religious groups and organizations* are *collective actors* which have a central reference to a religion – for example, they represent a religious ideology, offer religious goods, or perform religious collective activities. Examples are churches, religious centres, temple communities and prayer groups.
- *Religiosity* is an *individual* experience or action, insofar as it relates to one or more religions. Religiosity has different dimensions (action, experience, knowledge, belief, etc.).[68] Attending a religious service or a

---

[65] For similar positions on the definition of religion, see Pollack (1995), Geertz (1993a). For a defence of a narrow and substantial concept of religion, see Riesebrodt (2007). On the question of the boundaries between secular and religious phenomena, see Stolz & Usunier (2013).

[66] For a good discussion of this issue, see Riesebrodt (2007).

[67] The objects of incomprehensible or uncontrollable phenomena change with developments in society.

[68] A vast literature exists on the dimensionality of religiosity. See the classic Glock (1967) and, for an overview, Huber (2003). The dimensions of religiosity, though, are really nothing else than the basic dimensions of human behaviour in general, see Stolz (2012). Note that the concept 'alternative spirituality' that will be used extensively in the book is in this conception just a subtype of religiosity (see for the definition of alternative spirituality Chapter 3).

meditation course, praying, going on a pilgrimage, and believing in angels
are all examples of an individual religiosity as defined here.

By using these definitions, we can distinguish between the religious and the non-
religious. All cultural, social and individual phenomena which are *not* religious
are therefore for us *secular*. In reality, of course, there are also sometimes hybrid
phenomena and grey areas. In concrete sociological work, however, these
definitions allow us in most cases to classify phenomena clearly into either the
religious or the secular.

The changing advantageousness of religion

A further assumption of our theory follows from these definitions: namely, the
changing advantageousness of religion and religious structures during the course
of time. For long periods in the development of society, religious structures
enjoyed a high level of advantageousness because they enabled people to deal
with what seemed to be 'unsolvable' problems. In earlier societies, many illnesses,
the outbreak of diseases, natural disasters, personal poverty, the creation of the
world, and the origin of the human species, etc., could only be controlled and
explained with difficulty, and so were virtually predestined to be dealt with in a
symbolic-religious way.[69]

Since the modern era, though, it now appears that secular innovations
often allow people greater control and better understanding, with the effect
that phenomena have tended to be taken from the religious domain. Examples
here include the discovery of bacteria and viruses, the control of risks through
insurances, the discovery of the economic causes of poverty, the discovery
of the ongoing expansion of the universe, and the discovery of the theory of
evolution. However, these innovations do not lead directly and necessarily to
the withdrawal of issues and responsibilities from the religious domain. Rather,
they change the conditions of the competition in which different actors find
themselves. It is only with the expiry of the competition that very different
possible social outcomes can come about.

This explains why we observe in self-modernizing societies both a uniform
overall trend of secularization on the one hand and, on the other, the fact that
developments run their course so differently from country to country and from
region to region.[70]

---

[69] For such a perspective on religion, see, for example, Weber (1985 (1922a)) or
Malinowski (1984). Very similar is Stolz (2001).

[70] See Inglehart & Welzel (2005), Norris & Inglehart (2004).

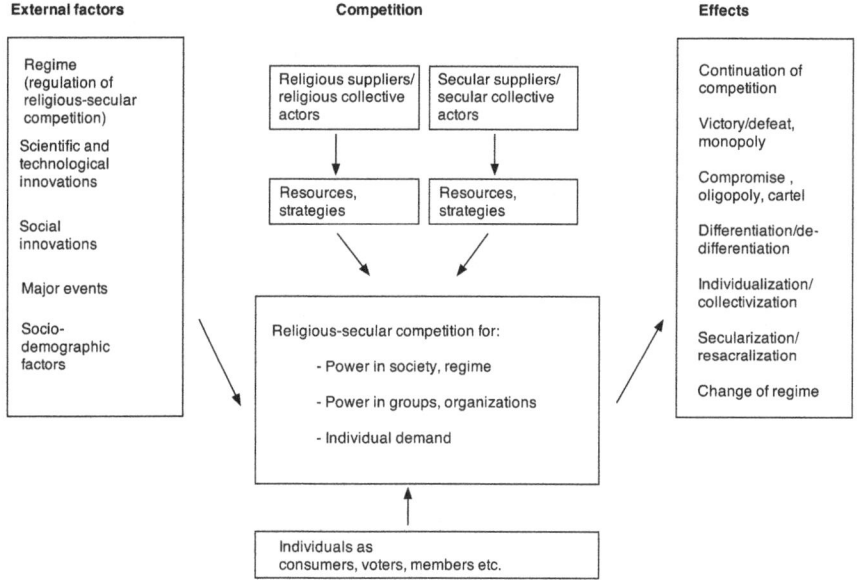

Figure 2.1　The theory of religious-secular competition

Social Competition

Religious and secular suppliers and collective actors

Our theory is centrally concerned with religious-secular and intra-religious competition. It is here that religious and secular suppliers, as well as collective actors, operate, and we are dealing with very concrete groups, organizations and milieus which are committed to the goals of their group. The type of groups, organizations and milieus is extremely diverse. They can be religious or secular professions (e.g., the clergy, doctors), organizations, political parties, elites, and even the state. According to our theory, these collective and individual actors compete for three highly desirable objects.

The first object competed for is *power at the level of society as a whole.*[71] Here, religious and secular actors contest the question of the prevailing order, the authority to interpret, the rules of coexistence, and the responsibility for solving problems.[72] On the one hand, this is about how the *competition regime* is configured, that is, about the question of the principles, norms, rules and

---

[71]　In such competition, religious components are almost always mixed with other diverse (political, economic, ethnic, status-related) components.

[72]　A conceptualization of power which is compatible with analytical sociology has been provided by Coleman (1990). See also Esser (2000b).

processes by which legitimate power, influence and the authority to interpret are regulated in society.[73] On the other hand, collective actors compete for power, influence and the authority to interpret *within* any given competition regime. Examples are easy to find. During the Iranian revolution of 1979, secular and religious parties fought for power in the country.[74] In Germany in the 1930s, Nazi and Catholic youth groups competed for influence over the German youth.[75] And, at the beginning of the twentieth century, clerics and neurologists competed for who was responsible for 'personal problems'.[76]

The second object competed for is *power, influence and the authority to interpret* at the second level of *groups, organizations and milieus*.[77] In the foreground here are questions concerning, for example, the general direction which the group should take, the legitimation of responsibility for important tasks, etc. In this way, various Muslim movements fought after the death of Mohammed over the question of his legitimate successor, which led to the split between Sunnis and Shias. During the Second Vatican Council, conservative and reform-minded Catholics fought over the range of reforms that should be implemented. And, in the late nineteenth century, there were bitter struggles in many Protestant communities in Switzerland between members of the same community over the question of whether the Bible should be interpreted in a 'positive' (supranaturalistic) or a 'liberal' (especially ethical) way.

The third object competed for is not so much power as *individual demand for goods*. What we mean here is that religious and secular 'suppliers' compete with each other for the individual's demand for goods, participation and financial support.[78] Competition arises because the goods offered by religious and secular suppliers often satisfy the same needs. If someone with depression needs help, then he or she can demand the religious good 'pastoral care' – but there is also available a secular competitor in the form of the secular good 'psychotherapy'. The need for social contacts can be satisfied by the religious good 'active membership in a religious community' – but there are also many secular competitors available, such as sports clubs, associations of all kinds,

---

[73] The term *regime* is often used in political science. It is appropriate here because it is intended to describe the configuration of how supply and demand are regulated. See classic Krasner (1982), Keohane (1982). The term is close to what Esser (1999) calls 'constitution'.

[74] For this example, see Beyer (1994).

[75] For this example, see Ruff (2005).

[76] For this example, see Abbot (1988).

[77] Again, in actual conflicts, religious elements are usually blended with other lines of conflict: between older and younger generations, women and men, ethnically differentiated elites, higher and lower classes, etc.

[78] For details, see Stolz (2009b, 2013).

neighbourhood networks, etc. Depending on the need, other competitors to religious suppliers come into view (Table 2.1).[79]

Table 2.1   Needs satisfied by religion, and religious and secular competitors

Needs satisfied by religion	Religious competitors	Possible secular competitors
Help with problems	Prayer, confession, pastoral care, diaconia	Psychotherapy, counselling, welfare state
Security, health, success	Salvation goods	Insurances, welfare state, career
Inner peace and harmony	Parish	Sport, family
Interpretation of the world, meaning	Sermon, interpretation of religious texts, dogmas	Science
Structuring of life	Life-cycle rituals, religious celebrations	Private celebrations, work-holiday cycle
Social identity, social capital	Parish as network	Career networks, new social media, clubs

Resources and power distributions
Suppliers of goods and collective actors have various resources at their disposal which they can employ in the competition – for example, economic capital, reputation, legitimation, technical know-how, electoral strength, etc.[80] Power is distributed differently in the competition according to differences in the resources available to the various groups. The regime itself is an extremely important resource. During the Iranian revolution of 1979, for example, the Shah Mohammad Reza Pahlavi had great resources at his disposal in the form of financial reserves and state power (the police apparatus and the military). His opponent, the revolutionary leader Ayatollah Khomeini, though, possessed resources in the form of great legitimacy and enormous popular support (demonstrations), and could ultimately employ these to overthrow the Shah.

---

[79]   For the suppliers in this kind of competition, it is about questions of so-called marketing: Which product should be offered? How much should it cost? At which place should it be brought to the man or woman? How should the product be made known to people and advertised? If the perspective of the customer is taken, though, such questions arise as: Will my child develop better if sent to Sunday school or to football practice on a Sunday morning? Should I join the church choir or a secular choir? Are religious/magical or biomedical forms of healing better?

[80]   The resources can be equated with Bourdieu's forms of capital. See Bourdieu (1983).

Strategies

The strategies employed by suppliers to survive in the competition are extremely diverse and therefore cannot all be listed here. Collective actors can, for example, *mobilize* their membership base to exert political pressure on people with decision-making powers or to intimidate political or religious opponents (e.g., through demonstrations, processions, press campaigns). Or a different strategy may lie in *withdrawal*, that is, they can draw boundaries to distinguish themselves from their environment (e.g., through a special hairstyle, emblems, food taboos). Another important strategy is *growth*, by which collective actors can increase their own influence (e.g., through recruiting, biological reproduction) or strengthen their own impact through increasing members' sense of *identification* (e.g., through socializing members, social control). When it comes to the demand for the group's 'products', a further important strategy lies in *price adjustment*, in *increasing attractiveness*, and in *raising the level of quality*. Religious groups may try to encourage more people to participate, for example, by offering religious services tailored to particular groups or by hiring outstanding musicians to play, etc. Here, as elsewhere, innovation often leads to success.

Individual action

In turn, individuals respond to each situation in the competition by adapting. They demand either religious or secular goods; they vote for more religious-oriented or more secular-oriented political parties; they join either religious or secular clubs or associations, etc. Here, we are assuming a 'restricted rationality' in Herbert Simon's sense. Individuals have limited information and limited resources of attention and calculation, and their behaviour very often runs in accordance with culturally prescribed habits. Nevertheless, in the face of changing conditions, they do often try to select that combination of (religious and/or secular) goods from which they can gain the greatest possible benefit.[81]

External factors of influence

The actual course that competition takes is influenced by various external factors. It is like when players in a game of Monopoly are constantly disturbed from the outside – new rules are suddenly introduced; some players are given

---

[81]   Our model makes do with the very weak assumption that individuals in general and in the medium term strive for a situation which they regard as being beneficial to them. There is no question that single individuals often react highly irrationally in particular situations. On the idea of interpreting rational-choice theories as 'medium-term theories', see Kroneberg (2011). There is also no question that real individuals differ in diverse ways from the *homo oeconomicus* posited by economists. See Esser (1999). Which option is chosen by the individual depends on the resources, the availability, the price and the productivity of the respective options.

additional resources while others have their resources taken away from them; there are enforced breaks, etc. External factors of influence can assume very different forms; we shall name only five of the most important here.

The first factor of influence is the *regime of religious-secular competition* (also abbreviated as *competition regime* in the following). This determines not only the legal channels but also the valid norms in society, whether and to what extent there may be intra-religious or religious-secular competition, and the rules by which such competition is to take place.[82] The regime of religious-secular competition can regulate both supply and demand. Examples of the regulation of supply are the hindrance of religious suppliers in the former East Germany, and the recognition under public law of some religious communities in Switzerland. Examples of the regulation of demand are norms that make religious practice socially expected (as was still the case in some French villages up until the 1950s) and legal norms which prescribe church marriages. The regime of religious-secular competition is therefore to a certain extent the sum of the 'rules of the game' which are valid in a society for a certain period of time. An important insight for our theory is that such rules never go unchallenged. They are based on distributions of power, on the relative sizes of different groups, etc., and are the constant subject of renegotiation. In some situations, there may then occur a so-called 'change of competition regime', that is, changes in the rules of the game are so great that a qualitatively new game comes into being (see below).

In line with recent economic and historical theories, our theory places a particularly strong emphasis on innovations.[83] Here, to begin with, we can think of *scientific/technological innovations*. By providing new opportunities to control and understand the world, these innovations change the resources and opportunities available to the various competitors.[84] The discovery of the theory of evolution by Charles Darwin, for example, changed the entire religious-secular field of competition, since it opened up for the first time the opportunity to explain the origin of the human species in a purely secular way.[85] The results of historical and critical Bible studies, initiated, for example, by Julius Wellhausen's work on the Old Testament and by David Friedrich Strauss' work on the life of Jesus, profoundly changed the religious-secular field of competition within Protestantism and within Western societies as a whole.[86] While such scientific

---

[82] The literature on regulation of religion is very important. Among others see the contributions in Sullivan/Beaman (2013), Beyer (2013), Chaves/Cann (1992), Fox/Tabory (2008), Fox (2011), Iannaccone (1991, 1992), Jordan (2002).

[83] See Müller & Veyrassat (2001), Caron (2001).

[84] The innovations also partly create new groups, which then participate in the competition.

[85] Darwin (1985 (1859)). On this, see Portier, Veuille & Willaime (2011).

[86] On Wellhausen's contribution to current understanding of the Hebrew Bible, see Römer (2004). On the contribution of David Friedrich Strauss, see Schweitzer (1966),

innovations affect religious thought directly, many act indirectly by modifying – at first barely perceptibly – the consciousness of people. They affect, to echo Peter Berger, people's general 'plausibility structure'.[87]

In addition to scientific and technological innovations, there are, thirdly, *social innovations*, which are also extremely important. The idea of universal human rights, for example, which prevailed after 1948 (after important stages of development in the natural law of the Enlightenment and the American and French revolutions), shows the possibility of establishing the value of the human being independently of God.[88] The welfare state, which was invented in the second half of the nineteenth century and expanded greatly in many Western countries in the 1950s, led to a previously unknown degree of individual security, a security that was independent of religious communities and ideologies.[89] The invention of modern professions in the nineteenth century, which replaced the guilds, led to the triumph of scientifically legitimated expert knowledge. The new careers that thereby emerged – in particular, journalists, doctors, social workers and psychotherapists – became key competitors to religious leaders (the clergy), who saw themselves as complete experts and who in turn had to transform themselves from bearers of an office already specified in the *ancien régime* to members of a profession.[90]

A fourth form of external factors of influence is *major events*. Examples are epidemics, wars, famines, exceptional meteorological conditions, migrations, etc. Thus, the massive wave of Islamophobia in the Western world since 2001 is almost certainly due largely to the attacks on 11 September and their consequences. Without these attacks, the debate on Islam and attitudes towards members of the religion would probably be very different.[91]

The fifth and final factor of influence is *socio-demographic changes*. Changes in birth rates, shifts in the numbers of mono- or inter-denominational marriages, the outnumbering of men by women (or *vice versa*) in society – these can all have an important influence on the religious-secular competition. Thus, for example, majority-minority relations between competing parties can be reversed within a few generations due to different levels of fertility. Finally, changes in how education, occupational status and income are distributed are important, too.

Theissen & Merz (2001).

[87]   See Berger (1990 (1967)).

[88]   On the development of human rights, see Beitz (2009).

[89]   See Kaufmann (1997).

[90]   On this, see Russell (1980), Abbott (1988), Conze & Kocka (1985).

[91]   Or, to give another example, the fact that in Switzerland it is the cantons which regulate the relationship between church and state, and not the federal government, cannot be explained without reference to the Sonderbund War of 1847.

Effects of competition

Our theory will now explain a number of phenomena resulting from these struggles.[92] Of course, it is possible for a competition simply to persist without either of the two sides being able to achieve a decisive victory. In many other cases, however, interesting changes in the overall system do occur.

If one party wins and the other loses, then *monopolies* or *quasi-monopolies* come into existence. Examples here are the enforcement of Christianity under Theodosius in the fourth century and the enforcement of Islam through the Iranian revolution of 1978/1979. In some cases, the losing party disappears, but more often victories and defeats are not absolute but gradual. They are reflected in shifts of power, in shifts of influence, and in fluctuations in the number of followers.[93]

Another solution to the conflict lies in reducing or avoiding struggle through agreed *compromises, collusions or cartels*.[94] For example, the competing Christian missionary societies agreed in 1910 in Edinburgh not to poach members from each other – and thereby founded the Ecumenical Movement.[95] And denominational splits after a period of conflict led in some Western European countries (Germany, the Netherlands, Switzerland) to a geographical and social division of society in which people lived side by side but separately.

Our theory, though, can explain not only the success or failure of suppliers, but also other social phenomena such as differentiation, individualization and secularization.

Thus, competition, in conjunction with other factors, can lead to *phenomena not only of differentiation but also of de-differentiation*.[96] Here,

---

[92] Of central significance here is how the competition itself unfolds, i.e., the so-called 'path dependence'. At every moment of the game, a variety of next moves are possible. But once one of the possibilities has been realized, this influences what is possible next. Thus, there may be strengthening effects, reaction effects, feedback effects, etc. On the concept of path dependence, see Esser (2000a).

[93] Interestingly, victories and defeats can have unexpected effects. Sometimes victory, i.e., the implementation of a group's concerns, leads to the disappearance of the victor – because it no longer has any reason to mobilize. For example, the Catholic milieu disappeared in Germany, the Netherlands and Switzerland in the 1960s – just as its most important concerns had been implemented. On the other hand, crushing defeats can hold the seed of future victories, because they have within them the symbolic material for future mobilizations (e.g., the crucifixion of Jesus).

[94] Peter Berger has analysed the ecumenical aspirations of the Christian churches in terms of cartel-building (1965).

[95] See Basset (1996), Braybrooke (1992).

[96] The current and dominant theories of a trend of ongoing (necessary?) differentiation of society are still too indebted to the biologistic thought of the nineteenth century, which assumes a differentiation of the 'social body'. With the concept suggested here, both differentiation and de-differentiation are possible, depending on our starting point.

differentiation refers to the fact that social life is dissected into functionally different, specialized parts (positions, roles, institutions) which now perform very specific functions that were once performed by a single institution.[97] An example is the battle waged by doctors in the nineteenth century concerning the autonomy of their profession – they vehemently rejected not only 'quacks' and 'witchdoctors', but also religious healers.[98] In effect, this competition led to an increase in differentiation between religion and medicine in society. The dispute concerning sovereignty over religious instruction, which resulted in a religious instruction independent of the church, also shows an increasing differentiation between churches and schools.[99] Interestingly, though, competition can also result in *de-differentiations*. It has been shown, for example, that the most intensely religious members of the Reformed and the Catholic Churches, as well as of the Evangelical churches, sometimes come together to fight against the common 'enemy' represented by the secular, consumerist society. In doing so, the differences between these communities, which had previously been so important, are blurred. Another example is charismatic churches which, faced with strong competition from the area of leisure activities, so strongly imitate the culture of pop music in their 'celebrations' that there is ultimately a blurring of boundaries between religious and secular 'product'. This can also be read as a process of de-differentiation.

Competition can also lead to processes of *individualization and collectivization*.[100] Expansion of competition leads to a multiplication of what is on offer and to the increasing opportunity for people to differentiate themselves from every other person through what they consume. Thus, the new – and, in part, strongly competitive – religious diversity that we have observed in many Western countries since the 1960s has led to an opportunity for religious choice and individualization that had never been there before.[101] For example, the emergence of a competitive market for Islamic clothing has meant that the headscarf has gone from being a stigmatized practice to being a highly individualized fashion item.[102] Conversely, though, competition can

---

[97] The literature on this subject is extremely broad. On differentiation from a system-theoretical perspective, see Parsons (1975, 1999). On the conception of differentiation within analytical sociology, see Esser (2000a) as well as the edited volume by Schwinn, Kroneberg & Greve (2011). A classic text on the differentiation of spheres of value is Weber (1988 (1920)). On the link between social differentiation and religious diversity, see Baumann & Stolz (2007a).

[98] On this example, see Abbott (1988), Fritschi (1990).

[99] On this example, see Frank & Jödicke (2007).

[100] See, for example, Beck (1983, 1986).

[101] See, for example, Baumann & Stolz (2007a), Bouma (1997).

[102] See Sandikzi & Ger (2010). On the emergence of a Muslim consumer society, see Haenni (2009).

also have a collectivizing effect. Many studies have shown how the most diverse religious groups – from Christian fundamentalists to Scientologists – react to competition precisely by strengthening the collective character of the group through special signs of membership and high 'admission prices'.[103]

Competition can also lead to both the *secularization* and the *re-sacralization* of entire societies.[104] For example, the struggle in France between the laicists and the Catholic Church during and after the French Revolution led to an unprecedented secularization of France – ultimately because the party of laicists emerged victorious from the struggle. Also, the competition between the leisure society and Catholicism in the Netherlands in the 1960s led to a strong secularization, because the religious suppliers of leisure pursuits were unable to offer anything comparable in return, and individuals chose the more attractive secular goods on offer. Conversely, the competition between the Communist regime and civil society in Poland in the 1980s led to a re-sacralization of society, since the opposition saw in religion the best opportunity of building resistance.[105] Incidentally, widespread religious indifference can also be explained by way of the idea of competition: when a particular religious-secular competition ended in favour of the secular side, and the end of the competition already lies further back in history (as is the case at present in the new federal states of Germany), then many people do not even come into contact with religion, and show no particular interest in religious questions.[106]

Finally, a particularly interesting effect of competition is *change of competition regime*. As we have already seen, the collective actors are constantly struggling for power, influence and the authority to interpret in society, by, among other things, trying to change the competition regime in force. Since various forces are constantly at work, there can often be longer periods of stability in spite of this competition. Sometimes, however, the competition regime in force is so strongly altered (partly due to the results of the competition and partly due to external influences) that a qualitatively new 'social game' comes into being. It is in such a case that we can speak of a change of competition regime. In this exceptional situation, 'the cards are reshuffled' to a certain extent. Resources that once had a lot of value suddenly become worthless, and *vice versa*; social groups that once led are suddenly downgraded; those seeking influence must suddenly proceed in a completely different way. In the next section, we shall discuss in detail such a change of competition regime.

---

[103] See, for example, Kelley (1986 (1972)), Iannaccone (1994), Olson (2005). Scientology is also a good example here, if we consider the transition from dianetics to scientology. See Wallis (1995).

[104] Concrete secularizations and resacralizations are usually due to complex combinations of mechanisms at different levels.

[105] On this example, see Borowik (2002).

[106] For this addition, we are grateful for a question posed by Detlef Pollack.

What we have outlined here shows, we hope, that a theory built on notions of competition has important advantages over the previous theories (modernization theory, individualization theory, and market theory). In particular, it introduces an actor perspective and establishes clear causal mechanisms. To provide useful explanations and hypotheses, though, the theory must also be socio-historically concretized. That is our goal in the following sections.

2.3 Socio-historical Concretization[107]

The central thesis of our book is that the cultural revolution of the 1960s led to a new regime of religious-secular competition. Religious-secular competition for domination and individual demand existed both before and after this revolution, but the form that this competition took changed significantly in the 1960s. Before the revolution, religion and religiosity were viewed as public matters, and society as a whole saw itself as bi-denominational, that is, despite all denominational difference, as Christian. This led to various intra-religious and religious-secular struggles – above all, for power, influence, and the authority to interpret. After the change of competition regime, though, society came to be seen as essentially pluralistic, and religion and religiosity increasingly as private matters, which led to new forms of competition – and, above all, new forms of competition for individual demand. It goes without saying that we cannot provide here a comprehensive history of these struggles in Switzerland. Our goal, rather, is to outline the main events in this competition so as to make plausible our general theory and our thesis of the change of competition regime, and then to derive some hypotheses.

Religious-secular Competition in Industrial Society

Since the sixteenth century, Switzerland has been a loose confederation of cantons and regions in which (most) cantons belong fully to one or the other denomination. The power relations were very different in urban cantons

---

[107] For the general history of Switzerland, we rely on Im Hof (1997), Maissen (2010). The materials available on the history of religion in Switzerland are distributed very unevenly. In particular, Catholicism has been much better researched than Protestantism. This is primarily due to the extensive work of Urs Altermatt and his school, which lacks a counterpart on the Protestant side. A wide field lies here for important historical research. On the general history of the church in Switzerland, see Pfister (1984), Vischer, Schenker, Dellsperger & Fatio (1995). On the history of Catholicism in the nineteenth and twentieth century, see Altermatt (1981, 1988, 1989, 2009), Dora (1997), Schweizerisches Pastoralsoziologisches Institut [Swiss Pastoral Institute of Sociology] (1986). On Protestantism, see Lindt (1988), Guggisberg (1971), Reymond (1999), Aerne (2006), Barth (1981), Schweizer (1972).

(aristocratic rule), rural cantons (some direct democracy), and peasant areas (the whole area assigned to another canton). From the start of the nineteenth century (Napoleon's invasion in 1798, the Helvetic Republic, Mediation, Restoration), Switzerland began to democratize and industrialize more and more. In the 1800–1950 period, which we shall refer to as the 'competition regime of industrial society', various intra-religious and religious-secular relationships of competition existed in a Swiss society that saw itself overall as Christian.

A first central relationship of competition existed between *liberal-Protestant and conservative-Catholic forces*. There had already been conflicts between the denominationally different cantons in the confederation. In the nineteenth century, however, these conflicts assumed new dimensions. The conflict between supporters of the new, democratic and liberal social order and advocates of the old, pre-modern social order ended differently in the different cantons. While the liberals prevailed in the Protestant urban cantons, the conservatives triumphed in the Catholic rural cantons, which meant that the liberal/ conservative opposition became denominationalized. Increasing tensions and provocations on both sides (dissolution of monasteries by Protestant cantons, the calling into existence of the Jesuit Order in Catholic Lucerne) eventually led to the Sonderbund War of 1847. This war ended in victory for the liberal-Protestant side and the founding of the Swiss federal state in 1848. With the constitution that was then adopted, the two-tier system determining the church-state relationship that is still valid today came into being. The constitution guaranteed religious freedom, and left the responsibility for determining the relationship between church and state to the cantons, each of which chose a very different form of the relationship (from separation to strong entanglement). The anti-modernist stance of Rome, manifested in the Syllabus of Errors of 1864 and the dogma of infallibility of 1870, led to a resurgence of tensions and a 'culture war' in Switzerland, which again was won by the liberal side. In the revised constitution of 1874, anti-Catholic articles were then also adopted (e.g., the prohibition on building new monasteries and the banning of the Jesuit Order). As a consequence, Catholic-conservative Switzerland lived in a kind of 'special society' which was in a permanent state of tension with regard to liberal-Protestant Switzerland, and it only let itself be integrated slowly.[108] The Catholic milieu, with its own cantons, newspapers, political parties, associations, universities, etc., played a very important role in society. It had one last flourish in the 1950s, before then collapsing in the 1960s. The Catholic milieu was a negative foil for the Reformist denomination. Because of their liberal credo, the Reformists were united on virtually nothing – except *not* being Catholic. The

---

[108] On the Catholic milieu in Switzerland, see Altermatt (1989, 2009), Dora (1997).

Catholic-Reformed conflict was therefore very important in creating identity for both sides up until the 1950s.[109]

A second important relationship of competition lay in the confrontation between *liberal and conservative directions within the denominations themselves*.[110] On the Catholic side, liberals fought against ultramontane Catholics loyal to Rome, which led at the height of the conflict in 1872 to the founding of the liberal Christian Catholic Church. Within Protestantism, a dominant liberal direction fought against a positive direction, one conservative and true to the Bible, throughout the nineteenth century.[111] Then, towards the end of the century, a further religious-social issue appeared, with liberals and positives clashing over the question of whether and to what extent the Bible can be read from a historical-critical perspective, and to what extent the Bible can be interpreted supranaturalistically. While liberals such as Alois Biedermann and David Friedrich Strauss rejected all supranaturalism (e.g., the miracles wrought by Jesus), abolished mandatory confessions, and interpreted the Christian message in essentially ethical terms, the positives held fast to their belief in the supernatural potency of God. Since the positives usually had to concede defeat, and since religious freedom had come in the meantime, they often left the churches to establish their own Protestant free churches. In this way, the 'Réveil' arose in Romandie.[112] Many of the communities created then are still an important part of the 'evangelical milieu' today.

A third relationship of competition existed between *social democracy and the (Christian) establishment*. Industrialization in the nineteenth century led to the impoverishment of the working class, which was described at the end of the century as being the 'social question'.[113] Workers began to organize themselves; in 1880, the Swiss Federation of Trade Unions came into being; in 1888, the Social Democratic Party was founded. Within unions and the party, Marxist, militant and atheist ideas were indeed controversial, but they managed to gain the upper hand at the beginning of the twentieth century. The conflict reached its climax during the general strike of 1918, which was crushed with the help of the army. As a consequence, however, many of the workers' demands were gradually met, so that tensions could be reduced.[114] This competition was extremely important

---

[109]   See Altermatt (1988), Lindt (1988).

[110]   See Gäbler (1999), Vischer et al. (1995, p. 212).

[111]   On individual aspects, besides the literature already cited, see Schweizer (1972), Barth (1981), Aerne (2006).

[112]   This period saw the founding of the *Eglise libre vaudoise* (1845), the *Eglise évangélique libre de Genève* (1849), and an independent faculty for theology at Neuenburg (1873). See Vischer et al. (1995).

[113]   Im Hof (1997, p. 128).

[114]   When the Social Democrats received their first federal councillor in 1959, they were then fully integrated into the political system.

for the religious field in Switzerland, since this was the first time that a large popular movement had explicitly represented a Marxist-atheist ideology and had confronted (sometimes with great hostility) the churches.[115] The religious and social movements in both the Protestant and the Catholic camps tried to deal with this problem by representing the interests of the working class from a decidedly Christian perspective.

A fourth relationship of competition developed between different *occupational groups*, especially in the nineteenth and twentieth centuries. This concerned the question of legitimate responsibility with regard to various activities. In particular, teachers, social workers and nurses sought to free themselves from the control of the clergy.[116] Schools, for example, were originally exclusively organized by the church, and were then later often church-controlled institutions. One of the most important educational goals of the school system in the nineteenth century was still making proper Christians of children, and that also meant at the same time making proper citizens of them.[117] Increasingly, however, the school and the educational sphere developed goals independently of religion and, together with the educational sciences, its own system of self-reflection: namely, pedagogy. And then, in around 1900, the general (primary) school was introduced, which was free and under state supervision.[118]

A fifth and final relationship of competition came about between *religious activity and employment*.[119] In the nineteenth century, entrepreneurs tried to enforce work on Sunday so as to be able to generate higher profits. Barth,[120] for example, cites a report by the Zurich Synodical Commission for Home Missions, which states:

> It is not uncommon that apprentices or servants cannot attend church service because they are working and would then have to forfeit their position. In other areas, it is the silk weavers who are busy because they are threatened with deductions.

The churches, together with the socialist forces, successfully countered these attempts. This was a competition, though, that would continue underground throughout the whole of the twentieth century.

---

[115] See Barth (1981).

[116] A history of these struggles *as struggles* in Abbott's sense (1988) remains to be written for Switzerland. For hints at least, see, for example, Schmidt-Rost (1988), Fritschi (1990), Späni (2003).

[117] Späni (2003). Similar relations can be found in Germany, too. See, for example, Kolping (1952, p. 16): the 'good citizen', the 'good Christian', and the 'good businessman'.

[118] Grunder (2011).

[119] Barth (1981, p. 130).

[120] Barth (1981, p. 129).

If we view all these struggles between 1800 and the 1950s together (in the 'competition regime of industrial society'), what becomes clear is that religion and the churches were severely weakened internally during this period. At the federal level, the liberal state had introduced denominational neutrality, the cantons had taken on many functions that had previously belonged to the churches, the demands of the Catholic submilieu had largely been met (meaning also that the milieu was no longer necessary for survival), various competing ideologies (nationalism, socialism, liberalism) had appeared on the scene and had relieved religious truths of their former monopoly position, and new professions had taken tasks away from the religious specialists.

Swiss society, though, was not, or was only partly, conscious of this decline. Up until the end of the 1950s, Swiss society still believed that it was, itself, a Christian society. That was justified on the one hand by the fact that over 97 per cent of the population belonged to a Christian denomination (1900: 99.4 per cent, 1950: 97.8 per cent), and that belonging did not appear to be a matter of individual choice.[121] As had been the case for centuries, the individual was 'born into' his or her religion, was baptized as a child, socialized within his or her own denominational milieu, made into a full member of society and the church through a rite of passage (such as confirmation), and buried according to the ritual of his or her own denomination. On the other hand, the two world wars had played an important role. Switzerland had been miraculously spared the carnage of war. A strategy during this period had been the so-called 'spiritual defence', that is, an emphasis on the specific Swiss characteristic with respect first to the German ideology of blood and soil, and then to communism.[122] In both cases, Switzerland was represented as a bastion of democracy, of multilingualism, of freedom, and not least of freedom also of the Christian faith – in stark contrast to the atheist Nazis and Communists.[123]

The 1950s allow us to view once more, as though through a magnifying glass, this paradox whereby religion becomes weaker in the background and stronger in the foreground. In the 1950s, phenomena appeared that led to the imminent

---

[121] Choice was also normally excluded within each denomination. According to where he or she lived, the individual was assigned to a parish or church community and could not choose a different one. Moreover, the denominational milieus were strictly separated from each other not only geographically but also socially. Before 1848, the Swiss cantons were, with exceptions and each with its own unique historical development, monodenominational and dominated by the church. Civil rights depended on denominational affiliation. Relationships differed considerably between Protestant-Reformed, Catholic and bipartite cantons. In the Protestant cantons, there was an extremely close relationship between church and state. In the Catholic areas, the Pope and bishops exercised great power. On this, see Kuhn (2007), Pfister (1974).

[122] On spiritual defence, see Loderer (2012).

[123] Also Vischer et al. (1995, p. 264).

cultural revolution and paved the way for it. Of particular importance here are the economic boom and mass consumption related to it. An ever increasing number of new products entered the market, such as the vacuum cleaner, the washing machine, the food mixer, the television, fully automatic heating, etc. Thanks to rising incomes, they could also be bought by the great mass of the population.[124] It is no coincidence that the population spoke of the 'Volkswagen' (the people's car) and, at least initially, also of the 'Volkskühlschrank' (the people's fridge).[125] The car had a particularly strong effect, enabling as it did a completely new level of mobility with regard to where people worked and spent their leisure time.[126] The magazine *Touring* wrote enthusiastically in 1952, for example:

> Is there a more enjoyable way to criss-cross Switzerland than by car? Hardly! By car, the leaps have become even smaller; people have been given seven-league boots, as if in a fairy tale. (Touring, 15/1952)[127]

This new culture of mass consumption also influenced teenagers and young adults in particular. They could now be consumers and had become their own distinctive group that business and advertising could target. New youth cultures (such as Teddy Boys) and leisure activities (dance halls, movie theatres) developed (to some extent, they had already begun developing in the 1950s).

The new opportunities open to people multiplied, however, not only because incomes rose overall, but also because the state had an important influence. Due to economic growth, government revenues increased, which enabled the state to provide an unprecedented amount of collective goods. These included, to name just two examples, the introduction in 1948 of the AHV (an insurance protecting the elderly and the widowed), and the development of an extensive road and rail network.[128] These state initiatives, then, also greatly increased the secular options open to individuals.

At the same time, the second half of the 1940s and the 1950s were a time of (at least apparent) stability with respect to existing values, and moral and religious attitudes.[129] After the war years, people seemed to have a need for normality, security, peace, order and conservative values. People wished to find such normality especially in the family, which was still organized according to traditional gender roles. It was logical, then, for an article protecting the family to be included in the constitution in 1946. This value-laden conservatism dovetailed perfectly with the positions then being taken by the churches (in

---

[124] On this, see the excellent book by Buomberger & Pfrunder (2012).
[125] See Schumacher (2012).
[126] See Buomberger (2012).
[127] Quoted from Buomberger (2012, p. 42).
[128] Buomberger (2012).
[129] For Europe in general, see McLeod (2007, p. 45).

all their denominational variety), and explains in part the religious renaissance which (again: at least apparently) occurred at the time. The churches participated in the general economic recovery; their memberships grew (in absolute terms) due to the strongly growing population; they built new churches; and they stood for the legitimization of values of duty and acceptance which were so important during this time. The Catholic Church in particular showed itself to be, up until the Second Vatican Council, a relentless defender of conservative moral and religious values. And, at the same time, the churches were able to gain an advantage by presenting themselves as guardians of the peace.

An example of the conservatism of the 1950s is the scandal surrounding the painter Kurt Fahrner,[130] who publicly displayed his painting 'Image of a crucified woman of our time' (a naked woman on a cross) at the *Barfüsserplatz* in Basel on 29 April 1959. He was arrested by the police; the picture was confiscated; and Fahrner was sentenced to three days in prison on probation and fined 100 francs. The judges stated in their verdict: 'such [a] representation bordering on obscenity, with the redemptive death of Christ placed in parallel [...], does injury in the meanest way to the religious beliefs of others'.[131]

There seems to have been precisely this contradiction in the 1950s: the new opportunities to do things due to economic recovery and mass consumption and, at the same time, the preservation of the traditional (moral, value-laden, religious) corset, this contradiction leading to the outbreak of the revolution of the 1960s.

To summarize: within the old competition regime, there were, as we have seen, fierce struggles both between different denominations and between religious and secular groups. Yet, despite a sinking number of functions performed by churches due to these struggles, the assumption of a fundamental Christian legitimacy of the entire system remained. This was to change in the 1960s.

The change of competition regime in the 1960s
In Switzerland in the 1960s, as in almost all Western countries, there was a cultural revolution that was not a religious-secular conflict as such, but which would nonetheless so change the entire fabric of society that the intra-religious and religious-secular struggles would now have to run their course in a different way.[132]

---

[130] For an illustration of this example in the context of contemporary history, see Skenderovic & Späti (2012).

[131] See   http://de.wikipedia.org/wiki/Bild_einer_gekreuzigten_Frau_unserer_Zeit, downloaded on 21.7.2013.

[132] On the revolution of the 1960s in connection with religion in general, see McLeod (2007), Putnam & Campbell (2010). On the 1968 revolution in Switzerland, see Skenderovic & Späti (2012). On the influence of 1968 on religion in Switzerland, see Campiche (2008).

The cultural revolution of the 1960s was initially a conflict between generations: a young generation turned against the older generations and their – as they thought – stale, stuffy and boring ideas on life and values. The 1968 revolution crystallized around a number of issues, with the actors criticizing in particular the Vietnam War, colonialism, imperialism, militarism and fascism. They opposed any authority, whether government, university, parent or church. A central issue closely related to this was individual freedom: the individual should be allowed to choose free of all pressure and be able to live out his or her individual wishes, especially in the realm of sexuality.[133] For many teenagers and young adults, this period was a time of great emotion, a time when the world seemed to be coming apart at the seams and everything seemed possible. The Beatles summed this feeling up in their song 'All you need is love', while Cat Stevens sang in 1971: 'If you want to sing out sing out / and if you want to be free be free / there's a million ways to be / you know that there are'.[134]

Young people now consumed in particular a new, proudly alternative and countercultural music (Beatles, Rolling Stones, Doors; and, in Switzerland, Les Sauterelles around Toni Vescoli), alternative clothing and hairstyles (colourful, loose clothing, long hair for men, short for women), and alternative leisure activities (sit-ins, happenings, alternative art). The young generation in the *cities*, and in particular students, was especially caught up in the revolution.[135]

The new individualistic values and lifestyles by no means remained restricted to young people living in cities and to young adults, though. Rather, they spread from the young to older generations, from the cities to the countryside, and from those with higher levels of education to all levels. The expansion to all age groups occurred not so much because older people accepted the new values, but because older generations with traditional ideas simply died off and the succeeding generations upheld the new values from the beginning. The spread from the city to the country was greatly helped by the new opportunities available to be mobile (car, development of rail transport): more and more people were living in an urban agglomeration or living in the countryside and commuting to the city to work and to pursue leisure activities.

---

[133] In the whole Western world, though, sexual norms seem to have loosened subliminally before the 1960s. See, for example, McLeod (2007), Barbagli, Dalla Zuanna & Garelli (2010).

[134] Cat Stevens, 'If you want to sing out, sing out'. The song was first heard in the film *Harold and Maude* (1970/71).

[135] For individual details on culture in Switzerland in the 1960s, see Skenderovic & Späti (2012). On youth cultures in Switzerland, see Stapferhaus Lenzburg (1997).

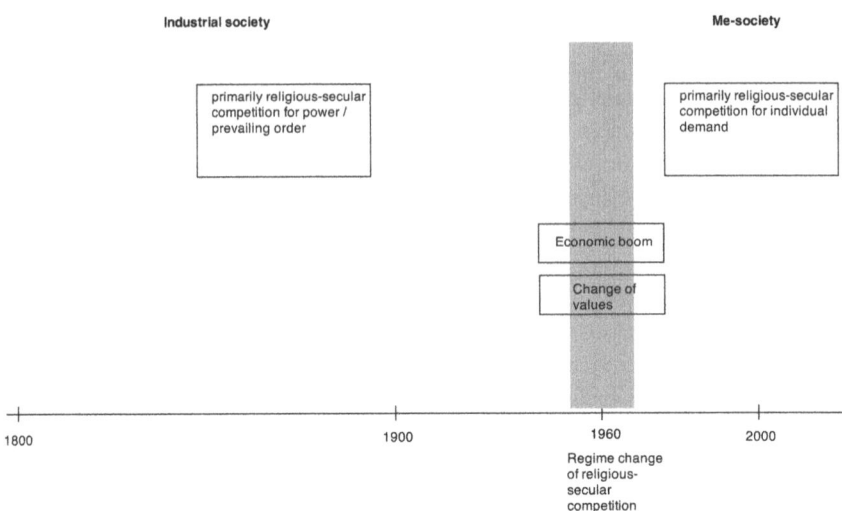

Figure 2.2   Schematic representation of regime change of religious-
secular competition

The revolution of the 1960s had several extremely important implications for religion, and we can group these under three central points. First, it meant that teenagers and young adults attacked and challenged religion and the churches as one of the various authorities. In the previous few decades, the churches had certainly steadily lost functions, but, up until the 1950s, they had always been able to legitimize Swiss society as a whole. With the cultural revolution of the 1960s, this function was denied them – from both without and within.[136] Second, the new living conditions of the 1950s and 1960s, with extreme increases in income and the new leisure activities available, meant that the youth work of the churches – which had always played an important role – was undermined by what the secular competitors could offer. It had already become apparent in the 1940s and 1950s that church-organized leisure activities would have a difficult time – now, they were often simply swept away. Third, there were also, interestingly, actual revolutions within the main churches themselves. On the Catholic side, the Second Vatican Council was a decisive event which led to huge expectations of change; and, on the Reformed side, there was an upswing in ideas which were extremely critical of the institution, as well as the idea of the

---

[136]   This side of the 1960s still has to be researched. See the issue by Reformiert.info from 30.5.2008: '1968: Der Protest, der (auch) aus der Kirche kam. Rückschau/Was fast vergessen ging: Auch die Kirche war 1968 für die Jugend prägend: als heimat, Plattform und ... Negativfolie'. http://www.reformiert.info/artikel_4674.html. Downloaded on 22.8.2013.

'death of God'. In 1971, the church historian Kurt Guggisberg wrote about the previous decade:

> When the extensive 'Handbook of Reformed Switzerland' proudly paraded Protestantism in 1962, the churchly structures discussed there still appeared unchallenged. Since then, though, everything has been thrown overboard as outdated and in need of improvement by revolutionary-minded theologians and lay people.[137]

Interestingly, the 1960s was not a particularly secular decade. On the contrary, these were years of great, albeit critical, religious interest. The churches may have been criticized, but at least they were talked about. Many people considered the decade as a period of new religious awakening, and few foresaw the impending collapse of the churches.

Religious-secular competition in the me-society

Through the revolution of the 1960s, the old regime of religious-secular competition of industrial society was replaced by that of the me-society. In both competition regimes, we find religious-secular competition at all three levels: for power in society, for power within groups/organizations/milieus, and for individual demand. However, the central point around which competition revolved changed completely. Since the new competition regime, individuals now possess a relatively large amount of resources and a great deal of security. On this basis, they make their own decisions regarding education, choice of career, choice of partner, sexual orientation, lifestyle – and religion and religiosity, too. Religious affiliation is therefore regarded essentially as being something that people can choose, and leaving the church is no longer a taboo. Individuals increasingly consider themselves to be not so much members of a religious community from birth onwards but much more as 'customers' purchasing goods from religious 'suppliers'.[138] This does not mean that, in this competition regime, there cannot also be religious-secular competition for power. But, in such cases, people also now adopt as a matter of course a fundamentally individualistic worldview.

Relationships of competition

The most important relationship of competition in the competition regime of the me-society is certainly *religious-secular competition for demand*. In literally

---

[137] Guggisberg (1971, p. 307).

[138] Or, formulated differently: many still see themselves as Protestant or Catholic 'from birth'. But it is precisely because they themselves did not choose the religion/denomination that it does not appear to be particularly important to them.

every area where they had previously enjoyed a monopoly, the churches and religious communities are now confronted by secular suppliers offering similar goods. A *first* area of this relationship of competition is leisure time. Because the norms which secured religious practice have lost their binding force, religious practice has now become a 'leisure-time decision'. This has a particularly strong impact on how Sunday is organized. For many people, the 'Lord's Day' has become a secular weekend. Leisure-time competition is also very clear with regard to young people. From the end of the nineteenth century, the churches tried to provide leisure-time activities for young people, so as to guarantee a continuous transmission of the Christian faith. In the 1950s, and then in particular in the 1960s, these activities found themselves subjected to strong competition from secular activities of all kinds. The competition for demand is, *second*, also strong in the area of children's upbringing, where parents have to ask themselves the question of how much space should be granted to religious upbringing in comparison to secular upbringing and to other possible uses of time. A *third* aspect of this competition concerns the 'demand for a religious career'. Due to the economic recovery and the improved educational opportunities for broad segments of the population, the profession of priest or pastor has become less attractive than it used to be. This profession was once one of the few opportunities for social advancement that children from poorer and more rural areas had. With the disappearance of this advantage, the profession has lost some of its attractiveness.[139] A *fourth* and final area of competition concerns life-cycle rituals, which were still long considered as the last bastion of the churches, and which are now the subject of competition whenever secular suppliers of rituals appear on the scene.[140]

Religious-secular competition for demand leads to important effects not only for those supplying but also for those demanding, the latter usually choosing the product on offer that appears most attractive to them. Since secular products have been greatly expanded and are also more accessible due to people's greater purchasing power, many individuals are now undergoing a so-called 'secular drift', that is, they are sliding slowly into secular waters.[141] This often happens less as a conscious decision *against* religious products, and more as a byproduct of the decision *for* secular products. The fact that individuals themselves decide on their religious-secular demand also leads to an increasing individualization (individuals increasingly differ with respect to their individually chosen religious-secular 'shopping basket'), and to an increasing consumerism (individuals

---

[139] A point also made by McLeod (2007, p. 113).

[140] However, many individuals seem not to need such suppliers, either. Rather, they themselves create the form of the rituals marking important stages in life. For such possibilities, see, for example, http://www.ritualnetz.ch.

[141] In coining the term 'secular drift' we have been influenced by Long/Hadden (1983) who talk about 'social drift'.

increasingly regard the religious-secular world as consisting of 'products' to be judged according to performance and price). For religious suppliers, the new competition regime of the me-society means that they have to make great efforts in order to 'stay in the market', that is, in order to motivate people to make time, energy and money available for religious (and not other) purposes. Hence, churches are increasingly trying to use different strategies from marketing (e.g., needs analysis, quality assurance, and advertising).[142] A key strategy is also to reach a certain size in order to be able to survive in the competition (hence, the phenomenon of mergers and megachurches).[143]

One struggle that has been extremely important for religion in society concerns the *emancipation of women*,[144] which is a struggle that began in the nineteenth century and that pervaded the whole of the twentieth century, increasing in virulence in the 1960s, 1970s and 1980s. While it was normal in pre-industrial times for both men and women to work,[145] industrialization, the widening separation of home and workplace, and the invention of the traditional family unit led to a strong division of labour between the sexes. In this ideology, the husband was responsible for earning a living outside the home, while the wife stayed at home to take care of the children and household. The very fact that the woman did not need to work was a sign of the status of the family. Men and women were assigned different 'innate' characteristics. Men were rational, tough, courageous, decisive – and potentially endangered by 'vice'. Women were motherly, tender, loving, pure and pious.[146] On the basis of this ideology, women were excluded from political and most other public activities. In working life, they could pursue only certain professions, could only rise in their profession to a very limited extent, and usually received less pay for equal work. In marital law, the wife was not considered equal to her husband, who had financial jurisdiction and could decide whether or not to allow his wife to work. Even in matters of sexuality, there was no equality. The women's movement demanded equality in all these areas. For us, what is interesting is that the traditional gender-specific division of labour in the nineteenth and early twentieth century led overall to a feminization of religion.[147] On the one hand, women were shut out from a

---

[142] On religious marketing, see Famos & Kunz (2006), Stolz & Usunier (2013), Mottner (2007), Einstein (2008), Sengers (2009). On the relationship between religion and consumer culture, see Gauthier/Martikainen/Woodhead (2011).

[143] On the phenomenon of megachurches, see Chaves (2006), Fath (2008). For the existence of megachurches in Switzerland see Stolz/Chaves/Monnot/Amiotte-Suchet (2011), Monnot (2013).

[144] On this with regard to Switzerland, see also Campiche (1996). For Western Europe, see McLeod (2007). For Eastern European countries, see Sammet & Bergelt (2012).

[145] See Schnegg (1988).

[146] See, for example, Fritschi (1990), Mesmer (1988), Brown (2001).

[147] See McLeod (2000), Brown (2001).

number of areas of activity which could have competed with religion, and which men effectively did (employed work, leisure activities, sport, etc.). On the other hand, they were given a role as wife and mother which directly focused on the mediation of religiosity. The wife, especially in Catholicism, had to take care of the religious upbringing of the children and to rule as 'priestess of the family'. If they were active in public life, this was usually in the context of charity work.[148] In the fight for equality, which progressed more slowly in Switzerland than in other Western European countries, these two pillars of female religiosity were destroyed. On the one hand, women fought for equal political, economic and social rights. And so they won the right to vote in 1971 (comparatively very late, as we have said); equality between men and women was included in the constitution in 1981; and the Marriage Act of 1985 no longer considered the husband to be head of the family.[149] On the other hand, the traditional gender-specific role images were destroyed, and especially so in the (also, sexual) revolution of the 1960s and in the subsequent women's movement.[150] Women fought vehemently against the traditional stereotypes and rejected the religious legitimacy of the role images. Interestingly, women could pursue the struggle for new freedoms and a new identity not only in conflict with religion, but also precisely with the help of a new, alternative spirituality, one which originated in the 1960s and came to full bloom in the 1970s. In effect, both developments meant that women were now confronted by the same factors in competition with religion as men.

A further struggle within the competition regime of the me-society relates to the *standing of the churches recognized (in most cantons) as public and legal institutions*. We are no longer concerned here with individual demand, but with questions of power and influence on the prevailing order in society. Since the number of people with no religious affiliation is rising, as well as the number of non-Christian religions, the practice of granting exclusive recognition to the national churches is appearing ever less legitimate. The standing of these churches is therefore becoming vulnerable to attack – for example, by secularist groups and by religious communities which have not been granted such recognition.[151] Thus, there have been repeated attempts in recent decades to bring an end to such exclusive recognition for the national churches in different cantons, or to curtail certain privileges that they enjoy. The cantons have also then gradually amended their constitutions, either to loosen the church-state relationship, or to offer the possibility to other religious communities of gaining legal recognition.

---

[148]   As an instructive example, see Moser (2004).

[149]   See Maissen (2010, p. 297 f.).

[150]   See Skenderovic & Späti (2012). On the link between religion and sexuality using the example of Italy, see the interesting contribution by Barbagli, Dalla Zuanna & Garelli (2010).

[151]   See Famos (2007), Pahud de Mortanges (2007, 2012).

In this context, it is also interesting to note that the major churches are limited in how they respond to this competition, for wrestling openly for dominance with other denominations or religions is not appreciated in the new competition regime. They can strengthen their public standing instead by supporting issues that serve the public interest overall, such as peace, inter-faith dialogue, and commitment to human rights.[152]

Finally, we can identify an important *struggle around Islam*. Here, those who oppose Islam because they see it as something threatening are in conflict with actors who want to give Islam the same rights as all other religions in Switzerland. The anti-Islam activists are made up of different groups: right-wing conservatives around the Swiss People's Party, right-wing members of Evangelical churches, and feminists who object to the traditional ideas on gender held by many Muslims. The activists on the other side consist of representatives of the major churches, practitioners of inter-faith dialogue, and supporters of the multicultural society.[153] In the referendum of 2009, the opponents of Islam managed to enforce a ban on minarets in Switzerland, which is now in Article 72 of the constitution.[154] It is obvious that the majority of those voting for a ban on minarets did so not so much because Islam is not a Christian religion, but rather because they see Islam as a religion which threatens the prevailing pluralistic and democratic order.

2.4 Hypotheses

If the general theory and the socio-historical concretization of the last few pages are true, then should they also not be observable empirically? This question leads us to make several central hypotheses that we will be testing in this book. We can distinguish hypotheses regarding the transition to the me-society, individual adjustments, major groups (milieus), and religious-spiritual suppliers.

Transition to the Me-society

H1   *Transition to the me-society, economic growth and religious indicators.* We should be able to show that a great change in different dimensions actually did occur in the 1960s (which we call the transition to the me-society or the change of competition regime). In this period, we

---

[152] See Könemann & Jödicke (2012).

[153] On Islam and criticism of Islam in Switzerland, see Behloul & Lathion (2007), Behloul (2007), Schneuwly-Purdie, Giann & Magali (2009). On the prohibition of minarets, see Haenni & Lathion (2011). On Islamophobia in Switzerland, see Stolz (2006), Helbling (2010), Lindemann (2012).

[154] Article 72, Paragraph 3 states: 'The building of minarets is prohibited'.

should find a marked increase in living standards for the vast majority of the population (real income, personal security, mobility, leisure options), and at the same time a marked decline in religious practice.

H2   *Transition to the me-society and cultural change.* Individuals born before 1960 should differ markedly in various cultural respects from those born later. The former should still report of a strong, enforced religious socialization which bears the features of the old competition regime. We should find with the former less individualization and religious consumerism, a stronger denominational identity, and a lower rejection of anti-individualistic religion (insofar as this applies to their own religion). This group should on average also be more religious than later generations. The generation born in the 1940s should have often experienced the change of competition regime as a biographical break with their own parental home. In contrast, the later generations should report a much freer religious socialization and display strong values of the new competition regime.

H3   *Transition to the me-society and gender.* Men and women should be clearly different in several respects. People born before 1940 should still report of very different religious socialization for boys and girls. The women of these generations should also still be clearly more religious than the men. Women born between 1940 and 1970 should report to a greater extent of a freeing from traditional religious patterns of thought and partly of experiments in alternative spirituality. After 1970, an alignment between the genders with regard to religion should be noticeable.

H4   *Transition to the me-society and the urban/rural distinction.* The differences between urban and rural areas should initially increase in terms of religion, since the transition to the me-society (or to the new competition regime) began in the urban areas. As the new lifestyle spread from the city to the countryside, so should the differences decrease again.

Individual Adjustments

H5   *Secular drift.* Individuals should show a secular drift, that is, they should, on average, become less religious, and that is because, since the 1960s, individuals see that they are no longer forced into religion, that they have many resources and very many secular options, and that (in their opinion) they can often better satisfy their needs through secular institutions. Secular drift should be observable between generations in particular, since religiosity and spirituality are strongly influenced by socialization and each new generation grows up in a world which is even more strongly marked by secular alternatives.

H6   *Individualization and consumerism.* We should be able to observe across the whole society an increase in individualism and consumerism during the last few decades, which means that individuals increasingly think that they can and must decide for themselves in religious/secular matters, and increasingly choose the options which bring them (subjectively) the greatest 'benefit' or the most 'satisfaction'.

Major groups

H7   *Different patterns of growth and shrinkage of major groups.* Major groups with a traditional Christian religiosity should shrink, while those with a distanced religiosity and secular views should grow. We should be able to observe a major group with an alternative spirituality from the 1970s. This hypothesis requires a more exact description of the major groups, which is what we shall be providing in Chapters 3 to 8.

Suppliers

As our investigation has collected data primarily on individuals, we can test the hypotheses concerning religious and spiritual suppliers only partly and only indirectly (particularly in Chapters 7, 8 and 9). Again, we ask what would have to be observed empirically if our theoretical description is correct.

H8   *Religious marketing.* Churches and religious communities should increasingly be using religious marketing. Since they notice that individuals no longer have to be members and there are no longer any norms sanctioning religiosity, suppliers are forced to adapt to the needs of individuals. For this purpose, they will increasingly try to use the same techniques as other organizations (market research, surveys, studies of milieus, quality assurance, diversification, focusing on a core product, advertising, etc.).

H9   *Megachurches and fusions.* In order to be able to survive in the competition, and particularly when competing with secular suppliers, many religious suppliers will try to reach a critical mass, either through a megachurch or fusions of existing communities.

H10   *Accommodating vs. withdrawing.* If suppliers wish to appeal to many people (i.e., remain 'national churches for the people'), then they will adapt to the values and moral ideas of the new competition regime and absorb these in the long term. They will therefore stress the freedom of the individual person, human rights, equality between men and women, etc. They will also be weakened if they try to control the behaviour and moral ideas of their members. Elements of the ideology of suppliers which do not fit in to the new competition regime will appear as highly illegitimate in society. On the other hand, if suppliers are not willing to adapt to the new competition regime, they will then have to practise a form of social withdrawal. By creating closed milieus or social groups with clear boundaries, they will have to isolate their members to such an extent that they do not, or hardly, hear criticism from the outside world.

***

We have now presented our theory and the hypotheses that emerge from it. Anyone familiar with the literature will have noticed that most of the ideas presented here are not new. Nonetheless, we wish here to make a new systematization, one which shows in a general way how religious-secular competition, in conjunction with other factors, can explain the most diverse religious phenomena. As we have already mentioned, this theory has several advantages over previous theories. By highlighting the contribution of (individual and collective) actors and identifying the causal mechanisms of the action, the theory is not only descriptive but also explanatory. In other words, it does not simply provide descriptive labels such as 'secularization', 'differentiation', 'rationalization' and 'individualization', but actually traces these processes back to a few basic explanatory mechanisms. In contrast to market theory, the advantage here is that we recognize intra-religious competition as a special case among many other possibilities. Furthermore, the theory is able to explain both the secularizing macro-trend as well as historical and geographical variations. At the most diverse points, it allows us to a certain extent to 'step into history', so that from there we can make visible the next stages.

How much evidence supports this theory, though? This question is addressed in all the following chapters. Chapters 3 to 8 will first describe the major groups quantitatively and qualitatively. Chapter 9 will then take up the explanatory question again and show whether and how these hypotheses can be empirically verified.

Chapter 3
Four Forms of (Un)Belief

Jörg Stolz, Mallory Schneuwly-Purdie

(...) let every man seek heaven in his own fashion. (Frederick the Great)

Anyone setting out, as we are, to explore for the next few years how people in Switzerland discuss their religiosity, spirituality or irreligiosity first faces an immense diversity. The complexity of the different forms of belief, religious views, spiritual or secular experiences, and histories is as impressive as it is overwhelming. How can such an immense diversity possibly be represented in a comprehensible way in just a few pages?

The aim of this chapter is to introduce a new typology, one which helps us to bring order to the complexity of individual religious experiences and actions. We are not the first to propose such a typology.[1] Previous attempts, though, usually referred only to sub-areas of religion and were supported only by quantitative data, which sometimes impaired comprehensibility. By that we mean that it was difficult really to imagine the different types. In contrast, we looked for as clear a typology as possible, one which covers the most important religious dimensions (i.e., beliefs, practices, values, etc.), is based on qualitative as well as quantitative data, and can be linked to an explanatory theory.[2]

3.1 A Typology on Two Levels

We can explain the typology[3] most easily by way of a figure (Figure 3.1). The typology is based on two dimensions, a dimension of institutional religiosity (vertical axis) and a dimension of alternative spirituality (horizontal axis). By *institutional*

---

[1]   Earlier typologies can be found, for example, in Krüggeler (1993), Dubach & Campiche (1993), Campiche (2004), Bréchon et al. (1997), Höhmann & Krech (2006), Benthaus-Apel (2006), Rodriguez (2005), Höllinger & Tripold (2012), Siegers (2012).

[2]   We also see a function of our typology as being to bring into a common framework the greatest variety of findings from quantitative and qualitative studies, findings which have previously seemed to contradict each other.

[3]   The typology arose from an iterative interplay of qualitative and quantitative analyses. On the quantitative side, we carried out a cluster analysis with SPSS, on the basis of which we grouped the respondents according to similarities and differences with regard to

religiosity, we mean individual religiosity which is connected to the products and teachings of Christian churches. By *alternative spirituality*, we mean individual beliefs, forms of practice and experiences which are related to the products of alternative-spiritual suppliers, and which are at the same time distinguished from the Christian churches.[4] Figure 3.1 shows that we distinguish four types within the two dimensions: an institutional (I), an alternative (A), a distanced (D), and a secular (S) type. These four types differ not only in terms of beliefs and religious practices, but also in terms of their identity, socio-structural characteristics, values, relationships to religious suppliers, and perceptions of other religions.

The number of types which we can distinguish depends primarily on the 'sociological altitude' from which we observe society. The types mentioned are a result of looking at society from 'way up above'. If we were to swoop down and look at the situation close up, though, new subtypes within the four general types would suddenly appear (Figure 3.2). The subtypes occur in two forms: as milieus and as aggregates. First, by *milieus*, we mean major groups organized around religiosity and spirituality which have their own group identity.[5] Thus, we find an evangelical milieu, an established milieu (which includes core members of Catholic and Reformed religious communities), and an esoteric milieu (in which we find the highly active in the esoteric domain). On the other hand, there are also subtypes that can only be described as *social aggregates*, that is, as collectives of people resulting from statistical combination, which have similar religious or secular practices and attitudes. Social aggregates have neither their own group structures and suppliers, nor a group identity, and include, for example, the 'Sheilaists and alternative customers', as well as the different subtypes within the distanced and secular types.[6]

---

their churchly-religious or alternative practices and their religious beliefs. For more details, see Appendix.

　[4]　Our definition of alternative spirituality is, in comparison to other definitions, rather narrow. The literature on spirituality is very large. See, for example, Giordan (2007), Rose (2001), Höllinger & Tripold (2012), Siegers (2012, 2014), Streib/Hood (2013). Note that our concept of alternative spirituality is seen as a subphenomenon of the more general phenomenon of religiosity (see Chapter 2).

　[5]　We use a similar concept of milieu to Schulze (1995, p. 210), but (re)construct here very specific religious-spiritual milieus which do not appear in Schulze's work in such a form. Using the concept of milieu in this way is quite common in the literature of the sociology of religion – see, for example, for the Protestant milieu, Stolz, Favre, Gachet & Buchard (2013); for the fundamentalist milieu, Riesebrodt (1990); for the holistic or alternative-spiritual milieu, Höllinger & Tripold (2012), Campbell (1995 (1972)); for the Catholic milieu, Altermatt (1989). Marcel Proust (1896) already wrote more than a century ago that the milieu of fashion is characterized by the fact that everyone forms a personal opinion on the basis of everyone else's opinion. But what if everyone has an opinion which fundamentally contradicts everyone else's opinion? Then, says Proust, we find ourselves in the literary milieu.

　[6]　But there are also communities with their own group identity within the secular milieu.

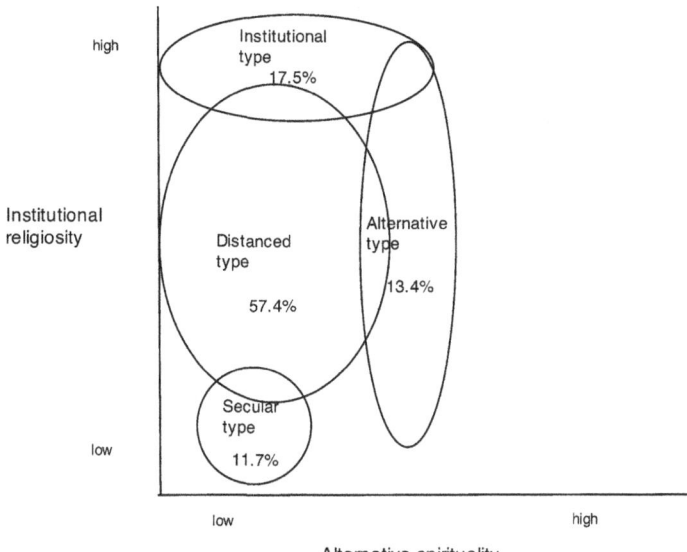

Figure 3.1   Four types (higher level)

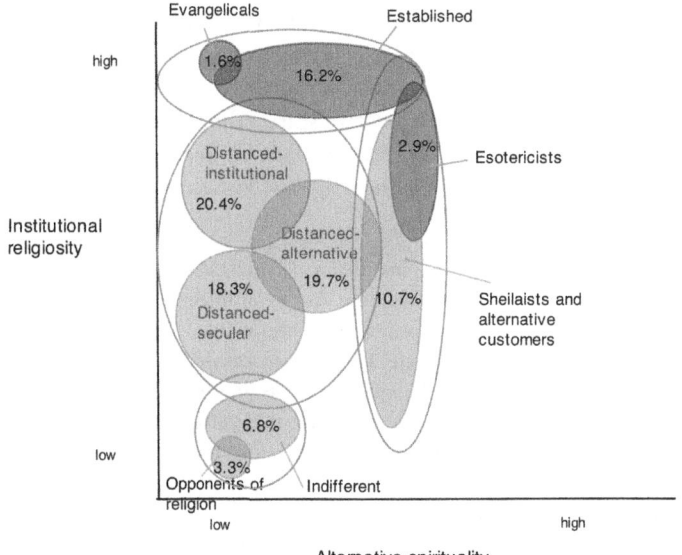

Figure 3.2   Nine subtypes: aggregates and milieus (lower level)

We shall now present the beliefs and religious practices (if any) of the types and subtypes. With our methodological approach, we can divide into types and subtypes not only the participants in our representative study but also the conversation partners in our guided interviews. Thus, when we talk of the 'institutional' (a type on the first level) or the 'opponents of religion' (a subtype of secularist on the second level), we always have in mind exact people that match this type or subtype. We are also quite sure that readers will have no trouble allocating their friends and acquaintances to one of the different types, subtypes or milieus.[7]

3.2 Institutional

The *institutional*, comprising 17.5 per cent of our sample, attribute great value to the Christian faith and Christian practice in their own lives (Table 3.1). These are core members of the Catholic and Reformed religious communities, as well as the great majority of members of Evangelical churches. The institutional *believe* in a single, personal and transcendental God. Around 99 per cent believe (quite or completely) that this God cares for each individual person, and most are convinced that life only has meaning through God and Jesus Christ. 63 per cent believe in life after death. Some (especially Evangelicals) are very critical of secular or atheist attitudes, and also vehemently reject alternative-spiritual beliefs. Other members of this type can accept secular attitudes and are sometimes very open-minded towards alternative spirituality. The institutional have a pronounced *religious practice*, which is usually linked with the ideas and products of the churches and their core religious communities. Of those

---

[7]   In naming the types and subtypes ('institutional', 'alternative', 'distanced' and 'secular'), we looked for names which were as simple and as intuitively comprehensible as possible. However, accidental associations cannot always be avoided. The institutional, for example, are given that name because they are in close contact with a major church or Evangelical church – and in this sense with a 'religious institution'. On the other hand, we could argue, though, that the Evangelical churches distance themselves from the national churches, which they see precisely as 'institutions', and therefore the term is somewhat infelicitous. The members of the alternative type are so-called because their religiosity or spirituality often sees itself as a 'counter-proposal' to what they perceive as the dominant churches. Some critics have argued that the term is judgmental, because it does not represent alternative religion as 'normal'. Others still have claimed that what we mean by spirituality is really the mainstream today and can therefore no longer be considered 'alternative'. We spent the most time naming the 'distanced'. We have in mind here a phenomenon which British sociologists of religion have called 'fuzzy fidelity'. But 'fuzzies' seemed an unfortunate name. We finally settled on 'distanced', a term which was promptly criticized, particularly by some church representatives, for setting out with a 'false understanding of the church'.

belonging to this type, 72 per cent go to church at least once a month, while 69 per cent pray daily.

Institutional

Nathalie (41, subtype 'established') is a housewife and mother. She is very involved in the Catholic Church. As coordinator of the catechesis, she is actively involved in the organization of mass, and is also involved with parents in the religious instruction of their children. She believes not in a punitive God, but in a God of love who lives within every person. Nathalie goes regularly to mass, not because of external coercion, but because of an inner need.

François (55, subtype 'established') is a male nurse. He is a Protestant and grew up in a Methodist family which went to church every Sunday. François has been married to a Catholic woman for many years. He believes in God or in a higher power that somehow influences his life, as well as in life after death, which is, though, difficult to put into words. Moreover, the values of solidarity and humanity are extremely important for his faith, which is why he is strongly committed to refugees and concerned with hunger in the world. François prays alone and every fortnight accompanies his wife to Catholic mass (his wife goes to mass every week).

Willi (40, subtype 'evangelical') is managing director of a small company. As a child, he attended an evangelical community with his mother, and converted during a tent mission at the age of 16. This conversion kept him from leaving school early and steered his life in a new direction. He is a member of a congregation in which he also has a responsibility. Willi reads the Bible every morning for half an hour, prays regularly, and goes with his family to religious service on Sunday mornings. His faith in Jesus Christ, in God and in the Holy Spirit plays a central role in his life.

Within the type of the institutional, we can distinguish two important subtypes: the 'established' and the 'evangelical' (see the box entitled 'Institutional' with Nathalie and Willi as examples). The two subtypes can be distinguished quite clearly. The *established* (16.2 per cent) are core members of Catholic and Reformed religious communities; they have a very personal religiousness and are actively involved within their religious community. They have often been subject to strong religious socialization and the continuation of this tradition is an important motive for them. According to denomination, the specifically Reformed or Roman/Christian Catholic rituals are important for most members of this subtype. Within this subtype, we can still find certain clearly recognizable denominational differences. Catholics have often been subject to much stronger religious socialization, and sometimes it is the saints, Mary and the specifically Catholic elements of religious service that are important to them. The Reformed have usually been brought up much more freely and often emphasize the importance of *not* being a Catholic. Overall, though, the data show clearly that the very central denominational differences of earlier decades have lost much of their social importance – even in this highly religious group.

In contrast, the *evangelical* subtype (1.6 per cent) are (to state the obvious) mostly members of Evangelical churches, or they show an evangelical style of religiousness.[8] They always characterize themselves through a very particular style of faith, practice and living. Here, the individual conversion, that is, a turning to the saviour Jesus Christ, is central. This conversion, which occurs completely individually, is usually symbolized later in the forms of an adult baptism before the congregation.[9] Individuals see themselves as 'Christian' or 'true Christian', and usually distance themselves from Christians for whom their faith is not important in this way. Being a Christian means leading a life which is strongly shaped by faith, practising regularly, being actively involved in a religious community, converting non-Christians to the faith, and leading a clearly moral life. In contrast to those belonging to the established subtype, for the evangelical subtype, continuing traditions is less important. Within this subtype or within the 'evangelical milieu',[10] we can make out a classic, a Pentecostal and a conservative stream.

We can find many overlappings and sometimes also movements between the established and the evangelical subtypes. On the one hand, there have long been evangelical and charismatic movements within the pluralistic major churches. On the other hand, we can find many individuals who move from one milieu to another, go back and forth between them, or simply belong to both. We can take Barbara and Beat as examples. Barbara (58), whose husband is a permanent member of an Evangelical church, formally belongs to the national Reformed Church, but sometimes attends religious service in her husband's Evangelical church, and sometimes the service of her national Reformed Church. What she likes about the Evangelical church is the commitment, the fact that there are also many young people involved, and that the congregation is '*alive*'. What she is critical of, though, is its '*isolation*'. What she appreciates about the Reformed Church is its ecumenical openness – but what she does not like is the fact that there are only a few, and older, people there. The apprentice Beat, 18, is, with his entire family, a member of the national Reformed Church – but his style of faith corresponds very much to that of most Evangelicals. For him, religion is 'Christianity and faith in Jesus, life after death, and that he saved us all'. Beat

---

8   The study by Stolz, Favre, Gachet & Buchard (2013) can be read as an in-depth case study of this milieu – and it is also based on the same theoretical foundation as this book.

9   Despite all its individuality, evangelical conversion is also of course a social phenomenon and is socially determined. On this, see Stolz, Favre, Gachet & Buchard (2013).

10   See Favre (2002), Stolz, Favre, Gachet & Buchard (2013).

goes with friends to special religious services for young people and hasalready played in a band for the Alphalive course and it is also important to his girlfriend that Beat is a '*Christian*'. Beat is therefore also an example of the fact that there are many points of contact and overlappings between the established and the evangelical subtypes.

3.3 Alternative

A second type consists of the *alternative* (13.4 per cent of our sample). The people grouped together here have holistic and esoteric beliefs and practices. What can be noticed immediately is that the vocabulary that they use is very different to that used by the institutional type. For example, they speak in terms more of '*spirituality*' than of '*religion*', and, for them, it is less about '*belief*' than about '*experience*' and '*knowledge*'. Around 52 per cent believe that there is rebirth or reincarnation of the person in different lives. 58 per cent deem it probable that there are people who can predict the future. People of this type are interested in the law of karma, contacts with angels and spirits, cosmic energies, chakras, the skills of secret masters, and the healing powers of stones, plants, crystals, and of touch or laying on of hands. Among the practices of this type can be found, besides the reading of esoteric literature, techniques of divination (tarot, channelling, palmistry), spiritual healing (shamanism, *faiseurs de secret*), breathing and movement techniques (e.g., tai chi, kinesiology, Alexander technique, yoga, meditation), healing techniques that work through the hands (e.g., reiki, massage, acupressure), and various other techniques and rituals (e.g., nature rituals, hypnosis, female spirituality).[11]

The spirituality of the alternative type is extremely diverse and therefore difficult to put into subcategories. Nonetheless, we can specify three basic characteristics underlying their beliefs (knowledge, experience) and practices: holism, syncretism, and love of nature. Their spirituality is *holistic* because they reject reductionist dichotomies (distinctions), such as male/female, light/ dark, good/evil, God/Devil, and material/spiritual. To overcome thinking in opposites, they emphasize instead the interconnectedness of all things. The divine and the worldly form a single unit. This unit is both male and female, material and spiritual, and has both light as well as dark sides, etc. In the world of alternative spirituality, everything is connected to everything else. This spirituality is also *syncretic* because it mixes together influences from the most diverse cultural backgrounds: Far Eastern, Celtic, Jungian, environmental,

---

[11] See Fleury (2010), Schneuwly Purdie (2009), Mayer (1993), Bloch (1998), Heelas & Woodhead (2004), Spickard (1995). For interesting case studies of alternative spiritualities linked to Neo-Hinduism and Kabbalah in different countries see Altglas (2011, 2014).

Indian, Christian and other beliefs are brought together in permanently new combinations. Finally, this worldview is *nature-loving* because it usually sees nature as being vital, if not sacred. Seeing nature as being sacred is particularly strong among those adhering to ecospiritualism and Indian shamanism.

Alternative

Eliot (42, subtype 'esotericist') works for an NGO. He grew up within Protestantism, from which he distanced himself at an early age. After a serious life crisis, he came via Zen Buddhism and tai chi to qi gong, which he currently practises. Eliot has completed various courses and retreats, as well as a whole training course in different alternative-spiritual techniques, and has also taught these techniques in different places for years. For Eliot, qi gong is a philosophy of life which is one of the pillars of Chinese medicine. It is about achieving a mastery over breathing and the insight that the energy of the body goes through the meridians.

Maude (51, subtype 'Sheilaists and alternative customers') is a school head and teacher. Originally from Holland, she was brought up as a progressive Catholic. In her home, she surrounds herself with crosses, a crucifix, a rosary, candles and a smiling Buddha. Both the crucifix and the Buddha give her strength, each in its own way. Maude believes in God, whom she compares to a '*cushion*', and in life after death. She often prays for others and, when she meditates, she likes to light candles. Maude does not go to religious service, but likes going to churches – as long as she can be alone there. Sometimes she goes to a monastery in order to enjoy the silence there in solitude.

Angela (37, subtype 'Sheilaists and alternative customers') is a midwife. She has Italian roots, but grew up in Switzerland and was raised as a Catholic (baptism, communion, confirmation). Angela's attitude towards the church and religion in general is somewhere between indifferent and critical. She has nonetheless not left the church. Angela makes regular use of alternative medicines, such as reiki, acupuncture, shiatsu, homeopathy, essential oils, and also uses them in her work. She does not give these methods any particular spiritual significance, however.

We can distinguish two subtypes here, too. The examples of Eliot, Maude and Angela in the 'Alternative' box show these differences clearly. Eliot belongs to the first subtype: the *esotericists* (2.9 per cent).[12] These are people who very frequently use alternative-spiritual practices and see their whole lives immersed

---

[12]   The study by Bochinger, Engelbrecht & Gebhart (2009) can be read as an in-depth case study of some of our 'esotericists': namely, those esotericists who are still at the same time in a certain proximity to the churches. Even though Bochinger, Engelbrecht and Gebhart carried out their study in Germany (Franconia), the parallels of the findings are striking.

in an esoteric-spiritual light. Since they often attend and/or teach courses, shared rituals and spiritual workshops, they are part of a network of people who think and practise similarly.[13] While they are very much on their own individual path of personal development and put together their own unique 'alternative-spiritual mix', they very often do so together with other 'spiritual wanderers', and are thereby also significantly influenced in the way that they think and act. They are part of an esoteric *milieu*.[14] Maude and Angela belong to a far less distinct subtype, one which is composed of 'Sheilaists' and 'alternative customers' (10.7 per cent). The term 'Sheilaist' is sometimes used in the sociology of religion to refer to people who assemble their very own religion (after the name of a woman, 'Sheila', who claimed that this was the case for her).[15] Maude falls into this category, since she has developed her own forms of practice and faith – without being in contact with other people, however. Angela, in contrast, is more of an 'alternative customer', since she consumes and uses many products from alternative spirituality without having any particular spiritual intentions. This second subtype of 'Sheilaists and alternative customers' is in our view not a 'milieu', but a 'social aggregate', since, although the people grouped together here may share certain common forms of practice and belief, they are not connected with each other in social networks. To understand the alternative type, it is important to realize that only about a quarter belong to the 'esoteric milieu', while all the rest are connected with alternative spirituality in a more relaxed manner.

Our data also show that there are certain overlappings and movements between the institutional and the alternative types. Some people are both very churchly and interested in alternative spirituality. These are individuals who have been referred to by Bochinger, Engelbrecht and Gebhart as 'spiritual wanderers'.[16] We estimate that this group does not account for more than about 2 to 3 per cent of the population.

---

[13] This network comes about simply through the fact that esotericists meet other participants at courses, who then recommend *further* courses and techniques. Esotericists very often 'wander' along these recommended paths and often meet other wanderers several times. This creates acquaintanceships and friendships, which can be described as a network. See Höllinger & Tripold (2012).

[14] The esoteric milieu has already been described often – sometimes under different titles. Campbell (1995 (1972)) coined the term 'cultic milieu'. On the cultic (or esoteric) milieu in Switzerland, see Mayer (1993), Rademacher (2009). Bochinger, Engelbrecht & Gebhart (2009, p. 121 ff.) encounter the same phenomenon when they describe 'forms of communities among spiritual wanderers'. Van Hove (1999) talks about a 'spiritual market'. On this from an institutional point of view, see Hero (2010).

[15] See Bellah (1985, p. 221).

[16] See Bochinger, Engelbrecht & Gebhart (2009).

3.4 Distanced

The largest group in our typology is the *distanced* type (57.4 per cent).[17] In a way, this type comprises those who are least considered by the scientific literature and the public – but that is precisely what makes this type the most interesting. Who are these people; what do they believe; how do they live their religiosity, spirituality or secularity? The answer to this question is not so simple, because those belonging to this type can only be described with limited, attenuated or negative attributes. But we shall try nonetheless. First, they believe and practise *something*; they do have certain religious and spiritual beliefs and practices. But these are not particularly important in their life and/or are activated only in rare cases. They often believe that there is *'something higher'* (Quentin, Kaitline, Claude, Mélanie or Marcel) or some *'energy'* (Angela, Michel, Lucia, Simon), and they are concerned with the *'meaning of life'* and *'reincarnation'*, but do not want to, or cannot, be much more specific. They may perhaps go to church for major celebrations (especially at Christmas), but otherwise they are not drawn to places of worship. They may use one alternative technique or the other (e.g., yoga, reiki, fortune telling), but they usually do not attach any particular spiritual significance to this. They usually refer to themselves as members of one of the major denominations and pay church taxes accordingly – but religious affiliation has no great importance in their daily lives. For this type, the churches do not give them much personally, but they still feel a residue of connectedness which prevents them from leaving the church. People belonging to this type not only distance themselves from the Christian religion and the churches, but also are sceptical towards alternative ideas and practices. These middle positions are quantitatively demonstrated by the fact that the distanced type has the highest numbers of 'neither-nor' statements.[18] The sociologist of religion David Voas, on whose work our study is based (among others), describes the phenomenon as 'fuzzy fidelity'.

We can also divide this type into three subtypes, each of which comes near to one of the three 'poles' that we have already distinguished: distanced-institutional, distanced-alternative, and distanced-secular. However, the boundaries here are often very blurred (see in the box entitled 'Distanced' and the three examples of Kaitline, Claude and Elina).

---

[17]   The study by Plüss & Portmann (2011) on 'secularized Christians', which also uses the concept of distancing, can be read as a series of in-depth case studies of our 'distanced' type. See also Portmann & Plüss (2011).

[18]   See Table A7 in the Appendix.

Distanced

Kaitline (63, subtype 'distanced-institutional') is a retired sociologist. She was socialized in the Catholic faith and attended a state school run by nuns. As a teenager, she was very interested in the church and considered entering a convent – but without actually putting this idea into practice. She then married and had two children, only to divorce a few years later. Afterwards, she began studying sociology and religious studies, and completed her degree at the age of 49. Her divorce resulted in her excommunication, which shook her badly. Since that point on, she has not entered a church. She nonetheless retains a faith, which she brings together with values such as justice and respect.

Claude (39, subtype 'distanced-alternative'), who grew up in Germany, has a PhD in biochemistry and works in marketing in the pharmaceutical industry. Christianity has never interested him. Claude's mother is reasonably religious, but his father not at all so. Because of skin problems and allergies, he has tried alternative medicine and has come into contact with spiritual healers. In the process, he was confirmed as having a special aura and ability to empathize. Fascinated by the idea of being able to influence everything himself, Claude then learnt intensively all about mental training, and began practising sahaja yoga. In the meantime, though, the demands of everyday life have led to his dropping this practice.

Elina (24, subtype 'distanced-secular') is studying economics. She grew up in a small village in the canton of Ticino and was brought up as a Catholic, baptized and confirmed. She describes herself today as agnostic. When she returns to her village to celebrate someone's rite of passage or Christmas, and goes to mass, she sees this more as a concession to family tradition than as a religious act. She takes a critical and somewhat amused look at the religious traditions of her birthplace. Very rarely, in difficult situations, does she take refuge in a short hurried prayer. Overall, though, she finds religious claims implausible.

In all these descriptions, we should be careful not to forget that, for those belonging to this type, religion and spirituality are not that important. They only thought about religion and spirituality for an hour because we asked them questions on this issue – it is something that otherwise they rarely do. But this is precisely the point: it is the low importance that religion and spirituality have in their practical lives that gives this type its specificity.

3.5 Secular

The fourth type comprises *secularists*, who make up 11.7 per cent of our sample.[19] These are people without any religious practices and without any religious beliefs. Around 44 per cent claim not to believe in God, 83 per cent consider churches to be unimportant for them personally, 73 per cent never go to church, and about 50 per cent fully agree with the statement that religions lead more to conflict than to peace. All this does not mean that these people are without philosophical convictions – quite the contrary, in fact. In this type, we find people who often have very clear views on general issues such as the origin of the human species, questions of social justice, and the meaning of life. Only, the answers that they give are not religious, or are anti-religious. Again, we can distinguish two subtypes here: the indifferent and the opponents of religion. The former are completely indifferent to religion, the church and faith, but also to esotericism and spiritual healing. The latter are often strongly critical of both institutional religion and alternative spirituality – but also of non-Christian religions. Again, we shall introduce three people of this type: Daniela, Siegfried and Gregory (see 'Secular' box below). The first represents the indifferent subtype, while the second and third represent the subtype comprising opponents of religion.

Secular

Daniela (24, subtype 'indifferent') is studying physics. Although she was baptized in a Reformed church, she underwent no formative religious socialization. Her mother seems to be interested in certain alternative-spiritual practices like feng shui or tarot. Daniela describes herself as agnostic, as well as *'realistic'*, *'scientific'* and *'pragmatic'*. She is familiar with the sense of wonderment through beautiful music and brilliant scientific theory – but none of that has anything to do with religion for her. She does not reject religions completely, but does not have much use for them herself.

Siegfried (39, subtype 'opponent of religion') is an engineer; he is married and has three children. Siegfried and his wife left the church because they did not want to have their children baptized. He describes himself as a rational and scientifically-minded person, but accepts that there is something unexplained and inexplicable. Siegfried believes neither in a higher power, nor in a pre-ordained destiny. He sees religion as fundamentally problematical because, in his opinion, it excludes, it wreaks havoc, and it prevents people from thinking and acting for themselves.

---

[19]   We know of no in-depth case study of the secular type in Switzerland. In the international literature, see, for example, Cimino & Smith (2007), Voas & Day (2007), Day (2009).

Gregory (70, subtype 'opponent of religion') is an architect nearing retirement who has lived with his partner for 30 years. He was brought up as a Protestant and had to go to Sunday school, where he was often slapped. He subsequently refused to be confirmed and has never set foot in a church since. He has absolutely no religious practices or religious beliefs. He is very critical of religions and religious organizations: for him, all religions are only the false promise of a paradise to come and in actual fact lead only to war.

***

The aim of this chapter has been to enable the reader to understand the typology by way of an initial overview and examples. In the following chapters (Chapters 4 to 8), we use this typology to analyse identity, belief and practice, values, the relationship to religious-spiritual suppliers, and the perception of religion(s) in Switzerland. In Chapter 9, we will then explain the emergence and development of the types.

Chapter 4
Identity and Social Structure

Jörg Stolz, Mallory Schneuwly Purdie

I am a highly religious non-believer – that is something
of a new type of religion. (Albert Einstein)

The influential analyses of Pierre Bourdieu and Gerhard Schulze in the sociology
of culture have shown that groups often gain their identity by distinguishing
themselves from other groups through the use of cultural signs – but, in our
opinion, this insight has so far never been made fruitful for the description
of an entire religious landscape of a country.[1] In this chapter, we therefore
show how the types and subtypes describe *themselves* precisely by distancing
themselves from other groups. For this purpose, we analyse, first, how members
construct their religious affiliation; second, what members of the different
types mean when they call themselves 'religious' or 'spiritual' – or perhaps
neither; and, third, how they establish religious, spiritual or secular identities
by distinguishing themselves from other types. In this way, we make visible
a subtle game of identities, one which is played out between the types and
subtypes, and which has been ignored in the literature so far. Who the types
and subtypes 'are' is determined not only by their own distinguishing activities,
but also, and especially, by so-called social-structural features – for example, the
typical educational qualifications and occupations that they have, whether they
live mainly in a town, an urban agglomeration or in the countryside, whether
they are predominantly men or women, etc. We make such a description in the
second part of this chapter.

4.1 Types, Subtypes and Identity

Identity – Categorial, Collective, Personal

Research in the social sciences is in agreement that personal identity is
not essentially 'given', but is always 'constructed' by the individual in his or

---

[1] See Bourdieu (1979), Schulze (1995).

her interaction with the social environment.[2] By *identity*, we can therefore understand the totality of the generalized hypotheses which individuals maintain about themselves and their relationship to the social environment.[3] A woman can, for example, define herself as Swiss, a mother, a biologist, a cyclist, a wife, a pensioner, etc., and distinguish herself in each case from counter definitions and counter groups. Following a suggestion by the sociologist Hartmut Esser, we wish to distinguish here between categorial, collective and personal identity.[4] We can talk of *categorial identity* when an individual assigns him- or herself to a social category without (from a subjective point of view) also thereby thinking of group identities (e.g., 'man', 'cyclist'). We can talk of *collective identity* when the individual assigns him- or herself to a social group which (from a subjective point of view) has a group identity ('We fans of FC Zurich' or 'We Swiss'). Whether a particular attribute, for example, 'Swiss', is now meant categorially or collectively cannot be determined abstractly, but must be worked out empirically. *Personal identity* consists of properties and hypotheses about the self which (again from a subjective point of view) are also given independently of social relations. The talent shows which are popular at present, for example, show that many people derive an important part of their identity from the opinion that they have a particularly nice voice and a good sense of rhythm.

Denominational Identity

Analysis of our data shows, first, that the various types and subtypes differ greatly in the way that they 'construct' their own denominational identity. Our most significant finding is that, while the institutional often see denomination as a feature of collective identity, that is, as group identity, the majority of members of the other types see denomination only as a categorial feature from which they are more or less strongly distanced.

Let us first consider the *institutional* type and its *established* subtype. Here, we meet people who define themselves emphatically as either Catholic or Reformed. They see Catholics and the Reformed as separate groups with their own group identity – from which they in turn can derive part of their own personal identity. Thus, Gisèle, for example, says: 'I'm very Catholic' and she

---

     2   This construction is due to different mechanisms. It arises through primary and secondary socialization (Berger 1982 (1980)), only through comparative observation of self and others (Festinger 1954, Suls & Wheeler 2000)., through communication of identity-bestowing differences (so-called 'boundary making') (Barth 1969, Wimmer 2008), through identity management (Goffmann 1959), and also through allocation and choice of reference groups (Tajfel 1982).

     3   See Esser (2000d, p. 335), Mead (1967 (1934)).

     4   See Esser (2000d, p. 345).

never feels 'at home' in Reformed churches.[5] Such people speak very often in the *we*-form, whereby *we* can refer to Catholics in general, but also sometimes to their own family or to their marital partnership. Stephan, for example, says: 'The basic principle really is Catholicism, where we say: We believe in God, we believe in a higher power. Whether that is the whole Bible story, there are certainly doubts [attached](...), but we still believe that after death it also carries on' (Stephan, 45, Roman Catholic).

And Marc-Antoine says: 'We are very involved in our church. We are Catholic. We are traditional; we go to mass on Sunday. It's important for us; if we don't go, then we have a feeling that something is missing' (Marc-Antoine, 63, Roman Catholic).

Members of the Reformed Church can also have such a collective identity – although much less often. Wilma,[6] for example, would never change church and says (where again a 'we' appears and she also differentiates herself from Catholics): 'I experience and live (...) the Reformed faith as a free person, [as a] faith in which we have few prescriptions and I enjoy that as well (laughs), when I compare it now to the Catholic faith' (Wilma, 47, Reformed).

That members of the established subtype see their denominational affiliation at the same time as group affiliation is also shown quantitatively in the fact that they usually perceive themselves as members also of a local religious community, with 99 per cent considering themselves as 'belonging to a religion or denomination', but also 81 per cent considering themselves as being 'members of a parish, congregation or religious community' (Table A6 in the Appendix).

In the *evangelical* subtype, the situation is slightly different. Here, people identify not with the denomination, but with the fact of 'being Christian'. The we-group for these people is usually not only the local congregation, but also and especially the community of those '*who believe in Jesus Christ*' (Dorothée), of '*believers*', of people with a '*living faith*', of (in the emphatic sense) '*Christians*'.

In contrast, all other types and subtypes generally have a strongly distanced relationship to denominational affiliation: denomination is understood not in the collective, but only in the categorial, sense. Our respondents explain that they are Catholic or Reformed '*on paper*', '*by birth*', '*by upbringing*', to which they then add a proviso (a '*but*'). There are many such examples in our material. The respondent is indeed Catholic/Reformed, '*but*' it has '*never touched*' him;

---

5   What is particularly interesting about the case of Gisèle is that, because of her marriage, she had to go over to Protestantism and is therefore officially Reformed – but she personally sees herself as Catholic.

6   We assign Wilma to the distanced-institutional subtype and not to the institutional type in our typology. Generally speaking, quite a few who consider themselves emphatically as Reformed 'land' in our subtype of the distanced-institutional. This makes sense because the Reformed traditionally have a more distanced relationship to the churchly institution than Catholics.

it caused her *'great difficulties'*; it *'raised many questions'*, etc. Renato, for example, says:

[I] now simply came into the world as a Roman Catholic, but we have already seen in history all the things that have been done in the name of this religion. (Renato, 41, Roman Catholic)

Our respondents always acknowledge that the categorial identity is accurate or can be applied to them in certain circumstances – but at the same time they also wish to clarify that this categorial affiliation has only a limited importance for them and sometimes no importance at all. They usually do not feel either Catholic or Reformed; they see in the denomination no group affiliation which could make available to them as group members important identitary resources. Again, their distanced attitude towards their own denomination or religion is reflected in the quantitative data, with very many members of the non-institutional types and subtypes feeling that they belong only abstractly to a religion or a denomination, but not to the concrete religious community in their locality.[7]

But how have denominational identities changed in recent decades? A look at the composition of denominations (according to self-description) of the Swiss population shows that (in percentage terms) fewer and fewer people define themselves as belonging to one of the major denominations (for details, see Chapter 9). We can see a second change above all in our qualitative data, though, when we consider how our respondents talk about their childhoods. It turns out that many still understood denominational affiliation until the 1960s in a much more strongly collective way. The denominations appeared as major groups comprising very different mentalities. Niklaus, for example, explains:

[Our family] came here in 1962 (…) into the Catholic village and there were five of us then, Reformed, and we [children] were really picked on by the Catholics at school. We defended ourselves, though, us Reformed, and I always said to myself then: 'When I'm older, when I'm grown-up, whether you're Catholic or Reformed or whatever you are, religion doesn't matter at all. Everyone should believe in what makes sense for them, and then everything will be OK.' (Niklaus, 47, Reformed)

---

7   Whether a person presents him- or herself as being anchored in a denomination can all depend on the situation and occasion. An interesting example of such an 'identity politics' is provided by Elina: *'When I had to enrol at the University of Freiburg and had to write down what religion I belong to (laughs), I just wrote it down [denominational affiliation 'Catholic'], just like that, by accident. But then I was on Facebook recently, and I saw that friends, people that I know, are more religious than me, and that they had also given their religion or that others had written down 'secular'. I didn't write anything down, no answer (laughs)'.*

Quantitatively, we can read the same development in the fact that the proportion of people who think that 'between the Catholic and the Reformed faith there are important differences' clearly shrank between 1989 and 1999 – and in all age groups, too.[8] As a 'social boundary', denominational difference has, within a few decades, become ever more permeable and fuzzy.[9]

Traditionally, denominational identity was particularly important when it came to choosing a marriage partner. Our older interview partners mention this almost without exception. Today, though, denomination or religion seems to have become irrelevant in the choice of (marriage) partner for the great majority of our respondents – and especially for the distanced and alternative types (on this, see Chapter 9).

Religious-Spiritual and Secular Identity[10]

Another form of identity construction is people's self-description as 'religious' or 'spiritual' – or the simple rejection of both these terms. It is sometimes argued that today we should no longer talk in terms of religiosity, but of spirituality; and that research which still uses the concept of religiosity misses what is really happening, since people are increasingly understanding themselves no longer as religious, but as spiritual.[11]

We can deal with this question empirically by investigating whether our types denote themselves as 'spiritual' and/or 'religious'. In the quantitative survey, four possibilities were given – whether a person would describe him- or herself as being 'religious and spiritual', 'spiritual but not religious', 'religious but not spiritual', or 'neither religious nor spiritual' (the four possibilities arise through cross-tabulation).[12]

In Figure 4.1, we can see to begin with that our types of religiosity differ very strongly from each other according to how and whether they describe themselves

---

[8] Unfortunately, researchers, that is, ourselves, were so certain in 2009 that denominational differences in the population were no longer important that they did not include this question in their questionnaires.

[9] To use the terminology of Richard Alba (1999), this is a case of 'blurring'.

[10] For this section, we have carried out a triangulation of qualitative and quantitative data on the level of individuals. What appears is that, precisely for these questions, there is a very high diffusivity of answers, which means that we make the relations appear more ordered and free of contradiction than they actually are.

[11] See Heelas & Woodhead (2004), Rose (2001). The literature on 'spirituality' is very extensive. See especially the contributions in Flanagan & Jupp (2007), Giordan (2007), Höllinger & Tripold (2012).

[12] The item was formulated in a somewhat more complicated way: namely, 'I am committed to a/no religion and do/do not consider myself a spiritual person who is interested in the divine or the supernatural'.

as being religious or spiritual. Put very simply: members of the institutional type see themselves either as 'religious and spiritual' (47 per cent) or 'religious but not spiritual' (48 per cent); members of the alternative type see themselves most commonly as 'spiritual but not religious' (39 per cent); members of the distanced type describe themselves predominantly as 'religious but not spiritual' (49 per cent); and members of the secular type are, hardly surprisingly, 'neither religious nor spiritual' (69 per cent). It becomes clear in the qualitative interviews what importance the respondents attach to these different self-designations. Why do we find among the *institutional* type (and the distanced-institutional subtype) both 'religious and spiritual' and 'religious but not spiritual'? It is because 'spiritual' is interpreted by this type in two ways. On the one hand, we find respondents who interpret 'spiritual' positively, as the authentic, individual experience of their own religion. It is these respondents who describe themselves as 'religious and spiritual', and for them this inner life often appears to be much more important than the institutional side of religion. Nathalie, for example, says: 'Being religious, that sounds like a bit of a cliche, like a label. I think that's how people see me a bit, because I work in the church. I want to be spiritual; I want to be inspired by the spirit' (Nathalie, 41, Roman Catholic).

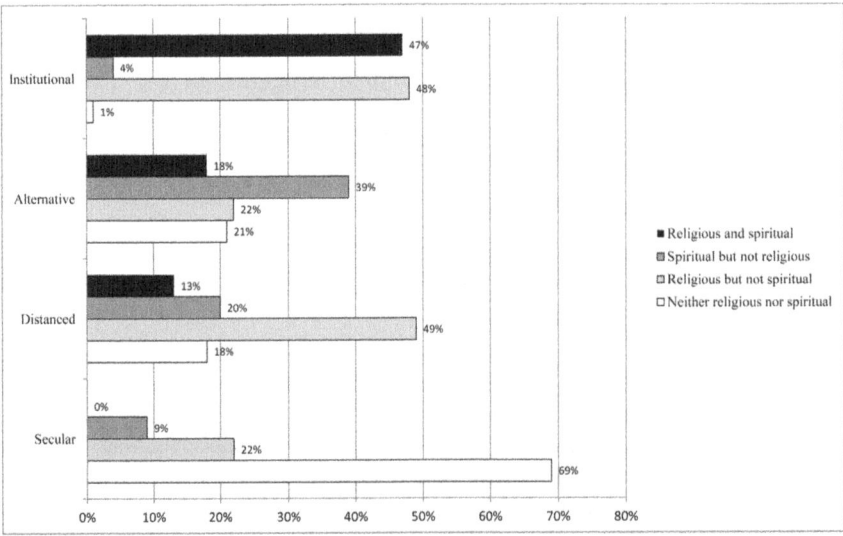

Figure 4.1   The four types distinguish themselves according to whether they describe themselves as 'religious' and/or 'spiritual'

On the other hand, though, we also see, among the institutional type, people who understand 'spirituality' negatively and reject it as being esoteric, magical and involving contact with spirits. Some members of the evangelical subtype even see such practices as being dangerous, since they build contact with 'dark forces'.

People of the *alternative* type often describe themselves as 'spiritual but not religious'. Here spirituality stands postively for them for an open and creative contact with higher dimensions of their own self, through which they can develop their own personality.[13] The goal is, almost always, to enable their self to become more authentic and to move to a higher state of being. Claude tells the interviewer the following: 'My key message: be responsible yourself for your life; you can have influence on it to a large, to a very large, extent – more than you think'. The positive view of spirituality is offset by a negative view of religion and religiosity among the alternative type. Religion is regarded as dogmatic, institutional, technical and power-obsessed. Eliot has 'a lot of trouble with the word religion'. For Michel, religion is a '*crutch*' that was once important at a certain stage of humanity but has now been replaced by spirituality.

Among the *distanced* type, the most common answer is 'religious but not spiritual'. A more detailed analysis of the semi-structured interviews shows that behind this answer are two cases in particular. Firstly, we find (as among the institutional type) people who believe in God and are connected – albeit in a distanced form – to the church, and who associate the spiritual with (negatively perceived) esotericism. Maia says, for example: 'So [I see myself as being] religious because I believe in God. (...) Spiritual – they're the ones that believe in magic, or what are they?' (Maia, 19, Reformed). Livia says: '[I see myself as being] definitely not spiritual. But as religious, yes. (...) Religion for me is really belief in God. Spiritual (...) for me are spiritual healer things, with incense sticks, with various stones, esoteric stuff' (Livia, 38, Reformed).

Secondly, there are those who interpret 'religious' only generally as meaning 'categorial affiliation' to a denomination; 'not spiritual', however, indicates that the respondents are personally not particularly strongly interested in religious, spiritual or esoteric questions, or do not know exactly what they should associate with 'spiritual'.

Finally, among the *secular* type, the overwhelming answer is 'neither religious nor spiritual', with respondents rejecting, often vehemently, the self-designations of both religiosity and spirituality. But what are these respondents, then, if not religious or spiritual? Here, they give us a whole list of terms. They describe themselves as '*realistic*', '*scientific*', '*factual*', '*pragmatic*' and '*rational*'. They are '*not dreamers*'. When asked whether he sees himself as a religious or spiritual person, Siegfried says: 'No, not at all (...) I am a thinking person who is oriented towards technology'. Sometimes, members of the secular type

---

[13]   The positive connotation of the concept of spirituality in the alternative-spiritual milieu is a universal finding of research. See, for example, Mayer (1993), Höllinger & Tripold (2012), Bochinger, Engelbrecht & Gebhart (2009).

describe themselves explicitly as atheist or agnostic. The rejection of religiosity and spirituality, and the self-designation as rational, scientific, etc., is also often accompanied by the claim that religion is an unnecessary, irrational, sometimes damaging way for people to deal with their problems. Many think that religious people do not go to the root of their problems, but rely on false solutions. For Karine, for example, religion is 'the opium of the people', the 'will of the person to hold on to something', a 'projection'.[14]

Positive and negative descriptions: me/us vs. the others
People gain identity not only by ascribing features to themselves, but also by distinguishing themselves from other social groups. In other words, people show who they are by making it clear who they are *not*. Seen this way, identity is highly dependent on the act of drawing boundaries.[15] From which social groups do our types distinguish themselves, then? As might be expected, there are other groups to which people simply do not wish to belong, and this varies from type to type (Figure 4.2). Since we deal with this subject in depth in Chapter 8 when we discuss the perception of religious diversity, we shall be brief here.

Members of the *evangelical* type generally distinguish themselves from all those who are not '*real Christians*', that is, from those who are not converted, born again, or religious. They reject very strongly not only a merely categorial affiliation to a denomination and a merely 'Christmas Christianity', but also atheism and esotericism. In contrast to these groups, they themselves possess a '*living faith*' that they can use to fight those '*dark forces*' which find expression in esotericism and atheism. Members of the *established* type, that is, core members of Catholic and Reformed religious communities, often distinguish themselves from the '*bigoted*' or '*strict*' behaviour of other members of the institutional type or of their own parents. They see themselves as '*open*' and '*religious of their own accord*'. While religious Catholics often distinguish themselves from an integristic Catholicism which is loyal to Rome, religious members of the Reformed faith use Catholics as a negative foil for their own self-description. Members of the *alternative* type distinguish themselves from the church with its rigid structures and dogmas. For them, it is the Catholic Church above all that represents everything that is negative about religion. People who go to mass, for example, are 'not all there' (Emily), and they 'just simply go along with the ceremonial aspect'. The alternative type opposes these dogmas and rigid rules with their own open spirituality. Members of the *distanced* type often distinguish themselves from several other groups. They stress that they do not

---

[14]   This argument picks up on the ideas of Feuerbach and Marx, of course.
[15]   On this, see classic Tajfel (1982), Barth (1969); for more recent literature, see Dahinden, Duemmler, & Moret (2010), Wimmer (2008, p. 335).

belong to the '*really religious*' who '*are forever running to church*'. Nadia, for example, explains:

> We're not really religious. Our neighbours behind us, for example – they're very religious, they're always going to church. But we don't go to church, except just (...) for our wedding or (...) when we had our children baptized. That was important for me, too. But otherwise religious, not really. (Nadia, 37, Reformed)

They also distance themselves from everything '*not normal*' and '*extreme*', and repeatedly name as examples Jehovah's Witnesses, unspecified sects, and Islamic terrorists. In contrast, they often see themselves as '*normal*', but also sometimes as '*not religious, in the sense you would expect*'. Members of the *secular* type distance themselves from the religious and the spiritual as a whole. Again, they often mention the Catholic Church, the Pope, Muslims, religious sects, etc. This act of demarcation is often articulated in particularly critical tones by the opponents of religion, for whom the religious is dangerous, a '*scandal*', '*brainwashing*'. Members of the secular type see themselves as rational, pragmatic and scientific; in contrast to irrational religious people, they solve actual problems rather than relying on religious pseudo-solutions.[16]

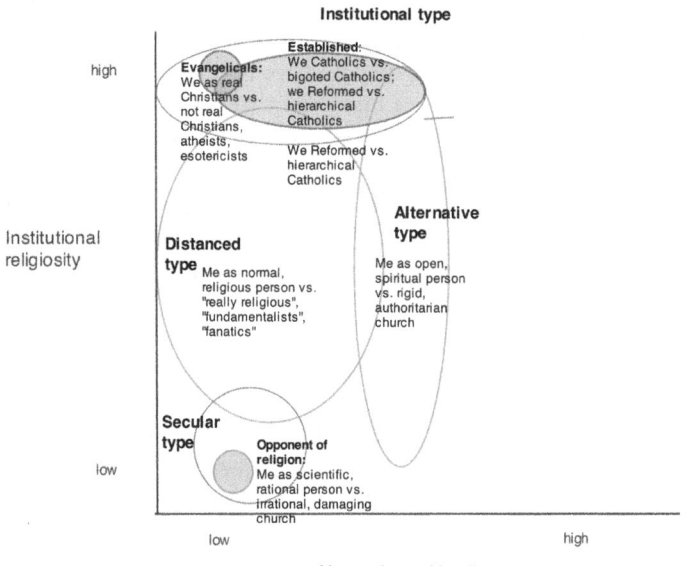

Figure 4.2   The types distance themselves from different negative groups

---

[16]   These descriptions are also greatly simplified. Behind the relatively simple general statements is hidden a great individual diversity.

4.2 Sociodemographic Features of the Types

Finally, we wish to inspect the sociodemographic features of the types in greater detail.[17] As is generally the case in this chapter, we are concerned here in the first instance with only giving a description of the types. Why the types look the way they do and not otherwise is a second question that we only touch on here. It is a question to which we shall return in Chapter 9.

The Institutional Type: Established and Evangelical

Within the institutional type, core members of Reformed and Catholic religious communities (the *established* subtype) are very different from members of the Evangelical churches (the *evangelical* subtype). The former are on average older people (39 per cent over 60) and predominantly female (59.3 per cent). Due to their high average age, many have already retired (26.5 per cent). They are often married or widowed and are more likely than average to have only had the compulsory amount of schooling (40.4 per cent). They are also somewhat more likely to live in the countryside and in very small villages, and are more likely than average to be Catholic (57.3 per cent) or Reformed (37.6 per cent). In addition, comparatively many feel very or quite connected not only to their own church, but also to a political party (31.2 per cent). In contrast, members of the latter subtype *(Evangelical)* are not older on average and are not predominantly female. However, they do have the highest number of married people (88.2 per cent), as well as a birth rate that is well above the average, an indication of their strong family centredness. By definition, they are members of Evangelical churches, or they have a similar style of religiousness to them.[18] They have an average level of education, although very low and very high levels occur somewhat less frequently than on average. To contradict a prominent sociological theory, we can see that members of this subtype do not live to a disproportionate extent in the countryside.[19]

The Alternative Type: Esotericists and Sheilaists/Alternative Customers

Within the alternative type, we can distinguish between esotericists and Sheilaists/alternative customers. What is immediately striking about the *esotericists* is the large proportion of people aged between 40 and 50 (48.5 per

---

[17]   On sociodemographic correlations between Christian religiosity and alternative spirituality, see Miller & Stark (2002), Rose (1998), Stolz (2009), Woodhead (2007).

[18]   On this, see Gachet (2013a).

[19]   These statements rely not only on our own data but also and above all on Favre (2002), Favre & Stolz (2009), and Stolz, Favre, Gachet & Buchard (2013).

cent) and of women (87.5 per cent),[20] something which can only be explained historically. Women born between 1960 and 1970 were strongly shaped by the New Age movement which broke out in the 1970s in particular, and have taken these views and practices 'with them through their lives'. Esotericists are quite often divorced (12.9 per cent), have a level of education which is well above the average (37.5 per cent), and very often work part-time (48.1 per cent). Esotericists are more likely than average to live in an urban agglomeration or a medium-sized town. Esotericists are often Catholic (43.8 per cent), less often Reformed (21.9 per cent), and 34.4 per cent have no religious affiliation. The *Sheilaists and alternative customers* have very similar typical characteristics to the esotericists – usually, though, to a less pronounced extent. They, too, are overrepresented in terms both of people aged between 40 and 50 (27.5 per cent) and of women (62.4 per cent). Again, too, they have a higher level of education than the average (32.5 per cent), and very many work part-time (32.4 per cent). Particularly striking is the high proportion of divorced people (19.0 per cent). As with the esotericists, too, the Sheilaists and alternative customers are more likely than average to live in an urban agglomeration or a medium-sized town (46.6 per cent). For the alternative type overall, the picture that emerges is of a fairly well-educated, strongly female, 40- to 50-year-old person who has been unable to turn her good education into a successful career.[21]

The Distanced Type

Sociodemographically, members of the distanced type have hardly any distinguishing features. They are more likely than average to live in villages with a population of between one and ten thousand, they are quite often Reformed, and they often do not feel close to any political party. As was already the case when we came to describe their religiosity and spirituality, so it is difficult here again to characterize this type succinctly. There are also only one or two differences of any note between the subtypes. What is noticeable at least is that the distanced-institutional subtype has a higher average age, are more likely to be Reformed, and are more likely to have had only the compulsory number of years at school. Not surprisingly, the three subtypes differ in terms of the proportion of people without religious affiliation: only 12.1 per cent for the distanced-institutional subtype, but 27.3 per cent for the distanced-alternative subtype, and 35.8 per cent for the distanced-secular subtype.

---

[20] On similar findings for Austria, see Höllinger & Tripold (2012, p. 126 ff.).
[21] See Benthaus-Apel (1998).

The Secular Type: Indifferent and Opponents of Religion

Within the secular type, we distinguish between the *indifferent* and the *opponents of religion*. The former are on average a younger subtype (50 per cent are younger than 40), which is reflected in the high proportion of those who have never married (42.1 per cent) and in the relatively high number of those still in education or training (13.0 per cent). Members of this subtype live more often than elsewhere in very large cities (21.3 per cent), while 50.7 per cent have no religious affiliation. The latter subtype, meanwhile, is overrepresented among those aged 18 to 30 (25 per cent) and those over 70 (19.4 per cent), while 69.4 per cent are male. They are more likely to be in full-time employment (61.5 per cent), and 88.9 per cent have no religious affiliation. Why we should find so many men among the opponents of religion is an interesting question. It is something which is noticeable in our qualitative material, too, where the most vehement critics of religion are men. We shall return to this gender puzzle in Chapter 9. In the next chapter, though, we shall be examining more closely the religiosity and spirituality – or, indeed, the unbelief – of the four different types.

***

In this chapter, we have examined our types and subtypes in relation to identity and social structure in detail. What has emerged is that people in society constantly observe and evaluate not only themselves but also each other. It is through these observations and evaluations – through what Bourdieu calls 'distinctions' – that identity comes about. The value of this chapter lies in the evidence that it provides that our types are characterized by special identities and underlying social-structural properties that can often only be reconstructed by in-depth analysis.

Chapter 5

Belief, Knowledge, Experience, Action

Mallory Schneuwly Purdie, Jörg Stolz

If triangles made a god, they would give him three sides. (Montesquieu)

Who or what is God? Is he *'a bearded man in the sky'*? Is he *'this presence that is there'*? Or is he more an *'energy'* or a *'power'*? Can he be felt as *'love'* within, or is he a *'sovereign God'* out there? Or perhaps we should be talking here instead of a *goddess*? In this chapter, we shall show that the great diversity of statements about a power that exceeds the sensual ('transcendence'), about a possible existence after death, as well as about religious and spiritual practices and experiences, can be better understood when they are ordered and interpreted according to our typology.

In terms of religiosity and spirituality, various 'dimensions' can be distinguished, one of which (that of identity) we dealt with in the previous chapter.[1] This chapter is now concerned with the dimensions of belief, knowledge, experience and practice. We are interested here not only in the *content* of these dimensions, but also in their *form* and their *manifestation* in everyday life. In other words, what we are concerned with is not just the *What*, but also the *How*.[2] To help you understand what follows, you should keep in

---

[1]   Since the important work of Charles Glock (1967), various dimensions of religiosity have been distinguished in the sociology of religion. Glock differentiated a dimension of 'religious experience', a 'ritualistic' dimension, an 'ideological' dimension, an 'intellectual' dimension, as well as a dimension of the consequences of religious beliefs. Glock's dimensions probably say less about the phenomenon of 'religion' or 'religiosity' as such than about differences between quite basic dimensions of human existence (acting, learning/feeling, believing, knowing). Considered this way, additional dimensions can also be easily found, such as the dimension of 'adherence to values and norms' and the dimension of 'being a member' (the well-known dimension of 'belonging'). For empirical research on the dimensions of religiosity, see Boos-Nünning (1972), Kecskes & Wolf (1995). Fundamental to the more recent state of research is Huber (2003).

[2]   In terms of 'belief' and 'practice', research in the sociology of religion (especially in its quantitative expression) has been accused of concentrating too much on the content and not enough on the form. In doing so, research has essentialized and distorted the positions of people described as religious. It is therefore important to describe also the *How*, the very concrete ways in which people, for example, actually believe, know, experience, practise. It

mind at all times the two-level structure of our typology (Figure 5.1). We shall be describing the four main types and the subtypes within each type.[3]

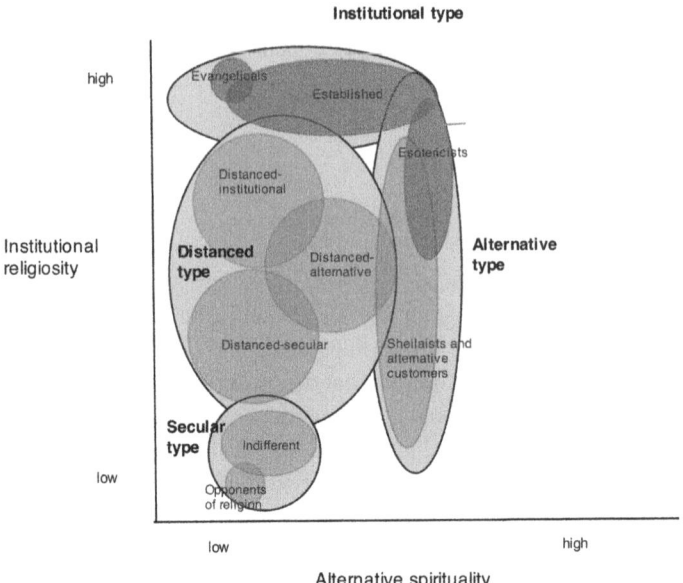

Figure 5.1   The types and subtypes

5.1 Institutional Religiosity

When we consider the religiosity of the institutional type, three commonalities spring immediately to mind. First, members of this type all believe in a characteristic way in *God*. For them, God has the form of a person that we have knowledge of through, among other things, the Bible. This God has the characteristic of personally taking care of each and every person, so that we can tell him in prayer about our own worries, hardships, joys and hopes. Second, they usually believe in *life after death and heaven* (less frequently in hell). Third, institutional religiosity is characterized by *strong Christian practice*, with 73

---

is only by doing so that we can understand, for example, the often ambivalent, ambiguous, wavering forms of being religious. On this with regard to the concept of belief, see Lamine (2008, 2010). For an ethnographic investigation that shows the *How* of practice in a Catholic community, see Piette (1999). In English-speaking countries, there is a great deal of literature on the subject under the heading of 'lived religion' (Orsi 2003).

3   Our approach is comparative and idealized: we compare the types and subtypes by way of different abstract dimensions (e.g., 'believing', 'acting'), and set out in particular what is specific to each type.

per cent of this type going to church at least once a month, and 85 per cent praying several times a week or more.[4] In their homes, there are often religious objects such as crosses, pictures of saints, and religious magazines and books. When we look more closely, though, interesting differences emerge within these commonalities – and particularly between the two different subtypes (established and evangelical).

Established

The established subtype sees God as a transcendental figure who listens sympathetically and kindly, who can be confided in with anything, and who welcomes every individual unconditionally.[5] For Nathalie, for example, God is an '*infinite presence*' whom she '*loves infinitely*'. She says that, when she was on the Way of St. James, she felt '*this presence of God within me, and no longer outside of me*'. And Béatrice explains:

> For me, [God is someone] you can say anything to and he listens. I believe that you really can tell him everything. It is a relationship of absolute trust. And he's someone who does not judge. We say that Christ is love, and I think that's it. He's not the God of punishment the church wanted us to believe in not so long ago. (Béatrice, 44, Roman Catholic)

From a distance, this God appears as a mixture of benevolent parents who accept their child unconditionally, and a psychotherapist who listens supportively to whatever the patient may present. As is already clear in Béatrice's quotation, this God does not behave in an authoritarian, power-conscious or judgemental way. Members of the established subtype are all convinced that we need have no fear of God (in contrast to what those over 60 were told in their religious instruction).[6] God seems to influence above all the mental and moral condition of the religious.[7] Through him, we obtain a '*foothold*', '*support*', and the opportunity to lead a meaningful life. On the other hand, though, God hardly

---

4   The tables containing the percentages used throughout this chapter can be found in the Appendix.

5   On a description of the 'presence' of God in the congregations of a Catholic parish, see Piette (1999, 2006).

6   Several respondents emphasize that God is 'someone who does not judge us; he is not the punitive God that we were supposed to believe in as children'. The fact that God no longer judges is a general finding in Western European countries. On this, see the excellent book by Ebertz (1993) on the 'Civilization of God'.

7   What is noticeable in the discourse of the established subtype is that God appears often, but not Jesus, Mary or the Holy Ghost. We had expected Mary to be mentioned more often, especially by Catholics.

seems to intervene at all in the physical and historical world, although, for most members of the established subtype, he probably could. God may have *'created the world'*, but his influence on current events in the world is indirect. It is here that we are confronted with the well-known question of theodicy.[8] If God really can intervene, then why doesn't he? Why does he allow Béatrice's sister-in-law to behave so terribly? Why does he tolerate mass murderers? Why does he allow a 17-year-old to die in a car crash? These are questions that many who belong to this subtype wrestle with, and they often solve the problem by simply continuing to trust in God.

Members of the established subtype usually have quite unclear and often fluctuating ideas about the *afterlife*, and the subject usually comes up only as a result of a question by the interviewer. Daniele believes in paradise, but has no idea what that will be like. François believes in life after death, but his ideas on this are *'vague'*. Gisèle believes that there is something after death, but sometimes has her doubts. What Marc-Antoine says is symptomatic:'I believe that there is something after life; I believe in the afterlife, but I don't know what it will be like there. I can't imagine what it will be like, but I still believe in it – that's how it is' (Marc-Antoine, 63, Roman Catholic). In the few places in our material where members of the established subtype do talk more concretely about the afterlife, this is usually depicted as a place where (hopefully) the deceased can be found again. It is a place where 'those who have gone before us live together' (François), a place 'where we can find again those we have lost, but not like here on earth, on another level' (Béatrice). Only rarely do members of the established subtype go further in their clarifications – and then usually to express doubt. Typical here is again Marc-Antoine's question concerning resurrection: 'There'll be quite a few people coming together there', he says, 'so where should they all go?'

If we turn to *religious practice*, then what becomes apparent is that members of the established subtype usually practise alone. Whether walking to religious service, praying, going on pilgrimage, or taking a religiously motivated action to help others – the individual almost always performs the activity as a single person. A prototype here is the older Catholic or Reformed woman who goes to religious service on her own. In some cases, though, we also find couples who go to service together or who pray together – but we hardly ever see whole families who practise religiously as a whole family. The most common form of practice outside the home for this subtype is going to religious service. Nevertheless, almost everybody in this subtype also says that going to service is *not* the most important factor in their religion, and that they do not have to go (any longer) if they do not want to. They go if and because it *'does [them] good'* or when *'something special'* is going on. On the other hand, it does not matter if they miss service every now and again – when, for example, a priest that they do not

---

8   On this, see classic Weber (1985a (1922)), Berger (1988 (1973)).

like is to say mass. Members of the established subtype very often still sing in a church choir, or at least link their practice of attending religious service with a strong love for church music. Only in exceptional cases do they justify going to religious service by saying that a 'salvation good' will be distributed (for example, a blessing, the sacramental bread). The most important individual form of practice for this subtype is prayer. They pray regularly, usually in the evening before going to sleep, but sometimes also in the morning before the day begins or at other times during the day. They very often mix '*traditional prayers*' such as 'Our Father' or the 'Hail Mary' (Catholics only) with a free prayer, where they express their gratitude for what has been given to them, and appeal on behalf of others or of themselves. Praying makes them calm, relaxed and full of renewed confidence, since they can pass on their problems to God. Béatrice prays every day, and thanks God for '*the many things he does for us and gives to us*'. So she thanks God, for example, for having been born in a country like Switzerland, for being healthy, for having her own home; and, at the same time, she also prays for the health of people that she both knows and does not know. Gisèle uses her walks through the woods with her dog to do her rosary prayers and to recommend other people to God. And François says: '(...) a silent prayer. (...) Particularly in the evening in bed, but it can also be during the day. It's about thanking God, asking for something for someone close to me, or for myself' (François, 55, Reformed).

The established subtype seldom reads the Bible. When the Bible does crop up in our material, it is usually in a *distancing form* – Stephan, for example, says that he has some doubts also about the stories in the Bible. Only sometimes do members of this subtype talk about special religious events such as going to Lourdes or on a pilgrimage to Santiago de Compostela. But when they do talk about such events, then they often do so with enthusiasm: they experienced here great religious emotions and a whole new belief. The established subtype usually sees no problem in resorting sometimes to alternative-spiritual practices, with 24 per cent using alternative medicine often or very often – Barbara uses Echinacea drops, Berta-Lisa has been to a faith healer with her husband, François uses homeopathic remedies, Marc-Antoine swears by lymphatic drainage, and Béatrice has already had ghosts driven from her home. However, these forms of practice that would otherwise be more associated with the alternative milieu are only mentioned in passing, and, in contrast to the Christian elements, they assume a very small place in the worldview of the established subtype. All in all, the religiosity of this subtype appears restrained, traditional and contemplative – which makes it different from the religiosity of the evangelical subtype.

Evangelical

The *God* of the evangelical subtype is a much more active figure than that of the established subtype.[9] On the one hand, he is in a very close personal relationship with the evangelical subtype, for whom he is '*like a mother*', '*my healer*', '*my Saviour*' and '*closest friend*'.[10] On the other hand, he is an eminent and omnipotent figure of authority: God is the '*Lord of all*', the '*boss*', the '*God of Creation who created all things*', and someone who '*holds the reins*'. Members of the evangelical subtype do not doubt that this God exists, with 95.5 per cent stating that they 'know that God really exists and have no doubts about it' (in comparison, only 70.3 per cent of the established subtype makes the same claim). For the evangelical subtype, God cannot be separated from Jesus, in whose form God redeemed people of their sins on the cross. It is he who gives access to paradise and who will return in the form of Jesus. This is Beat's explanation:

> [I believe] in Jesus. That he saves us, that he forgives us our mistakes. And the connection to life is simple, live as far as possible according to the Bible, (...) commit no sins (...). There is a song that (...) has a really interesting text by a punk band, which goes: 'If we all believed in heaven, then he [Jesus] would be down here within a year'. (Beat, 18, Reformed/Evangelical)

At the same time, members of the evangelical subtype believe that God also very actively intervenes in daily life. Everything that happens is an effect of God. He heals, finds people an apprenticeship, brings partners together and decides on life and death. The theodicy question can sometimes appear among the evangelical subtype, too, with the solution usually being to ascribe unknown rational reasons to God. God has 'an ulterior motive for everything; he understands' (Beat).

Members of this subtype usually speak with great conviction of heaven. For Barnabé, for example, there is no doubt 'that there is an eternal life, just as God is eternal'. Willi firmly believes that 'when you are done in the world, (...) you then enter the kingdom of God'. According to Beat, Jesus will lead 'us into paradise'. Our material shows among all members of this subtype a spontaneous juxtaposition of heaven and hell, and the idea that our life on earth can affect where we go when we die. Dorothée, for example, says:

> We rely on the fact that, if there is a God, then there are also two worlds thereafter. We believe in heaven and hell, and that there is life after death. Our life on

---

9   On this, see Stolz, Favre, Gachet & Buchard (2013).

10   Some of these comparisons are taken from the data in Stolz, Favre, Gachet & Buchard (2013).

earth influences where we will be spending our lives afterwards (laughs a little). (Dorothée, 32, Evangelical)

Religious practice for the *evangelical* subtype – going to church, praying, singing, etc. – is, unlike for the established subtype, usually not just a matter for the individual, but is something that involves the couple, or even the whole family. This is possible because members of this subtype usually marry someone who has also converted, and because the couple then bring up their children strongly in the faith. The whole family often goes to religious service, where children are also offered a varied programme. In our material, reference is sometimes made in particular to the '*dynamic*' character of these services, where there is not an organ playing, but a band with drums and guitar. An important point of evangelical practice is the individual conversion (a moment or process in which the individual 'decides for Jesus'). Following this conversion, the individual is baptized before the congregation, be it in the church or outdoors in a lake. Only when a person has been converted and then baptized is he or she a fully-fledged member of the religious community. From a sociological point of view, there is here a social drawing of boundaries and a membership criterion which the established subtype and their national-church structures lack in this form. Prayer is very important for the evangelical subtype (as it is for the established subtype, too) – they nonetheless practise and interpret prayer in different ways. First, members of the evangelical subtype not only pray at certain times of day and (partly) with set prayers; rather, it is much more the case that they can always and everywhere be in touch with God and Jesus: 'Whether on my tractor, in my car, with my cows – I can be in touch with my heavenly Father, like I'm in touch with my son, who works with me' (Barnabé, 56, Evangelical).

This spontaneous and constant saying of prayers (which only occurs occasionally among the established subtype) is a very typical lifestyle component among the evangelical subtype. A second important point is that this subtype uses prayer much more strongly to deal with very specific problems in life, and that they assign to prayer a direct effect. They think that prayer '*works*', that in prayer God provides them with the answer to very specific questions, and that it makes sense to pray for a future spouse, a new home, or advice regarding a relationship crisis.[11]

Unlike the established subtype, the evangelical subtype assigns a central role to reading the Bible, with all members of this subtype in our sample reading the Bible. Barnabé has read the Bible through four times. Willi reads the Bible every day. Dorothée reads a story from the Bible to her children every evening. Only Beat is an exception and reads less often – for which he promptly apologizes. Members of this subtype see the Bible as representing the Word of God in a

---

[11] See Stolz, Favre, Gachet & Buchard (2013).

relatively direct and comprehensible form, and they strongly reject any historical or critical exegesis. 50 per cent believe that the Bible is '*the Word of God and must be taken in a strictly literal way*'.[12]

Members of the evangelical subtype are very different from the established subtype in their conception of alternative spirituality, since they see esotericism, alternative-spiritual healing, yoga and meditation as being extremely dangerous. They do not dispute that such methods are effective; the problem, rather, is that, in alternative spirituality, evil powers, the devil, can always work their effects.

5.2 Alternative Spirituality

The universe of alternative religiosity or spirituality is very different from that of the institutional type. Members of the alternative type claim to about the same extent as the institutional type that there is '*a higher power*' (82 per cent), but what they have in mind here differs significantly from what members of the institutional type have in mind. Whereas 'God' appears to the latter as a supernatural person, for the former he is usually an energy which is all-pervading and which exists in every person and in nature, a light or a force. Whereas the former believe in life after death in a heaven of some kind, most members of the alternative type believe that reincarnation in ever-new lives is probable. And, while the practices of the institutional type mostly occur within the framework of Christian rituals and customs, the practices of the alternative type comprise a huge number of alternative-spiritual techniques deriving from a great diversity of sources, such as Buddhism, esotericism (Christian and Far Eastern), New Ageism, and alternative methods of healing.

Large majorities of the alternative type represent or use some forms of belief and practice. For example, 71 per cent think that 'some faith healers really have supernatural powers of healing', while 70 per cent believe that the 'signs of the Zodiac or the birth horoscope' can have 'an influence on the course of a person's life'. 70 per cent use therapies that work through breathing, relaxation or movement, and 67 per cent use techniques in which hands are used to influence the body, such as reiki, acupressure or massage. Nonetheless, the diversity of what is available to this type is so immense that many beliefs and forms of practice are represented or used only by minorities – yoga, for example, is one of the most important alternative-spiritual techniques, but it is practised by only 33 per cent of the alternative type.

Such diversity means that we can only describe alternative forms of belief and practice by way of long lists. What respondents mention in our material

---

[12]   On how members of Evangelical churches understand the Bible, see also Gachet & Stolz (2010).

are, for example, *belief* in karma, reincarnation, guardian angels, singing stones, fairies, star energy, light, power, energy, meridians, past-life regression, hidden meanings of Christian rituals, etc., as well as *practices* such as esoteric rituals in the forest, using LSD, yoga, colour therapy, Zen meditation, seminars about angels and positive thinking, autogenic training, qi gong, tai chi, homeopathy, kinesiology, acupuncture, reiki, reflexology, Chinese medicine, craniosacral therapy, family constellation, polarity, and many more. Just like institutional practice, alternative practice is also mainly a female phenomenon. In all areas of alternative practice – from the use of herbal remedies to the performance of esoteric rituals – women outnumber men by at least 2 to 1. But what are the differences *within* the alternative type, between the two subtypes?

Esotericists

Everything that we have written above about alternative religiosity or spirituality in general is particularly true for the subtype of esotericists, who are the virtuosos of the alternative type.[13] This can be seen to begin with in how and where they experience transcendence – namely, everywhere! Esotericists live in an enchanted world, a world permeated through and through by the divine. Klaus, for example, explains:

> just as air is everywhere, so also is power, or spirit. The divine is everywhere, in every atom. The only question is whether I actually perceive it at all, the reality, and of course if I'm locked out by my concepts, then I can't see reality. (Klaus, 62, no religious affiliation)

Since the divine is in everything, we also cannot, according to many esotericists, distinguish between an earth and a heaven, or between an immanence and a transcendence. There is, to quote Klaus again, '*no duality, there is only unity*'. As we can see, God here is not, as it is for the institutional type, a figure in the form of a person, but rather an impersonal power which our respondents also refer to as strength, love, colour, breath or life. What Emily has to say is typical: 'For me, God is not a father figure or any kind of figure, but an infinite power, an infinite energy; for me, God is light' (Emily, 62, Roman Catholic).

Since they are able to see the extraordinary in the ordinary, to perceive all of life as divine, esotericists live in a world in which they can receive special messages, insights and secrets from every direction. Michel, for example, knows about hidden meanings in the Christian ritual of baptism (it is about the opening of the seventh chakra), Eliot sees in his young daughter his '*master*', and Klaus

---

[13]   On descriptions of the spirituality of this type, see Bloch (1997, 1998), Bochinger, Engelbrecht & Gebhart (2009), Heelas & Woodhead (2004), Höllinger & Tripold (2012).

is convinced that he is in contact with spirits. All the esotericists in our data strongly believe in reincarnation and are convinced that there is predestination linked to karma. Both Emily and Klaus explain that they had chosen their own parents themselves so as to learn something very specific in this life. Klaus, for example, is convinced that, because of transgressions in past lives, he must learn in this life what it is like when the male is despised by the female. It is interesting that esotericists should generally be positive towards reincarnation, since, in its original Indian meaning, it was something that should simply be overcome. They mention neither the infernal cycle of reincarnation which the individual must break to reach nirvana, nor the possibility of being reincarnated as something non-human. Rather, our interview partners see reincarnation only as an opportunity for constant self-improvement and for the achievement of higher knowledge. Not least, esotericists encounter transcendence in the form of 'extraordinary people' who display supernatural knowledge and can perform incredible feats. All esotericists talk about such encounters – in our material, there is a bishop who is interested in hermeticism, various doctors who are interested in the spiritual world, a Zen master, a woman who is in contact with angels, and many others.

If we consider the *practices* of the esotericists in our sample, what we immediately notice is the strong social networking that exists. Esoteric ideology may be extremely individualistic: it is the individual who is to move forward spiritually along his or her own path, and the individual should and must only accept what is 'right' for him or her. But the fact is that esotericists are almost always integrated into a strong social network of like-minded people, a network which underpins the plausibility of each form of practice. Friends, partner and important acquaintances are usually just as esoterically minded as the individual in question. Esotericists attend many courses, seminars and training events. Emily, for example, has attended seminars on angels, positive thinking, autogenic training, homeopathy, fauna, marine biology, kinesiology, and many other subjects. Eliot first went to a Zen meditation class and then joined a tai chi group, before going for several years to a qi gong course – today, he himself is a qi gong teacher. From these events, esotericists learn what we could call, echoing Bourdieu, an 'esoteric habitus', a way of seeing the world, experiencing it and moving within it.[14] At the same time, they are taught that they themselves can and should pass on these techniques to others. In the alternative-spiritual milieu, people often feel able to become teachers themselves after just a short period of learning. In fact, both Michel and Eliot are now giving courses either full-time or part-time in the most diverse spiritual methods. Esotericists then also apply the techniques that they learn in their private lives, combining them in many different ways and then using them, whether at home or outside (often

---

[14]   On the concept of habitus, see Bourdieu (1987b).

in nature). What matters in general with regard to esoteric practice is that the salvation good is thereby acquired, and that the individual constantly develops further – and, in a certain respect, also higher. The individual is like a wanderer climbing a mountain who has to find his or her very own path.[15]

Sheilaists and Alternative Customers

In contrast to the virtuoso esotericists, Sheilaists and alternative customers assign less importance to alternative spirituality, which occurs in a highly attenuated and rarely contemporary form. As far as transcendence is concerned, for example, Sheilaists and alternative customers also believe in energies, guardian angels, fairies, and stars which determine our lives. They also see the transcendental more as '*life itself*' or '*a light*' than a God in the form of a person (who also crops up in our material sometimes). And here, too, there are special people, mostly healers and therapists, with extraordinary abilities. But, unlike the esotericists, the Sheilaists and alternative customers do not live permanently in this transcendentally charged world and are not part of a strong alternative-spiritual network. Sheilaists like Lucia and Maude have formed their very own alternative-spiritual views, which they do not share with anybody and which occupy a clear, though restricted, place in their lives. A nice example of a Sheilaist is Maude when she talks about God:

> God is the only God, yes, but he is made of different things. He is a comfort, like a cushion you can lie on. A cushion that can comfort you but can't give you bread, or anything to eat or drink. He can't give you a car (laughs) but maybe he can give you time to do things. Love. He can give you lots of things, but not material things. For me, it is a space where I can find myself, maybe we can put it that way. (...) God is not a person, because he can't answer you, but he can listen. It is a space for me, a little moment to pause where you can find yourself, because God, that is deep joy, that is something that carries you, that takes you forward. (Maude, 50, Roman Catholic)

Alternative customers on the other hand use alternative remedies primarily to solve very specific problems in life, with the spiritual side sometimes playing only a subordinate role or no role at all.

If we consider the *practices* of Sheilaists and alternative customers, what becomes apparent is that there is, in contrast to the case of the esotericists, an almost complete absence of an alternative-spiritual network. Members of this subtype 'believe', 'experience', and 'practise' alone. Mona cooks Indian food for herself (which comes from her mother's side), Simon pulls energy from stars

---

[15]   On the concept of the 'spiritual wanderer', see Bochinger et al. (2009).

and trees in solitude (which still comes from the time he spent with his strongly esoteric girlfriend). Félicia prays in secret: she has told neither her husband nor her daughters. Practice with others is limited to using the services of alternative-spiritual healers and specialists. Angela, for example, is being treated through reiki, and David has tried out reflexology, a hypnotist, acupuncture, phytotherapy and homeopathy. For this subtype, it is usually not so much a case of taking a habitus firmly into their entire life (as it is with the esotericists) as being occasionally treated and influenced by people with extraordinary abilities. David shows this way of being a customer very clearly:

> Oh, I've tried many things. I've done both parallel and natural medicine. I've been doing quite a bit of reflexology recently, I've been treated by a hypnotist, I've done Chinese medicine, acupuncture, Chinese phytotherapy, now I'm being treated by a homeopath. What else have I tried? One person had a kind of apparatus and they could explore more or less what's missing in the body, such things, I don't remember exactly what it was. I've also visited what is called a guru, a guy who reads you and who has a small pendant (laughs). (David, 30, no religious affiliation)

It is quite possible also that this subtype interprets these forms of practice only partly or not at all as being *spiritual*. Since Sheilaists and alternative customers are not involved in strong social networks, their practice not so much reflects the courses and groups which they have recently gone to, but consists of rituals which are only individually-based and whose elements can sometimes be traced far back into the individual's past. Overall, Sheilaists and alternative customers do not so much represent the idea that the individual shall become ever better and more highly developed as possess an openness for very different solutions to problems and an often deep awareness of 'other dimensions'.

5.3 Distanced Religiosity

Many of our respondents have not deleted religion from their lives, though, but have simply distanced themselves from it. Members of the distanced type do believe in something, but find it difficult to say exactly what that something is. When they are asked about God, life after death, energies, spirits or other transcendental things, then the answers that they give are characterized above all by a high level of uncertainty.[16] This is reflected quantitatively in the fact that, in questions about religious beliefs, members of this type have the highest scores in 'neither/nor' categories.

---

[16]   This uncertainty was expressed by Voas (2009) in his concept of 'fuzzy fidelity'.

Members of the distanced type certainly do have some religious practice: 20.8 per cent say that they pray at least once a day, and around 72 per cent pray at least once or twice a year, while 6.9 per cent go to religious service at least once a month, and 67 per cent go to religious service more often than once or twice a year – usually for an important event (especially Christmas) or life-cycle rituals (funerals, weddings, baptisms). Members of this type sometimes have contact with alternative spirituality, whose techniques can be interpreted more or less as 'spiritual': 42 per cent have used a method in the last year which is based either on the healing properties of plants or on an organic diet; 34 per cent have used techniques in the last year which use the hands to treat the body (e.g., reiki, acupressure, massage); 14 per cent have read in the last year at least one esoteric book or one esoteric magazine; and 12 per cent have practised yoga in the last year. Generally, though, these practices are not central to the lives of the distanced type – they are only needed occasionally and have a very limited importance. While religious practice for the institutional and the alternative types is often a central component of life, one which influences and determines many other areas of life, religious practice for the distanced type has, in the language of Stefan Huber, a minor 'centrality' (Huber 2003), which means that it is controlled and influenced by other, non-religious criteria, while it itself has barely any impact on other areas of life.

Again, we can distinguish three subtypes within the distanced type, and we shall try now to present each form of religious uncertainty. To enable us to do so, we shall assign each of the three subtypes to one of the three poles (institutional, alternative, secular). To a certain extent, we are therefore also dealing here with the 'distanced variants' of institutional, alternative and secular ways of life.

Distanced-Institutional

The *distanced-institutional* form a subtype within the distanced type which is close to the institutional type. Almost all of our respondents who belong to this subtype say that they believe in 'something higher'. In the background to their lives, there is clearly the Christian God – but the too-specific Christian ideas alienate the distanced-institutional subtype. That God is a supernatural power, perhaps a bearded man, who acts and intervenes in the world – that is something that, with the best will in the world, the distanced-institutional subtype simply cannot imagine. What remains for them is a feeling that there is 'a higher power', one which can certainly be called God, but need not bear this name. Kaitline, for example, says:

> I personally believe that there is something which dominates us. If you look at
> nature in its perfection – that cannot be the work of humans. The human can only
> add, renew, change, destroy, rebuild – what is already there. But to begin with

there is a power which is above us. Now, what we should call this power – I don't know. (Kaitline, 63, Roman Catholic)

Or take Renate, who names this higher entity *'something above'*: 'I have the feeling as though something were above us, something which doesn't exercise its power, though, but just provides the framework for us to develop in' (Renate, 51, Roman Catholic).

When asked about how this 'higher' entity works, though, the distanced-institutional are undecided. Does it work as a *'framework'*, a *'cushion'*, or more as a *'ground'*? Finally, it is very noticeable that the distanced-institutional often waver in their assessment of this higher form. Bettina is *'torn this way and that'*; Kaitline speaks of oscillating (*'coming and going'*); Maia cannot believe that God is sitting up there somewhere, and yet somehow still believes that he is; for Marcel, the things within are now very *'paradoxical'*. Karol, for example, says:

> At the moment I'm going backwards and forwards. At one moment, I believe, and then there are elements that make me not believe. I tell myself it's not possible. There are so many things that happen; there can't be a single cause somewhere. Well, you can get into the debate about free will (...) that's a very difficult question. But to answer your question, I waver between Yes and No, with some very strong moments and other moments of much less intensity. (Karol, 64, Roman Catholic)

Melanie tells a very similar story: 'Well, I believe that we can influence situations through our thoughts, our actions, our states of mind. And then – is there a supernatural power which controls us? Sometimes I tell myself, yes, and sometimes I tell myself, no' (Melanie, 33, Roman Catholic).

It appears that these members of the distanced type have within them various cognitive structures which contradict each other. Every now and again one or the other is activated, which they then experience as wavering or uncertainty. The reason that they have these different structures is primarily because they did have a strong Christian socialization in childhood, but, for various reasons, they have since distanced themselves from these beliefs. This has often led not to a complete replacement of the former beliefs, but to a 'coexistence' of the different, and sometimes contradictory, cognitive structures.[17] The same uncertainty and the same wavering are also apparent, incidentally, when many of the distanced-institutional subtype talk about a possible life after death. They often claim that there probably is 'something afterwards', but are unclear as to

---

[17]   On a theory of the coexistence of different cognitive structures within the individual, see Schulz von Thun (1998).

what exactly that could be. Other members of this subtype, though, tend to believe that everything is over after death.

Distanced-Alternative

The beliefs of the distanced-alternative subtype are also characterized by a high degree of uncertainty, which can be explained above all by the fact that our respondents do not find the questions on this subject particularly important. In this regard, this subtype is close to the alternative pole, that is, God appears to them to be not so much a person, but rather an energy, a positive thought, an influence that spirits have, or a potential within the 'I'. If they do believe in life after death, then it is most likely in the form of reincarnation. The practices of this subtype are also close to the alternative pole. They rarely go to church (or, if they do, then mainly to funerals or weddings), but they occasionally draw on what is available in the alternative-spiritual world, be it attending a course in an esoteric circle, reading a book about NLP, or having an esoteric LSD experience. But for this subtype, too, such practices have only a minor centrality: they are one activity among many, and they have no special significance in life as a whole.

An example of the distanced-alternative subtype is 39-year-old Claude (Reformed), who studied the natural sciences and now works in business. Claude has gone in the past to several alternative-spiritual seminars (e.g., mental training, the circle of a faith healer), and is convinced that he has '*a good aura*'. For him, spiritual practice is mainly an opportunity to '*tap into a power*', and thereby become more productive and more composed. However, as he told the interviewer, he is not involved in any religious or spiritual practice at all at the moment because he simply has too much to do:

> I start every now and then, and then maybe have a few small successes. But (...)
> I have quite a lot to do at the moment. I've recently set up another company
> with a few colleagues and there's not much time for me to spare. I do actually
> already know that I must build [meditation] into my schedule (...). But I haven't
> consciously practised meditation in the last two years. (Claude, 39, Reformed)

Distanced-Secular

This group of people are members of the distanced type who are near to the secular pole. They claim mostly not to believe in God, or, if they do, then in a strongly secularized form – for example, as '*collective unconscious*' or '*universal love*' or '*life*'. They normally do not believe in life after death. Members of this subtype have only a minimal level of religious practice. Although they are often (still) officially members of a church, their practice is mostly limited to going to religious services for life-cycle rituals or family celebrations. Elina, for example, goes to church at Christmas, when she visits her family in the small village she grew up in. She then '*plays along with the game of tradition*', as she puts it. Otherwise, she does not practise religion in any way. Among this subtype as a whole, we can find hardly any religious practice: they hardly ever pray and barely use alternative-spiritual techniques. Nevertheless, we can still find among all members of this subtype *something or other* that connects them with religiosity, spirituality or religious-spiritual suppliers. Unlike secularists, they have not turned their back completely on religion. An example is the 41-year-old Renato, a Spanish citizen who studied electrical engineering at university and who now works in IT-service management. Although he sees himself as an extremely rational person, he still says that not everything can be explained and understood through reason. Renato has no religious practice, except for the fact that he prays once or twice a year. He does so in extreme emotional situations, be they positive (such as the birth of his children) or negative (during his parents' divorce or the death of his mother-in-law). He is critical of the church as an institution, but would never officially leave. As a Spaniard, Renato was brought up as a Catholic, and his parents are much more Catholic than he is.

5.4 Secularity

Not surprisingly, members of the secular type have the fewest religious beliefs, with only 10 per cent believing in a higher power, and only 2 per cent in a God who takes care of each individual person. Secularists reject not only Christian but also alternative-spiritual beliefs, with only 10 per cent believing in reincarnation, only 5 per cent in the existence of 'transcendental forces in the universe that influence people's lives', and only 14 per cent in the supernatural powers of faith healers. Again not surprisingly, we find among the secularists the highest percentage of those with no religious affiliation (62 per cent) and of atheists (72 per cent). Again, it is fruitful to divide the secular type into two subtypes.

Indifferent

Members of the indifferent subtype in our sample usually claim not to believe in God, nor in life after death, but rather in something else, this 'something else' usually being the human and his or her abilities. Qasim, for example, claims '[to believe] in people', and in the fact that 'things can be changed if there are enough people of strong character'. According to Gustave, we should believe in people, even if doing so brings with it 'a lot of disappointments'.[18] And Karine is typical when she says:

> I don't believe [in God]. I believe in people. Despite everything that happens, despite all the terrible things that you can see going on. I still believe that there is something in people, their conscience, if you will, which pushes humanity on. That's what it's about for me. (Karine, 68, no religious affiliation)

But that 'something else' is not always the human being. This subtype can also believe in life, nature, evolution or poetic justice, beliefs which are, for them, not plucked out of thin air or quixotic, but can be combined very well with a rational, logical and scientific view of the world.

Although members of this subtype do not have religious beliefs, they are nonetheless usually not negative towards such beliefs. They do not complain about religion or try to convince religious people of the falsity of their views; and they do not represent any anti-religious ideologies. Some even reveal a slight wistfulness – it would be nice, say these respondents, if they *could* believe in, say, life after death or a benevolent God. But they simply cannot.

This subtype mostly has no religious practice. When Daniela takes refuge in a '*hurried prayer*' before a difficult exam, she addresses the prayer not to God but to herself, and says, for example: 'Hey, Daniela, if you do well (...) – then we'll go to the opera next week' (Daniela, 24, Reformed).

When Cécile goes into a church during her holidays, she does not stop for reflection – she simply visits the church '*like a museum*'. This subtype almost always describes this almost complete absence of religious practice or religious ritual as unproblematical. An exception, though, is Gustave, who grew up completely without religion and who lost both his father and grandfather in the same year. At that moment, he found it very difficult that there was no ceremony available that he could fall back on: 'I needed a ceremony, but not a religious ceremony. It's too difficult to invent things [for your own ceremony] when you're in mourning' (Gustave, 30, no religious affiliation).

Members of this subtype usually have little regard for alternative remedies. If they do use such remedies, though, they usually assume that how they work can be explained in a completely scientific way.

---

[18] This belief in the human being also means that secularists recognize Jesus as a historical person and can therefore certainly assign him a certain importance in this respect. Some see him as a revolutionary, as a disturbing presence. For Ernesto, Jesus 'spoke up against the powerful and for the people, and that is also why they crucified him'. And Cécile tells her daughter 'that the Romans crucified Jesus because he stirred people up', but does not like going into any kind of detail. Although she talks to her daughter about Jesus as God's son, she refuses categorically to speak of any divine order.

Opponents of Religion

Members of this subtype are characterized by very similar beliefs as the indifferent subtype. They do not believe in God, in life after death, in reincarnation, or in a divine 'I'; and nor do they usually have any regard for alternative healing. Where the two subtypes differ, though, is in terms of *emphasis*. While members of the indifferent subtype usually talk calmly about their non-belief or about their naturalistic or scientific worldviews, opponents of religion reply to our questions in a very emotional way. They maintain an *emphatic non-belief*; it is important for them to reject religion in front of others, and some use terms that are negatively loaded, derogatory metaphors and swear words to express their opinion. Peter has no use for these 'old wives' tales', while Siegfried does not believe in the 'happy hunting grounds'. And Ernesto says: 'Ha, a higher power! No, absolutely not!' (Ernesto, 68, no religious affiliation).

Opponents of religion do not believe in a transcendental power, but they do believe that churches and religions have a hugely damaging effect in the most diverse areas of society. Peter says that all previous wars were 'somehow based on religion'. Ernesto believes that religion is 'always on the side of the powerful'. And Gregory says:

> No, I think that it's a clever exploitation (I apologize if you're religious); a clever exploitation of human weakness. Because whether you take the Bible or the Koran, whether Catholic, Protestant, New Testament, Old Testament – they're all promises of a paradise. I don't believe in it. For various reasons. When you see the development of life, from birth on, or even before, when the child is still a foetus in the mother's womb, then I do not see where the hand of God is. And then this whole mess, this whole bullshit inflicted by the church, huh? (laughs) Wherever there is war, there is also the church: in the Middle East, Ireland, the Crusades – well, OK, that was a long time ago, that's not today. But take the Middle East with Israel and its neighbouring countries and then with these lunatics, the Taliban and so on. No, no, religion really can't be proud of itself, huh? (Gregory, 70, no religious affiliation)

Opponents of religion may have no religious practice in the strict sense, but they do have a practice which is *related to religion*: namely, they fight back against churches and religion, whether only on a verbal level, or through private or public actions. Some, like Siegfried and Erich, argue in a considered way. Others, like Gregory and Peter, show an almost missionary anti-religious zeal. Peter has even gone to religious events organized by Evangelicals and Scientologists on purpose:

I once spent some time finding out about sects. Evangelicals, Scientology, Moonies, and so on, for about four years. You have to stop at some point, otherwise you start going mad. And I even went there, (...) I sneaked in to a meeting of the Evangelicals (...), and also of Scientology, I've got a neighbour who's some kind of holy saint there (but he's left now, because it got too much for him) (...) [I did that] to see how it works. How they can trick people and take their money off them. That's rape, that's (...) brainwashing. (Peter, 65, no religious affiliation)

The negative interest that opponents of religion have in churches, 'sects' and religions can lead them to becoming publicly involved and building their own groups. However, in our sample, there is only one person – Ernesto – who has joined a group which is decidedly critical of religion (and this is communist-oriented).

***

In contrast to previous literature, this chapter has provided a 'thick description' of religious or spiritual belief, knowledge, experience and action in Switzerland.[19] In contrast to work which is only quantitative, our inclusion of different methods has enabled us not only to present percentages and correlations regarding religious faith, but also to link them to typical individual meanings. Research that is only quantitative knows, for example, that 71.6 per cent of the respondents believe in 'something higher', but it does not understand *why* so many people should agree *precisely with this* statement. With our model of types, it becomes clear that the evangelical, established, alternative and distanced types or subtypes can agree with this statement for quite different reasons – and why.

Even if there are, as we have shown, many differences between the types and subtypes, there are also transversal elements, properties which all types have in common. Everywhere we find, for example, unusual situations in which people stop and ask themselves, what is the meaning of this? Or who see great disappointments and breakthroughs as moments of beauty. Only a few types and subtypes interpret these moments religiously, however. In all types and subtypes, the 'I' is also important: the fact that the individual is seen as autonomous and can decide for him- or herself what (not) to believe in and how (not) to practise. Finally, what shines through in all the types and subtypes is a larger social process that we have called here the 'transition to the me-society', a process which brings with it a progressive distancing by people from institutional religiosity.

We shall return to these points in Chapter 9, when we come to explain social change. First, though, we shall continue our work of description and

---

[19] On the concept of 'thick description', see Geertz (1993b).

interpretation, and turn in the next chapter to the question of how the types and subtypes combine religion with values.

Chapter 6
Values and Change of Values

Jörg Stolz, Thomas Englberger

The true purpose of religion is to impress the principles of morality
deep into the soul. (Gottfried Wilhelm von Leibniz)

For centuries, religion, morality, and values were very closely linked in Western
societies. To lead a morally good life was to be a good Christian, and *vice
versa*. Only gradually, and especially with the religious wars in the seventeenth
century, with the Enlightenment in the eighteenth century, and with the civil
revolutions in the eighteenth and nineteenth centuries, did people become
aware that there could also be values which were not Christian.[1] But change
did not stop there. An extensive literature shows that a further profound
change of values occurred in the 1960s.[2] According to Ronald Inglehart, who
is perhaps the most well-known researcher of values, there has been a shift from
'materialist' to 'post-materialist' values.[3] A research group led by Helmut Klages
has the same thing in mind when they talk in terms of a transition from values of
duty and acceptance to values of self-development.[4] According to Klages and his
colleagues, values of duty and acceptance, such as obedience, subservience, duty
and loyalty, are losing their importance in Western societies, while values of self-
development, such as individualism, imagination, creativity and independence,
are becoming ever more important. A significant component of the change of
values relates to norms regarding the family and sexuality: women should now
have the same rights and opportunities as men, sex before marriage or without
marrying is becoming normal, and homosexuality is also gaining ever greater
social acceptance.[5]

What does this change of values which occurred in the 1960s, and which is
part of the transition to the 'me-society', mean, then, for religion and religiosity?[6]

---

[1]   See, for example, Böckenförde (1991), Taylor (2007).

[2]   See, for example, Inglehart (1977, 1997), Sacchi (1992), Inglehart & Baker (2000),
Klages (1985, 1988).

[3]   See, for example, Inglehart (1977, 1997), Inglehart & Baker (2000).

[4]   Klages (1985, 1988, 1994), Franz & Herbert (1987a, 1987b).

[5]   On the emancipation of women, see also Chapters 2 and 9.

[6]   By 'values', we mean, following Esser (2000d, p. 312), 'collectively shared ideas on
desirable conditions which are seen as binding'. By 'norms', we mean institutional rules

Surprisingly little work in the sociology of religion has been carried out to answer just this question, and we therefore wish to make a contribution here with the help of our typology. What we can see is that the change of values in the 1960s actually did have a profound effect on the relationship between values and religion in society – but that the effects vary greatly according to type and subtype. We first analyse the values of our types and subtypes by taking a kind of snapshot of them (in a cross-sectional study). We then address the question of how the change of values has affected religiosity in recent decades (in a longitudinal study). We are thereby preparing ourselves for Chapter 9, which is concerned with explaining religious-social change.

6.1 The Types and Their Values

Our religious types and milieus differ in a characteristic manner with regard to how they combine religion, religiosity and values.

Institutional

Members of the institutional type as a whole are characterized by the fact that they see Christian faith and practice as a very important value, one which gives rise to most or all other values. Whenever this type talks of values, then a religious justification is not long coming. Within the values held high by the institutional type are also values regarding sexuality and the family which are (or tend to be) conservative. In Figure 6.1, we can see how important religion as a value is for the institutional type in comparison to its standing for the alternative, distanced and secular types, and the extent to which the institutional type represents more traditional norms of sexuality and gender. They reject far more often than the others: sex before marriage, extramarital affairs, homosexuality, abortion, and equal roles for husband and wife in the family. They also have more 'values of duty and acceptance' and fewer 'values of self-development', that is, they attach more value to 'maintaining order', 'obedience' and 'thrift', and less value to 'imagination', 'independence' and 'participation'.

---

backed by sanctions (see Esser (2000c, p. 10)). By 'moral', we mean the way in which respect and disrespect are distributed in a society or social group on the basis of values and norms (Luhmann 1987, p. 320).

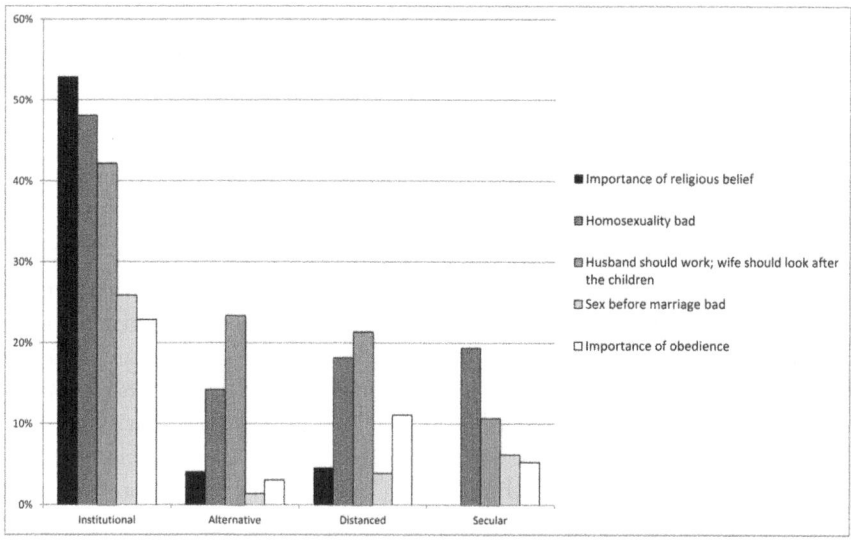

Figure 6.1   The institutional type sees religious faith as a value and has more conservative norms regarding sexuality and gender than the other types

Interestingly, though, there is a whole range of values where members of the institutional type do *not* differ significantly from the other types – values which they nonetheless derive from religion: tolerance and respect, generosity, a sense of responsibility, and good manners are not more important for the institutional type than for the other types. It seems, then, that the institutional type makes religion and faith responsible for what the other types also have, despite their lower level of religiosity. There are also no significant differences between the types in relation to work norms under difficult circumstances, such as 'work hard', 'do your best', 'keep up your level of performance', and 'determination and perseverance'.

A more detailed analysis shows, however, that there are clear differences *within* the institutional type (that is, between the established and the evangelical subtypes), with the two subtypes linking their religiosity with their values in a different way.

Members of the *established* subtype, that is, core members of Catholic and Reformed religious communities, link their religiosity with their values in a moderate form.[7] They believe that faith, the Ten Commandments and biblical charity lead to a general attitude towards life and to various values, such as

---

7   For similar findings in Australia, see Bellamy et al. (2002, p. 55).

behaving well, being patient and honest, and accepting others especially in their diversity and weaknesses. This is what Gisèle has to say, for example:

> If you believe in something, then you have many examples in the Bible, so that – I always say, if I'm good to other people, then that will come back to me in some way. Maybe not right now, but at some point it has to come back. I'm sure. (Gisèle, 63, Roman Catholic)

Although members of the established subtype are usually more conservative than other members of society in relation to norms covering sexuality and gender, we can also find among some members of the subtype some signs of progressiveness: they are in favour of the equality of the sexes, the use of condoms, and openness towards those who think differently. It is precisely this openness that quite often leads the established subtype to assume positions which are quite independent of what they perceive as 'churchly opinion'. Daniele is an example: only recently confirmed, the 46-year-old from Tessin embodies a new type of convertee, one who deals very seriously and deeply with religious questions. It is natural for Daniele that women want to continue their careers. Since he considers the sexes as being equal, he is struggling with the fact that the subordination of women to men is supposed to be God's will. Daniele's conclusion is that 'God is sexist'.

In contrast, members of the *evangelical* subtype make a much more direct link between their faith and their values. For them, values can often be derived *directly* and sometimes *literally* from the Bible. For Barbara, the New Testament is a '*rule*'; for Barnabé, '*the Bible teaches us*' values; and Beat draws his values from Biblical exemplars. This subtype also represents much more clearly, and sometimes vehemently, the traditional norms governing sexuality and the family. For this subtype, these values should be construed not so much as something '*forced*' on people, but as something which protects both individuals and society. In living these values, the individual can build a stable family and live a life full of faith in God. And, in turn, strong, stable families support society and keep them from imminent collapse. Barnabé explains:

> The Bible teaches us family balance. A father, a mother, and children who are brought up by their parents. This is something that today's society is losing. Look at the newspapers – and if you don't maintain the values – husband, wife, children – then you won't get far. (Barnabé, 56, Evangelical)

To conclude, we can say that many members of the institutional type have only gone along with the change of values to a limited extent, or have even consciously opposed the change. It is precisely for this reason that the positions which they take are sometimes viewed by the other types as being '*old-fashioned*' and '*no longer appropriate*'.

Alternative

Members of the alternative type (comprising esotericists, Sheilaists and alternative customers) differ greatly from the institutional type in terms of their values. For them, 'religious belief' is not important, and they are progressive with regard to issues of sexuality and gender. Otherwise, if we take account only of the numbers, then they appear to have fairly similar values as the distanced and secular types.

The most important point in relation to their values only reveals itself when we consider the qualitative material: namely, the fact that, like the institutional type, they make a close link between their own 'spirituality' and certain values which are widespread in society. These values, though, are modern, that is, they are values of self-development such as imagination, independence, tolerance, individualism, etc. It is precisely these values, though, that for the alternative type are highly spiritual. For this type, the individual with his or her needs is central. In cases of doubt, they deem their own body and their own feelings to have a higher authority than all external norms and rules. They believe that the individual should live out his or her needs, emotions and opinions as authentically as possible, and thereby reach a spiritually higher level. Because of this 'me-centredness', they take a critical view of anything that could restrict the individual. Klaus, for example, was strongly shaped by Catholicism, but he left the church to become one with himself completely. For Klaus, it was about 'taking away the net, so that I really risk everything and follow my own path entirely'. Eliot and Michel talk in terms of 'developing their own personality'. The alternative type also values tolerance, since one person should not restrict the authenticity and unique path of development of another. According to the alternative type, 'how the divine manifests and incarnates itself in the human being takes many faces and forms' (Klaus). For them, though, a 'non-value' lies precisely in the norms and dogmas which they see as emanating from the churches, norms and dogmas that force the individual to do something that does not correspond to his or her needs. All members of the alternative type vehemently oppose such norms and dogmas. 'On the day I had to be confirmed', Eliot says, 'I burned the Bible'. And Klaus explains: 'The paternalism (...) which is being manifested again by the Pontifical (...) is just not right for me' (Klaus, 62, Roman Catholic).

And Emily articulates her reservations concerning the rituals of the Catholic Church as follows:

> If you go to mass, then I never have the feeling that people are really themselves; they're just present, they do the ceremonial stuff, because that's what you do on a Sunday, (...) I really don't need that anymore. What I need is, (...) when I am with the divine together, mentally or energetically, (...) then I want to

enter into the peace and into the love. And what (...) goes on in the churches has for me nothing whatsoever to do with absolute love anymore. (Emily, 62, Roman Catholic)

The main point here, then, is not that members of the alternative type are much more fixed on self-development, individualism, etc. than other members of society – that is not the case. We all live in the 'me-society' and have such values. Rather, the point is that members of the alternative type are characterized by the fact that they link their self-development to their spirituality in a direct way. In this sense, they live a kind of *me-spirituality*.

Distanced

Interestingly, members of the distanced type do not talk often of values when they are questioned about religiosity and spirituality, the reason for which is quite simple: for many, the two areas are not particularly strongly linked.

Most of the values which are important to the distanced type seem to them to be self-evident, and therefore not necessarily in need of religious justification. The values that they name include, for example, charity, tolerance, acceptance of others, solidarity, always giving people a second chance, living well together with others, fairness, the stronger taking responsibility for the weaker, and acting responsibly. But very often they add: for this I don't need religion! Olga sees compassion as not being something that is specifically Christian: 'Good, but [compassion] I think [is] not necessarily a typically Christian value; (...) it is a common property' (Olga, 38, Roman Catholic).

For Nadia, behaving well has nothing to do with religion: 'So I just hope that my children (...) have a certain decorum so that they behave well. (...) But whether that's got anything to do with religion? I don't think so necessarily' Has it? (Nadia, 37, Reformed).

And for Fabio, too, fairness and the responsibility of the stronger for the weaker have nothing directly to do with religion:

> Yes, there are a few principles that I believe in. For example, I believe that a certain fairness should play a role in life, I believe that the stronger have a certain responsibility for the weaker. I believe that [a] certain openness, [a] certain honesty (...) are values that should definitely be pursued. (...) But that for me now doesn't have that much to do with religion. These are actually things that (...) for me would have a meaning in every religion, (...) if they really have anything to do with religion at all. (Fabio, 57, Roman Catholic)

The distanced type, though, often refers to the norms of the Catholic Church and the Evangelical churches governing sex, marriage and gender roles as being no longer '*contemporary*', and even often as being '*shocking*' (see Chapter 8).

Secular

Finally, the secularists are characterized in many respects by very similar values as the distanced and alternative types. The major difference compared to the institutional and alternative types, though, is precisely that they *do not* link these values to religiosity or spirituality. On the contrary, they often see religiosity and spirituality negatively, and oppose all religious-spiritual legitimation of what they themselves deem important. Again, we find the same values upheld as everywhere: honesty, justice, behaving appropriately, solidarity, respect, etc. To the question of whether his values have a religious basis, Siegfried, for example, says: 'No, it is (...) an idealistic notion that I (...) have, or where I hope if everyone behaved like that, then we would simply have (...) fewer problems, don't you think?' (Siegfried, 39, no religious affiliation).

The deeper reason for this rejection is that secularists give absolutely no plausibility to religious claims, and often also assume that religion is downright harmful for both the individual and society.

6.2 Change of Values and Religiosity

The most diverse authors agree that in the 1960s in all Western industrialized nations a quite extraordinary change of values took place (see Chapter 2).[8] This change can be seen in our data, too. It is a change that may be described as a decline in the values of duty and acceptance and an increase in the values of self-development. Linked to this change, sexual norms have become looser and the emancipation of women and homosexuals has come about. All of that is common knowledge. But what does it mean for religion and religiosity? To answer this question, we put forward three theses. First, religion and religiosity are themselves a possible value – but they have lost much of their importance within the canon of values due to the change of values that has taken place. Even as recently as the 1950s, it was clear to a majority of the population that religion legitimized the canon of values as a whole and that 'good behaviour' was

---

[8]   On the change of values during this period, see Klages (1985, 1988, 1994), Franz & Herbert (1987a, 1987b), Inglehart (1997), McLeod (2007), Putnam & Campbell (2010). On the individualization of values, see Bréchon & Galland (2010). For a comparison between countries with regard to the religious grounding (or increasing decoupling) of values, see Pickel (2001).

consistent with religion. For large swathes of the population, though, religion has lost this legitimizing function. Second, 'religion' is considered by many people to have something to do with 'old values', and is criticized accordingly. Above all, many of our respondents have Catholicism in mind, which represents for them outdated sexual norms and gender roles. Third, many of the values held by people are being increasingly seen as existing independently of religion. This applies to both traditional (but not regarded as outdated) values such as honesty and respect, as well as to 'new' values of self-development such as individualism and imagination. We shall now explore these three theses.

How Religion has Lost its 'Value' and its Legitimizing Function

There can be no doubt that religion has lost its importance as a value through the change of values that occurred in the 1960s. From what our older respondents say, it is quite clear that most people belonging to the pre-1960s generations considered the religious instruction of their children to be important. This was, on the one hand, because such instruction was '*simply part of life*', and, on the other, because these generations of parents believed that religion would make their children '*better people*'. They still saw religion and morality as forming a relatively strong unit, and even those parents for whom religion had little importance personally had their children baptized and confirmed as a matter of course. Religion had in all these respects a kind of cohesive function and was generally seen as the basis of moral conduct. Only very rarely do our respondents argue today how many thought then: that people's belief in a just reward or a just punishment in the afterlife would lead to their higher morality in this life:

> Yes, we do have a certain order, little crime, I think those are value concepts if someone steals from someone else (...) I think the thought is still there. (...) It is not just the police who punish, but also maybe then (...) that he must live with it (...) that maybe it's not all over with (laughs). (Stephan, 45, Roman Catholic)

The 1960s put an end to this cohesive function for large segments of the population. If we compare the oldest and the youngest generation in our data in terms of their values, we can see very clearly how the older generation give more value to working hard and obedience (values of duty and acceptance), whereas the younger generation give more value to imagination and independence (values of self-development). The key point for us, though, is that religious belief is being passed on to the next generation in a weaker state. This is considered to be a much more important value by the older generation than by the younger.[9]

---

[9]   The level of education and the socio-spatial context also play a role: the more urban (and anonymous), the more an egalitarian and liberal image of relationships and the family

The Criticism of 'Old' Values and their Link to Religion

The other side of the coin to the process that we have just dealt with is to some extent the fact that many people now associate 'religion' with 'old values', and criticize it accordingly. Religion and the values of the church are no longer appropriate, not authentic enough, exclude people, and constrict the individual. We can find such criticisms among all the types. One example is Klaus, when he criticizes Catholic sexual morality as follows:

> One thing in my life is now clear: I am the eighth of nine children. (...) Actually, I would have been superfluous if Catholic morality had not insisted that the woman has to be submissive to the man, even in bed. Then the mother would certainly not have had ten children, because that was a huge burden. (Klaus, 62, no religious affiliation)

Figure 6.2 shows in spectacular fashion how younger generations reject more strongly a traditional division of roles (the husband works, the wife looks after the house and children) than older generations, and how younger generations accept homosexuality and premarital sex more than older generations.[10] Most respondents, though, see sex before marriage, homosexuality and equality between men and women as quite normal, and also as being in direct opposition to the norms of the (mostly Catholic) church. Our respondents are particularly critical of the churches for their conservative attitudes in these areas, with many respondents blurring denominational differences and taking the Pope and the Catholic Church to represent the 'church' as a whole.

---

is propagated. In the rural and village context, in contrast, traditional ideas are given more support. Generally, women are much more likely to reject the classic allocation of gender roles than men.

[10]   Again, it is natural to understand these differences in age as generational differences. It is unlikely, in other words, that the younger people now will become more traditional and develop conservative views regarding sexuality, marriage and family roles as they grow older. These values depend not only on age but also on level of education, gender and the urban-rural feature. The more highly educated women and those living in urban areas are, the more likely they are to reject traditional sexual norms and gender roles.

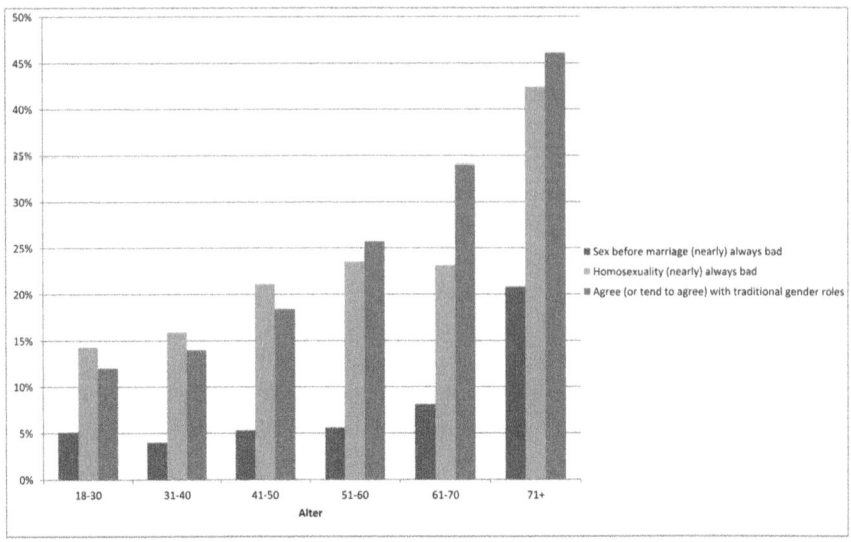

Figure 6.2   Older people have clearly more conservative norms regarding
sexuality and gender roles than younger people

The Release of 'New' Values

A third facet of the same process is that people considered many of the 'new' values to be independent of religion from the very beginning. Our respondents rarely associate individualism, imagination and creativity with religion. *One* exception, though, can be found among members of the alternative type, who legitimize values of self-development through alternative spirituality. Klaus left the church to be able to pursue his Sufi journey in an authentic way. For Michel, yoga leads to a spiritual evolution of the personality. What is particularly striking about members of the alternative type is the extreme value that they place on individual authenticity. Whatever they do, it must be right for their own 'I'. The 'I' must remain authentic to itself or develop in such a way that it becomes even more authentic.

***

What we can conclude from this is that the 'revolution of the 1960s' profoundly changed the relationship between values and religion across the whole of society – but that the effects of this vary considerably from type to type and subtype to subtype. In short, three main things occurred in the change of values of the 1960s. First, 'old' values such as obedience, subservience, and traditional roles of gender and sexuality were destroyed. Second, 'constant' values such as sense of duty, striving for success, honesty, and good manners were also rejected in the heat of battle of 1968, but prevailed in the end and have been maintained overall. Third, 'new' values such as self-development, individualism, creativity were added to the canon of values and have since prevailed in the whole of society. The different types now saw the relationship of these values to religion and spirituality very differently. A majority of the population – the distanced and secular types – vehemently rejected the old values, and saw the constant and new values as being independent in principle of religion and spirituality. For them, it was not necessary to be religious to have these values. This is an interesting historical first, for, in Swiss society until well into the 1950s, values were legitimized in the final instance by religion. In contrast, three groups continued to have a close relationship to religion. The evangelical subtype still upheld the old values (traditional gender roles and sexual norms) and legitimized this through their belief based on the Bible. The established subtype mostly came to terms with the destruction of the old values in society, but still believed that their own values were built on their belief and that society needed religion, especially to maintain the constant values, such as sense of duty, striving for success, honesty, good manners, etc. The alternative type also saw a close relationship between values and religiosity/spirituality, and believed that it was only the new, alternative spirituality that could justify the new values of self-development, individualism, and creativity. For them, the spiritual task would be the individual, creative and self-directed pursuit of happiness and personal development.

Chapter 7

Major Churches, Evangelical Churches and Alternative-Spiritual Suppliers

Jörg Stolz, Thomas Englberger

I believe in God; I just don't trust anyone who works for him. (Author unknown)

The religious landscape of Switzerland consists not only of individuals but also, and significantly, of 'religious suppliers', that is, groups or single people who practise, offer and disseminate religious-spiritual rituals, beliefs, values, and methods of healing.1 It is they who, according to our theory, are in competition both with each other and with secular suppliers (see Chapter 2). In this chapter, we shall address the question of which 'salvation goods' and 'benefits' our respondents perceive with regard to these suppliers and what they offer, on what basis they choose between what is on offer (or simply reject what is on offer), whether a 'religious-spiritual marketplace' comes into being, and how they evaluate and criticize the suppliers and what they offer. We shall deal here with three different suppliers: the major churches, that is, Roman Catholic and Reformed churches, Evangelical churches, and alternative-spiritual suppliers. Our perspective, though, always remains that of the customer, that is, we analyse how our respondents perceive, evaluate and make use of the religious-spiritual suppliers. Through the special nature of our data, which are both qualitative and quantitative, we are able to arrive at several new insights which in part diametrically contradict the ideas of prevalent theories of the religious market (Iannaccone 1998, Stark and Bainbridge 1989) and of 'vicarious religion' (Davie 2006).

---

1   We may ask ourselves whether the term 'supplier' is well chosen here. Does it not already imply that we are dealing here with a 'market' with 'suppliers' and 'customers'? For our purposes, though, the term does not already imply a market. After all, a religious community acting as a 'supplier' can supply its own members and their children with 'salvation goods', without a 'religious market' coming into being. We should also point out again here that we have excluded the non-Christian 'suppliers' from our analysis for purely methodological reasons. On such suppliers, see the various studies of NFP 58; for an overview, see Stolz, Chaves, Monnot & Amiotte-Suchet (2011).

7.1 Three Types of Suppliers

Major Churches, Evangelical Churches, Alternative-Spiritual Suppliers

Let us recall briefly some of the key characteristics of the three religious-spiritual suppliers that we wish to deal with here. First, there are the *major churches*, which are Roman Catholic and Protestant-Reformed cantonal churches whose local communities consist of church congregations and parishes.[2] These major churches are (in most cantons) recognized under public law, which bestows on them certain rights and obligations. For example, they have the right to collect church taxes and to offer pastoral care in schools, hospitals and the army. On the other hand, they are also forced to adopt a democratic structure of organization and to accept some state monitoring.[3] These local church communities have existed for several hundred years; they are territorial communities (i.e., membership is not a matter of choice, but determined by place of residence); and most of these communities have a building especially constructed for religious purposes, that is, a church. The membership structure is characterized by the fact that a large number of people are 'passive members', that is, they pay church taxes, but do not actively participate in rituals or other activities of the church community. According to the first census, which was carried out in 2008, there are 1094 Reformed, 1750 Roman Catholic, and 35 Christian Catholic local religious communities.[4]

A second type of suppliers is *Evangelical churches.*[5] They are Protestant or at least situated within Protestant surroundings, and are not recognized under public law. They therefore finance themselves not through church taxes, but through member donations. Most of these communities emerged in the nineteenth and twentieth centuries. Most are not territorial, but voluntary communities, with members joining the community on their own initiative and quite independently of place of residence or parental origin.[6] Some Evangelical churches have buildings specifically constructed for religious purposes, while others perform their rituals in secular buildings, such as former supermarkets, residential buildings, commercial buildings, factories, etc. The membership structure of evangelical communities differs significantly from that of the major churches, since with the former the number of official and active members is

---

[2]   In some cantons, the Christian Catholic Church is also recognized under public law. Due to its low membership, though, it cannot be classified as a 'major church'. See Pahud de Mortanges (2007).

[3]   On this, see Pahud de Mortanges (2007), Winzeler (1998, 2005).

[4]   See Stolz, Chaves, Monnot & Amiotte-Suchet (2011, p. 13).

[5]   On this, see Favre (2002), Stolz, Favre, Gachet & Buchard (2013).

[6]   This does not mean that parental socialization is not important. The opposite is in fact the case. On this, see Chapter 9.

often roughly the same. The reason for this is that evangelical communities are usually small and consist of 'confessing members': joining the community implies a high religious commitment. According to the census of 2008, there are 1423 evangelical communities.[7]

A third type is *alternative-spiritual suppliers*.[8] These are often individual people who offer courses, seminars, trainings, retreats and therapies, as well as healing or counselling services. What they offer covers a very wide area: from yoga, tai chi, qi gong, family therapy, reiki, NLP, chromotherapy, Zen meditation and acupuncture, to homeopathy, reflexology and seminars on angels. Some of these suppliers form loose groups and communities around them, while others maintain a pure supplier-client relationship. Alternative-spiritual suppliers usually have no building constructed for spiritual purposes. They are financed through participation fees or payment for individual healing sessions, but also through donations. As far as we know, there are no exact data on the number of alternative-spiritual suppliers in Switzerland. Magali Jenny and Riti Sharma have published lists with over 250 healers in Romandie and over 200 healers in German-speaking Switzerland.[9] It is especially in German-speaking Switzerland, though, where the actual numbers may be much higher.[10]

In Figure 7.1, we have drawn in a fourth type: the secular suppliers. These exist, of course (free thinkers, atheist groups, etc.), but our material provides too little for us to be able to make any accurate statements here.[11]

Anchoring and Presence of the Three Suppliers

Each type of supplier is, roughly speaking, anchored in one of the three milieus that we have identified: the major churches with their church communities and parishes in the established milieu; the Evangelical churches in the evangelical milieu; and the spiritual entrepreneurs in the esoteric milieu (see Figure 7.1). By 'anchoring', we mean here that the suppliers recruit their leadership figures and professional or semi-professional practitioners, as well as their most loyal participants in rituals, in the respective milieu.

---

[7]   Stolz, Chaves, Monnot & Amiotte-Suchet (2011, p. 13).

[8]   On this, see Mayer (1993), Hero (2010).

[9]   Jenny (2008), Sharma & Jenny (2009).

[10]   It is clear that there are also anchored suppliers within the secular type: for example, the *Freidenke Vereinigung* (Association of Freethinkers), the *Giordano Bruno Stiftung* (the Giordano Bruno Foundation), sceptics, and communist-oriented groups in which atheist aims are also pursued. In our material, though, these groups are too marginal for us to be able to analyse them properly here.

[11]   A larger research project on this is currently being planned. For preparatory work on this, see Ramsel, Huber & Stolz (2013).

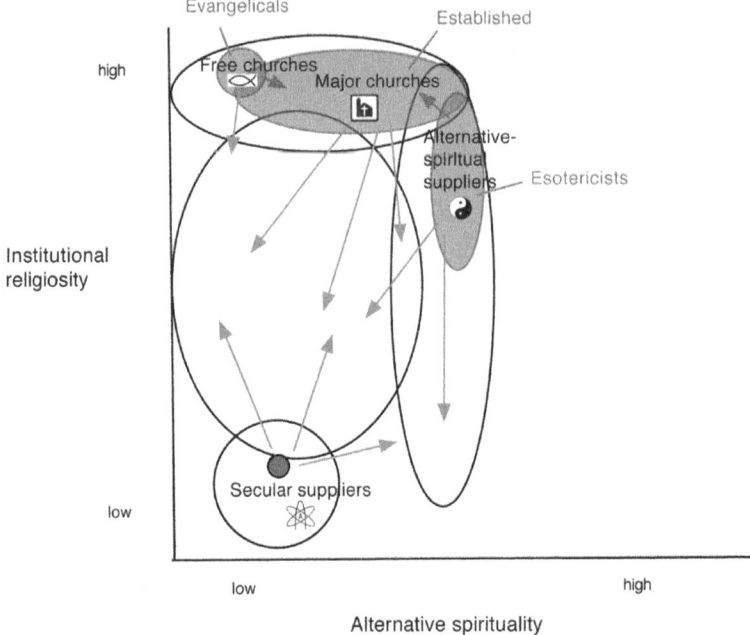

Figure 7.1   Major churches, Evangelical churches and alternative-spiritual
suppliers are each anchored in their own milieu

However, religious-spiritual suppliers offer their 'products' not only in the milieu
in which they are anchored; rather, they have a presence throughout society as
a whole and try to appeal to wide sections of society (indicated by the arrows
in Figure 7.1). The major churches, for example, can count on the fact that the
'institutional' will come to their religious services. Nonetheless, they still offer
life-cycle rituals, values, support, religious instruction, etc. to all their members
(and to members of society in general). Here, they are concerned above all with
the distanced type, and also partly with the alternative and secular types. Figure
7.2 makes this fact clear. As we can see, of all those defining themselves as 'Roman
Catholic', only 27 per cent belong to the institutional type, while the majority
belong to the distanced type (58 per cent), 11 per cent to the alternative type, and
4 per cent to the secular type. There are similar relations among those defining
themselves as 'Reformed'. Among members of the Evangelical churches, though,
the situation is very different, with 86 per cent belonging to the institutional
type, that is, the membership of these churches is made up of people who are
very involved in the life of the church. In these religious communities, 'official
members' correspond to 'participants'. Although Evangelical churches can also
have a 'presence' with regard to society as a whole through their missionary

activities, charitable works and appearances in the public domain, they can do this to a far lesser extent than can the major churches.

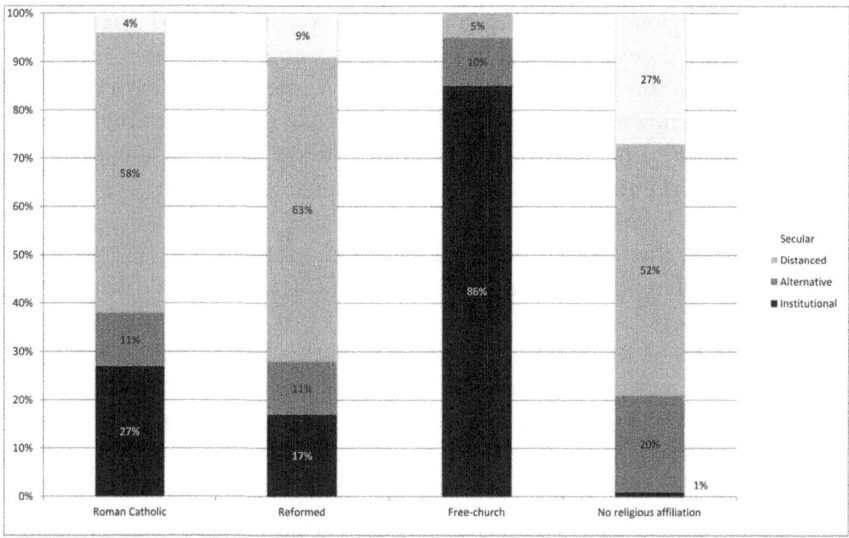

Figure 7.2   Most members of Evangelical churches belong to the institutional type; among Catholics and the Reformed, the institutional type is very much in the minority

As we have already seen in Chapter 4, many *alternative-spiritual suppliers* also manage to reach a wide public that goes well beyond their own milieu. Many of the customers of these suppliers usually demand the particular services (remedies, massages, predictions for the future) for very concrete and practical reasons, and it is only in a few cases that they link these services to a specific spirituality.

7.2 'Salvation Goods' and 'Benefits' of the Goods on Offer

What, though, do churches, Evangelical churches and 'alternative suppliers' offer exactly? Or, in the language of the great sociologist Max Weber, what 'salvation goods' do they promise?[12] And what other benefits do people see in belonging to a major church or an Evangelical church, or in using the services of an alternative-spiritual supplier?

---

[12]   See Weber (1985a (1922)) and Stolz (2006b).

Churches: Strength, Support, Tradition, and Benefit to Others

When it comes to the question of what churches offer, most of our respondents think of the religious service, church music, life-cycle rituals, and 'good works'. People who use these goods (in our typology, the 'established' type) often give different reasons for doing so. Some respondents enjoy continuing a tradition that they have known since childhood. Others say that these goods give them '*strength*', '*support*', and '*comfort and security*'. Others still are convinced that they can maintain and deepen their faith through the church. For Bettina, it is a matter of finding '*strength*': 'I have the feeling that I get strength when I'm in church. I then concentrate hard and listen carefully (...) and go home afterwards a different person and go to work a different person' (Bettina, 40, Roman Catholic).

A second set of reasons relate to '*church music*', with many people in close contact with churches participating because they can find an environment there in which they can sing and make music. The '*very beautiful hymns*' give them '*joy*', and they experience '*great emotions*' and moments of happiness.

It is noticeable that most of the reasons given are related to psychology and inner mental states, with the individual participating on account of his or her own religious, psychological and traditional needs. Our respondents rarely associate what churches offer with strong 'transcendental salvation goods'. No member of the established type, for example, believes that God thinks that people must go to church, and nobody says that going to church increases the likelihood of an eternal life, etc. And, apart from church music, our respondents hardly ever mention any other inherent advantages to going to church, such as seeing their friends, meeting interesting people, or getting support in bringing up their children better. Finally, they barely mention (any longer) a 'social control' which could force people to use what churches offer, a point which is particularly important since it shows how much conditions have changed since the transition to the me-society (see Chapters 2 and 9).

Overall, frequent churchgoers believe that what the church offers is important not only for them personally but for society as a whole. In particular, churches provide life-cycle rituals and provide society with important values. They also consider churches to be trustworthy institutions and believe that society as a whole would benefit from more religion and from churches having a greater influence.

In contrast, the *alternative* and *distanced* types generally see the benefits of the churches as lying in quite different areas. Many see some benefit to life-cycle rituals and festive religious services, and they can well imagine using the services of the church for when they or their children marry, or for baptisms, confirmations and funerals: these are '*the high points, the celebrations*'. According to Beryl: 'So, yes, I do think that the church is important. These ceremonies –

that you are accepted into life when you are baptized or get married' (Beryl, 64, Roman Catholic). Some also say that their main point of contact with the church is the religious service at Christmas: 'I think of Christmas mass: that's the only time I go to mass, and I like going then' (Elina, 25, Roman Catholic).

Other respondents again see churches as providing a psychological support. Although Livia has no contact whatsoever with the church at the moment, the fact that she could turn to the church if ever it were necessary is something positive: 'I think that if I need someone to talk to or whatever – then I can go to the pastor. But I can also go to church and have the feeling that I can find shelter there. Yes, that's true. That's what the church gives you' (Livia, 38, Reformed).

But by far the most frequent answer to the question, 'Do churches provide something that is beneficial to you?' is: 'not beneficial to me, but to others'. These respondents do not need churches themselves, but they still see churches as definitely being of benefit to others, and to three groups in particular. First, the religious, that is, people who 'wish ultimately to find explanations in the church', and who are 'given support when they go to a sermon'. Second, the disadvantaged, 'those in need', 'people with emotional problems who are on the edge of despair'. Third, many of our respondents see a benefit to society as a whole in that the church provides it with a moral foundation. They say, for example, that churches are 'a safety railing for society', 'a polar opposite in today's competitive society', 'a brake on the violence and sense of derailment in society'.

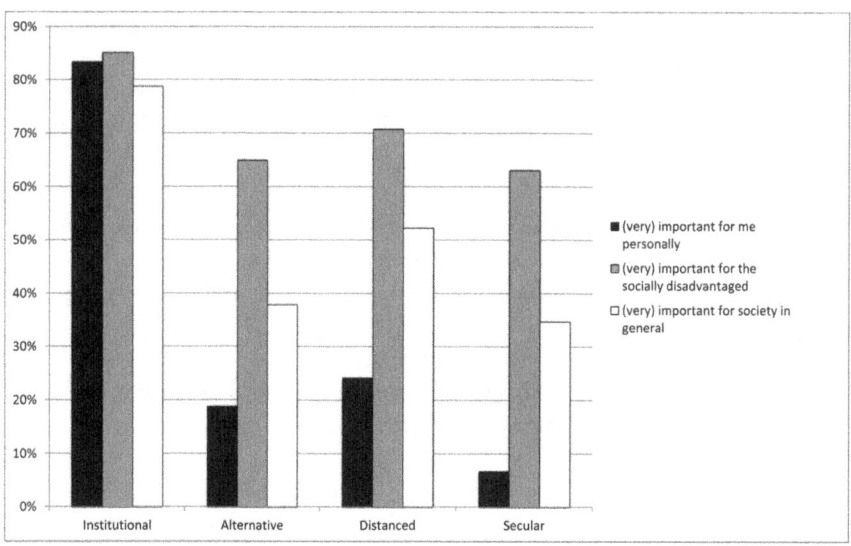

Figure 7.3   Among the alternative, distanced and secular types, churches are primarily 'important for others'

Our quantitative findings show this very clearly, too (Figure 7.3). Not only the distanced type, but also the alternative and even the secular types, see the churches as not particularly important for them personally, but as nonetheless very important for the disadvantaged and (albeit to a lesser degree) for society as a whole. It is here that one of the main sources of legitimacy for the churches still lies.[13] Regardless of personal religious viewpoint or religious affiliation, the majority of the population perceives and recognizes the churches as, so to speak, providers of relief.

Evangelical Churches: Living with Jesus and with Other Christians

Compared with the major churches, Evangelical churches seem to promise a significantly different kind of 'benefit' and different 'salvation goods'. What is in the foreground here is not a religious, psychological, traditional 'support', or church music, or the provision of life-cycle rituals, or a corrective function for society. Rather, for the evangelical subtype, the religious community is an *essential component of a whole Christian lifestyle*, at the centre of which is life with God and Jesus Christ full of miracles, the forgiveness of sins, and the hope of an eternal life. For the evangelical subtype, such a lifestyle, though, is only possible in a community with other 'Christians' (in the emphatic sense). For them, the Evangelical church is therefore not a distant institution, but a very close community. It is where they can see their friends again, gain personal support, and talk about their faith, a place that they need to be able to bring up their children as Christians, to maintain their faith, and to overcome doubt. Barbara tells of how her religious community prayed for her when she fell seriously ill, and Willi explains how friendly and familiar everything is in his religious community:

> We all know each other, of course; it's not a big community. There are about sixty of us, and so we all know each other almost personally; and we also go out together and we have colleagues. Yes, there is a closer relationship, more of a family group. (Willi, 40, Evangelical)

And Dorothée explains how conversations in small groups can help members to see how to apply their faith in a very practical way:

> Yes, I think that it's useful in the sense that you meet other people and discuss things with them. You are then confronted with the problems of other people (...), problems that you don't necessarily know about. That's how you learn. (Dorothée, 32, Evangelical)

---

[13]   For earlier work on this, see Dubach & Campiche (1993), Campiche (2004).

For members of Evangelical churches, then, the question of 'benefit' is different from how it is for members of the major churches. From the perspective of the former, it is a *necessity* to belong to a religious community, even if it is usually less important *which* community – as long as this community represents a 'true' faith.

Alternative-Spiritual Suppliers: Spiritual Growth and Problem-Solving

The 'benefits' and 'salvation goods' of alternative-spiritual suppliers differ again from those of the major churches and Evangelical churches. The consumers here expect a veritable flood of individual benefits, with the core group (our 'esotericists') looking to complete and perfect their own transcendental self, and being concerned with *'growing spiritually', 'developing personally'*, discovering *'the divine within me', 'regenerating', 'becoming more whole', 'letting everything become spiritual, like breathing'*. The individual draws on the most varied methods and techniques to achieve a higher state of being, a state that is expressed spiritually, mentally and physically. According to Michel, for example, yoga brings

> a physical suppleness, which is the first phase. This brings an increased sense of well-being at the level of health – that's not to be sneezed at. And then at the level of mental equilibrium, it leads to a certain inner balance, a certain peace, and then it helps you to develop yourself spiritually. (Michel, 63, no religious affiliation)

Many other respondents (such as 'Sheilaists and alternative customers', and the 'distanced' type), though, see the benefits of what alternative-spiritual suppliers offer more in terms of *ad hoc* solutions to quite specific problems. Berta-Lisa tried homeopathy to stop her fainting fits. Julie has back problems and goes to an osteopath with amazing psychic abilities. Deborah's partner went to a specialist on colours to help him choose between her and his then wife (but later ex-wife). David employs a whole range of alternative-spiritual remedies to treat his various illnesses. In all these cases, it is not 'spiritual development' that our respondents are looking for, but the solution to a very specific mental or physical problem. In drawing on these remedies, they are willing to believe that alternative-spiritual suppliers possess exceptional abilities that could be used to solve their problems.

Different religious-spiritual suppliers not only offer different products, but also make available different forms for members or customers in order to bond with them. This is the subject of the next section.

7.3 The Relationship of Members to Religious-Spiritual Suppliers

According to an important theory in the sociology of religion (the so-called 'market theory'), people in Western societies generally choose their membership of a religious group in the same way that they choose a product. Depending on their own resources and the price-performance ratio of the suppliers available, they will then choose the membership that promises them the greatest benefits, or switch from one supplier to another if a better deal is available. But does this theory work in practice?

Major Churches: Staying or Leaving

Interestingly, the theory does *not* apply to the majority of church members. The question that church members ask themselves is certainly not which religious community they should choose or whether they should *switch* from one community to another. This applies both to religiously active church members (those belonging to the 'established' subtype) and to less active church members (those belonging to the 'distanced' type). Active church members choose consciously from what their church has to offer and are sometimes unhappy with much of what their church does have to offer. Nevertheless, they do not consider whether changing church would be possible, nor inform themselves about other options or weigh up other appropriate options.[14] The reason is usually that they experience their membership as part of their identity, and a change of church or religious community usually does not even appear as an option in their consciousness. Even the less active church members give no consideration at all to 'changing their supplier'. But their reason is usually different: namely, insufficient demand for religiosity. Many respondents explain that they do not want to change because they are too little interested in religion. They have '*in any case no intention of ever being active*'. Blandine, for example, says: 'If I'm not inside [in the community] anyway, then I don't see why I should look around for something else' (Blandine, 63, Roman Catholic).
The question that the respondents concern themselves with in our material is not whether to *change* their church, but whether *to leave the church* completely.[15] Church members think long and hard about this question, and it is a question that is subject to much discussion.

Most of our respondents explicitly reject the possibility of leaving the church – and often even do so when they strongly criticize their church, do not

---

[14]   We meet here the finding from the social sciences that markets build on typical perceptions and rules which explain market behaviour as normal.

[15]   On the issue of leaving the church, see Pollack (2001), Need & de Graf (1996), Birkelbach (1999), Stolz & Ballif (2010).

(really) believe in God, and have not been to church for a long time. The reasons for remaining in the church are complex. In most cases, church membership seems to be traditional and something that people simply take for granted, with respondents seeing '*no reason*' to leave. While many respondents give no further reason for seeing church membership as a matter of course, others cite specific reasons, these being very wide-ranging and including arguments relating to identity and needs, social control, and public goods. Leaving the church is not a possibility because, for example, '*I've been a Catholic since a small child*'; the church is '*part of my journey through life*'; we '*need the saints*', otherwise people '*would look at you strangely*'; we need the '*institution*' in society. Members of the institutional type in particular, but also many of those belonging to the distanced type, therefore consider leaving the church as '*not even being an issue*'.

Other respondents state that they have already considered leaving the church, but have not done so yet. They are weighing up the reasons for leaving and staying in the church. The possible *reasons for leaving* can be grouped into three categories. First, it might be the case that people consider the church and the Christian faith as no longer having anything to say to them; that they have grown indifferent to the questions that the church poses. Second, it may be that people are annoyed or angry with the church (too dominant, authoritarian, etc.). Third, people may want to save on taxes. While our respondents classify leaving the church for reasons of indifference or annoyance as being socially acceptable, most seem to consider leaving for financial reasons to be unacceptable. While one respondent referred to his church membership as being his '*most expensive subscription*' and another asked why it was that he did not notice his membership more when he was paying so much, most respondents who discussed church tax felt that this was simply not a valid argument for leaving the church. Renato's line of argumentation is typical:

> So to change is not an option for me. Oh, to leave [the church] – the question is justified. It is (...) something I would not do for financial reasons, because then I would have to see only the benefits. But then I do it not so much for selfish reasons, not for reasons related to me, but for everyone. I think that if nobody did this (...) then something would be missing. (Renato, 41, Roman Catholic)

As we have said, though, the possible reasons for leaving the church are balanced by important and wide-ranging *reasons for staying*. Sometimes the spur to leave is missing. Sometimes the annoyance or anger with the church is not great enough, and is quickly forgotten again. In many cases, there remains a certain bond, a '*little feeling*', a '*residual belief*'. Often it is the life-cycle rituals that seem to be an important reason for people to stay in the church: our respondents want to be able to marry in church, to be buried and to bury their nearest and dearest, to have their children baptized. With some we find a kind of 'stand-by mode', with respondents arguing that we can never know if one day we might need the church after all. Laurence says: 'I don't know what the future may bring. Perhaps we'll be pleased one day to be able to go there [to church]' (Laurence, 40, Roman Catholic).

Those who have already left the church also give all the reasons already mentioned, but often make the financial argument very forcefully, too.[16] People can, says Peter, 'save a shedload of money' by leaving. And Erich says: 'Then I finally just said: for that [for the church] I'm not paying any money. I'm not supporting it anymore' (Erich, 40, no religious affiliation).

We can complement the picture that we have painted so far of the tendencies to stay in and to leave the church by analysing the quantitative data. According to these data, thinking about leaving the church is more common among younger people, men, people living in urban areas, couples cohabiting, people with no or few children, and the better educated. It is striking that, in our material, there is much more talk of leaving the church than of joining it. The only respondent to have rejoined the church is Nadia, who did so because she wanted to marry in church and have her children baptized. We can again see here in the background the process of secularization and distantiation that we have already encountered repeatedly in this book.[17]

Evangelical Churches and Alternative-Spiritual Suppliers: Competitive Markets for Members and Customers

The situation is quite different when we turn to Evangelical churches and alternative-spiritual suppliers. In contrast to the major churches, what we find here are (very different) market forms in the sense of people changing their religious supplier.

---

[16]   It is interesting that it is mainly men who discuss the question of church taxes, regardless of whether they see them as legitimate or illegitimate.

[17]   A relation that first appears to be paradoxical emerges when we consider language regions and thoughts of leaving the church. In the French-speaking areas of Switzerland, we find more people without religious affiliation, but fewer people who have thought about leaving the church than in the German-speaking areas. This might be connected to the different church-state relations in the different cantons. The French-speaking cantons have (usually) no church taxes (Geneva, Neuchâtel), or at least no taxes which could be saved on by taking this step (Vaud, Valais). Thus, for people in French-speaking Switzerland it is often less clear whether they are 'officially' affiliated to a particular denomination, which might push the number of people without religious affiliation upwards. Moreover, they have less incentive to consider leaving the church, since doing so would not save them any church taxes – which could explain the low proportion of those willing to leave the church.

Members of Evangelical churches are quite willing to change their religious community.[18] Members of the evangelical subtype certainly believe that people should be loyal to their own religious community, and not immediately '*run away*' from every problem. And they also criticize what they perceive to be a Christian '*consumer mentality*'. Nevertheless, many members of evangelical churches are very willing to change their community if that would give them the opportunity to live their faith better, to bring up their children in a more Christian way, or if other circumstances make a change beneficial. From their point of view, it is not so much a question of *which* religious community they belong to, but rather the fact that they belong to a community which strengthens and deepens their own faith. This is very clear in the case of Dorothée, who says: 'We are here [in this community] because we think that we belong here, but at the same time we wouldn't have any problem changing, provided that the new community has the same values and the same faith' (Dorothée, 32, Evangelical).

It is very clear that many members of evangelical churches change their community several times during the course of their life; that, when they move address or when they have to change their community for other reasons, they look at several possible communities before making their choice; and that, particularly among younger people, there is a lively game of 'supply and demand' going on. We can also find a number of people who switch back and forth between Reformed and evangelical communities.

When we consider *alternative-spiritual suppliers*, then different relations appear again. These suppliers operate in an almost typically ideal market. Most are individual religious-spiritual undertakings that sometimes form 'circles' or 'communities' around themselves. They often see their consumers not as 'members', but as 'participants' or 'customers'. They have internalized the constant 'wandering' by people from one product to another. Emily, who has participated in various seminars about angels, aura, positive thinking, homeopathy, and autogenic training, and who has been trained in craniosacral and polarity therapy, explains that she has '*succeeded*' because she has '*never stuck to one particular thing*'. And, after providing a long list of things she has already tried (reiki, shiatsu, natural diets, etc.), Félicia explains: 'And it may well be that I'll do other things in the future. Depending on what I come across' (Félicia, 55, Reformed).

In the me-society in particular, many people have only a loose membership relation or no membership relation at all, to one or more religious or spiritual supplier(s). In such a situation, questions of public perception and 'image' become extremely important for suppliers. It is to this issue that we turn in the next section.

---

[18]   This point is analysed in great detail in the chapter on changing churches by Caroline Gachet in Stolz, Favre, Gachet & Buchard (2013).

7.4 The Perception of Religious-Spiritual Suppliers

The Image of the Major Churches: Useful, but Outdated and Conservative

For our respondents, the major churches as 'religious suppliers' have a very ambivalent image.[19] On the one hand, as we have already seen, large sections of the population agree that the churches do good for the disadvantaged and that they can represent important values for society. Many people are also happy to take advantage of the life-cycle rituals and festive services offered by the church and think that, if the church were to disappear, then there would be '*something missing*'. These positive assessments are, however, counterbalanced by very different, and much more negative, views. Church services are often seen as '*bland*', '*tedious*' and '*stuck in the past*'. They are attended only by a few elderly people, who are, though, according to Mona, '*mega-happy when they can go to church*'. People talk of a community, but it does not actually exist. Even if people did want to be involved, the churches are simply not attractive. Barbara, for example, explains:

> But if there are so few people in the local church and only elderly people go to church, then I think that's a shame, right? I always hope that I can get involved in my local church one day, but if it has so few people, then I don't fancy it. (Barbara, 58, Reformed)

Vanessa went to a Christmas service with her children and was disappointed at how boring it was. She had trouble keeping the children reasonably quiet for an hour. 'I then told my sister-in-law that I wasn't surprised any more that people don't go to church; it's so boring' (Vanessa, 41, Reformed).

The image of these churches is also affected negatively by the fact that their values are seen as conservative and no longer appropriate, and sometimes even as being un-Christian (see Chapters 6 and 8). Very many respondents speak at length about issues such as the conservatism of the Pope, the celibacy of priests, the fact that women cannot become priests, the rejection of contraception. As we will show in detail in the next chapter, most respondents consider these attitudes as being '*no longer appropriate*', '*no longer relevant in today's world*', and '*outdated*'. For many, the church is as guilty of causing famine and the spread of AIDS in Africa as it is of paedophilia among its priests. Even though these points all pertain to Catholicism, many respondents blur the denominational borders and usually associate these conservative values with '*the church in general*'. Where people refer to the Reformed Church in our material, however, they often note positively that they are probably more open than the

---

19   On the image that major churches have, see Stolz & Ballif (2010).

Catholics. Many respondents therefore think that the churches should '*do things differently*', that they should '*blow away the cobwebs*' and '*the dust*'. Apart from the recommendation (to Catholics) of allowing priests to marry, admitting women to the priesthood, and allowing contraception, our respondents did not give clear ideas, though. Respondents also usually do not know '*what should be done there*'.

We can evaluate the image of the church from a different perspective again if we compare its image with that of other institutions. In Figure 7.4, we present the degree of trust (total trust or large trust) that our four types have in various institutions. We can see that, particularly among the institutional type, churches enjoy a comparatively high degree of trust (higher than do national and local governmental bodies, trade and industry, and the law courts and legal system). On the other hand, the alternative, distanced and secular types have less trust in the churches than in all the other institutions mentioned. A comparison over time (not presented here) reveals an overall decline in the trust that people have in the churches, which, though, is comparable to the decline in the trust that people have in other institutions. Here also we can see the transition to the 'me-society': individuals emancipate themselves from institutions and assume a distanced and critical or evaluative stance towards them.

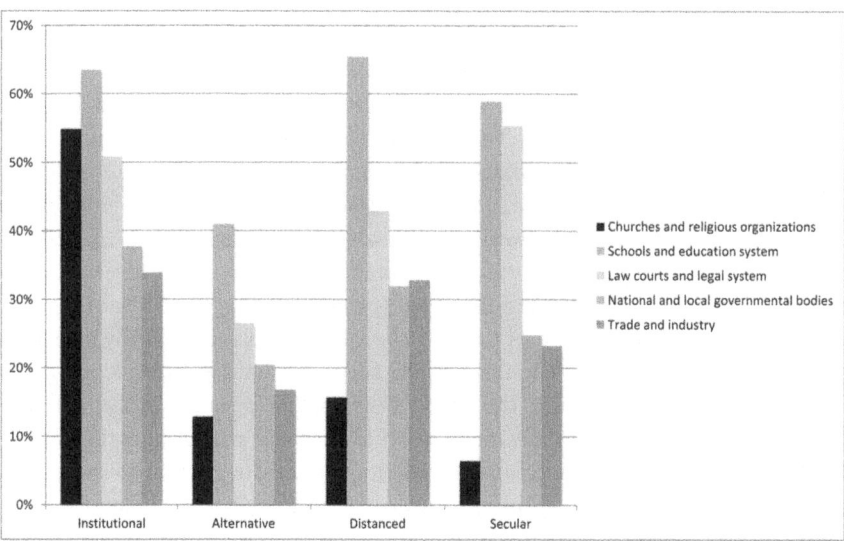

Figure 7.4   With the exception of the institutional type, people have less trust in the church than they do in other institutions

Note: what is shown here is 'total or large trust' in the respective institutions.

Church Pastors and Priests: From Old-fashioned to 'Cool'

Pastors, priests and other church specialists are considered no less ambivalently than the major churches for which they work.[20] It is striking that, across all types and milieus, very stereotypical images of good and bad pastors or priests appear in the material. The typical bad pastor or priest is described as an older, *'bigoted'*, *'stubborn'*, *'hypocritical'*, *'insensitive'* and *'authoritarian'* man who implements the norms and *'dogmas'* of his church in a conservative and authoritarian manner. He delivers sermons *'that say nothing'*. Our respondents have encountered this type of pastor or priest in their religious socialization or have had something to do with him at a church wedding or funeral. This man does precisely what religion, according to the respondents, should not do: namely, he tries *'to force'*, *'to hammer'*, *'to ram'* his beliefs home. He may not be completely responsible for his unfortunate behaviour, though, since he is part of a *'scandalous organization'*, one which does not allow him to marry and start a family. This man lives *'in his own world'*, he *'doesn't wash-up'*, he *'doesn't make his own bed'*. Since he is not married, there are many things in life that he knows very little about. Blandine would not ask a priest for advice, because: 'Knowledge of life – I think we have more of it than them [the priests]. Family? What have they got? They give us nice sermons! But what have they experienced? Nothing!' (Blandine, 63, Roman Catholic).

Our material is full of stories and encounters with (predominantly Catholic) clerics whom our respondents perceive in this manner. The good pastor or priest, on the other hand, assumes two stereotypical forms. On the one hand, they may be *'young'*, *'cool'*, *'dynamic'* people who defy all churchly norms and are *'normal'*, *'very open'*, *'very nice'*. He *'plays football with the children'*. People would like to get to know him better, *'as a person'* and *'completely outside of religion'*. And, on the other, we find an *'old'*, *'wise'*, *'special'*, *'bearded'*, *'solitary'*, *'very religious'* man. He is *'gentle'*, *'looks into your eyes and knows everything'*, *'sees what you are feeling'*. People can ask him for advice and feel uplifted. In both cases, however, it seems as if the respondents are seeing the *'good pastor'* as being positive not *because of*, but *despite*, the institution of the church. The good pastor skilfully overrides the *'dogmas'* and *'rules'* of the institution, and deals with people as people. It is precisely because he applies the gospel fully that he does not come across as being a pastor or priest at all. Daniele says: 'He is a priest who applies the gospel; he doesn't look like a priest at all. Because he applies the gospel too much. He leaves all the institutions behind him, he doesn't like any rules; he likes to go his own way' (Daniele, 46, Roman Catholic).

---

[20]   On the development of the pastor profession, see Willaime (1996, 2002).

The good pastor or priest carries the load of being a cleric alone because he as a person is how he is. The institutional connection is rather a hindrance than a help.[21]

For all the ambivalence, though, one point is beyond doubt: the specialists in the church have less authority now in the me-society than they had in the past. We would find a similar phenomenon with regard to non-religious specialists – in the religious sphere, though, the decline seems to have been particularly marked. The Catholic clergy above all have suffered an extreme loss of authority. Berta-Lisa says:

> The priests – they're also all human beings like us. In the past, when we were little, they were so high up. And at some point we suddenly realized: yes, they are the same height as us, or we're the same height as them. And that just removed some of the priestly aura. (Berta-Lisa, 62, Roman Catholic)

On the one hand, then, priests are no longer *'special, higher'* people; and, on the other, their university education does not seem to give religious specialists any special expertise in which our respondents can have confidence. Pastors and priests usually know *'no more than we do'*.

The Image of Evangelical Churches and Their Pastors: From Lively to Dangerous

The image of *Evangelical churches* is ambivalent, too. This ambivalence, though, stems from the fact that different groups of people have very different views on Evangelical churches. Put very concisely and somewhat exaggeratedly, members of Evangelical churches almost always draw a positive picture, while former members and non-members often have a rather critical view. The former speak of their Evangelical church as a *'family community'*, as a place where they meet their friends, where they can talk about their faith, where *'one person can learn from another'*, where their children can find an ideal environment to live their faith. In a way, these people are so close to their communities that we can speak in terms of an 'image' in a limited sense only. They see their communities not as something external to them; rather, they see themselves as part of these communities. Outsiders, though, often have a very different impression. On the basis often only of brief contact or media reports, they are usually critical of Evangelical churches. They often refer to them as *'sects'* and mention them in the same breath as new spiritual communities which have attracted controversy. As a child, Maia had classmates who were in a *'Evangelical church, a sect'*, who *'were looked at strangely by everyone'*, and whose *'parents were weird'*. For that reason, Maia did not go to this family's home. Peter refers to members of Evangelical

---

[21]   On the same finding, see Bruhn et al. (1999).

churches as *'fishies'*[22] and places them in the context of *'fishies, uh, things, Scientology, Moonies, and so on'*. Daniela talks about a friend

> who goes to some kind of sect, that's I think very, very terrible, or not a sect, I think I'm exaggerating now, but some kind of Evangelical church and they also have witness accounts from people who have talked with God. I find all that really, really bad. (Daniela, 24, Reformed)

Not surprisingly, the opinions of former members of Evangelical churches or of people on their periphery are much more differentiated. What Barbara, for example, likes about Evangelical churches is the fact that many young people also go to religious service and that it is very *'lively'*. What troubles her, though, are *'the rules'*, the *'isolatedness'*, and the fact that they are not really ecumenical.

Members of Evangelical churches usually see *Evangelical-church pastors* in a positive light.[23] They are seen as people with a specific task, who on the one hand function as an example of an exemplary life with God, and on the other teach biblical knowledge and a Christian way of life. The authority that evangelical pastors have among members is usually much more pronounced than the authority that pastors of the major churches have. It is based on three combinable sources. First, theological knowledge is seen by members of Evangelical churches as being something quite significant. Studying theology or knowing the Bible well can bestow prestige on the pastor. Second, evangelical pastors achieve authority through their strong networking within the evangelical milieu. Third, a very specific 'charisma' may be attributed to them, one which extends to miraculous powers (especially in the Pentecostal-charismatic submilieu).

The Image of Alternative-Spiritual Techniques and Suppliers: From Neutral to Extraordinary

The image of alternative-spiritual suppliers is very different again. Such suppliers are usually not associated with an institution, community or church which would provide them with a certain image. Rather, they use certain techniques which are accompanied by a particular image. Among consumers, these techniques have on the whole a neutral to good image. Reiki, qi gong, craniosacral therapy, yoga, and lymphatic drainage are usually talked about by our respondents as being things that they have used and which in some cases have had positive effects. Alternative-spiritual specialists are often referred to as

---

22   In German 'Fischli', a derogatory name for Evangelicals, in reaction Evangelicals putting a stylized fish on the back of their car.

23   This paragraph is based on Emmanuelle Buchard's chapter 'Jeux et enjeux de l'exercice de l'autorité' in Stolz, Favre, Gachet & Buchard (2013).

'*special*' and '*extraordinary*'. They have '*amazing skills*', '*feel an enormous amount*', '*can read you like an open book*', may even be '*all-knowing*' and a '*living proof of reincarnation*'. They gain their good reputation from different sources. One source of legitimation is, interestingly, a certain scientific veneer. They are invited to universities, they teach at '*institutions*', their techniques are '*rather scientific*', and sometimes they have a doctor title. Second, they are recommended by '*good friends*', who testify to the effectiveness of their techniques and skills. Third, our respondents themselves often say that the teachings and treatments have helped them. Fourth, many techniques enable learners and those treated to become teachers or practitioners themselves. This 'empowerment' leads many to having increased confidence in the relevant techniques.

What is sociologically interesting here is the fact that the supplier, as a person, and the techniques have an image, while most alternative-spiritual communities around them do not. The social reality of the alternative-spiritual world is hidden, although, as the material shows clearly, it is latently extremely important. In other words, members of the alternative type very often have unusual and mostly positive experiences, especially in courses, seminars and therapies, that is, especially in the presence of others. But the fact that this sociality enables the experience in the first place is usually ignored.[24] The explanation for this seems on the one hand to be the very fluid character of these communities ('courses', 'lectures', 'retreats', 'circles'), and on the other the very strong individualism of esotericists and people in the alternative domain.

Criticism of alternative-spiritual specialists and techniques does occur in our material – but, compared with the criticism of the major churches, it is surprisingly very restrained. Respondents are mostly content to say that they do not use any alternative-spiritual techniques because they do not believe that they work. How can this be explained? Assuming that usually there is no scientific basis to the techniques, and that the rates of healing are, at least according to biomedical standards, often likely to be on the low side, then why are the techniques not criticized more?[25] There seem to be several factors that protect the alternative-spiritual scene from criticism. Since the scene is set up like a market, criticism always fixes on individual products. Even if one supplier is revealed as a 'charlatan', then many others can still offer high-quality products. Also, among the more frequent users of alternative-spiritual techniques, the principle of 'epistemological individualism' applies:[26] the individual is the sole authority when it comes to whether something is 'true' or 'effective'. Therefore, everything depends on whether something is 'true for me' or 'effective for me'.

---

[24]   This point is described very clearly in Bochinger, Englberger & Gebhart (2009).

[25]   On the effectiveness of alternative-spiritual remedies, see Singh & Ernst (2008). On the case of Christian healing services, see Stolz (2011).

[26]   See Wallis (1977, p. 14).

***

In this chapter, we have shown how our respondents perceive, evaluate and use three types of religious-spiritual suppliers – the major churches, Evangelical churches, and alternative-spiritual suppliers. We have seen that the typical salvation goods of these suppliers differ. Formulated very schematically, the major churches offer strength, support, tradition and benefit to others; Evangelical churches provide a highly norm-determined lifestyle for converted Christians; and spiritual-alternative suppliers offer spiritual growth and solutions to specific problems in life.

A second insight concerns the relationship that members have with these suppliers. Our results here blatantly contradict market theory. According to this theory, all people in modern society choose their memberships of religious groups like a product – what then emerges is a membership market and a general competition between the religious and spiritual suppliers. As we have seen, though, we hardly find any evidence among the members of the major churches of the existence of a membership market. Neither the core nor the distanced members consider whether or not to switch to another supplier – at most, they think of leaving the church altogether. However, we do find membership and customer markets with regard to Evangelical churches and alternative-spiritual suppliers. The error of market theory is obviously to consider only intra-religious competition. In the current competition of the me-society, though, individuals are free to choose between religious and secular options, with many showing a preference for the secular options (see Chapter 2). Most members of society therefore belong to the distanced type and do not see why they should switch suppliers if they are in any case only members in a very weak way.

Finally, we have also seen that suppliers are perceived very differently. To summarize very schematically again, we can say that people see the major churches as being useful but outdated and conservative, Evangelical churches as dynamic but potentially dangerous, and alternative-spiritual suppliers as unusual and possibly effective. Again, we can relate this finding to a well-known theory. Grace Davie, one of the most influential sociologists of religion today, has claimed in several publications that there is such a thing as 'vicarious religion'. According to Davie, people themselves are not religious, but advocate explicitly or implicitly that others be to some extent religious 'in their place'.[27] As plausible as this argument may seem to be, it is in fact contradicted by our data, since such reasoning never appears in our material. The fact that others and not they themselves are religious is seen and described by our respondents, but in a different way: namely, they see that churches are a public good, and, while I do

---

[27]   Davie (2006a, 2006b, 2007). Our criticism complements the arguments in Bruce & Voas (2010).

not need them myself, others do – and perhaps I will need them myself one day, too. In our view, it is here that the 'core of truth' of Davie's observation lies.

Chapter 8

The Perception and Evaluation of Religion(s)

Jörg Stolz, Thomas Englberger

Nobody is so atheistic that they do not help celebrate
the Christian holidays. (Friedrich Hebbel)

In contrast to the situation at the beginning of the twentieth century, Switzerland is no longer a country of almost exclusively Christian character. Rather, we find, particularly since the 1960s, a rapidly growing number of people without religious affiliation on the one hand, and a new religious diversity consisting of members of non-Christian religions on the other.[1] This new situation has, together with other factors, led to an unprecedented distancing of people from the phenomenon of 'religion(s)', and raises controversial questions that have vexed the Swiss public in recent years: Is religion socially valuable or does it do more harm than good? Are all religions essentially equal? Is Christianity to be understood (still) as the basis of Swiss society? Is the migration of non-Christian religions to Switzerland a loss or a gain? Should the building of minarets be allowed or forbidden? And how should the principle of religious freedom be applied? In this chapter, we look more closely at how the population of Switzerland thinks about these questions, and at how we can explain their perceptions and evaluations.[2]

8.1 Perception and Evaluation of 'Religion Itself'

Let us first consider what the population thinks in general about 'religion itself', without referring to specific religions.[3]

---

[1]   For an overview, see Baumann & Stolz (2007a), Bochinger (2012), and especially the chapter Mader & Schinzel (2012).

[2]   For a similar investigation, see Pollack (2011b). For a study of prejudices and stereotypes of outgroups in Switzerland, see Cattacin et al. (2006), Stolz (2000). On the history of the perception of religious diversity in Switzerland, see Forclaz (2007), Baumann & Stolz (2007b).

[3]   Different terms are used in the literature to discuss the social perceptions and evaluations which we examine in this chapter. A series of publications have used the terms

Truth Relativism and the 'Equality' of Religions

A first important insight is that the relativism of truth and the assumption of the fundamental equality of religions have prevailed in the me-society.[4] Only about 5 per cent of our respondents think that there is truth in only one religion. The claims to truth of Christianity, which once motivated early crusades, inquisitions and decade-long wars, and which still apply at least officially in the Catholic Church,[5] are no longer accepted. Much like Lessing's 'Nathan the Wise', there is instead an overwhelming majority of about 79 per cent who believe that there are 'basic truths in many religions'. Finally, 17 per cent of our respondents believe that the truth content of each and every religion is very low. Figure 8.1 shows that the relativists make up the majority in all of our four main types. Among the institutional type at least, 15 per cent believe that truth is to be found in one religion only, while among the secular type, approximately 43 per cent tend to deny truth to any religion.

---

stereotype, prejudice, xenophobia, Islamophobia, anti-Semitism, etc., where what is always meant are some kind of 'pathological' perceptions; see, for example, Zick (1997). Another branch of literature uses the concept of *discourse*, e.g., van Dijk (1993), Behloul (2007), where what is always implied is that a ruling group oppresses another group. Different again is the literature around 'Boundary Making', e.g., Wimmer (2008), where an us/them distinction must necessarily always be made. The literature perhaps closest to our point of view speaks in terms of 'social representations', a term which implies neither pathology nor imbalances of power nor an us/them distinction; see, for example, Moscovici (1981), Farr (1990).

    4   The trend of a decline in the number of people who only believe in the truth of their own religion can be found in the USA, too. See Chaves (2011).

    5   Although religious freedom was recognized by the Second Vatican Council, the Catholic claim to absoluteness 'Extra ecclesiam nulla salus' (Outside the Church there is no salvation) is still valid. On this, see the encyclical Lumen Gentium, 14: 'This Sacred Council wishes to turn its attention firstly to the Catholic faithful. Basing itself upon Sacred Scripture and Tradition, it teaches that the Church, now sojourning on earth as an exile, is necessary for salvation. Christ, present to us in His Body, which is the Church, is the one Mediator and the unique way of salvation. In explicit terms He Himself affirmed the necessity of faith and baptism (see Mk 16:16; Jn 3:5) and thereby affirmed also the necessity of the Church, for through baptism as through a door men enter the Church. Whosoever, therefore, knowing that the Catholic Church was made necessary by Christ, would refuse to enter or to remain in it, could not be saved'.

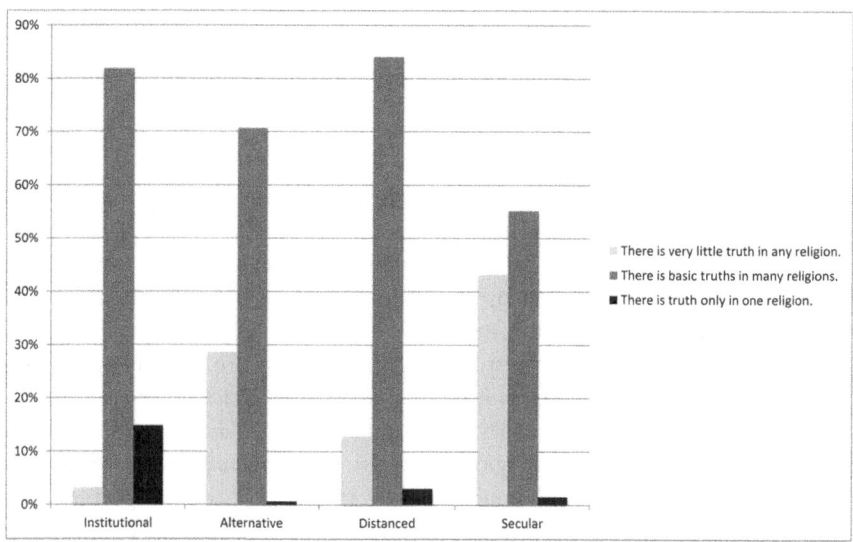

Figure 8.1   In all four types, a relativistic position predominates regarding whether there are 'basic truths in many religions'

The relativism of the claim to truth corresponds to the prominent opinion in our qualitative material that 'all religions are somewhat similar', an opinion which we can group into three categories. A first group of respondents are convinced for purely intellectual reasons that, with all religions, we are dealing essentially with the same phenomenon. Both strongly religious and also distanced people believe what Cécile formulates here: 'The forms of appeal differ. The buildings are different. (...) But it's always the same thing, always – in theory – the same God, expressed each time in a different way' (Cécile, 38, Reformed).

The idea that we are always dealing with the same phenomenon when it comes to religion leads many respondents to the view that disputes or even wars over religious questions are pointless. They themselves would *'never fight for a religion'*; they find religious wars *'totally absurd, stupid'*. A second group, consisting primarily of core members of the alternative type (the so-called 'esotericists'), has the same opinion on account of their own syncretic spiritual experiences. Around 91 per cent of the esotericists think that there are 'basic truths in many religions', and, seen overall, this group display the most positive attitudes towards all world religions. A third group, consisting mainly of secularists, believes that all religions are equally unnecessary or harmful.

What is noticeable overall is how few respondents answer in an exclusivist way. While many people in Switzerland quite naturally assumed up until the middle of the twentieth century that their own religion was 'true' or at least 'better',[6] today only small minorities argue in such a way – above all, those belonging to Evangelical churches.

Criteria for Assessing 'Good' or 'Bad' Religion

The assumption of a 'fundamental equality of religions' and truth relativism have a very important consequence: namely, individuals begin to evaluate 'religion itself' as 'good' or 'bad' in comparison to other social phenomena and institutions.[7] The criteria used by our respondents to make these evaluations turn out to be remarkably uniform. They see religion as being 'good' if it has positive social effects – for example, if it alleviates social problems by helping the needy and the marginalized, if it is committed to peace and international understanding, and if it acts as society's moral conscience.[8] For our respondents, all this is only possible if religion is *'open'*, *'not extreme'*, *'not judgmental'*, *'ecumenical'*. From the personal point of view, religion is good if it gives people *'support'*, *'strength'* or *'values'*. Our respondents name different people who incarnate 'good religion': the Dalai Lama, Sister Emanuelle, Abbé Pierre, Pastor Sieber, Mother Theresa and Ghandi. On the other hand, religion is 'bad' if it has negative effects on society – for example, if it leads to wars, discrimination, exclusion, terrorism, overpopulation. According to our respondents, these effects arise when religion is *'fanatical'*, *'intolerant'*, *'dogmatic'* and *'not contemporary'*, when it insists on an exclusive claim to truth. From the personal point of view, religion is bad whenever it limits the freedom of its members in any way, and if it imposes beliefs and feelings of guilt on its members or forces them to behave in certain ways (e.g., clothing, religious practices). These few criteria to assess 'religion itself' can be used later in this chapter to explain the attitudes of the majority of respondents with regard to religious diversity and specific religions (Islam, Buddhism, Christianity, etc.).

If we consider with the help of the above criteria what our respondents say about the phenomenon of 'religion itself', we find, as might be expected, the most diverse individual evaluations. Some respondents regard religion as fundamentally good, most are ambivalent, and others primarily see the

---

[6]   On this, see Baumann & Stolz (2007b), Altermatt (2009).

[7]   In the following, we try to work out the criteria that are used here. Later in this chapter, this will be useful to explain why certain religions have such a good or such a bad image. For essays from many disciplines with answers to the question of what a 'good' religion is, see Wenzel (2007).

[8]   It should be noted that this form of reasoning is itself of course full of presuppositions. Before the Enlightenment, people would have made not society but God their final point of reference. It was not religion and God that would have been measured according to the needs of society, but society according to the prescriptions of religion and God. On the related cultural changes, see, for example, Böckenförde (1991), Taylor (2007).

problematical sides of religion. As we will see below, the attitudes also very much depend on whether we are dealing here with people's 'own' or with 'foreign' religions, whether the 'prevailing order' is affected by the religion, which religion is being considered exactly, and which general political attitudes a person otherwise has.

The Return of Criticism of Religion

We wish first, though, to address the fact that we were surprised by the frequency and vehemence of critical attitudes towards 'religion(s) itself/themselves'. Criticism of religion itself is comparatively old. It was developed first by the Enlightenment thinkers and then in its most well-known forms by Feuerbach, Marx, Nietzsche and Freud.[9] But those who believed that the debate about the truth and utility of religion belonged to the past, and that the main problems had been solved, were mistaken. The work of modern critics of religion such as Richard Dawkins, Sam Harris and Christopher Hitchens are regularly on international best-seller lists.[10] The movement of the freethinkers is experiencing a strong upturn in different countries, and their actions, such as the slogan 'There probably is no God, so stop worrying and enjoy your life', attract huge media coverage.[11] We can therefore talk with much more accuracy of a 'return of criticism of religion' rather than of a 'return of religion'.

But we encounter very powerful criticism of religion not only in the international media, but among the Swiss population, too. According to many of our respondents, religion has often played a very dark role in the course of world history. For Cécile, everything done in the name of religion has been '*totally abhorrent*'. Respondents point to the crusades, the Inquisition, the conquistadors, and the wars in the former Yugoslavia. Peter says:

> Name me a war that has not somehow been based on religion. Or just tell me of a neighbourly dispute which is not based on religious belief. Everything on religious belief, always religious belief under an assumed name. (Peter, 65, no religious affiliation)

It is not only in the past, though, but also in the present that religion can be used by people to '*gain power*', to '*influence people negatively*', to ignite violence and war. 85 per cent of our respondents agree fully or quite with the statement, 'If you look at what is happening in the world today, religions lead more to conflict

---

9   For an overview, see Weger (1979).

10   Dawkins & Vogel (2008), Hitchens (2007), Harris (2004).

11   On this action first initiated in 2008 in England, which found imitators worldwide and caused great controversy, see http://de.wikipedia.org/wiki/Atheist_Bus_Campaign.

than to peace', and 82 per cent think that 'strongly religious people are often too intolerant towards others'. Here, it is interesting to note that all of our types are willing to admit that 'religion' has aspects that are problematical.[12] If we consider criticism of religion a little more closely, though, we soon see that it is only the particularly critical subtype of secularists, the so-called 'opponents of religion', who reject religion completely. All other groups are willing to recognize the problematical aspects of religion, but also often see a positive or neutral aspect. Their criticism is then directed not so much at religion in general, but at specific phenomena. The most important issues mentioned by our respondents are religious (especially Islamic) extremists, the failure of Islam to adapt in Switzerland, sects, and the conservative attitudes of the Catholic Church. We will analyze these points in greater detail later in the chapter.

8.2 Perception and Evaluation of Specific Religious Groups

In a context of plurality, the 'image', that is, the evaluative perception of religions and religious communities, becomes ever more important. A positive image and the prestige of a religion or religious community is an important resource for such communities, while a negative image can greatly impede their activity and lead to discrimination against their members. Our data show a uniform picture, with our respondents using the criteria outlined above to distinguish between 'their own' and 'foreign' religions, and also between 'good', 'neutral' and 'bad' religions.[13] They consider Christianity as their own religion, and have a relatively positive relationship to it despite all their criticisms of the church, while they perceive all other religions as 'foreign'. Figures 8.2 and 8.3 show how positively or negatively our types evaluate members of different religions. Let us consider these attitudes in detail.

---

[12] This point is also all the more interesting because it was ignored by our precursor studies. This criticism is not mentioned anywhere in the books *Everyone a special case?* and *The two faces of religion*.

[13] See Portman & Plüss (2011). For a collection of philosophical/theological answers to the question of when a religion is 'good' or 'bad', see Wenzel (2007).

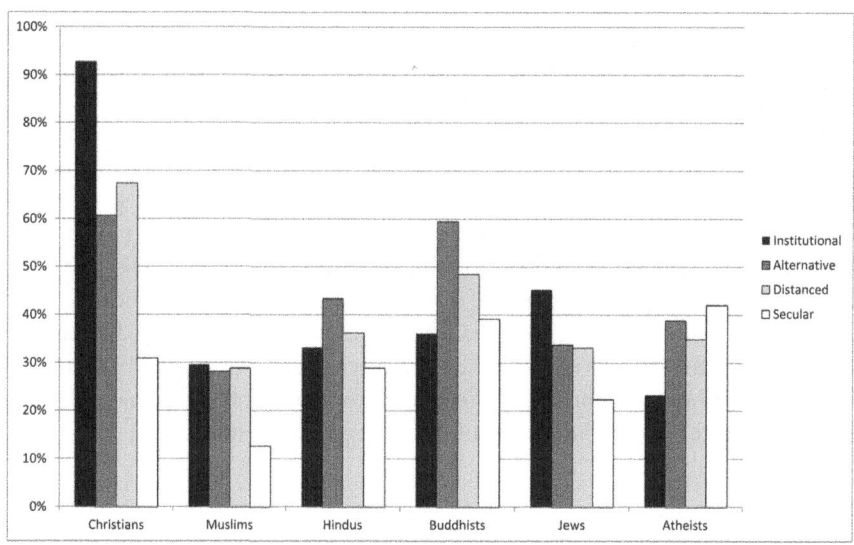

Figure 8.2   Christians and Buddhists attract the most very and quite positive attitudes

Note: only very and quite positive attitudes are shown here.

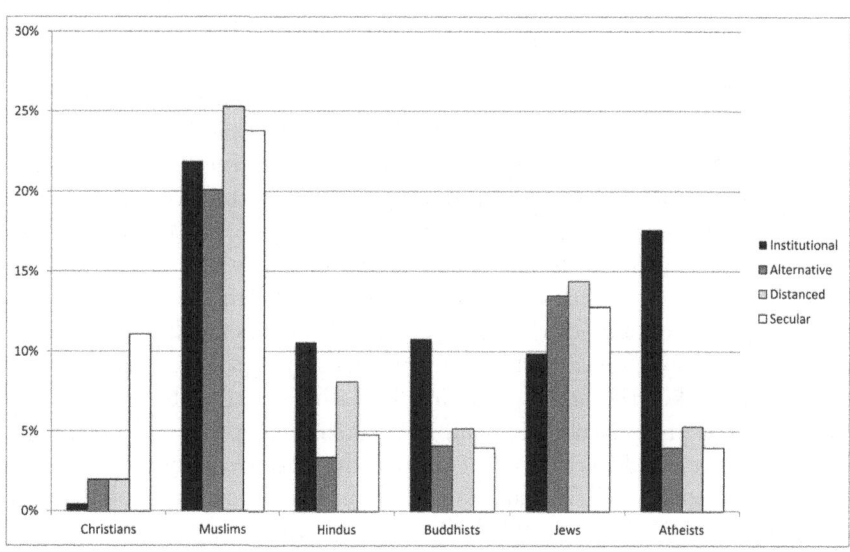

Figure 8.3   Muslims attract the most very and quite negative attitudes

Note: only very and quite negative attitudes are shown here.

Christianity

Our respondents see Christianity as 'their own religion'. When asked about their positive or negative attitudes towards 'Christians', most of our respondents say that they have a very or quite positive attitude, with the institutional type in particular showing a very positive attitude (Figure 8.2). We can see here an example of the very general finding that people feel positive towards what they know and what is similar to them.[14] The qualitative data support this, but they also show that respondents perceive different Christian groups very differently, and that, particularly in the case of Christian denominations, they distinguish between members of the religions and the churches as institutions. We shall deal here with Catholicism and the Protestant Reformed Church; we have already dealt in Chapter 7 with the 'image' of the Evangelical churches.

Catholicism

Catholicism tends to have a negative image among the population. Put simply, many respondents see the Catholic Church as a conservative, rigid, hierarchical, authoritarian, morally intolerant, hypocritical institution which contradicts the meaning of a true religion. It is almost incredible how many respondents – especially practising Catholics – make the most serious accusations against the Catholic Church as an institution.

The most important criticism concerns its *conservative attitude, which is perceived as being no longer appropriate*. For our respondents, this attitude manifests itself in many different ways. They claim the Catholic Church represents obsolete and absurd dogmas such as the infallibility of the Pope, the notion of original sin, and the exclusive truth of Catholic doctrine. The Church also defends obsolete norms and punishes the fallible through ostracism or exclusion. Our respondents provide a flood of examples in which they have experienced the Catholic Church as an authoritarian and intolerant institution: Katherine and Kaitline were excommunicated because of their divorces, something which they regard as scandalous. Renate tells of a clergyman who judged suicide as 'botching God's handiwork'. Diane and Ingolf found the Catholic clergy to be authoritarian when they were not given a free hand in organizing a baptism and a marriage. Many of our respondents find it *'idiotic'* that the Catholic Church forbids the use of contraception in Africa, and therefore contributes to overpopulation and the spread of AIDS. Practising Catholics in particular, but also many others, do not understand why the Catholic Church adheres to the idea of celibacy. This is *'not biblical'* and cannot be *'God's will'*. Celibacy is *'nonsense'* and, according

---

[14]   On this, see Stolz (2000), Gergen & Gergen (1986), LeVine & Campbell (1972), Zick (1997).

to various respondents, leads among other things to the fact that priests have no idea of the actual living situations of many believers. Two respondents (Blandine and Rebecca) also express the view that celibacy leads directly to paedophilia among some priests. The Catholic Church also has a *'scandalous'* view of women and withholds many rights from them. Fabio thinks that *'women still hardly exist in the church'*, and that the church is *'totally macho mania'*. The strong emotions of many respondents, the fact that they are downright angry, can be explained by the fact that they see this conservative behaviour as contradicting 'true religion'. For many of our respondents, it is (at the time) the reigning Pope Benedict XVI who represents all these negative points.

The anger is exacerbated by a second, widespread, reproach: that of *'hypocrisy'*. While the previous point was concerned with the fact that what the Catholic Church preaches is wrong, we are concerned here now with the view that the church itself does not adhere to its own rules and prescriptions, and that it only constructs a beautiful, but fake, facade. On the one hand, the church preaches peacefulness, tolerance, good works and poverty; and, on the other, itself behaves in an intolerant and discriminatory way, covers up its sex and paedophilia scandals, and enjoys huge wealth. Erich, for example, states:

> ... hypocrisy, when you hear what happens, a priest is suspended if he has a relationship with a woman, but when he performs sexual activity with a child, then it is covered up. (Erich, 40, no religious affiliation)

If, as we shall see below, Islam is for many the 'bad foreign religion', then Catholicism is clearly 'our very own bad religion'.

These negative points are, though, also counterbalanced by positive assessments. Many respondents view positively the social commitment of the Catholic Church (see Chapter 7), some know a priest or parish leader themselves, and in some cases Catholicism represents a very natural part of their own life stories and their own social environments. 'Catholics' are for many respondents people like you and me, and it is precisely in their normality that they can be seen in a positive light.

Reformed

The Reformed Church struggles less with an ambivalent image than it does with having no image at all.[15] It hardly crops up as a distinguishable group in our material at all. While Catholics attract a wave of criticism, hardly anybody is annoyed at members of the Reformed Church. No one makes them responsible

---

[15] On the image of the Reformed, see Stolz & Ballif (2010).

for abuses and scandals. No one gets worked up about them.[16] We can divide the comparatively rare statements about the Reformed into three types. First, they occur in lists when it comes to the presentation of religious diversity: Catholics, Reformed, Buddhists, Jews. They are considered here as 'part of the religious landscape', but are given no further consideration. Second, they are used as a positive counter-image to the – actually interesting, but negatively depicted – Catholic Church. The Reformed are *just a bit more intelligent* than Catholics; they have more *'critical sense'*, and are *'fairly open'*. Our respondents are positive towards the Reformed because, in comparison with Catholics, they appear better adapted to the present – since they allow women to preach, permit the use of contraception, have fewer prohibitions, etc. Cécile, for example, says:

> The Reformed are fairly open in many regards. In terms of – the fact that women can lead a religious service, in terms of their views on contraception, their general views, they're fairly open. Because I think it's scandalous that for example the Catholic Church rejects women, and especially that it opposes the use of contraception in African countries. (Cécile, 38, Reformed)

Third, they are referred to as not being able to interest people in what they have to offer. Their religious services come across as being *'bland'*, they attract *'few people'*, if you look at how empty their services and talks are, then it gives you *'cause for concern'*. Katherine says: 'It's going badly for the Reformed, they're losing a lot of people' (Katherine, 61, Roman Catholic).

The Reformed are therefore seen as better adjusted to today's society, but also as not very interesting. They are talked about neither positively nor negatively. While it is clear that they are not like the Catholics, it is unclear exactly *what* they stand for. To modify Musil's well-known book title, we could speak here of a 'church without features'.

Buddhism

The prime example of a 'foreign' but 'positive' religion is Buddhism, which is typically portrayed as being non-violent, peaceful, welcoming and undogmatic. Buddhists do not *'hurt anyone'*, and they are *'for world peace'*. In Buddhism, there is the *'Zen attitude (zénitude)'*, and nothing is *'forced'* on anyone. Several respondents explain that, although they do not know Buddhism particularly

---

[16] That is put too strongly, perhaps. There are of course the occasional people who criticize things about the Reformed (in our material: Peter and Siegfried). But these are very much the exceptions. There is no such 'critical discourse' on the Reformed Church as there clearly is on the Catholic Church.

well, it makes a very positive impression on them, and is a religion that they could at least potentially find attractive. Erich explains that Buddhism has

> ... good points in contrast (...) to Islam or Christianity, so if I had to choose, it would certainly be better for me. (Erich, 40, no religious affiliation)

And Rebecca says:

> Buddhism is actually a religion that also accepts everything else. So (...) if I converted now (...) it would be [Buddhism] that I could imagine converting to. (Rebecca, 45, Roman Catholic)

Not surprisingly, we find the most positive attitudes towards Buddhism among the alternative type (and in particular among the subtype of esotericists). We can explain the positive image of Buddhism with the help of the criteria which we developed above for the evaluation of religion(s). Buddhism seems to embody everything that is now regarded as 'good religion': peacefulness, lack of dogma, openness, spirituality.

Islam

In stark contrast to Buddhism, Islam is seen as the very epitome of a negative religion.[17] What is this religion accused of by its critics? First, it is a religion in whose name extremism, hatred, violence and holy war could arise. Vanessa typifies attitudes here:

> Islam has become a red rag for me and that simply has to do with fear. What do I think of when I hear Islam? Then I think of war, of violence (...). I'm doing great parts of Islam a disservice here, certainly, but those are the first thoughts that come to mind. (Vanessa, 41, Reformed)

Second, for our respondents, Islam treats women badly – they are forced to wear a veil, to have arranged marriages, and girls are not allowed to have swimming lessons at school. Gregory, for example, says: 'That ruins people, in the name of Allah and company, and also I think that the religion treats women very badly. Yes, it's tough in the Muslim world. No, no, I don't agree with it at all' (Gregory, 70, no religious affiliation).

---

[17]   On the perception of Islam in Switzerland on the individual level, see Stolz (2006a), Helbling (2010). On the representation of Muslims in the media, see Schranz & Imhof (2002). The literature on 'Islamophobia' is extensive; see, for example, Allen (2001), Halliday (1999), Stolz (2006a), Helbling (2010).

Third, according to many of our respondents, Islam is a religion which oppresses the native population and upsets the prevailing order. In doing so, it typically violates the laws of hospitality. The reasoning here is that, although foreign religions have a right to practise their faith freely, they are nonetheless guests in a foreign country and therefore, as guests, have to behave in a proper and discreet manner. Many Muslims, though, 'abuse the hospitality that is shown them', 'hang their washing out on Sunday', 'stick up some mosque somewhere', 'run around with a headscarf on', 'exempt their children from school', 'expand and grow', 'constantly demand more things'. The native population itself has to 'adapt', and is given 'the feeling that it's not allowed to be itself'.

Fourth, in the perception of many of our respondents, this infringement of the rules of hospitality is exacerbated by the fact that it is the Muslims themselves who carefully monitor compliance with these rules and hand down severe punishments for infringements. Respondents use the following argument with startling regularity: when we are with them as guests, we have to adapt and, if we do not, then *'we are locked up'* or *'stoned to death'*. But, when they are with us, we make concessions, while they do not adhere to the rules at all. Niklaus, for example, says: 'So I have to be honest, I don't need any kind of mosque. Each to their faith, but if we go down there to them, we can't put up a church, can we?' (Niklaus, 47, Reformed).

The very fact that it is people with a foreign religion who are seen as rule breakers and troublemakers also explains why so many of our respondents react so emotionally to this subject. These accusations are sometimes made without any restriction, together with the demand, for example, for limits to be set on *'Islamism'*. Respondents do often limit their assessments, though, by on the one hand recognizing the freedom of religion, and on the other by pointing to their limited knowledge and to the internal diversity of Islam – and some even point to the possibility that they themselves have prejudices. This is expressed in formulations such as 'I think I'm doing it [Islam] a great disservice here, certainly, but ... '; 'maybe that's a prejudice, because I do not understand it better, but ... '; 'they've also got very good points, I'm sure, but ... '. It may be the case, though, that these statements simply show that our respondents think that their criticisms of Islam are not socially desirable, and that they therefore mollify their criticisms when talking to the interviewer.

New Religious Communities

Besides Muslims, new religious communities are also often seen in a very negative way.[18] Respondents speak of *'sects'*. While small religious communities with

---

[18]   Stolz (2000) has already shown people's extremely negative attitudes towards 'sects'.

unusual practices and beliefs are just as legitimate or illegitimate for scholars of religion as large, well-known religious communities, most respondents see matters quite differently. Sects are, in their opinion, groups which practise '*brainwashing*', where members have a '*blind faith*', people can '*fall into their trap*', members are '*ripped off by their holy ones*', and '*can't escape*'. Sects can '*destroy families*', practise '*incest*', and sexually abuse their members. Renato says: 'Where I do have an aversion is [against] sects; that really jars with me. These strange sects, I can't get along with them. If someone [from a sect] shows up again at my house, I'll simply tell them to go, because I really don't need [that]' (Renato, 41, Roman Catholic).

Not all respondents have such a negative image, though – but the term *sect* is always used negatively. Nobody points out that in many cases sects could simply consist of people with a strong faith who, for subjectively good reasons, are together in small, unusual spiritual minorities.[19]

Several examples of 'sects' are named in the interviews – Raelians, Scientology, Evangelical churches, Order of the Solar Temple (OTS). But one group is always named by an overwhelming majority: the *Jehovah's Witnesses*. For our respondents, this is the prime example of a 'sect', and it is so well-known precisely because its members visit the population on their doorstep. Our respondents have a negative view of Jehovah's Witnesses, who '*are always ringing the doorbell*'; '*always coming to pester us*'. A number of respondents give anecdotes on how best to get rid of Jehovah's Witnesses.

8.3 Sources of Perceptions and Evaluations

How, then, do our respondents come to their assessments of the various religions? How can their perceptions and evaluations be explained sociologically? Since this was not the main focus of our investigation, our analyses have certain limitations here. Our data, though, do allow us to make the following claims.

Religious (Sub)Milieu

Quite clearly, members of different (sub)milieus have different typical assessments of the religious groups. Particularly interesting here are the highly religious and highly spiritual milieus. Members of the *established* subtype within the institutional type are, to state the obvious, positive towards their own

---

[19] We do not at all wish to deny here that problematical relationships could prevail in new religious communities. But the point is that this could also be the case in large communities, too. We therefore wish here to reject the crude contrast between 'good religions' and 'bad sects'.

religion, Christianity. Among Catholics in particular, though, we can also find a lot of criticism of their own church. Catholics often take a position of religious dialogue with regard to other religions and religious diversity, and argue that the plurality of religions, beliefs and sacred sites should be seen as something positive. Every person should therefore be allowed to live their religion in order then to enter into an accepting, interested and respectful relationship to other religions. It is therefore important here that the individual partners in the dialogue clearly know what they believe and communicate this clearly to their opposite number:

> We Christians should show more clearly that we are here and that we maintain our religion – but the Muslims also have the right to practise their religion. (Marc-Antoine, 63, Roman Catholic)

The goal here is better understanding, a more peaceful world, and possibly also an approximation to a deeper religious truth. To echo the title of a bestseller from the 1970s, we could say that the respondents take an 'I'm OK, you're OK' position.[20] In this regard, they are very close to the positions of the major churches, which also place great emphasis on inter-religious dialogue.[21]

In contrast, members of the *evangelical* subtype within the institutional type show a very different typical reaction to other religions. They reject all religions regarded as 'foreign', and especially Islam.[22] They reject these foreign religions with a barrage of arguments. Since they typically assume the truth of only one religion (their own), and since, with regard to other religions, they are oriented towards missionizing (rather than dialogue), they see other religions – and especially Islam – as competitors.

Members of the *alternative* type, and especially its core group (the so-called *esotericists*), have the most positive assessments of other religions of all kinds. While they strongly reject all dogmatic and rigid forms of religion (especially the Catholic Church as an institution), they are willing to recognize religious truths everywhere, and, if this appears worthwhile, to incorporate these truths into their worldview. Around 91 per cent of the esotericists think that 'there are basic truths in many religions'.

In contrast, the core group of the *secular* type (the so-called *opponents of religion*) is, unsurprisingly, negative towards all religions and religious communities.

---

[20]   Harris (2012).

[21]   On the Reformed, see Stolz & Ballif (2010).

[22]   As well as non-Christian religions, members of Evangelical churches also often very strongly reject esotericism, since it seems to them to venerate 'dark forces'. See Stolz, Favre, Gachet & Buchard (2013).

To conclude this section, then, we can say that a person's assessment of his or her own and of foreign religion(s) is always strongly influenced by the religious (sub)type to which that person belongs, if this type has a high 'centrality' within the person's own personal identity.

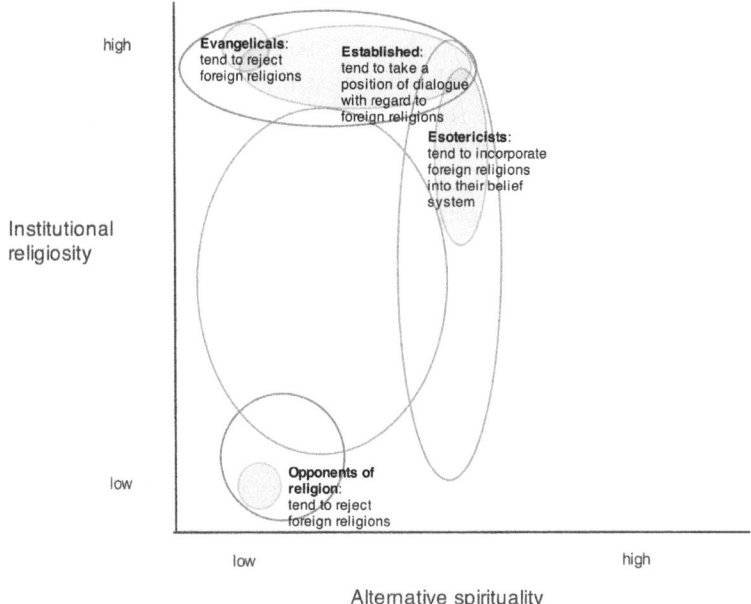

Figure 8.4   Different subtypes have very different attitudes towards foreign religions

Mass Media and Discourses in the Immediate Environment

There can be no doubt that our respondents' consumption of mass media has a huge influence on how they construct their perceptions.[23] As the well-known sociologist Niklas Luhmann puts it: 'What we know about our society, and indeed the world in which we live, we know through the mass media.'[24]

The mass media, and especially television, crop up in our material in many places and show that the respondents have indeed acquired a large part of their knowledge about religions through this channel. How Jews eat kosher meat,

---

[23]   A broad area of research has examined how religion and religions is/are represented in the mass media. For the Swiss context, see Schranz & Imhof (2002), Imhof & Ettinger (2007). What has not yet been said, however, is what effects this reporting actually has on individual perceptions and evaluations.

[24]   Luhmann (1996, p. 9).

how people convert to Judaism, how Christians practise self-flagellation in the Philippines, how Buddhists meditate, how we can communicate with the spirits of the dead, how young men blow themselves up as martyrs for Islam, how the Pope acts in Africa – our respondents have seen all these things on television. Only a few respondents reflect on the mass-media contingency of their perceptions and evaluations. Nicolas, for example, says that he does not see the Reformed as '*extreme people*', but as actually '*quite moderate*', and justifies this observation with the image that he has acquired through the mass media: 'Why do I see them [the Reformed] that way? I don't know. It seems to me that I don't see negative headlines about them all the time' (Nicolas, 36, no religious affiliation).

In some cases, we also encounter criticism of the media. For Cécile, for example, there are currently many prejudices about Islam, because on television we only see the '*worst things*'. For the vast majority of our respondents, though, how the mass media condition our perceptions remains opaque and must be interpreted by us. What is interesting here is that information provided by the mass media is not taken over in a direct one-to-one ratio, but is perceived very selectively and is incorporated into conversations with people in the immediate environment.

Personal Contact

In addition to the mass media, personal contacts and concrete experiences can also influence how people perceive and evaluate religions.[25] These experiences can confirm stereotypes conveyed by the media, or indeed contradict them. Our respondents mention personal contacts and concrete experiences that they have gained through travelling, at work and in their family.

The respondents generally indicate that the concrete experiences have helped them to develop a 'more differentiated' perception of foreign religions and a greater tolerance, and that this has also changed their view of their own religion. Through her numerous trips to Asia, for example, Olga has acquired '*more openness*' towards various religions. The picture that Cécile has of both Islam and Buddhism is based on her trips to Islamic countries and Asia. She deplores the negative portrayal of Islam in the media, and thinks that it is important to distinguish between the '*major religion*' of Islam and what an extremist minority makes of it. During a visit to Egypt, she not only visited mosques, but also deepened her knowledge of Islam by reading literature about the religion: '[Islam] is also a major religion that is perhaps more open in some respects. But now there are some extremists who are making something terrible out of it. This

---

[25] On the so-called *contact hypothesis* in the case of attitudes towards foreigners, see Zick (1997).

is very bad because people just throw everything into the same pot' (Cécile, 38, Reformed).

Cécile relativizes not only the negative image of Islam, but also the positive image of Buddhism. While travelling in Buddhist countries, she experienced how the religion is actually practised there: 'And Buddhism, you have to relativize there, too. You have to be realistic. People pray to win the lottery! (laughs). They're very pragmatic there, they pray so as to earn more money, and that's shocking' (Cécile, 38, Reformed).

All in all, Cécile has come to realize, from the various perspectives of architecture, religious traditions and beliefs, that the actual conditions contradict completely the picture constructed by the mass media. While working for four months in a hospital in Cameroon, Renate learned about Christianity anew. What impressed her was the religiousness of the Africans: 'They played the whole Easter story from Thursday to Easter. Really everything – the crucifixion, laying the body in the tomb, everything. And of course that was really impressive' (Renate, 51, Roman Catholic).

Our respondents also report that their personal contacts at work and within their family circle have a similarly relativizing effect. Quentin, a 50-year-old administrative clerk, has a Muslim in his immediate family: '*My sister was married to one; they are very nice, very kind*'. This experience has helped Quentin to develop a more positive view of Islam, one which is independent of the media: 'The image that I got was not the image they show us on television; it was completely different' (Quentin, 50, Reformed).

Travelling, as well as work and family contacts, can obviously lead people to developing an attitude in which understanding for the other religion can grow. We can also often see an enlightened and critical distancing from all religions, and also from Christianity. The people we have referred to here represent mostly the distanced type (Olga, Niklaus, Wilma, Quentin), but also partly the secular (Cécile) and the institutional (Bénédicte).

However, contact does not always lead to more openness. A number of respondents with particularly pronounced opinions on religion(s) report of contacts that obviously merely confirmed their own stereotypical perceptions.

Political Stance and Attitude Towards Foreigners

Finally, what also significantly influences people's perception of religions is their general political stance, and especially their attitude to the openness or closedness of Switzerland and their attitude to foreigners. Several authors have put forward the thesis that especially Islamophobia and the fear of an 'Islamization of Switzerland' are nothing other than a rehash of the old fear of foreigners and asylum seekers. Once it was the Italians, and then the Turks and people from the former Yugoslavia, who were perceived as being 'other', 'not capable of being integrated' and 'too foreign', and now it is the Muslims who have assumed this position. In this respect, the talk of 'over-foreignization' (*Überfremdung*) in the 1970s has its exact counterpart in the talk of 'Islamization' today.[26] From our data, we can make no final judgment here. There can be no doubt, however, that, among many of our respondents, the perception of non-Christian religions is strongly linked to issues related to foreigners, asylum seekers and Swiss identity. People who are politically more right-wing and nationalistic, who wish to preserve the neutrality of Switzerland and reject becoming a member of the EU, who call for a tougher line to be taken in dealing with asylum seekers and are in favour of giving preference to Swiss people over foreigners on the labour and housing markets, see non-Christian religions significantly more negatively than people who take a more left-wing position with regard to these matters.

What is also very clear in our material is that the respondents see such a critical attitude towards foreigners and Muslims as 'socially undesirable', and, while they express their opinion, they at the same time distance themselves from possibly being labelled 'racist' or 'anti-foreigner'. Here, the respondents laugh sometimes, which also indicates their distancing. This manifests itself in asides such as '*but I* don't belong to the SVP [Schweizerische Volkspartei], not that (laughs)', 'I'm not a racist, but (...)', 'this is now maybe a bit right-wing, but (...)', 'I'm a bit of a patriot (laughs)'. After saying that for her Islam 'has now become a red rag', as well as criticizing headscarves and wondering whether 'our children will always have to take a back seat', Vanessa tells the interviewer: 'So I hope you don't see me now as being anti-foreigner (laughs); I don't want to make any value judgments'(Vanessa, 41, Reformed).

Age and Generation

We can also establish an interesting correlation between a person's age (or generation) and their perception of religions. Older people are more positive than average towards Christianity (as their own religion) and more negative than average towards 'foreign' religions. These perceived differences between religions tend to decrease with the age of the respondents. If we then interpret these age differences as generational effects, we can see that society is increasing its distance from religion in general and also from Christianity, while increasing its acceptance of religious diversity.

***

The transition to the me-society has also profoundly changed people's perception of religion(s) (see Chapters 2 and 9). What was laid down in the Enlightenment

---

[26]   On discussion of this hypothesis, see Lindemann (2012).

and in the criticism of religion which followed it has now reached in a radicalized form the broad mass of the population. While up until the 1950s, Switzerland could be spoken of as a 'Christian country' where denominational differences were an important social marker that strongly influenced people's perceptions, religion in the new competition regime of the me-society is now seen by the overwhelming majority of the population in a completely new way: from this perspective, religion(s) is/are subordinate to the primacy of society and the individual. Religions cannot make demands themselves, but instead must serve society and the individual. If they do not do so, or even have harmful effects (e.g., extremism, fanaticism, intolerance), then they are rejected. The idea of a fundamental equality of all religion(s) is accompanied by a truth relativism and a distancing from religion. The majority of our respondents believe that at least the core of religion(s) is the same so that no single religion has exclusive truth.

Unlike before the 1960s, people now reject foreign religions not so much because they differ from their own 'true' and 'normal' religion, but because they seem to run against the social order which is independent of religion. Religions, and especially Islam, seem problematical because they question the 'prevailing order', which itself has not much to do with religion. Foreign religions abuse hospitality, contradict the liberal order, and disregard individual freedoms (e.g., of women), etc.

Against this background, we can explain why it is that people classify some religions as 'good' and others as 'bad', why in particular Buddhism and the Reformed Church are perceived quite positively, and Islam and Catholicism quite negatively. The former do not seem to disturb the prevailing order and leave all freedoms to the individual, while the latter impinge on society and restrict the freedoms of individuals.

Chapter 9
The Change in Religiosity, Spirituality and Secularity

Jörg Stolz, Thomas Englberger, Michael Krüggeler, Judith Könemann, Mallory Schneuwly Purdie

Margaret: Say, as regards religion, how you feel.
I know that you are a dear, good man,
Yet, for you, it seems, it has no appeal.
Faust: Leave that alone, child! You feel I'm kind to you:
For Love I'd give my blood, my life too.
I'll rob no man of his church and faith.
Margaret: That's not right, we must have faith.
(Johann Wolfgang von Goethe)

In this book, we have presented not only a typology of religious and secular groups, but also a new theory of religious and secular competition, one which explains the growth and shrinkage of these groups. While in chapters three to eight we were concerned in particular with describing in detail the different types and milieus, we are concerned in this chapter with examining the explanatory theory. Here, we try to show with the help of the available data how the transition to the me-society (or the change of competition regime) took place in the 1960s, and what impact this had on religion and spirituality: how it changed religious socialization, people's choice of partner, and norms and values, how these changes worked out differently for men and women, and how the developments spread from urban to rural areas. Finally, drawing together all these mechanisms, we are concerned here with explaining how the current distribution of institutional, alternative, distanced and secular types and milieus have come about through processes of growth and shrinkage.

As in the previous chapters, we use here a mixed-method strategy and triangulate four types of data. First, we compare the surveys from 1989, 1999 and 2009, each of which is a representative cross-sectional study. Second, we evaluate certain questions from these surveys retrospectively, these questions being those related to the childhoods of our respondents. Since the respondents were born in different decades, this information stretches back to the 1920s. Third, we draw on our own qualitative study in which the respondents reported on their childhood. Again, we can obtain information here that dates back as far as the 1920s (when they report things they know about the life of their parents and grandparents). Fourth, we use census data (since 1900), and various other state and church statistics. By triangulating these different data and drawing on what has been written by historians and social scientists about the development of Swiss society in the twentieth century, we try to reconstruct the historical course of events of this development.

In relation to the qualitative interviews, it is important that we locate our data with great historical accuracy. The oldest generation for which we have interviews are the 60- to 70-year-olds, who were born in the 1940s. These are precisely the people who would later as young adults initiate the transition to the me-society. They had experienced the old form of society, represented above all by their parents, teachers and other forces of socialization. Some of our respondents had at the time rebelled against the norms which they regarded as outdated and against the newly emerging consumer culture, and, in doing so, initiated a cultural upheaval that strongly affected religion and spirituality.

We follow the hypotheses set out in Chapter 2 (see Figure 9.1). The first four hypotheses relate to the transition to the me-society with regard to economic growth, cultural change, gender roles, and the urban-rural contrast (9.2). Two further hypotheses relate to how individuals adjust to the situation in the me-society, and we address here the issues of secular drift and religious individualization and consumerism (9.3). The final hypothesis relates to changes that types and milieus have undergone over the course of time (9.4).

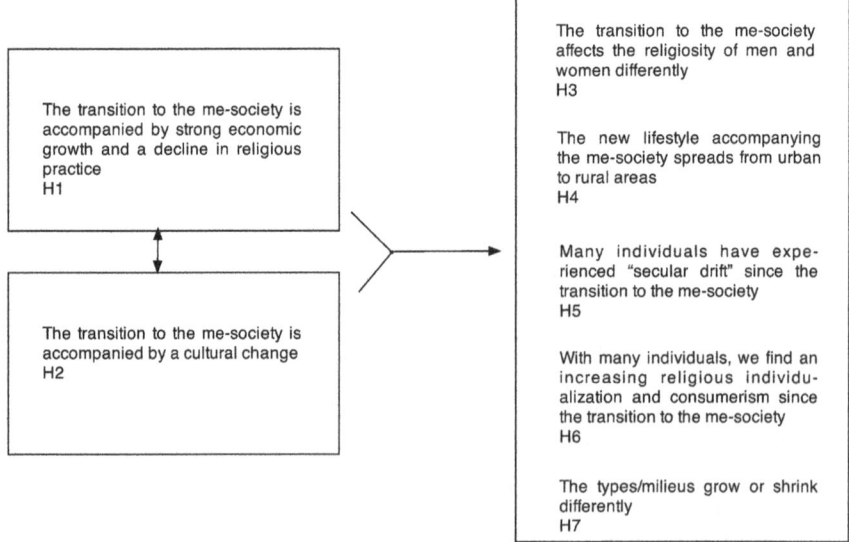

Figure 9.1   An overview of the seven hypotheses

9.1 The Transition to the Me-Society

The Me-Society and Economic Growth

Our first hypothesis is that the transition to the me-society (or the change of the religious-secular competition regime) that took place in the 1960s was accompanied by a strong economic upswing. It was precisely this economic upswing, together with the rise in living standards for the vast majority of the population in terms of real income, personal security, mobility, leisure options, etc., that was one of the most important reasons for the change in attitudes towards religion and spirituality.

Figure 9.2   There was an economic boom in Switzerland between 1946 and 1973

Note: the period of 'economic boom' between 1946 and 1973 is coloured grey

Source: data are taken from the internationally comparative Maddison Project; http://www.ggdc.net/maddison/maddison-project/home.htm (consulted on 15.8.2013). GDP measured in 1990 GK dollars.

Unlike most other European countries, Switzerland did not have to rebuild itself after the war, but could enter the post-war period with its full production capacities intact. The available data show very clearly the economic upswing that took place at the beginning of the second half of the twentieth century, with the real gross domestic product per capita doubling between 1946 and 1973 together with a growing population (see Figure 9.2), which represented an average annual growth rate of 5 per cent.[1] This boom was not exceptional in Europe, with Germany, France and England experiencing a similar phenomenon.[2]

The economic upswing manifests itself in our qualitative data, too, with different people from the oldest generation of our respondents remembering from their childhood a society that was poorer overall – where the farming family would pray during a thunderstorm as there was no lightning rod (Emily); where the mother had to work so much and had such little time because she had so many children (Klaus); where the mother never took a holiday except to go on a pilgrimage to Einsiedeln (in Switzerland) and where the children had to help with the work (Berta-Lisa); and where children had to start their working lives early (Kaitline). Juan was part of the influx of Spanish 'guest workers' who came to Switzerland in the 1960s to do seasonal work and who made a significant contribution to the economic boom, and he tells of the discrimination to which these workers were sometimes exposed. Such accounts disappear from the stories that subsequent generations tell, although some could of course still find themselves in financial difficulty. Mass affluence and mass consumption had set in.

The most diverse indicators show that it was precisely in the 1960s, that is, during the economic boom, that institutional religious practice changed dramatically. People with no religious affiliation appeared for the first time in the census of 1960 – at 0.7 per cent, an absolute minority phenomenon, but this figure would rise rapidly to 20.1 per cent by 2010 (see Figure 9.3). While the Reformed denomination has lost a huge number of members since 1950 (since 1950, as a percentage of the total population; since 1970, in absolute terms, too), the percentage of Catholics increased initially from 1950 onwards, which was due to the influx of Italian and Spanish workers (mostly men at first, and then later the rest of the family). Since 1970, the proportion of Catholics in Switzerland has sunk in percentage terms, but has managed to remain stable in absolute terms due to population growth. From 1960 onwards, we can also see the emergence of a new religious diversity caused by the growth in the number of Muslims, the Christian Orthodox, Hindus and Buddhists in Switzerland – a diversity that, although numerically small, has been very significant for society as a whole.[3]

---

[1]   See Strahm (1987, p. 54 ff.). Between 1946 and 1973, economic development was by no means uniform, however. For a classification of more precise economic cycles, see Hotz-Hart et al. (2001, p. 167). See also Skenderovic & Späti (2012), Siegenthaler (1987).

[2]   McLeod (2007, p. 102 ff.). Zürcher (2010) arrives at annual growth rates for Switzerland of 2.3 per cent (1.7 per cent pro capita) for 1920–50, of 4.4 per cent (3.1 per cent pro capita) for 1950–73, and of 1.5 per cent (0.9 per cent pro capita) for 1973–2008.

[3]   See for an analysis of this religious diversity in Switzerland: Baumann/Stolz (2007a), Stolz/Chaves/Monnot/Amiotte-Suchet (2011), Monnot (2013), Monnot/Stolz (2014).

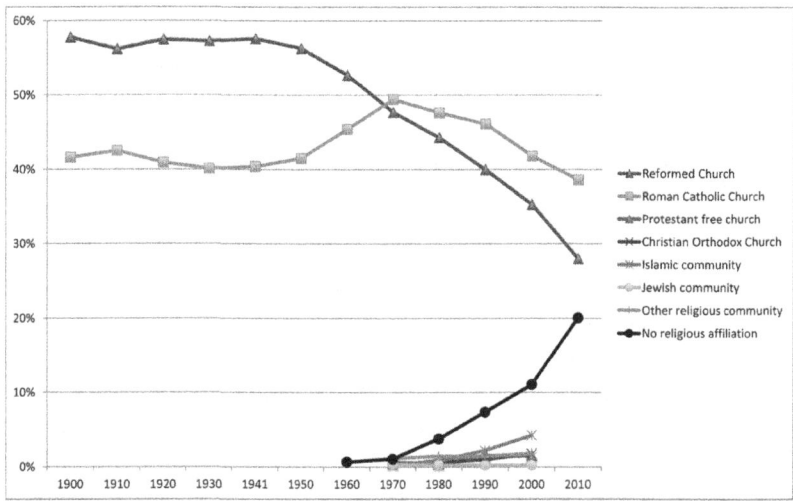

Figure 9.3   Religious affiliation in Switzerland: the number of people with
no religious affiliation has increased rapidly since 1960

Source: Bovay (2004, p. 11), press release FSO (corrected version from 11.10.2012):
Structural survey of the population census of 2010. One fifth of the population now has no
religious affiliation. The press release does not allow us to make any conclusions regarding
the development of the smaller religions.

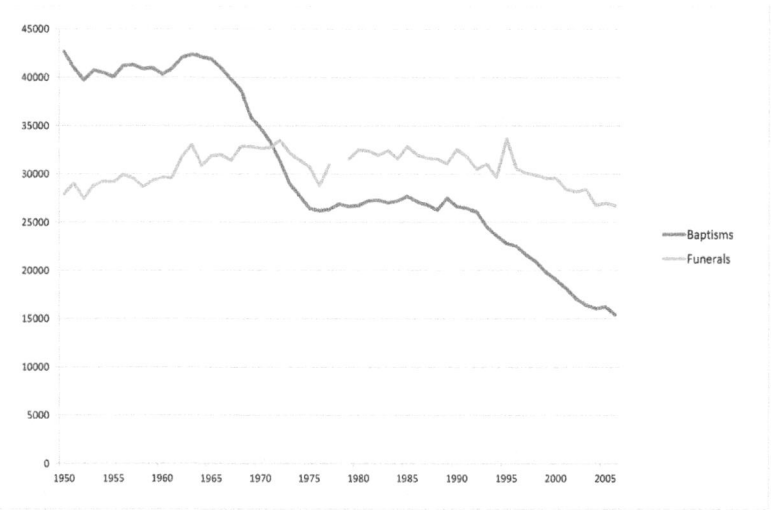

Figure 9.4   Baptisms and burials of the Reformed between 1950 and 2005.
The number of baptisms fell rapidly in 1965

Source: Stolz & Ballif (2010, p. 61).

When we also consider baptisms – represented here for the Reformed (Figure 9.4) – then we can again see that a collapse occurred in the 1960s. In a study of behaviour surrounding life-cycle rituals, Charles Landert has come to the conclusion that, in the period between 1970 and 2000, an important part of this decline can be attributed to the declining birth rate of children among Reformed families.[4] Nevertheless, there can be no doubt that a trend began in the 1960s in which Reformed parents no longer necessarily had their children baptized. Mixed-denominational couples also play an important role here, since they baptize their children much less frequently than do mono-denominational couples.

If we consider what our respondents say about the churchgoing of their parents (Figure 9.5), then what we notice immediately are the huge denominational differences, with Catholics going much more often to mass than do members of the Reformed Church to their religious service. We can see here also the well-known 'gender gap' with regard to Catholics, with Catholic women having always gone more frequently to mass than their male counterparts. This same gender difference is not observable among the Reformed, though. With respect to our central question, we can state that there was, indeed, and especially for Catholics, a massive collapse in religiosity in the 1960s and 1970s; and that there had already been a certain decline in religiosity in the 1940s.

---

[4]   On this, see Landert (2001). The birth rate in Switzerland as a whole dropped rapidly after 1963 and the so-called baby boom. In 1963 there were 2.67 births per woman at childbearing age, sinking to 1.55 in 1980. This decline also shows that society as a whole underwent in this period a significant structural and cultural transformation. See data: su-d-01.02.02.03.01.01.xls. at http://www.bfs.admin.ch/bfs/portal/de/index/themen/01/06/blank/data/01.html (downloaded 16.8.2013).

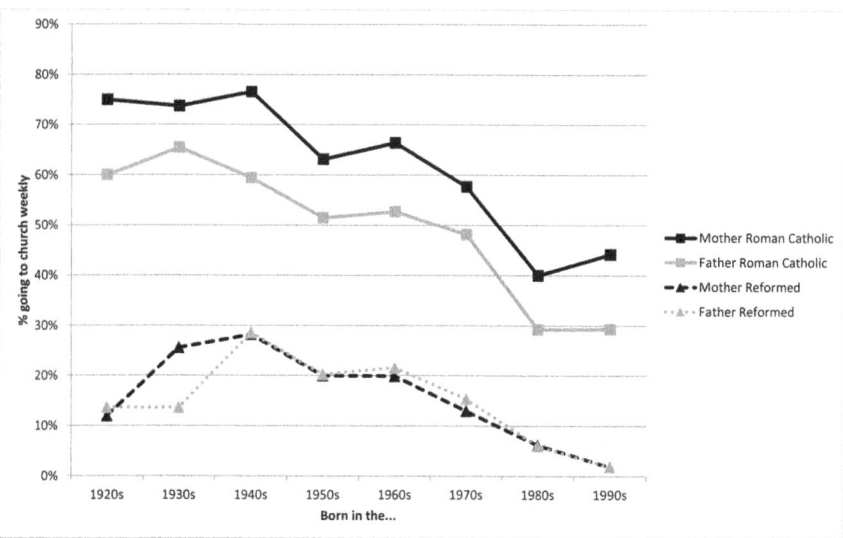

Figure 9.5   Weekly church attendance of parents when the respondents were between 12 and 15. Catholic parents went to church much more often than Reformed parents. In the 1940s, and then especially since the 1960s, we can see in both denominations a clear decline in religious practice

Source: Retrospective data on church attendance of respondents' parents, pooled data from records of 1989, 1999, 2009.

The transition can also be seen if we arrange our respondents according to year of birth and type (Figure 9.6). It is the oldest generation consisting of 71-year-olds and above (born in 1938 and earlier) who still make up the largest share of the institutional type (34 per cent). The generation of 61- to 70-year-olds, that is, the real '68ers' (those born between 1939 and 1948), were still socialized in the old form of society, but the share that they make up of the institutional type is much smaller (13 per cent). If we interpret these data historically, we can also make out the emergence of the alternative type. They appear in the generation of post-68ers, that is, in the generation of people born in the 1950s and 1960s. This type is particularly well represented among the 41- to 50-year-olds at the time of our study (and especially among women of this age).

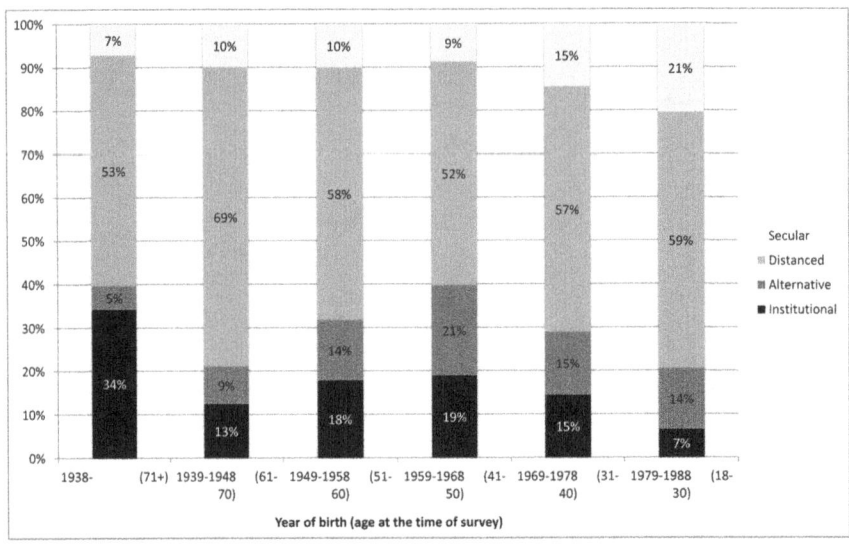

Figure 9.6 The institutional type is particularly common among those aged 71 and above; the alternative type is particularly common among 41- to 50-year-olds; secularists, among 18- to 30-year-olds

Source: Survey 2009.

To conclude, then, we can say that there is ample evidence for the argument that in the 1960s there actually was an extreme expansion of the financial opportunities open to the individual and, simultaneously, a decrease in religious practice.

The Me-Society and Culture

The transition to the me-society was triggered not only by economic, but also by cultural, factors – and this transition resulted in further profound cultural transformations (see Chapter 6 on change of values). According to our second hypothesis, therefore, older people (especially the generations born between 1940 and 1960) should be clearly distinguishable in a number of ways from people born later. The former should talk about a normatized religious practice and a strong, enforced religious socialization which bears the features of the previous form of society. Among these respondents, we should also find a stronger influence of denomination on choice of partner and marriage behaviour. In contrast, the later generations are likely to have experienced in their childhood hardly any normatized religious practice, and should report a much greater degree of freedom with regard to religious socialization and choice of partner.

Normatized vs. Optional Religious Practice

A phase of normatized religious practice does in fact appear when older people (60+) talk about their childhood. Life-cycle rituals – baptism, confirmation, wedding, and funeral – were self-evident and necessary elements of social life. Going to mass or religious service was socially expected, particularly in Catholic areas. In Protestant areas, adults did not have to go to church, but their children had to attend religious and confirmation classes. The two major denominations drew much of their identity from distinguishing themselves from the other denominations, with several older respondents reporting rejection and discrimination arising from this. The mother of Gisèle (63) had as a Protestant (before her conversion to Catholicism) a difficult life in the Catholic canton of Schwyz; her Catholic sister-in-law avoided her and left the house whenever she came in. Berta-Lisa (62, Roman Catholic), together with her fellow pupils, was instructed by the nun at school not to bother with the only Reformed girl in the class. As one of the few members of the Reformed Church living in a Catholic village in a central Swiss canton at the beginning of the 1960s, Niklaus (47, Reformed) was constantly teased by Catholic pupils at school. For Catholics, it was often no better in traditionally Protestant cantons, Victor describing how he witnessed as a child in the canton of Zurich the competition between the two denominations:

> So of course we had a really ostentatious Corpus Christi procession to show the Reformed that we've got a special festival. And then also of course they had to use jackhammers to remove the asphalt from all the streets used for the route to show that they are industrious and hard-working. (Victor, 55, Roman Catholic)

Some respondents describe these norms and denominational identities in retrospect as being claustrophobic, while others explain that they were simply '*quite normal*'.[5] Another striking feature of this time is that the religious specialists – bishops, pastors, priests, monks, nuns – still had a very natural authority which was appropriate to their office and vocation.

In the aftermath of the 1960s, though, we increasingly find a situation of 'normlessness and competition', where the new message is that religious practice, life-cycle rituals and belief are matters for the individual. Religious people now practise their religion, as they themselves say, 'because they feel like it', 'off their own bat', because 'it gives them something', when 'they have the need for it'.

---

[5]   Our description should not give the impression of monolithic relations here. Not all of our older respondents speak of such strong social control, and there were large geographical, denominational and individual differences. Nonetheless, our data point unambiguously to a normative world which developed significant cracks in the 1960s at the latest.

Berta-Lisa makes a quite explicit comparison between the situation now and the situation in the past: 'I don't want to say now that I go to church every Sunday like I used to, simply (...) because you go; rather, it's usually like: yes, I want to go' (Berta-Lisa, 62, Roman Catholic).

For these respondents, then, religious rituals and collective activities have become 'goods' that they can use or not use in accordance with their own preferences (although other, secular products always play a role here, too). Those who do not practise simply do not see the benefits of religious participation, and, just like those who do practise, also feel no social compulsion to do so. Maude is amused that she lives '*in sin*' (she is a Catholic who has remarried), and, although she knows that those who have remarried are excluded by Catholic doctrine from communion, she is not concerned: '[My husband] and I, we do not actually have the right to receive communion. (...) [But] I receive communion nevertheless, which doesn't bother me at all!' (Maude, 50, Roman Catholic).

With the exception of those belonging to Evangelical churches, all our respondents also think that it is not at all necessary to go to church or otherwise practise to be a Christian. Also, consensus is that the individual has an absolute right to determine what he or she believes and practises. Under no circumstances may the churches impose their 'dogmas' on the individual. Priests and pastors thereby lose their specific authority to enforce norms, and any attempts on their part to do so are regarded as being highly illegitimate.[6] When a priest wanted to forbid Diane to be baptized outside the church, she simply changed priest and went ahead anyway. For the priest, God is only in the church; but for Diane, she says laughing, 'God is everywhere'. When a priest suggested to Ingolf that he participate in a Bible weekend to prepare for his wedding ceremony, Ingolf replied: 'I can't make it'. When the priest then became '*annoyed*', Ingolf and his future wife looked for another priest. In general, as Béatrice says, it is important that a priest 'listens, that he doesn't judge'. Finally, as we shall also see below, what also counts is that the individual freedom of religion is also extended to children. They should also '*decide themselves*' whether they want to be confirmed, whether they want to go to religious classes, and whether they want to be religious later in life.

Overall, we encounter a situation in which, once religious norms have been eliminated, competition between the religious and the secular can develop freely. Religious choice is, like every other choice (political, economic, sporting), completely privatized and a matter of individual choice.

---

6   Since the 1960s, priests in Limerzel, France, have also lost much of their authority (see Lambert 2007 (1985)).

Normatized vs. Optional Religious Socialization

However we measure religious socialization, we always find that institutional religious socialization *decreased dramatically* around the time of the transition to the me-society in the 1960s.[7] This finding is reflected both in the quantitative data and in the qualitative study when we analyse the life stories of the respondents. The older respondents went to church more often with their parents, were sent more often to Sunday school, had more intensive denominational religious instruction, prayed more frequently, and had more contact with pastors, priests, nuns and other religious specialists. Of the 18 people between 61 and 70, four were in church schools led by religious people, and two attended a college that was specifically geared to the training of priests.

In contrast, the religious socialization of the younger respondents has decreased steadily in all these dimensions, an important exception being, however, in the Evangelical milieu. Here, children receive consistently strong religious socialization, and that appears to be one of the most important reasons for the numerical 'success' of this milieu.

Religious socialization has not only decreased, though; its *status* has also changed fundamentally as a consequence of the new competition regime of the me-society. It has gone from being a social practice that was deemed *natural* and *necessary* to being one that is considered *optional*. This change appears clearly in our material.

Up until the 1950s, religious socialization was a matter of course, and participation by children in religious services and religious instruction was imposed by force if necessary. It was '*strict*', '*enforced*', and there was '*no discussion*'. Prayers at table and in the evening were simply part of the daily routine in many (and especially Catholic) families. Sunday school, first communion, catechism and confirmation classes were unquestioned components of people's life biographies. A deviation, for example, refusing life-cycle rituals, was subject to strong social ostracism. According to Diane, it was a case of 'every child must be baptized'. And Gisèle says about confirmation then: 'You had to, otherwise it would have been a public scandal'. (Gisèle, 63, Roman Catholic).

It was not an issue, therefore, whether children agreed, whether they liked catechism, or whether they wanted to be confirmed or not. Since participation was general and a matter of course, the actual compulsion to participate was not always perceived as such. Religious teachers at school and church possessed an authority that was recognized generally, and they were also sometimes perceived as authoritarian. Part of their authority also resided in the fact that they represented an occasionally punitive God who would later decide who

---

[7]   However, socialization (operationalized as church-going of parents) is still the strongest predictor of current institutional religiosity. See Table A29, Appendix.

entered paradise and who did not. Religious socialization seems in most cases *not* to have consisted in parents giving their children a 'personal belief'. Instead, there was a division of labour between parents, church and school, with parents following the norms and expectations deemed natural, and delegating religious instruction to the church and school. All three, together with social control by society, forced through the religious norms. Fabio puts it this way:

> Authority has (...) played a relatively important role in my life. Too important, I think. (...) My parents were authoritarian, not in the sense that they exercised authority over me, but because they gave me to understand that this is important and that (if you don't mind) you have to obey authority. For them, it was the most normal thing that you respected authority. (...) So first we of course hardly ever talked about such issues [religion, spirituality] (...). You used to have this nice and clear division of tasks still: when you come home at four o'clock, then we are the parents, we are responsible, and when you are at school from two to four o'clock, the teacher is in charge and so you had virtually the two supplementing each other, intertwining (...). And so of course religious themes were passed on to the school, and weren't really talked about at home, well (...) at least not verbally, but maybe just in one way or another, because there was certainly a cross hanging up somewhere. And my parents certainly also went to church and wanted me to go to church and certainly also wanted me to dress well for church on Sunday, but that was all really just external stuff for something or other that didn't have anything to do with religion in the narrow sense. (Fabio, 57, Roman Catholic)

This division of labour seems to have worked for both Catholics and the Reformed. The major difference between the denominations lay in the fact that going to church and the lived religiosity were much more strongly anchored in everyday life among Catholics than among the Reformed.

Since the transition to the me-society in the 1960s, though, religious socialization has been seen increasingly by both parents and children as *optional*. Many parents, for example, do not have their children baptized or confirmed, so as to *'let them decide for themselves'* later. More generally, people do not wish *'to impose any thoughts'* on children in religious matters; children may *'choose what they want'*; we simply *'open a door for them to religion, and then they can do with it what they want'*. This also has to do with the fact that many parents have themselves already lost touch with the self-evident religious rituals of everyday life, and no longer automatically grant authority for religious socialization to church institutions.

This new optionality has led to religious-secular competition, with religious socialization being compared with other, secular options in terms of its 'leisure value' and 'benefit', and having to survive in this competition. Rebecca says: 'So in terms of what's on offer in general, for children anyway, it's huge. So you have to (...) crystallize what you really want to pick out (...). How will I choose here, and in the church, at school, in music, sport (...)?' (Rebecca, 45, Roman Catholic).

Parents and children think about all the things that children could otherwise do in the time required for religious socialization. The children of Maude (50, Roman Catholic), for example, do not want to spend so many weekends attending confirmation classes, and would prefer to go dancing or swimming. Many children resist if they are nonetheless forced to do so. It is precisely the resistance of children that is one of the most striking and clear findings in our material. The children *'don't want to'*, and *'oppose everything'*. Parents who still want to socialize their children religiously then often use monetary incentives. The son of Mona (48, no religious affiliation), for example, agreed to be confirmed *'only because of the money'*.

Religious socialization is also opposed by secular alternatives with respect to its plausibility. While the authority of religious socialization was simply enforced by the religious specialists before the 1960s (and despite the criticism of religion which had existed since the Enlightenment), a very different situation has appeared since the transition to the me-society, with many children now viewing religious stories and dogmas from a modern scientific perspective, and considering them to be wrong. This is what Elina says about her teacher of religion: 'He thinks that Adam and Eve exist, and that Paradise existed (...) and I've asked, but what about Darwin, what about monkeys? He said: 'No, no, you must not speak of that here' (Elina, 25, Roman Catholic).

And Blandine tells of how her 7-year-old son came home indignant from a religious class at school:

> He came home and grimaced, and I asked him: 'What's wrong? What happened?' He says: 'Look, the priest was at school (...) he should stop telling us nonsense'. And I said: 'Why?' And he says: 'Do you know what he told us this morning? He told us that Jesus once came to the sea with a horde of people and he told the sea, 'Open up', and they all went through on foot and after that the sea just closed up again'. He said to me: 'As if we believe that!' So, it is true – you can't make children today believe those stories any more. (Blandine, 63, Roman Catholic)

In general, our respondents often report that in religious instruction there is nonsense of all kinds going on, that children *'mess around'*, and that the teachers have problems with discipline.

Again, a comparison with the evangelical milieu is revealing; here, an intensive religious socialization takes place and parents try to pass on to their children a *'living, personal faith'*. In doing so, they guard against *'imposing'* anything, since this could provoke negative reactions. Instead, 'they live the faith' and present their religion in an attractive form (e.g., with cassettes of Bible stories and Christian children's music). Members of Evangelical churches also often deliberately choose a community with a strong programme for children and young people, so that their children will grow up and be socialized with other Christian children. Finally, the parents filter the child's environment by shutting out various environmental influences which they regard as being '*not Christian*' (e.g., television, internet, secular clubs, etc.). We can see here, then, an interesting response to the me-society: the milieu deliberately shuts out secular competition for religious socialization by retreating in on itself and offering its own socialization opportunities which it then makes as attractive as possible.

Choice of Partner, Marriage Behaviour, Influence of Partner

We can also see quite astonishing changes associated with the transition to the me-society in relation to people's marriage behaviour and their link to their partner.[8] Put as succinctly as possible, a marriage before 1960 was a matter not just between the two spouses. Rather, the parents, the church and society in general had a certain influence on the choice of partner, the official form that the partnership would take, the way of life of the married couple, as well as the upbringing of the children. The older respondents report that before 1960 a church marriage in their own denominational milieu was socially expected. Under certain circumstances, the parents had an important say in the choice of partner. If a person were to choose a partner from the other denomination, this often caused problems with their own parents or in-laws. Gisèle (63, Roman Catholic) had to convert from Catholicism to Protestantism in order to marry her husband. For most members of society at that time, it was only a church marriage that counted as a 'real marriage'.[9] Interviewer: 'Did you have a church marriage?' Blandine: 'Yes, yes, because for my parents you weren't married unless you got married in church' (Blandine, 63, Roman Catholic).

Also Mima, for whom a civil wedding ceremony would certainly have sufficed, had a church marriage '*to satisfy my mother's wishes*'. In general, marrying in church was the normal and socially expected lifestyle form. Living as a single person with children, living together as man and woman ('cohabitation') with or without children, a patchwork family and sharing accommodation with others – these were all frowned upon. The pregnancy of an unmarried daughter was a huge moral issue and the cause of great anxiety among all parents, and could usually be solved only by the immediate marriage of the daughter to the father of the child. If this did not happen, then both the daughter and the family as a whole suffered a loss of status.

---

8   See for an analysis of (mixed) religious marriage in Switzerland: Bovay (2004).
9   For the 63-year-old Gisèle, that is still the case.

With the transition to the me-society, the situation changed radically. In particular, the pill and other contraceptives, but also the idea of 'free love' propagated by, for example, the hippies, Herbert Marcuse and Wilhelm Reich, led to a liberalization of sexuality, particularly among women. The question of with whom and in what form a partnership should be entered into was now only a matter for both partners. This view has now become established and is one that is voiced by almost all our respondents. Karol (64, Roman Catholic) puts it succinctly when he says that, if two people are suited to each other, '*religion nowadays also shouldn't be a problem*'. Sex before marriage, cohabitation, single parents and patchwork families – all these are completely normal now. Blandine says: 'So now everyone is free, people get married or don't get married, people have children although they're not married, so that now happens as quickly as anything!' (Blandine, 63, Roman Catholic).

Marrying is no longer necessary for the cohabitation of a man and a woman to be socially recognized – and certainly not a *church* marriage, even if many couples still choose the form of at least a civil marriage. The norm of denominational homogeneity of the couple has also almost disappeared completely and is now considered obsolete. The question of the importance of religion for the choice of partner often provokes a lack of understanding among our respondents or even amusement. If the partner belongs to a different denomination, '*you make a note of it*' (Ingolf) – but it usually has no further significance. Since in the me-society only the partners themselves have the right to determine their relationship, any influence of third parties – the parents, society, the church – is viewed as being highly illegitimate and is blocked. The priest's questions on sexual matters during confession, which were still deemed normal in the 1960s and 1970s, are increasingly perceived as a gross interference in the private sphere.[10] Catholic norms which forbade divorce and remarriage under penalty of excommunication (or which made them subject to special permissions) seem to respondents to be outrageous and to contradict what they understand to be a true religion. Not least, individualization has become clearly reflected in life-cycle rituals, and especially in the marriage ceremony. Here, too, the partners themselves want to determine as much as possible of the ceremony. They are reluctant to be '*subject to the schedule of the church*' (Ingolf). In the material, then, there are also various stories of (sometimes bitter) negotiations between priests or pastors and couples in regard to the form of the church ritual.

Quantitatively, 60 per cent of people who were born up to and including 1938 (those aged 71 and over at the time of the survey) specify that denomination was

---

[10]   In some interviews, it becomes very clear how respondents perceive control by the church of their personal morality – especially through confession – as no longer plausible or justified.

an important factor in their choice of partner, while a little more than 20 per cent of the youngest generation say the same (Figure 9.7).

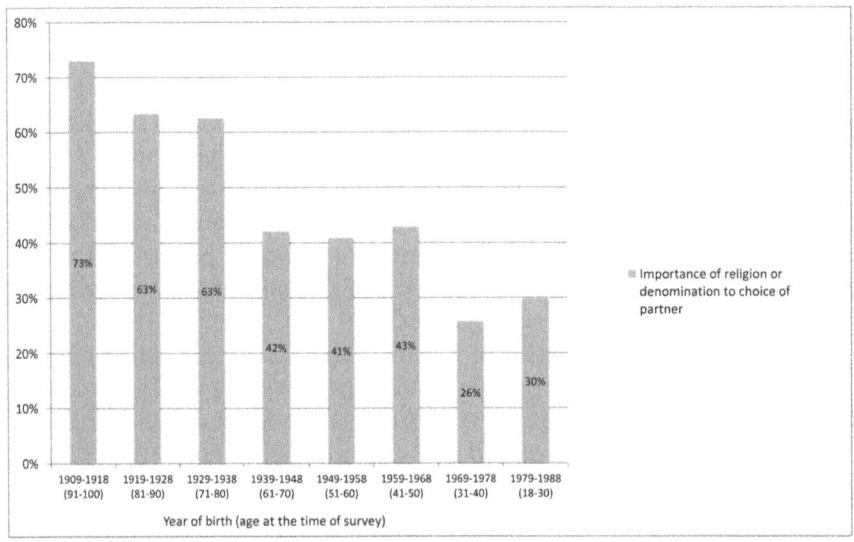

Figure 9.7   Religion is more often of greater importance in the choice of partner for older respondents than for younger respondents

Source: Retrospective data, pooled data from records from 1989, 1999, 2009.

Again, we can observe a large discrepancy between the majority of our respondents (including the established subtype) and those belonging to Evangelical churches; a norm persists for the latter which states that a '*Christian*' needs a religious partner. Even if the norm is often packaged as a purely pragmatic piece of wisdom, it is clear that the whole milieu insists very much on compliance. Barnabé is beside himself at the fact that his daughter is living with an unbeliever and sharing his bed (the partner is a '*delinquent*', and for his daughter this represents a '*failure for her life*'). All our evangelical respondents are therefore also married to, or friends with, other religious people. Nothing of the sort can be found among the alternative type. Although alternative spirituality can be very important for them, they seem to be so individualized that their partner does not necessarily have to share their beliefs and practices. Among the *secular* type, we find very often that the partner is also secular. Secularists state that it would be very difficult to be with a partner who practises a religion. This does not seem to be a question of norms, however, but rather a practical consideration – the fact that things could become difficult for a couple in a practical sense if the partners have different views and values.

The fact that in the me-society external normative influence on the partnership is considered undesirable leads to a situation in which people's partners have an unprecedented level of importance for their own values, their own behaviour, and their own religiosity or secularity. This crops up in our material in various places. Couples *'develop together in one direction'*, *'construct themselves together'*; it is important that it is *'right for both partners'*. This influence is very apparent in religious terms, too, with the religiosity or secularity of one partner affecting that of the other partner. In some cases, the influence leads to greater religiosity: Willi's wife has also converted, François accompanies his wife to mass every fortnight (he would otherwise go less often), Barbara often goes to religious service because of her husband. And Quentin sometimes faintly detects a spiritual *'presence'*, something that is obviously heavily influenced by his wife, who is regularly and intensively in contact with the spirits of the dead:

> I have the impression that there are certain people who have died that we know, when I have things to do (...) then I sometimes have the impression that [the deceased] is leading us or that he is there. It's like a presence. (...) But my wife is a lot more involved in that than I am. She is really certain. I myself have manifestations, but never real manifestations. (Quentin, 50, Reformed)

The mechanism acts more frequently in the secularizing direction, however: Marc-Antoine's sons, who used to go regularly with their parents to mass, stopped doing so as soon as they found secular partners, the wife of the secular David is slowly losing her Orthodox practice, and Peter's wife said, *'you're right in principle, we can save a lot of money there'*, and also left the church.

Changes in Coping Strategies

Another interesting change concerns how people cope with personal problems. While the pastor or priest was still a natural focal point for personal problems for many people before the 1960s, the competition between the religious and the secular since the 1960s seems to point increasingly to a displacement of religious specialists by secular ones. On the one hand, people are turning increasingly to coping strategies which are not part of the institutional-religious domain. For example, Félicia says: 'But it wouldn't occur to me to trust a pastor with a problem. (...) They're not psychologists'. (Félicia, 55, Reformed). And, similarly, Elina: '[The church used to be] a psychological support. (...) The priest was [like today is] our psychologist'. (Elina, 25, Roman Catholic).

On the other hand, pastors and priests in particular seem, according to many respondents, not to have any 'special knowledge' anymore which could help people if they have problems in life. Their 'expertise' in such cases is becoming less and less plausible. On the contrary, respondents often even claim that Catholic priests have only a limited knowledge of '*normal life*' because they live '*in their own world*', do not '*wash-up themselves*', and are not married. In addition, many respondents see religious coping as increasingly *implausible*. It does not solve the real problems. More effective is to approach problems '*rationally*', '*factually*', '*scientifically*', and to discuss them '*with friends*'.

Unlike institutional-religious coping, alternative-spiritual coping seems to have remained stable overall in the last 20 years, although specific techniques and strategies have undergone very strong fluctuation. This form of coping seems to be able to survive better in the religious-secular competition and is regarded as *plausible* for several reasons. The most important arguments in our material are that the effectiveness of alternative coping strategies has been experienced by the individual him- or herself or by others, that these strategies are based on mechanisms which have been (supposedly) scientifically researched, and that they are '*natural*' and '*gentle*' (in contrast to '*aggressive medicines*').

The Me-Society and Gender

According to our third hypothesis, the relation of gender to institutional religiosity and alternative spirituality can only be understood if it is placed within the context of developments during the last few decades, and therefore also within the context of the transition to the me-society. Again, the cultural revolution of the second half of the twentieth century proves to be central: in the 1960s, a sexual revolution occurred because of the invention of the contraceptive pill. In the 1970s, women in Switzerland were given the right to vote. And, in the 1980s, the so-called second women's movement occurred. Overall, these developments led to a transition from a social structure in which men and women clearly occupied separate gender roles (one which gave men pre-eminence), to a situation of (at least theoretical) equality in which both sexes have exactly the same rights. This was accompanied by a change in gender roles. Within the traditional situation up until and into the 1950s, the gender role of women was the classic role of mother and housewife, which was characterized by ideal properties such as industriousness, humility, subservience, helpfulness, chastity before marriage, etc. What genuinely belonged to this female role was religiousness, and therefore also the responsibility for religious matters in the family, especially the religious upbringing of the children.[11] In a sense, the distinction and separation of the gender roles were themselves legitimized religiously in that the religious prescriptions on sexuality, marriage and gender roles made the *status quo* appear natural and 'correct'. This system of gender roles was profoundly shaken by the transition to the me-society.[12]

---

[11]   This description of gender roles is still religiously legitimized for the Catholic Church on the doctrinal level today.

[12]   See Woodhead (2007).

Our data cannot prove all these hypotheses beyond reasonable doubt. However, there are many findings that make our causal story appear at least plausible. It is very clear in the qualitative interviews that, before the 1960s, traditional gender roles with a very strong gender-specific division of labour still prevailed. Here, bringing up the children, and especially their religious upbringing, were the exclusive responsibility of the mother. Almost all of our older respondents report that it was their mother who had given them a strongly religious upbringing. Mima explains in typical fashion:

> My mother was really very religious (...) she always went to church regularly; she did everything according to what her religion said. (...) She went on Sunday (...) and (...) also on every other day. My father didn't (laughs). My father went on Sunday, more out of habit or to make my mother happy. But there were no great discussions. Each lived in their own way. (...) Logically enough, our mother tried to teach us [the religion] and to send us to church. (Mima, 59, Roman Catholic)

The traditional gender roles derived from different male and female characteristics which were deemed to be biologically determined; these characteristics were then consolidated through socialization. The older female respondents tell of how they were brought up in this way; they often internalized the relevant characteristics and made them parts of their own personality.[13] Emily was taught that girls are *'not proud'*, that they should be modest, and that they may *'never outdo other people or be something better'*. If someone asks Mima for help now, she is *'incapable of saying no'* and does everything in her power to help. Gisèle learned from the nuns at boarding school that girls should never argue and should always love everyone – something that has had a decisive effect on her current personality. She says: 'It is in my nature not to argue, to love everybody. And sometimes other people say that I get on their nerves (laughs), when I ask them for the tenth time: would you not like some more to eat (laughs)?' (Gisèle, 63, Roman Catholic.)

The purity of the woman was also, and especially, to be understood in the sexual sense. Sex before marriage was, as Gretchen in Goethe's *Faust* had already learned, an absolute taboo. Compliance with norms governing sex was controlled among other things in confession, which seems, though, to have no longer been legitimate by the 1950s. Two Catholic women among our respondents tell indignantly of how questions about sex in the confessional box stopped them confessing ever again.

Both women and men of the '1968 generation' tell of how they slowly freed themselves from religious constraints, which for women was not only a casting off

---

[13]   The male gender roles are less easy to grasp in the material. One example perhaps is when Barbara says that the teacher of religion beat the boys (but not the girls) if they did not do what they were told.

of religious norms, but also at the same time a rejection of traditional gender roles. When asked why she is less religious than her older sister, Mima answers:

> Well (...) my sister is almost 20 years older than me. She was more used to accepting things imposed on her, even in the family. Maybe I'm more the rebel in the family (laughs). I am a 68er, that's the reason (laughs). A time of great upheaval, which may have changed how I am a bit (laughs). (...) You broaden your horizon, you don't believe any more that you have to do things simply out of habit. You do it if you feel like it, otherwise you don't. This change came and affected everything. (Mima, 59, Roman Catholic)

In the 1970s and 1980s, alternative spirituality emerged, which held a great fascination for many people. It was the time of the 'gurus', of the so-called 'youth religions', of the 'New Age'. Many people, and especially women, who had been brought up in a strongly religious way sought to combine a need for religious experience with the new freedoms. The generations that were socialized during this period remain very strongly alternative-spiritual today. For many women, this new kind of spirituality was a way to emancipation. Emily, who had been strongly socialized in the Catholic faith, talks about this self-discovery:

> As a woman [I] later learned [through] various seminars (...) that now I'm simply more how I really am. And those in my circle of friends and acquaintances who don't like that very much just don't belong to my life. (...) In yoga, I've learned a lot about my body, and about mind and soul, in meditations, a lot about my soul, and in polarity, I removed the blockages. And that's always very difficult, when you start removing blockages, because then something happens to you. And that is usually not very nice for the family, because you (...) begin [to change] very subtly. And then there are certain situations [where] your wife or mummy is no longer quite how you really know her to be. (...) That (...) then led me to where I really want to be. (Emily, 62, Roman Catholic)

We can no longer find any such comments among the younger respondents. Fewer and fewer respondents talk about traditional gender roles, and not at all about male and female characteristics (according to traditional ideology). The respondents (male and female) neither think that women have to be especially tender, loving, helpful and pure, and nor do they mention religiousness as a positive virtue of being a woman. The ideal of the 'nurse' has clearly outlived its usefulness. While it is still usually the mother who has the most important influence on the children's upbringing, she imparts religion much less often. When respondents do talk about gender roles, then they do so in stories about the lack of gender equality in, say, the Catholic Church or in Islam. Exceptions here are the evangelical members and a few of the older established type, who still wish to maintain traditional gender roles.

Other facets of change can be seen in the quantitative data. We can see very clearly here how women between 51 and 60, and especially between 41 and 50, show particularly strongly alternative-spiritual practices (Figure 9.8).[14] This supports the hypothesis that alternative spirituality for these generations of women is a kind of coping strategy in relation to the changes brought about by the new model of society. What we can also see (not shown here) is that there is a clear relationship between female employment and religious practice, with housewives practising institutional religion to a far greater extent – something which speaks for the competition thesis. Finally, we find (again, Figure 9.8) the well-known 'gender gap' once more: women in all age groups are both institutionally more religious and more alternative-spiritual.[15] Precisely this last finding is a problem for our theory, however: from our theoretical considerations, we would have expected the gender gap for both institutional and alternative religiosity/spirituality to be narrower for younger generations. There is clearly a need here for further research.

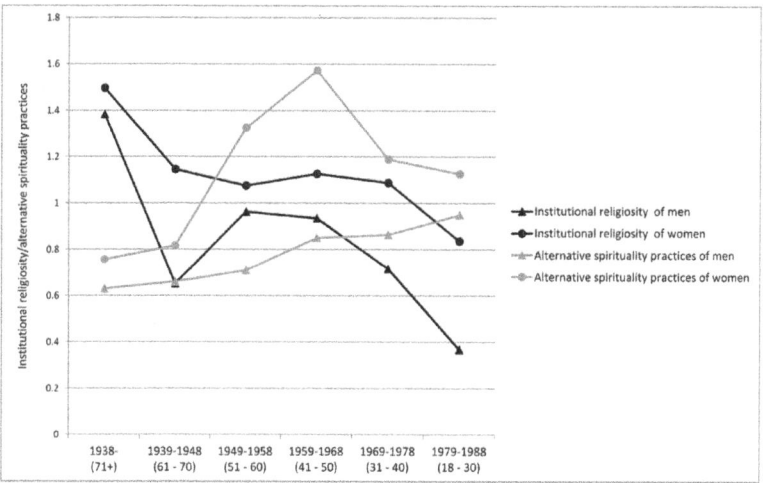

Figure 9.8   Women of all age groups are both institutionally more religious and show more alternative-spiritual practices than men. Women between 41 and 60 show alternative spiritual practices especially often

Note: This table shows the standardized values of the scales for institutional religiosity and alternative spirituality practices. The values have all been set +1 for better readability. For details on the scales see the Appendix.

---

[14]   We concentrate here on alternative spirituality *practices*. We do not find significant differences between men and women concerning our scale of alternative spirituality *beliefs*.

[15]   This finding holds when controlling for all kinds of control variable. See Table A29, A30, A31 in the Appendix. It is also one of the stable findings across all former representative surveys in Switzerland. See Table A25 and A26 in the Appendix.

The Me-Society and the Urban/Rural Contrast

According to our fourth hypothesis, the new modern individualized lifestyle and the religious-secular competition for demand have spread from urban areas to the countryside since the 1950s and 1960s. To begin with, these developments affected a younger, better educated, and urban layer. Due especially to the increasing mobility brought about by the car, though, they soon spread more and more to the countryside. We have in our material only limited opportunities to test this hypothesis; nonetheless, we do have enough to make a few plausible observations at least.

At certain points in our material, we still find remains of the phenomenon which often occurred before the 1960s – that in (especially Catholic) villages, there was a strong social control that supported church attendance, life-cycle rituals and denominational identity. Bettina, a farmer living in the Catholic canton of Valais, says that the church is important for her; that the life-cycle rituals of the church are a matter of course for her; that she wants to pass on her religion to her children; and that leaving the church would be unthinkable. After a further question by the interviewer, she then says that there is also still a certain social pressure in the village to be in the church: 'So I think here in the village, where everyone knows each other (...) we would probably still be looked at in a funny way if we were to leave (laughs), as a long-established farming family'. (Bettina, 40, Roman Catholic).

Stephan (45, Roman Catholic), also from the Valais region, tells of how the fire brigade still maintains very good relations with the church, and holds an annual mass for the patron saint of firefighters. And how new buildings in the village are also placed under the protection of God. Mima says that people in her village start to talk if you do not go to church: 'If you don't go to church here, people say things, they talk among themselves'. (Mima, 59, Roman Catholic).

Unfortunately, our quantitative data regarding the urban-rural feature do not reach back very far into the past. Comparing the three sets of data from 1989, 1999 and 2009 shows, however, that a still quite clear correlation between the urban-rural distinction (or number of inhabitants of the place of residence) and institutional religiosity seems to have weakened since 1989. While in 1989, smaller villages are clearly more institutionally religious than large towns and cities, in 2009 only the smallest villages are still more religious than all other categories – we can otherwise find no differences here anymore. This can be interpreted cautiously as showing that the spread of the individualized lifestyle from the city to the countryside is slowly coming to an end, at least where religion and spirituality are concerned.[16]

---

[16]   This finding holds when controlling for various control variables. See Table A29 in the Appendix.

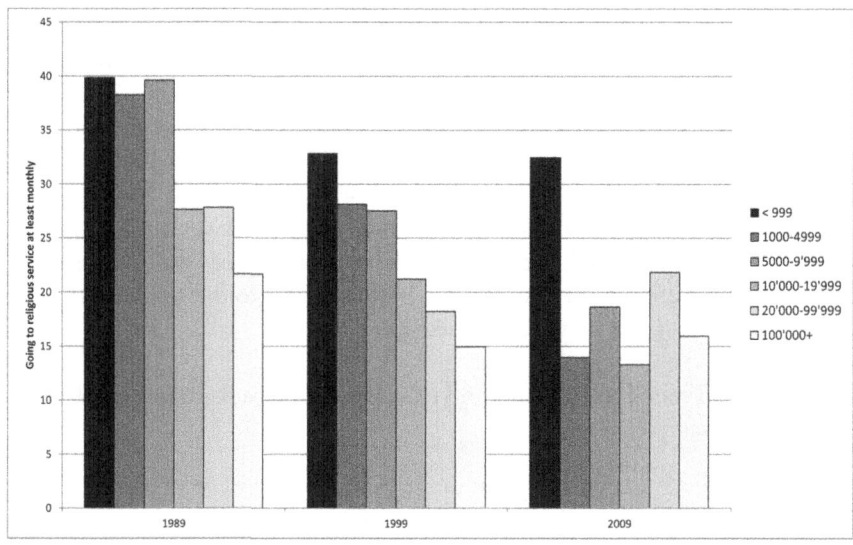

Figure 9.9   The urban-rural distinction with regard to institutional
             religiosity tended to lessen between 1989 and 2009

Source: Surveys 1989, 1999, 2009.

9.2 Individual Adjustments

Secular Drift

According to our fifth hypothesis, we should be able to see both an intergenerational and intragenerational *secular drift* among our respondents. Intergenerational secular drift means that children will on average have a certain probability to drift to less religious types than their parents. Intrareligious secular drift means that individuals will become on average less religious during their lifetime.

The reasons for both types of secular drift have been stated in detail in our theory chapter. Since the 1960s, individuals see that they are no longer forced to practise a religion, that they have many resources and very many secular options, and that they can (in their opinion) often satisfy their needs better by using secular institutions. Parents observe that their children do not need to be socialized religiously in order to succeed in society and they judge costs and benefits (in terms of time, money, conflict) of religious socialization in comparison to other types of socialization. This leads to the fact that each new generation grows up in a world which is even more marked by secular alternatives. In our data we find ample quantitative and qualitative evidence for both types of secular drift.

Let us turn to *intergenerational secular drift* first. If we take our qualitative sample and compare which 'parental background type' each individual grew up in and which type he or she now belongs to, then secular drift becomes very apparent (Table 9.1). As we see, individuals with an institutional parental background may stay in the same institutional type (31.6 per cent). More often, however, they will drift to a distanced type (42.1 per cent) or end up in an alternative type (21.1 per cent). If the parental background was distanced, then individuals will with a high probability either stay distanced (66.7 per cent) or become secular (25 per cent). And if their parental background was secular, then it is very likely that they stay secular (66.7 per cent).[17]

Table 9.1   Type of respondents and type of parental background (qual-sample, in per cent)

Type parental background	Type respondents						
	institutional	alternative	distanced	secular	Total %	N	p
institutional	31.6	21.1	42.1	5.3	100%	38	***
alternative	0.0	100.0	0.0	0.0	100%	1	
distanced	7.1	7.1	60.7	25.0	100%	28	
secular	0.0	16.7	16.7	66.7	100%	6	
Total	14	12	34	13	100%	73	

Intergenerational secular drift also becomes apparent when we compare the generations in 1989, 1999 and 2009. For any indicator, be it formal religious membership, subjective religious membership, frequency of church-going, or subjectively perceived importance of religion we find the same pattern: younger generations have drifted in a more secular direction than older generations. This can be seen in Figure 9.10 for formal religious membership and subjectively perceived importance of religion.[18] This intergenerational secular drift has often been noted in the literature seems to currently exist in all western societies (Voas/Crockett 2005; Voas/Doebler 2011, Voas/Chaves 2014) .

---

[17]   We have tried to do the same analysis with the quantitative sample (see Table A27 in the Appendix). The reconstruction of the parental type is more difficult, however. Overall, the same secular drift appears.

[18]   See Table A28 in the Appendix for additional evidence of intergenerational secular drift.

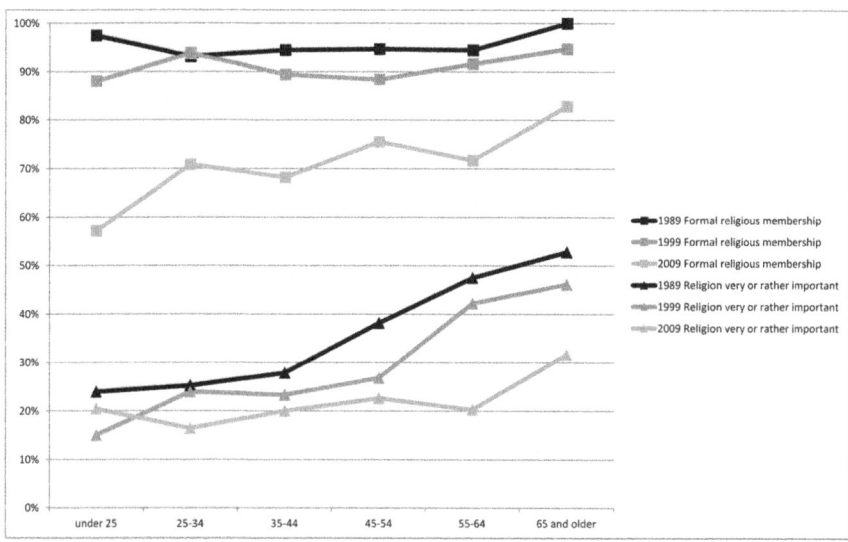

Figure 9.10   Younger generations are less often formal members of religions and give less importance to religion than older generations

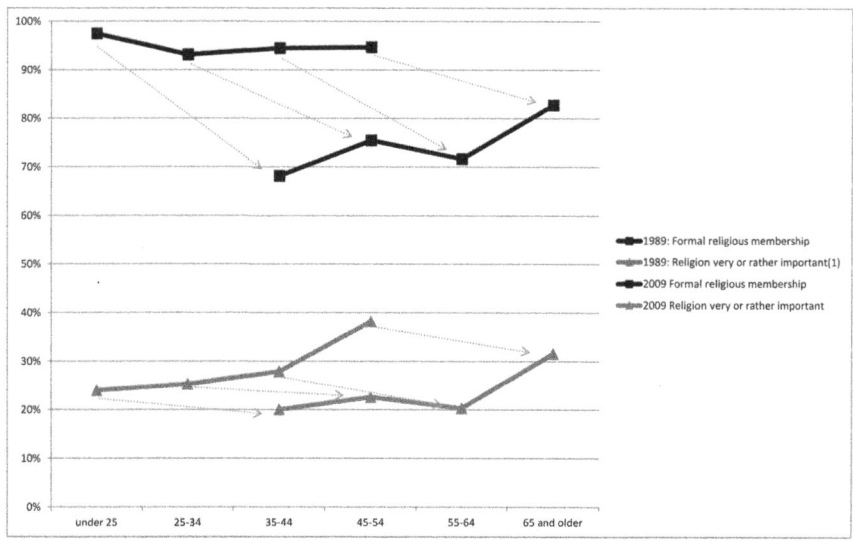

Figure 9.11   Different generations show declining percentages of formal religious membership and declining subjective importance of religion over time (1988 vs. 2009)

However, our data also very clearly point to *intra*generational secular drift. This type of drift shows up quantitatively if we follow different age groups over time in the 1989, 1999 and 2009 surveys as is shown in Figure 9.11 concerning formal membership and subjectively perceived importance of religion. For example, 97.5 per cent of the generation under 25 in 1988 were formal members of a religion. Two decades later, only 68.2 per cent of the same generation (now aged 35–44) are still formal members. Likewise, 24.0 per cent of the generation under 25 in 1988 thought that religion was very or rather important. Two decades later, only 20.0 per cent of the same generation (now aged 35–44) thought that religion was very or rather important.

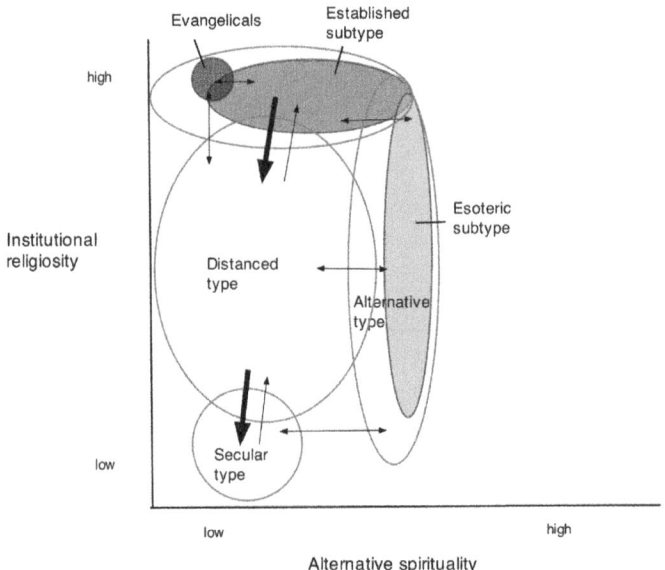

Figure 9.12   Change of type occurs especially from the established to the
distanced, and from the distanced to the secular

If we try to visualize what happens with the help of our picture of the types, we get something like Figure 9.10. The thin arrows indicate that people can make the most diverse changes of type (we have not shown here all the options possible). Empirically, though, what becomes apparent is a significant accumulation of secularizing changes of type, represented here by the thick lines: from the established milieu to the distanced type, and from the distanced type to the secular type. In other words, people who grew up in a parental home belonging to the institutional type are very likely either to remain in the same type or to migrate to the alternative or distanced type; those growing up in a parental home belonging to the distanced type will either remain in this type or migrate to the secular type; and those growing up in the secular type are very likely to remain in this type.[19]

A closer analysis of the qualitative material shows that the secular drift – both of the inter- and intragenerational type – can be *active or passive*, or can at least be represented in such a way. Some respondents explain that they had actively distanced themselves from religion: Lea (36, no religious affiliation) '*decided*' against her mother's will to '*turn her back on*' the church. After a bad experience with a priest, Blandine said: '*Enough is enough*'. Kaitline finished abruptly with her religious practice when she was excommunicated due to her divorce. For most of our respondents, though, secular drift is not so much a matter of making a decision (whether single or multiple), but is rather something that just seems to happen by itself. This is shown by many formulations such as: '*it happened naturally, it was not conscious*', '*it disappeared*', and '*I gradually stopped doing it*'.

What are the most important subjective reasons which the respondents give for secular drift? A *first* set of reasons relates to the fact that individuals may not necessarily have much against religion, but *in fact are simply more interested in other things*. Since they are not (or no longer) forced into religious behaviour, they are only religious when they feel like it – and for many that is hardly ever or never. Many respondents report that, after the obligatory religious lessons and confirmation, they simply stopped going to church and have barely been interested in religion since (e.g., Ferdinand, Renato, Deborah, Victor, Laurence). Deborah had always preferred having a lie-in to going to church, and stopped going to church once she no longer had to. And Laurence says:

> I have some beliefs, but recently I've hardly had any time to think about things. There was a time when I asked myself whether there is a God, a force. But now, in the last few years, it is quite intense, with the children, with the whole organization of family, work and everything. It's true (laughs), you set priorities. And [religion] is just not on my list of priorities. (Laurence, 40, Roman Catholic)

Even and especially when the individual is still interested in religion and church activities, he or she now constantly weighs up whether to do something else instead, because of the lack of norms (Bettina, Gisèle, Berta-Lisa). These reasons for being interested in something else are often connected to migration or relocation, with a number of respondents saying that they or their family had no longer gone to church since moving house (Juan, Beryl, Maude, Elina).

With a *second* group of people, secular drift is due primarily to *privately experienced disappointments* with the church. Here we find deep injuries due to

---

[19]   It is noticeable that there is only one 'alternative-spiritual' parental home in our qualitative data. This is due partly to the fact that the alternative-spiritual type did not become strong until the 1970s, but is partly also down to random error.

personal rejections by priests, anger at being prohibited from skiing on Sunday (Blandine), and memories of being clipped around the ear or experiencing other authoritarian behaviour at Sunday school and during religious lessons (Gregory, Stan, Félicia, Norbert, Lea). Kaitline, for example, says: 'I was a very diligent churchgoer into adulthood. My practice eased somewhat due to lack of time, when I had my children. And it stopped completely when I was excommunicated from the church [due to divorce]'. (Kaitline, 63, Roman Catholic).

For a *third* group of people, secular drift is based above all on an *increase in their own critical thoughts and a collapse of the plausibility* of the Christian religion. These people say that they have moved increasingly away from religiosity through their own critical thinking (Erich, Fabio, Siegfried, Ingolf, Angela, Félicia, Olga, Karine). Karine, for example, says: 'I don't know; it has happened gradually. I find it very difficult to explain. I started to think about certain things. Scientifically, I couldn't believe in it; I think that's it, but I have to say it came very slowly'. (Karine, 68, no religious affiliation).

An interesting case is Ernesto (68, no religious affiliation), who drifted from Catholicism through liberation theology to an atheist and Cuba-oriented communism. In three cases, it was experience of the question of theodicy that led to their faith being profoundly shaken. The illness of a close friend, the accumulation of accidents in a year, the death of a husband – all these led some respondents to doubt the existence of God (Marcel, Melanie, Mima).

Compared with the very many examples of people reporting secular drift, the cases of people becoming closer to institutional or alternative religiosity or spirituality can be counted on one hand. Two people from a parental home of the distanced type have migrated to the institutional type – in both cases, due to a strongly religious partner (Daniele, François). In three cases, people from a parental home of the distanced or secular type have migrated to the alternative type (Diane, Eliot, David) – in two of the three cases because of illness and deprivation, solutions to which were sought in the alternative-spiritual realm.

Overall, the mechanisms described above provide an environment that pushes individuals more and more in the direction of secularism, although the individual forms that this distancing then takes can be very varied.

Religious Individualization/Consumerism

According to our sixth hypothesis, we should be able to observe during the last few decades an increase in individualization and consumerism across the whole of society, that is, that individuals increasingly believe that they can and should make their own decisions with regard to religious/secular issues, and increasingly choose the options that from their point of view give them the greatest 'benefit' or the greatest 'satisfaction'.

In actual fact, our qualitative material shows that religious individualization and consumerism have now captured the entire social field – not in the sense, however, that every person behaves all the time as if they were in a spiritual supermarket. Rather, individualization and consumerism are expressed differently according to type/milieu.

Among the *established* type, individualization and consumerism are directly shown in the fact that the motivation to participate has changed in comparison to the 1940s and 1950s, and to some extent to the 1960s, too (e.g., Berta-Lisa, Gisèle, Marc-Antoine, Nathalie). The respondents say that they used to participate in religious events because they were forced to do so by religious specialists, but that they do so now (albeit somewhat less frequently) of their own accord. The fact of faith and practice is represented in an individualized way as a quite personal, conscious acquisition of an array of traditions, as an act that brings personal benefit and satisfies personal needs. All those of the established type make just the point that they do not practise to follow a norm. They go to church not *'because of the pastor'*, and not *'because they have a new coat'* to show off. Rather, they describe themselves as being completely directed from within: they *'go because they feel like it'*, *'they feel the need to'*, they *'like going'*, *'they feel good afterwards'*, and they *'benefit from it'*. These people could be called 'traditional for personal reasons'. Nathalie says: 'When I was young, I went to mass also because I was afraid, you had to go to mass – or else ... Today I say to myself, I go because I want to and I need it'. (Nathalie, 41, Roman Catholic).

In addition to the motivation to participate, the relationship to God and the form that God takes have also become individualized among many members of the established type. They have discovered that they can address God informally, that they can talk freely to him, and that they can find him especially in nature in their own unique way (e.g., Béatrice, Berta-Lisa, Gisèle). For those belonging to the established type who were still socialized according to the old form of society, we often see a period of personal rebellion against the cultural norms perceived as constricting and against the values of duty and acceptance of their parents, as well as against the religious prescriptions and certainties imposed with them. Berta-Lisa says: 'And I started to rebel and said: it's not all good, what comes from Rome' (Berta-Lisa, 62, Roman Catholic).

Or we hear Nathalie again, who tells of how her revolt led her from a strict Catholicism to a free (Taizé) spirituality:

> I come from a very, very committed Catholic family. We always prayed at the table, in the evening, during Advent, Lent (...). Every Sunday we went to mass. And when I was 15, I had a bit of a revolt (...) and then I was in a youth group (...) and I discovered another kind of spirituality, this free spirituality. (Nathalie, 41, Roman Catholic)

Among the *evangelical* type, there has always been a highly individualistic component. Here, too, the emphasis is on personal experience and making decisions completely individually. People have to choose Jesus '*themselves*', '*say yes to belief*'; people have a '*personal relationship [to Jesus]*', they '*live it*'; people talk '*very spontaneously*' to God. People experience together with God the whole of their own life in all its smallest details. But even in this milieu we can find a strengthening of individualism and consumerism since the 1960s, which is reflected in a (slightly) declining level in acceptance of participatory norms, in an increasing mobility between Evangelical churches, and in the success of megachurches, which strongly emphasize consumerism.[20]

The *alternative* type, who, in the aftermath of the 1968 revolution, reached full bloom in the 1970s, can be seen as an expression of an increase in spiritual individualization and consumerism. The type unites people with a highly individualistic system of values in which personal authenticity and self-development are the highest goods. These people consume spiritual products, courses, books, objects, etc., and gather them together to create a mix of spirituality that appeals to them. This manifests itself in statements such as: they have '*their own thing*', they '*make their own religion*', they '*have cobbled together their religion themselves*', what '*does them good they take*'. Angela, for example, takes ethical principles from different religions: 'I can make a melting pot, I take what I find good in this [religion], what I find good in that, and I make a mixed salad out of it all' (Angela, 37, Roman Catholic).

Increasing individualization and consumerism can be seen among many members of the *distanced* type, too. While it may well be the case that the distanced type put together their diverse beliefs individually, the important point here is that religiosity and spirituality are usually not considered to be particularly important. Rather, they often leave in a kind of stand-by mode what they have at some point been given as a belief or practice; they '*have it running in the background*', while they take care of other things. Ingolf, then, says this about his membership of the Reformed Church:

> What's positive I still think is that, should I at some point in my life experience something dramatic and have the feeling that the power [of God] is real, then the door is open. Otherwise I would have to make an effort for the door to open. That also maybe makes things easier, and it's also to do with inner comfort – not to want to break with something that I can't really deny from the depths of my conviction. (Ingolf, 51, Reformed)

This is accompanied by the fact that these members of the distanced type often think, also with regard to life-cycle rituals, that they themselves can select exactly

---

[20]   Gachet (2013b).

which elements they want to use. According to many of this type, they can go to church activities when they feel like it or when the opportunity lends itself. Thus, when asked whether he would go to church again, Karol says:

> Yes, why not? If that does you good. For some, it's sitting in a restaurant, for others, it's (...). That's the question, what kind of quality of life does the one person or the other have. There are lots of people who say, now I have to have my inner peace of mind and how do I do that? Some do yoga, some meditate, and some say, I've got to go to the fitness centre, that's what I need. (Karol, 64, Roman Catholic)

Finally, religious individualization and consumerism also manifest themselves in the opportunity taken by many *secularists* not to be religious at all, and not to have any interest whatsoever in religious or spiritual matters.

9.3 Effects on Types and Milieus

Growth and Shrinkage of Types and Milieus

According to our seventh and final hypothesis, large groups with traditional Christian religiosity should have shrunk since the transition to the me-society; large groups with distanced religiosity and secular views should have grown; and a large group with alternative spirituality should be observable from the 1970s onwards. We can also confirm this hypothesis by and large, and we have already presented the most interesting data in the course of this chapter. We shall briefly summarize the most important points again.

There can be no doubt that the *institutional type* has shrunk since the 1950s. All indicators show the same basic trend. Official membership has decreased (Figure 9.3) and while many church members think about leaving their churches, almost no non-church members think about joining a church (Table A22, Appendix). Church-going has plummeted among Reformed and Catholic both when looking at retrospective data (Figure 9.5) or when inspecting the findings of all available representative surveys in Switzerland (Table A18, Appendix), frequency of prayer has decreased (Table A19, Appendix). Institutional religiosity beliefs like the belief in god have likewise declined and there are in every age group more people who have lost their faith than who have come back to believing in God (Table A20, Appendix). Between 1988 and 2009, the importance individuals give to religion has decreased significantly, just as has the number of individuals who feel being a member of a parish (Table A23, Appendix).

The data available on the development of *the evangelical milieu* shows, however, that it seems to have grown within the institutional type. The census data show a rather spectacular growth of Evangelicals from 36,945 in 1970 to 112,964 in 2000 (Bovay 2004) but this growth is surely overestimated (Favre/Stolz 2009; Stolz/Favre et al 2013: 32). When taking into account both census data and the membership records of evangelical churches, however, there can be no doubt, that the evangelical milieu has, at least since the 1970s, been able to hold on to its members or has even been slightly growing (Stolz/Favre et al 2013; Polo 2010). Also, religious practice, belief in God and Jesus Christ, importance of the faith as well as strict sexual morals have all been rather stable on a very high level (Gachet 2013b). This has to do with its strong emphasis on homogamy within the evangelical milieu, a relatively high birth rate, a strong religious socialization of children, as well as the recruiting successes of the charismatic churches in particular. To sum up what happens with the institutional type we can say that it shrinks due to a very strong shrinking of the established subtype, while the evangelical subtype slightly grows. This may in time lead to a strong internal change of power due to changing majority/minority relations.

It is less easy to judge the development of the *alternative type* – principally because we have much less data. One way to look at the question is to look – as we have done above in Figure 9.6 – at the importance of the alternative type in different age groups. This makes plausible the emergence of the *alternative type* in the 1970s. After the 1968 revolution, which itself was strongly political, some of the revolutionaries became increasingly religious and/or spiritual. It is the group of 41- to 50-year-olds at the time of the study, those born in the 1960s and socialized in the 1970s, and especially the women among them, who make up the majority of the alternative type. The proportion belonging to this type decreases in later generations which would lead us to believe that the alternative type might be shrinking again in the long run. On the other hand, when we look at repeated cross-sectional data of alternative spirituality beliefs and practices from 1988, 1998, and 2009 (Table A24, Appendix), we get a sense of a certain stability. Some indicators show growth, others decline, others no significant changes. This leads us to the overall judgment that the alternative type has in recent decades been able to remain rather constant.

The combined quantitative and qualitative, retrospective, intergenerational, and cross-sectional data also shows without a doubt that the distanced and secular type combined have been strongly growing since the 1960s. Clearly, in Switzerland, it is especially the distanced type that has so far benefitted from secularization. Most individuals still have some link to the churches, to institutional religiosity or alternative spirituality suppliers. But all indicators show that it is not probable that – in the long run, distanced individuals and their children will find themselves rather in the secular than in the distanced group. The megatrend in the background is clearly one of secularization.

If we conduct a thought experiment based on the assumption that the mechanisms described will continue to work as before, and evaluate what the types in our scheme looked like in 1950, and then try to estimate what they could possibly look like in 2030, then we arrive at the results depicted in Figure 9.13. For 1950, we see a large group of the established type and a smaller group of the distanced type. The religious landscape is split into two, with a Reformed milieu and a Roman Catholic milieu. The evangelical milieu is somewhat smaller than it is today, and the alternative type also constitutes a very small group.[21]

If we then move to 2012, we can see that it is the established type in particular that has shrunk, while the distanced and alternative types have grown enormously. We can say that Switzerland witnessed during this phase what David Voas calls 'the rise of fuzzy fidelity'. We have set out in this book to describe this situation in great detail.

If the processes of modernization continue to work in the same way, then we can expect the established type to continue to shrink rapidly in the future, as the generations representing this type will simply die off. The alternative type should be able to hold its own more or less, although its core group will grow ever older. The distanced type will tend to shrink again, and instead the secularists will become the largest group. We can therefore expect a certain polarization between very religious members of Evangelical churches and esotericists on the one hand, and a very large group of people who are either totally indifferent to or critical of religion on the other.

***

In this chapter, we have attempted with the help of seven hypotheses to explain which processes have led to the current religious-spiritual situation in Switzerland. The mixed-methods strategy chosen here shows clearly that it is not helpful, as is now often done in the literature, to play off secularization theory, individualization theory and market theory against each other. In fact, we can see that, since the transition to the me-society in the 1960s, there has been a decline in religiosity and spirituality, and a strong secular drift. At the same time, there has been a profound individualization in all types and milieus, as well as a very significant increase in religious and spiritual consumerism. The key to understanding lies here in the transition to the me-society, when there was a change of regime of religious-secular competition. Now, due to the decline in the formative power of religious norms and values and the increase in material and temporal resources that took place in the 1960s, individuals can behave as consumers in a market where religious goods are only several among many other goods on offer. This development has led to the simultaneous growth of the three phenomena mentioned here: secular drift, religious individualization, and religious consumerism.

---

[21] The typology by Krüggeler (1993: 127) that uses the 1988 data, see Table A32, Appendix, can already be very well mapped on our current typology and shows very nicely what we mean: a situation with a larger institutional group, a smaller secular group, and a roughly stable alternative group.

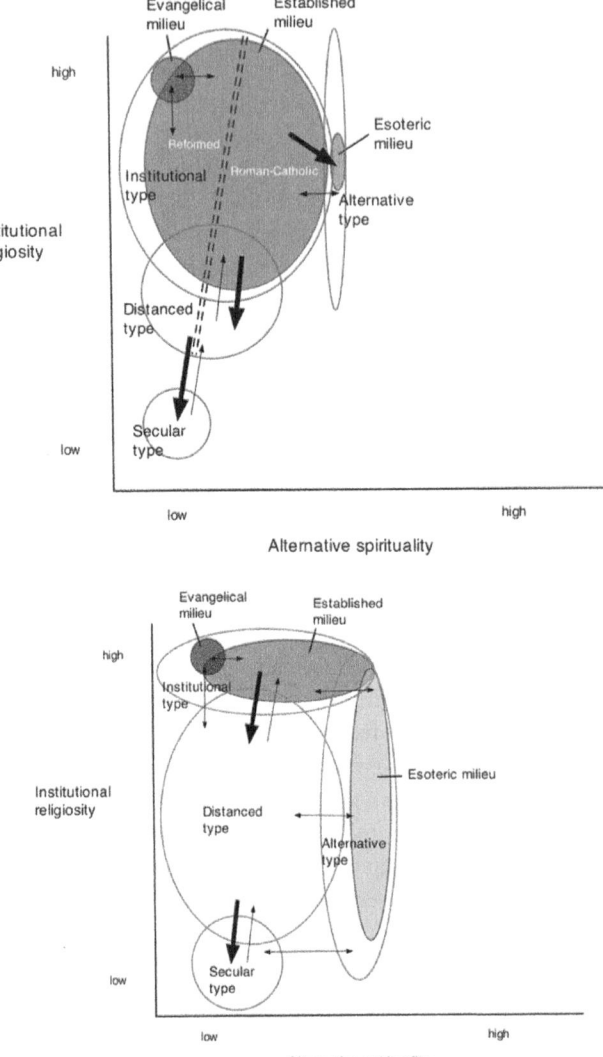

Figure 9.13   The types in 1950, 2012 and 2030. For 2030, we can
               assume a significant shrinkage of the established and
               distanced types, as well as a growth of the secular type:
               [9.13a] 1950 (Reconstruction) [9.13b]2012 [9.13c]2030 (Prognosis)

Note: the reconstruction and prognosis graphs only want to give a general impression of
possible past and future developments. There is a problem with these kinds of graphs in
that the size of the ellipses tries to capture both the number of people in the type and the
extension of the type in the diagram (which may vary independently). A three-dimensional
graph would be more adapted – but also less easily readable.

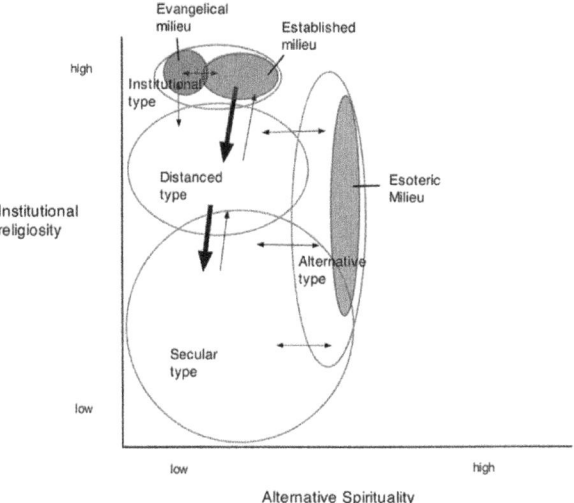

Figure 9.13   Concluded

Chapter 10
Conclusion: (Un)Believing in Modern Society

Jörg Stolz, Judith Könemann

Love God and do what you please. (Augustine)

10.1 Retrospect: So What?

In this book, we have tried to answer a classic question through new means. We have aimed to describe and explain religiosity and spirituality in modern society (what we have called the 'me-society'), and have drawn on quantitative and qualitative data to trace their development over the last few decades and up until the present. Our book consists of a description, a general theory, and a specific explanation.

A New Description

A large part of our discussion has centred on a new *description* of the religious-spiritual landscape of the me-society. In combining quantitative and qualitative elements, this description has provided a wealth of insights that support some existing theories, diametrically oppose others, and in many cases lead to a more differentiated view than previously existed. First, we have developed a new *typology*, one which describes each different religiosity, spirituality and secularity that people have (Chapter 3). In this typology, we have distinguished four types – the institutional, the alternative, the distanced and the secular. As we have seen, each of these types can be further distinguished into subtypes, with three of these subtypes forming their own religious-spiritual milieu (the evangelical, established and esoteric milieu) with their own producers, identity and boundaries. For us, the advantage of such a typology is the '*thick description*' which it enables, one which makes clear and understandable the characteristics of the members of the different types, as well as how they think and behave.

Second, we have also been able to show that the different types and subtypes differ markedly from each other in terms of '*identity construction*' (Chapter 4). This is something that has been completely overlooked in the literature on types of religiosity. Some subtypes, such as those belonging to Evangelical churches and Catholics in the established subtype, have a collective identity (i.e., they employ an emphatic 'we'). Other types and subtypes are only use much weaker, categorial self-descriptions – as, for example, when members of the distanced type say about themselves that they are Catholic or Reformed '*by birth*' or '*on paper*'. The types also differ from each other in how they describe themselves as '*religious*', '*spiritual*' or '*secular*', and in the meanings that they assign to these terms. Finally, the types create a religious/spiritual/secular identity by delimiting themselves from different negative groups. For example, the evangelical subtype, as '*Christians*', delimit themselves from the '*non-converted*'; committed Catholics, from '*bigoted*' Catholics; committed Protestants, from Catholics; the distanced type, from '*extremists*', '*fundamentalists*' and the '*very religious*'; and opponents of religion, from '*dreamers*' and '*weaklings*'.

Third, we have created with the help of our types and subtypes a '*thick description*' *of the symbolic forms and contents of religiosity, spirituality and secularity* in Switzerland (Chapter 5). In doing so, we have been able not only to show the statistical distributions of statements about God, angels, life after death, reincarnation, yoga, etc., but also to analyse the different meanings that these symbols have in each of the types. For example, we found major differences between the types and subtypes in terms of their understanding of concepts such as 'God'. While the evangelical subtype sees God as a supernatural friend, Lord and worker of miracles, the established subtype sees him as a mixture comprising father-mother figure and transcendental psychoanalyst. In contrast, the alternative type understands God mostly as a light-force-energy, while the distanced type does not quite know how to imagine God. In addition to various differences with regard to belief, knowledge, experience and practice, we have also been able to identify interesting commonalities. In all types, for example, we find unusual, uplifting and perplexing experiences, but only some types and subtypes interpret such experiences religiously. Similarly, all types and subtypes consider the self to be important: the fact that individuals are autonomous, and can and should decide for themselves what to believe (or not) and how to practise (or not).

Fourth, through combining cross-sectional and longitudinal analyses, our typology has enabled us to look anew at the changed *relationship between religion and values* since the 1960s (Chapter 6). What we found here is that the transition to the me-society profoundly changed the relationship between values and religion across the whole of society – but that the changes are very different according to type and subtype. While most members of society, and especially the distanced and secular types, increasingly see their own values as being independent of religion, three groups in particular maintain a different relationship between values and religion: members of the evangelical subtype continue to adhere to 'old values' (e.g., traditional gender roles and sexual norms) and legitimize them through the Bible; members of the institutional type legitimize 'constant values' in particular through their religion (e.g., those of honesty, sense of duty, striving for success); and members of the alternative type believe that so-called 'new values' (e.g., self-development, individualism) are very closely related to their own alternative spirituality.

Fifth, we have been able to show in Chapter 7 on the *relationship of individuals to religious suppliers* that the major churches, Evangelical churches and alternative-spiritual suppliers each offer (from the perspective of our respondents) very different 'salvation goods'. In short, the major churches offer strength, support, tradition and welfare for the needy, Evangelical churches provide a highly normatized lifestyle for a converted Christian, and alternative-spiritual suppliers offer spiritual growth and solutions to specific problems in life. As far as *image* is concerned, we can say, again very schematically, that the major churches are perceived as being useful, but outdated and conservative; Evangelical churches, as dynamic, but potentially dangerous; and alternative-spiritual suppliers, as unusual and possibly effective. Our typology also sheds new light on two well-known theories. In contradistinction to market theory, we can see that the majority of the population (who belong to the distanced type) do *not* see themselves in any way as being part of a religious market, and it is only with regard to evangelical and alternative-spiritual suppliers that we can really talk in terms of membership markets and customer markets. And, in contradistinction to Grace Davie's theory of 'vicarious religion', we do *not* come across any people at all who are happy that others are religious in their place. Nonetheless, there may be a kernel of truth to Davie's theory in the sense that, because many people see churches as producers of public goods, they therefore think that churches are important not for themselves but for others.

Sixth, we have been able to show that the transition to the me-society has also radically changed people's *perception of religion(s)* (Chapter 8). While, as late as the 1950s, Switzerland could still be regarded as a 'Christian country' where denominational differences were still an important social marker, religion is now considered completely differently by the overwhelming majority of the population. From the current perspective, religion(s) must serve the 'prevailing order' of society and the individual. If it does not do so, or even has adverse effects, then it is rejected. This attitude is accompanied by the idea of the fundamental equality of all religions and by a relativism with respect to religious truth. Against this background, we can explain why many of our respondents view Islam in particular so negatively: for them, Islam calls the 'prevailing order' into question, abuses the hospitality shown to it, runs against the basic liberal order, and violates individual freedoms (e.g., of women). The second religion which is the subject of strongly negative stereotypes in our data is Catholicism, which many of our respondents judge negatively because it legitimizes values that no longer appear to be appropriate (celibacy, no women as priests) and have negative consequences for society (prohibition on the use of contraception). In contrast, most of our respondents see Buddhism in particular as being positive, since this is a religion that does not seem to disturb the prevailing order and simply leaves all freedoms to the individual.

A General Theory

We have also presented here a *new general theory of religious-secular competition* (Chapter 2). This theory uses general principles from analytical sociology, and combines results and insights from very different areas of research, such as history, sociology, marketing theory and economics. The theory views religious change as resulting from religious-secular and intra-religious competition and struggle at a number of different levels. The competitors facing each other are religious or secular specialists and occupational groups, organizations, political parties, elites, and even the state (according to the agenda that it is pursuing at the time).

According to our theory, these actors compete for three desirable objects. First, they compete for *power, influence, and the authority to interpret at the level of society as a whole*. This competition can just as well occur in the official political domain (the Catholic conservatives fought against the liberal FDP and the socialists in Switzerland in the first half of the twentieth century) as lead to open civil war (as in the current conflicts between the Muslim Brotherhood and the military in Egypt). Second, the collective actors compete for *power, influence, and the authority to interpret within groups/organizations/milieus*, exemplified by the current battles within the liberal and conservative elites of the Catholic and Protestant milieus in different European countries. Third, they compete for *individual demand*. As soon as freedom of choice rules in principle in society, religious and secular 'suppliers' – communities, occupational groups, institutions – compete with each other for the demand that individuals have for goods, for their participation, time, energy and donations. Psychotherapists are therefore in competition with pastors, Sunday school with football, the church choir with the choral society.

The competitors use a large number of *strategies* in this struggle, such as mobilization, social withdrawal, recruitment, biological reproduction, socialization of their own members, price adjustment, improving attractiveness and quality, etc. They employ these strategies in an attempt to survive in the competition or even to score a decisive victory.

Various *external factors* influence the competition. What is important first of all is the rule system or regime provided by the state or society which regulates religious and secular competition in a particular social structure. The rules of this competition regime determine, for example, which religious and secular groups with their goods can appear on the market, and whether demand is directed or free. Other external factors of importance are scientific/technological innovations (e.g., the invention of the car), social innovations (e.g., the invention of the professions), major events (e.g., wars) and socio-demographic factors (e.g., different birth rates). The struggles within the competition can have different outcomes – they can lead to compromises and stalemates, to processes of differentiation and de-differentiation, of individualization and collectivization, and to secularization and re-sacralization.

An important argument of the theory is that the *advantageousness of religion has changed over time*. During long periods of social development, religious structures had a high advantageousness because they enabled people to deal with 'unsolvable' problems. Since the modern era, though, secular innovations have often allowed people greater control and a better understanding, which has tended to lead to the removal of phenomena from the religious domain. However, these innovations (e.g., the discovery of bacteria, the theory of evolution, etc.) do not lead directly and necessarily to a removal of issues and responsibilities from the domain of religion. Rather, they change the framework of competition in which the different actors find themselves. It is only with the expiry of the competition that quite different possible social outcomes can come about. This explains why we can observe in modernizing societies a uniform trend of secularization on the one hand, and such extreme differences in how these developments take place in different countries and regions on the other.

A Specific Explanation

A historical concretization of this general theory (Chapter 2) and an examination of the hypotheses arising from it (Chapter 9) have led to the central thesis of our book and therefore also to a new *specific explanation* of religious change in Switzerland. The thesis is that the cultural revolution of the 1960s brought about a *change of competition regime*, with the competition regime of 'industrial society' being replaced by that of the 'me-society'. While we can find both before and after the 1960s religious-secular competition for power, influence, and the authority to interpret, as well as for individual demand, the rules and form of this competition changed significantly in the 1960s. Before the cultural revolution, religion and religiosity were viewed as public matters, and society as a whole saw itself as bi-denominational, that is, as Christian, despite all denominational diversity. This led to various intra-religious and religious-secular struggles, especially for power, influence, and the authority to interpret. After the revolution, though, society came to be understood as essentially pluralistic, and Christianity as just one religion among others. Struggles between denominations for power, influence, and the authority to interpret are now considered illegitimate, while religion is seen as a private matter and consigned to the area of leisure pursuits. The most significant religious-secular competition is now therefore simply competition for individual demand.

We can elaborate the thesis further. In the *competition regime of industrial society* (from the nineteenth century to the middle of the twentieth century), there were various struggles for power, influence, and the authority to interpret. For example, the Catholic milieu fought against liberalism, the Christian establishment against socialism and its tendency towards atheism, the various liberal movements within the denominations against the conservative movements, the new professions (doctors, social workers, teachers) against the clerics. As a consequence of all these struggles, the churches may have forfeited more and more of their functions and may have been weakened internally, but they were not, or were only partially, aware of this, and Switzerland still considered itself to be a Christian society up until the end of the 1950s, with over 97 per cent of the population belonging to a Christian denomination and membership appearing not to be a matter of individual choice.

The religious situation in the competition regime of industrial society comes alive in the narratives of our older respondents (60+), when they tell of a strongly normatized religious practice even in the 1950s. Performing life-cycle rituals in the church was taken for granted. Going to mass or religious service was socially expected, particularly in Catholic areas. The religious socialization of children was deemed necessary and was imposed by force if required. People sought their marriage partner primarily in their own denominational group, and mixed-denominational marriages were frowned upon. Many respondents speak of a strongly perceived denominational identity, and of skirmishes, negative stereotypes and discrimination between the two major faiths. What is also very clear is how the traditional gender roles were legitimized religiously, with women being encouraged towards religious practice.

We can understand better the *transition from the competition regime of industrial society to the new competition regime of the me-society* if we make clear the events that occurred in the 1950s, 1960s and 1970s. The 1950s saw the beginning of a period of economic boom that would continue until 1973 and that would give Switzerland an average annual growth rate in GDP of 5 per cent. This greatly increased the secular options available to people, and put pressure, at least potentially, on the religious options. A wide range of people could now afford a standard of living in terms of leisure activities, mobility, quality of housing, security, etc. that would have been unthinkable just a few years earlier. In particular, young people now also constituted their own layer of affluent consumers. Nonetheless, despite this intrusion of the 'American way of life', the 1950s remained within the bounds of a strong conservatism and moralism. Traditional gender roles, the values of duty and acceptance, as well as religiosity and denominationalism – at least superficially, all these remained intact.

In the 1960s, there was in Switzerland, as in almost all Western countries, a cultural revolution which included religion, a revolution which ensured that intra-religious and religious-secular battles would now be waged in a different way. There was to begin with a generation conflict, with a young generation rebelling against the older and their outdated, stuffy and boring ideas on life and values. In religious terms, it meant that teenagers and young adults attacked and challenged religion and the churches as one of the various authorities, deeply anti-institutional ideas gained a foothold within the churches themselves, and youth work within the churches was plunged into a deep crisis. All three effects would often be described later by church leaders as a 'break with tradition'.

In the 1970s, the new *competition regime of the me-society* then prevailed. Now religion and denomination were simply private and optional features of identity, and Christianity was treated more and more as just one religion among others. There were still of course power struggles at the level of society and within groups/organizations/milieus – for example, over the recognition of the major churches under public law, and over the acceptance or non-acceptance of Islam in society and of women and homosexuals within different religious groups. Nonetheless, *by far the most important religious-secular struggle in the me-society was over individual demand.* Since religious practice was no longer socially expected, what religion had to offer was relegated to the realm of leisure pursuits, where it was forced to compete with other forms of 'leisure activity' and 'self-development'.

The qualitative and quantitative material of our study shows the effects of this new competition regime very clearly. Our respondents see religious practice as being fundamentally optional and ask themselves constantly how religious practice 'benefits' them in comparison to other activities. The religious socialization of children is judged in exactly the same way, with parents thinking about what benefits such a religious upbringing has in comparison to other, secular possibilities. In addition, parents do not want to impose anything religious on their children, so that children often have the opportunity to choose themselves. They often decide against religious activities, which appear less attractive to them. When people choose a partner in the new competition regime, denomination is usually no longer a criterion of selection. Moreover, neither marriage itself nor a church marriage is now a prerequisite for a man and a woman to live together.

As a whole, the transition to the me-society and the radical emancipation of women have largely destroyed traditional gender roles. Religiousness as an element of the female gender role and barriers to employment are things of the past. With their disappearance, very important reasons for the high religiosity of women in the competition regime of industrial society were eliminated, and so women have also become strongly secularized. As our data show, many women initially sought the path of alternative spirituality especially in the transitional period of the 1960s and 1970s so as to satisfy their spiritual needs and to be able to liberate themselves from traditional gender roles. Our data also show that the situation in the new competition regime of the me-society has led many people to experience what we have called 'secular drift'. Since their resources and secular options have increased greatly, they are, be it in their own biography, be it in relation to their parental home, slowly entering more secular waters. The fact that individuals themselves decide on their religious and secular needs also leads to an increasing individualization (individuals increasingly differentiate themselves with respect to their individually chosen religious-secular 'shopping basket') and to an increasing consumerism (individuals increasingly regard the religious-secular world in terms of 'products' which they then judge according to performance and price). In effect, this has led to a radical shift in the comparative sizes of the different types, with the established type having shrunk considerably since the 1950s, and the distanced and alternative types in particular having grown. The evangelical subtype, meanwhile, has been able to hold its own through isolating itself and being strongly competitive – in fact, if anything, this subtype has grown slightly. The new competition regime of the me-society means that religious suppliers can no longer wrestle publicly for power, influence, and the authority to interpret, but must nevertheless make great efforts to 'survive in the market', that is, to motivate people to make time, energy and money available for religious purposes. The churches are therefore increasingly trying to make use of various marketing strategies (e.g., needs analysis, quality assurance and advertising). A key strategy also lies in reaching a certain size in order to be able to survive in the competition (hence the phenomenon of mergers and megachurches).

As we already noted in our introduction, our study also has *limitations*. First, our testing of the theory relates only to the perspective of individuals. In the future, however, we should also test through studies that look at the competition from the perspective of the collective actors involved. Second, although we have attempted to take into consideration all the data available to us on religiosity and spirituality in Switzerland, it is precisely this approach that has shown a complete absence of important data. For example, while institutional religiosity can be fairly well traced back into the past, our claims concerning alternative spirituality are, as far as the available data are concerned, based on much shakier ground. Third, we have had to ignore a very important part of the religious diversity of Switzerland – namely, non-Christian religions. This was done deliberately in the design phase of the study, as an overall assessment would have gone well beyond the scope of the study. In any case, at least there are now available for these religions the results of many other research projects of National Research Programme 58. Fourth, our data are strictly limited geographically: they concern only Switzerland.

10.2 Outlook: The Future of Religion and Spirituality in the Me-Society

What, then, does this all mean for people, for religious-spiritual suppliers, and for society as a whole? For *people in our society*, it probably means that they will have to exist in the long term in a world in which they can and must decide for themselves what they want to believe in and practise. This does not mean that there will not continue to be powerful forces that affect them in this regard – socialization, education and the mass media, for example, will remain important. But in contemporary society the individual person will become ever more responsible for what he or she does, and will be able to rely less and less on mere 'tradition'. If the mechanisms of religious-secular competition prevail and the secular alternatives will continue to rise in attractiveness, the numbers of individuals who tend towards unbelief will steadily grow; the group we have called 'seculars' will eventually become the largest group of all.

For *religious-spiritual suppliers*, it means that they will have to adapt constantly to a situation in which individuals belong to them or make use of their products and services no longer because of tradition but because of the choice that they themselves have made. They will increasingly come to learn that they are in a competition in which they have to be attractive to their members, participants and sponsors. For churches, it means that the national church will increasingly make way for the membership church. There will also probably be more and more *hybrid phenomena* – packages that are only partly spiritual or whose spirituality is not immediately visible. When the great religious answers to phenomena that seem to people to be inexplicable and uncontrollable are neither convincing nor necessary, then there will remain a situative and occasional need for religious and spiritual symbolization. This need can attach itself to phenomena such as sport, psychological help, sexuality, consumerism or work – and then it is no longer even clear whether we should still be speaking of religion at all.

For *society* as a whole, it is likely that there will be a new polarization. The days when denominational differences led to heated debate are long gone. Instead, it is now becoming apparent that the melting of the 'natural' and traditionally based popular religiosity is leading to a new opposition and to a new line of conflict. On the one hand, there are those who believe and practise strongly and with great commitment – for example, those belonging to Evangelical churches, who actively oppose the secular tendencies of modern society and who are seeing their numbers steadily increase. On the other hand, we find an increasing number of militant secularists, who fight religion as an unnecessary by-product or even as a mistake of evolution. Whether the philosophical discussions about a 'post-secular society' will help here remains to be seen. What will be important in any case will be to focus on what has brought our society inner peace over the last few decades: the mechanisms of democratic debate, the constitutional state, and the never-ending quest to integrate social oppositions.

10.3 On Generalization: A Variation on a Common Theme?

An international readership will be interested to know the generality of the present findings. Does the Swiss case teach us something about the fate of religion and spirituality in other contexts? We believe that this is the case.

First, the *theory of religious-secular competition* is clearly applicable to western societies in general and has been used to explain phenomena in a large number of countries and regions of the world (Gruber/Hungerman 2008; Hirschle 2010, 2011; Stolz 2009b, 2013).

Second, our *description of the 'change of the regime of religious-secular competition' in the 1960s* can be observed in a large number of other western societies, such as England, France, Germany, the US and others (McLeod 2007). The secularizing tendencies described in this book can equally be found in very similar forms in most other western countries (Bruce 2002; Chaves 2011).

Third, the *typology here presented – and its quantitative-qualitative description – seems to be surprisingly generalizable*. Our institutional, distanced and secular types can be found in the analyses of a large number of western societies in Voas (2009) (where our distanced type is called 'fuzzy fidelity'). And Siegers' (2012) 'class' of alternative spirituality in different European societies can be easily mapped on our alternative type.[1]

Reading the work of our colleagues who analyse other countries or who do international comparative work, we therefore think that what happens to religion and spirituality in current western societies comprises a large number of variations on a common theme (to use an expression by Voas 2004). What we present here on Switzerland can be seen as one of those variations. While the socio-historical context is specific, the three main contributions we make can – to a more or less important extent – be generalized to a wider context.

---

[1] It has to be noted, though, that Siegers (2012) uses a different methodology and comes up with class-sizes that differ in some important ways from the type-sizes in our study.

Appendix

A1 Method

In the following pages, we present the essential methodological steps of the research project.[1]

Mixed Methods Approach

Our study takes a *mixed methods approach* (Bergman 2008, Bryman 1988, Tashakkori and Teddlie 1998, Kuckartz 2014). The views we take on mixed methods in general are explained in Stolz (2015).[2] We make four brief points.

- First, this research takes what may be called a 'realist' philosophical stance (Maxwell 2005, Miles/Huberman 1994). According to this view, there is such a thing as a 'world out there' or 'reality', where real things happen. We cannot observe this 'reality' directly and we cannot embrace it completely, which is why we necessarily have to resort to some sort of sampling and to (more or less structured) data collection, for example, interviews, observation, document analysis etc. On the basis of the analysed data, we then make inferences, that is, we draw conclusions about what we think is true about the world. Inference can be descriptive or explanatory. It can point to facts (existence of objects, attitudes, values, subjective constructions) or causal relationships (we infer something about causal mechanisms).
- Second, on the basis of a realist worldview, the distinction between qualitative and quantitative methods and data should *not* be made on *epistemological* grounds (as is often done; see for example Mahoney/ Goertz 2006). Rather, there is only a *technical* difference in that 'quantitative and qualitative research are simply denotations of different ways of conducting social investigations and which may be conceived of as being appropriate to different kinds of research question (...)'. (Bryman 1988, p. 5). According to this position, some of the most important differences are that qualitative research uses relatively small

---

[1] The following paragraphs partly follow Stolz (2015) very closely.
[2] For a very thorough treatment of mixed methods that is close to our views see the excellent book by Kelle (2007).

N's, (mostly) text, an only nominal level of measurement, and relatively unstructured instruments, while quantitative research uses relatively large N's, (mostly) numbers, all kinds of levels of measurement (from nominal to metric), and relatively structured instruments. Often, these and other distinctions are to be seen not as implying either/or choices, but as continua. Researchers can design their instruments as more or less structured; they can vary their N etc.

- Third, being only different in a technical sense, quantitative and qualitative methods have to use the *same underlying logic of inference* (King/Keohane/Verba 1994, Goldthorpe 2000). This means rejecting the idea often heard that quantitative methods generalize to populations and qualitative methods to theory (Yin 2002: 10); or that quantitative methods want to generalize while qualitative methods do not (Lincoln/ Guba 1985). Rather, from this realist point of view, *all* methods, quantitative or qualitative, will *always* want to infer something about some state of the world. Just as a detective might use qualitative evidence such as footprints or testimonies as well as quantitative evidence such as results of DNA profiling in order to judge the probability of a certain individual being the murderer, a social scientist will use, say, qualitative interviews and census data in order to see if a certain sociological theory (e.g. rational choice theory mate-choosing) holds up in the social reality.
- Fourth, the main rationale for mixed methods is that *quantitative and qualitative methods have non-overlapping strengths and weaknesses,* leading to non-overlapping validity threats (e.g. black box problems, small N problems etc.).[3] As a result, an intelligent combination of methods and data may lead through triangulation to *better inferences,* that is, more valid descriptive and explanatory results (Kelle 2007, Onwuegbuzie/ Teddlie 2003).

Mixed Methods Design and Rationale for Mixed Methods

Mixed methods studies can take many different designs (Tashakkori and Teddlie 1998). The general design of this study can be called a *concurrent mixed methods design* (Kelle 2007, p. 285, Stolz 2015). In such a design, the quantitative and qualitative parts of the research are conducted simultaneously in order to triangulate the different data types. This is usually done when researchers feel from the outset that a mono-method study would create important black-box

---

[3]   A black box problem is given when we know the inputs and the outputs of a model – but we do not know how and why the inputs are transformed into the outputs. A small-N problem is given when the analysis of a small number of cases does not permit to make statements about the generality and/or significance of the findings.

and small-N problems (Goldthorpe 2000, Stolz 2015). The rationale for a mixed methods study in our case was that, descriptively, a rather large number of typologies of religious types have been presented (e.g. Bréchon et al. 1997; Campiche 2004: 89ff.; Dubach 2004: 129ff.; Dubach/Fuchs 2005; Krüggeler 1993: 127; Rodriguez 2005), but that these typologies have lacked credibility due to only quantitative methodology. Also, the explanation of religious change in Switzerland has in the past been conducted with too little attention to concrete historical detail and too much abstracting from the points of view and strategies of individual and collective actors. We thought that a mixed methods study might help us to obtain better descriptive and explanatory results concerning these research goals.

Quantitative Data Collection

The quantitative data were collected through FORS (Swiss Foundation for Research in Social Sciences) in 2009 as part of the MOSAiCH study.[4] The MOSAiCH study comprised two parts:

1. A questionnaire, which was carried out face-to-face (CAPI: Computer Aided Personal Interviewing). In this questionnaire, we used the ISSP (International Social Survey Program) module 2008 for religion, a scale for the alternative religiosity of our research group, and socio-demographic variables.
2. A questionnaire, which the respondents filled out at home and then sent to the Research Institute (PAPI: Paper and Pencil Interviewing). In this module, we asked diverse questions on religion that we had selected, with the selection being made according to the following criteria: (a) replication of previous studies, (b) completion of dimensions of religiosity used by ISSP, and (c) collection of indicators to test the theories explaining religiosity. The new questions were extensively pretested.

The *population* of the study consisted of all persons of 18 and over who reside in Switzerland and who speak German, French or Italian. We carried out a *stratified random sampling*. The stratification was based on seven major regions (NUTS2). The concrete survey was carried out by MIS Trend. A total of 1229 valid face-to-face interviews and 796 valid written interviews were obtained (Table A1). The *response rate* for the face-to-face survey was 46.6 per cent, and for the written survey, 30.2 per cent.

---

[4]   See Sapin, Pollien & Joye (2010) *Rapport Technique Intermédiaire 17.02.10*, Mesure et Observation Sociologique des Attitudes en Suisse 2009.

Table A1   Individuals recruited for the qualitative part of the study

	N	Response rate
Gross sample	2640	
Net sample	2572	
Face-to-face interviews (CAPI)	1229	46.6%
Written interviews (PAPI)	796	30.2%

In practice, for comparison with the qualitative data, we excluded individuals with non-Christian religions, giving us an N = 1186.

The data were *weighted* with the variable t-weight created by FORS. This weight is the combination of two separately created weights (weight and p-weight) for the face-to-face survey (CAPI) and the written interviews (PAPI) respectively.[5]

Apart from our central 2009 quantitative data, we also drew on other quantitative data sets:

- The representative data sets from the studies in 1989 and 1999 that were in part replicated in the present study (for the methodological details see Dubach/Campiche (1993), Campiche (2004)).
- A compilation of 22 representative surveys on religion in Switzerland from 1968 to 2009 in order to be able to describe trends in religious practice and belief (see Stolz/Könemann/Schneuwly Purdie/Englberger 2011).
- The National Congregation Study Switzerland that gives a representative view of all local religious groups in Switzerland as well as some information on aggregate religious practice (Stolz/Chaves/Monnot/Amiotte-Suchet 2011).
- Data compiled in a study on Reformed churches in Switzerland (Stolz/Ballif 2010).
- A representative mixed methods study on Evangelicals in Switzerland (Stolz/Favre/Gachet/Buchard 2013).
- The Swiss census data since the beginning of the 20th century (Bovay 2004).

Qualitative Data Collection

The interview partners for the qualitative interviews were selected using a random-quota procedure. People residing in Switzerland were telephoned at random and, if they met the previously selected criteria, were recruited for an interview. Since, for statistical reasons, the quantitative study could only make

---

[5]   See the internal note 'Pondération'.

statements about Christians and those with no religious affiliation, we also restricted the qualitative study to these groups. To enable us to compare selected groups, we also determined the following quotas: (1) 50 per cent from German-speaking and 50 per cent from French-speaking Switzerland;[6] (2) 50 per cent men and 50 per cent women; (3) 50 per cent 40 years of age and younger, 50 per cent older than 40; (4) 50 per cent living in urban areas, 50 per cent living in rural areas.

The research institute LINK was commissioned for the practical implementation of the study. LINK recruited respondents by telephone on the basis of the random-quota procedure already mentioned. People who agreed to a qualitative interview were written to personally by the interviewer, and then telephoned again so that an interview date could be arranged.[7] Recruitment took place in four phases between October 2007 and March 2009, which allowed us to adjust the quotas so that we could achieve the group sizes that we required. Overall, the quotas were achieved quite satisfactorily. Only with regard to age was this not the case, since there was a significant over-representation of older people (44 respondents over 40) compared with younger (29 respondents 40 and below), which was due to the subsequent refusal of younger respondents to participate in the study.

The *interview guidelines* consisted of an initial question that had nothing to do with religion and that simply served as a general impulse for the respondent to talk, 17 open-ended questions which the interviewer could use to explore issues more deeply through further questioning, and nine questions about socio-demographic characteristics. The questions were constructed in parallel to the quantitative study. At the end of the interview, all respondents were given a written questionnaire with selected questions from the quantitative questionnaire, and asked to complete this and to send it back.

In this way, 73 interviews were conducted in all three language regions of Switzerland. These interviews had a mean length of 71 minutes (ranging from 30 minutes to 131 minutes).

The interviews were *transcribed* according to specified transcription rules and read into the ATLAS.ti programme. All interviews were anonymized.

Alignment of Sampling and Data Collection

In order to permit useful triangulation, a number of measures were taken in order to *align* the qualitative and quantitative data sets. Aligning (or parallelization) is the practice of combining the sampling and the data collection such that: (a)

---

6   Once it became clear that we would increase the number of respondents, we then also included six people from Ticino in the sample.

7   Refusals could occur again at this second stage.

the resulting qualitative and quantitative data may be used to answer a common research question; and (b) triangulation permits eliminating validity problems (Stolz 2015).

1. *Central question.* We took care to ensure that the qualitative and quantitative parts of the study were closely responding to the common central question and the subquestions of the study described in the introduction of this book.
2. *Sampling.* We used a random procedure drawing on all people living in Switzerland for both the qualitative and the quantitative parts of the study. Although we introduced additional selection criteria and quotas in the qualitative part (see above), the fact that the procedures were broadly parallel for the two parts allowed for a meaningful comparison of the two samples.
3. *Operationalizing.* The questions in the standardized questionnaire for the quantitative study and in the topic guide for the qualitative study were aligned. We ensured that for each interesting theme there were available various closed indicators (quantitative) on the one hand, and at least one open central question and various probes on the other (qualitative).[8]

Comparison of the Quantitative and Qualitative Samples.

To be able to establish a relationship between the data from the quantitative survey (MOSAiCH09) and from the qualitative interviews (RuM), and to take any distortions into account, interviewees in the qualitative interviews were also presented afterwards with selected questions from the standardized survey, including all questions on socio-demographics. The items were restricted to a reasonable number with regard to religion/religiosity. 64 of the 73 respondents returned the questionnaires, which represents a response rate for the qualitative sample of 88 per cent.[9] It was therefore possible to create a common data set of the qualitative (RuM) and quantitative (MOSAiCH09) data and to compare both samples (Table A2). We find no significant differences regarding gender, age, political orientation, subjective social class, the urban/rural distinction,[10] and the number of children. With regard to the denominational affiliation of respondents, Catholics and people from Protestant Evangelical churches are more strongly represented in the qualitative sample than in the quantitative survey,

---

[8]   See the internal working paper 'Tableau comparatif des questions au qualitatif et quantitatif'.

[9]   See the internal 'Research report 7'.

[10]   Measured with a dichotomous variable. Among the interviewees in the qualitative interviews, though, there are relatively few people from large (and the largest) Swiss cities.

while the Reformed are more weakly represented in the qualitative sample than in the quantitative survey. With regard to education, people with a higher (but not university) level of education are over-represented in the qualitative sample in comparison to people with a simple apprenticeship. In terms of linguistic region, people from the French-speaking regions of Switzerland are voluntarily over-represented in our qualitative sample. The sizes of the types in our central typology are remarkably similar in the quantitative and the qualitative sample.

Keeping in mind the existing differences concerning some of the dimensions mentioned, we think that we can well make the case to treat our qualitative sample as a subsample of the larger quantitative sample which in turn is representative of the general population. In other words, there seem to be good reasons to believe that the quantitative and the qualitative sample capture the same social reality and that we can therefore triangulate the different data types in order to make better inferences about religion and spirituality in society. In Table A2, we compare several important indicators from the two samples.

Table A2 Comparison of the quantitative and qualitative sample

	Quantitative sample		Qualitative sample		p
	N	%[1]	N	%[1]	
German-speaking Switzerland	778	70.3%	31	43.1%	0.000
French-speaking Switzerland	319	28.8%	35	48.6%	
Ticino	10	0.9%	6	8.3%	
Urban	569	50.6%	36	49.3%	n.s.
Rural	556	49.4%	37	50.7%	
Male	499	44.4%	35	47.9%	
Female	626	55.6%	38	52.1%	
below 30	167	14.8%	10	13.7%	n.s.
31–40	201	17.9%	19	26.0%	
41–50	234	20.8%	13	17.8%	
51–60	202	18.0%	13	17.8%	
61 and above	321	28.5%	18	24.7%	

	Quantitative sample		Qualitative sample		p
	N	%[1]	N	%[1]	
Obligatory education	268	23.8	8	13.3%	0.000
Apprenticeship	454	40.3	12	20.0%	
Federal diploma	127	11.3	20	33.3%	
Higher education / university	277	24.6	20	33.3%	
Roman Catholic	382	34.7%	32	43.8%	0.006
Reformed	394	35.8%	18	24.7%	
Evangelical	20	1.8%	5	6.8%	
No religious affiliation	305	27.7%	18	24.7%	
Swiss	936	83.2%	65	89.9%	n.s.
Non-Swiss	189	16.8%	7	11.0%	
Total	1186	100.0%	73	100.0%	

Notes: For this table, in the quantitative sample, we have excluded individuals with non-Christian religions and weighted by t-weight. In the qualitative sample, we have used all information both from quantitative and qualitative data to create the table.

(1) We identify here valid percentages, i.e., we omit the 'missings' and 'others'.

Quantitative Data Analysis

On the quantitative side we used standard quantitative data analysis techniques, progressing from univariate to bivariate and multivariate analyses. We relied on standard quantitative techniques such as crosstabs, multiple regression, logistic regression, ANOVA, factor analysis, and two-step cluster analysis conducted with SPSS (Wonnacott/Wonnacott 1990, Fox 2008, Kim/Mueller 1978). The differences we report in the book are, if not otherwise specified, all statistically significant (at least with $p < .05$, but mostly with $p < .01$), and we have always analysed our data in multivariate (linear or logistic) regression models, 'controlling' for all kinds of background variables (these analyses have not been included in this appendix for lack of space). Our standard control variables were age, sex, education, urban-rural, nationality, language region, and confession/religion. Depending on the specific research questions, additional control or intervening variables were used. In the analyses using the typologies, we routinely analysed the data with both levels of the typology.

Qualitative Data Analysis

On the qualitative side we used both sequential techniques and transversal thematic coding (Maxwell 2005, Spickard 2007). The qualitative data analysis software used was Atlas.ti (Friese 2014). All interviews were subjected to a *sequential case-specific analysis*, i.e., we tried to answer the research questions on the basis of the interview, and we created a short summary report. The interviews were then *thematically coded*, with different codes being fixed from the beginning by the research question and the main questions of the interview guidelines (on coding see Strauss 2003(1987), Mayring 2014). Other codes emerged inductively during coding, and the coding scheme became ever more solid during the coding process. Once the coding scheme was stable, the whole material was again coded according to this final coding scheme (a selection of our most important codes is presented in Table A3). Themes were then compared across case variables, for example, sex, age, urban-rural, our 'types' etc. with the help of what is now often called 'segment matrices' (Kuckartz 2014). The analysis switched continually between case- and code-perspective in order to get a comparative sense of the processes individual actors might go through as described by Miles/Huberman (1994: 207).

Mixed Data Analysis – Triangulation

Data analysis in analytic mixed methods research takes the form of triangulation (Creswell et al. 2003, Tashakkori/Teddlie 1998, p. 41, Kelle 2001). Triangulation may be defined as a kind of data analysis that uses different types of data in order to make better – more valid – inferences to an unobserved reality (Stolz 2015). We can distinguish descriptive triangulation (that combines different data sources in order to better describe a social fact) from explanatory triangulation (that combines data sources in order to make inferences to a causal mechanism or narrative).[11] Both types of triangulation were extensively used in our study. Concretely, in our analysis, we clarified for each question whether there were significant differences between the MOSAiCH09 and the RuM samples. If this was *not* the case, then we could assume that a triangulation of the evidence of both samples was unproblematic. If there *were* significant differences, though, we tried to dig deeper into the data in order to see just why there were (apparent or real) contradictions.

---

[11] This distinction is made in analogy to descriptive and explanatory inference in King et al (1994).

The mixed data analysis was performed iteratively, back and forth between the qualitative and the quantitative data, with the theoretical principles (the assumed 'social facts' and 'social mechanisms') acting as a *tertium comparationis*. In this way the intermediate results of quantitative and qualitative data analysis influenced each other. For example, quantitative analysis had an influence on the selected final coding scheme, and qualitative analysis had an influence on quantitative model selection concerning the final typology.

Although a series of general hypotheses were established from the beginning (especially from Stolz 2009a), the formation of the central typology and the concrete forms of the social mechanisms were only established 'en route'. This way of analysing data may be called *abductive* in the sense that one tries to explain given data by assuming a certain hypothesis to be true (Peirce 2006). Abduction, as Peirce conceives it, is not an alternative but a complement to both deductive and inductive reasoning. It needs '*deduction* of the consequences of that hypothesis; and *inductive* testing of those consequences to determine how likely it is that the hypothesis is true' (Haack 2006).

Table A3   Examples of codes of the final coding scheme and central case variables

Codes		Case variables
Belief	Spir_rel	– Male
– Belief_god	– Definition_religion	– Female
– Belief_life_after_death	– Definition_spirituality	
– Belief_mode	– Religious_not_spiritual	– Urban
– Belief_inst	– Spiritual_not_religious	– Rural
– Belief_alt	– Religious_and_spiritual	
– Belief_dist	– Not_religious_not_spiritual	– under 25
– Belief_sec	– Spiritual_religious_unclear	– 25–34
	– Alternative_medicine_spir	– 35–44
		– 45–54
Practice	Suppliers	– 55–64
– Practice_ritual	– Major_church	– 65+
– Practice_prayermed	– Free_church	
– Practice_bible	– Alternative_supplier	– German

Codes		Case variables
– Practice_conversion	– Integrating_leaving_ church	– French
– Practice_mode	– Function_suppliers	– Italian
– Practice_event	– Funct_suppl_for_society	
– Practice_inst	– Funct_suppl_for_myself	– Institutional
– Practice_alt	– Funct_suppl_for_needy	– Established
– Practice_dist	– Positive_exper_w_ suppliers	– Evangelical
– Practice_sec	– Negative_exper_w_ suppliers	– Alternative
	– Differ_evangelic_ mchurch	– Esoteric
	– Goodpriests_badpriests	– Sheilaist/alt. client
Identity	– Religious_specialists	– Distanced
– Identity_personal	– Rel_spec_churches	– Distanced-inst
– Identity_collective	– Rel_spec_freechurches	– Distanced-alt
– Identity_nominal	– Rel_Spec_altsuppliers	– Distanced-sec
– Identity_negativefoil	– Supplier_Rituals	– Secular
		– Indifferent
		– Opponent

A Factor Analysis

A relatively large number of items measuring religious beliefs and practices were standardized and analysed with the help of a factor analysis (principal axis factoring with oblimin rotation; this allows factors to correlate) (Kim/Mueller 1978, Field 2000: 423ff.). This gave three well interpretable factors: institutional beliefs and practices, alternative practices, and alternative beliefs (Table A4). The factor analysis explained 37.1 per cent of the total variance. Factors 1 and 2 were not significantly correlated, factors 2 and 3 were (not surprisingly) correlated with r = −0.283.

We excluded items that did not load more than 0.5 on one of these factors (in grey in Table A4). This left us with the variables in bold black shown in Table A4 measuring the three different dimensions. These factors were then used in order to impute missing values, in order not to conduct the subsequent cluster analysis on a much reduced subsample. Individuals that had a missing value on a variable received (on this variable) the mean of the other variables of the respective factor.

Table A4   A factor analysis and selection of variables

		Factor 1	Factor 2	Factor 3
Institutional belief and practice				
rs1_01_q	Belief: There is a God that has made himself known in Jesus Christ (5-step)	0.844		
r19_01q	Belief: God is interested in every human being (5-step)	0.805		
r19_03q	Belief: Life has a meaning because God is interested in every human being (5-step)	0.755		
rs1_04_q	Belief: There is a higher power (5-step)	0.538		−0.298
r18_02q	Belief: Do you believe in heaven (4-step)	0.769		
r18_04q	Belief: Do you believe in religious miracles (4-step)	0.756		
r18_01q	Belief: Do you believe in life after death (4-step)	0.657		
r18_03q	Belief: Do you believe in hell (4-step)	0.636		
d38p4	Practice: Taking part in religious service) (9-step)	0.799		0.408
r28	Practice: Taking part in other church activities (9-step)	0.599		0.368
r27	Practice: Praying (11-step)	0.738		
r30	Visiting a holy place (5-step)	0.470		
rs3_03q	Belief: Some healers have God-given powers	0.421	0.273	
r19_04q	Life does not have a precise meaning			
r19_02q	People cannot change their lives			
Alternative practice				
rs4_01	Practice: Read a book or magazine on esotericism in last year (2-step)		0.633	
rs4_02	Practice: Ordered a horoscope or used a clairvoyant in last year (2-step)		0.520	

		Factor 1	Factor 2	Factor 3
rs4_03	Practice: Used techniques of spiritual healing or been to a healer last year (2-step)		0.602	
rs4_04	Practice: Used a method of breathing technique, relaxation or movement) (2-step)		0.647	
rs4_05	Practice: Used a method where the body is treated with hands, e.g. Reiki (2-step)		0.550	
rs4_10	Practice: Oriental meditation, e.g. Zen (2-step)		0.614	
rs4_07	Practice: Participation esoteric ritual (2-step)		0.499	
rs4_11	Practice: Other type of alternative healing (2-step)		0.492	
rs4_08	Practice: Healing with plants / biological nutrition (2-step)		0.474	
rs4_06	Practice: Healing objects (e.g. stones) (2-step)		0.472	
rs4_09	Practice: Yoga (2-step)		0.427	
rs3_02q	Belief: Some fortune tellers can really foresee the future		0.292	
Alternative beliefs				
rs1_05_q	Belief: Higher power is an eternal cycle that unites man, nature and cosmos (5-step)			−0.662
rs1_03_q	Belief: God is a cosmic energy that influences our life (5-step)			−0.623
r19_06q	Belief: Own way of connecting with God without churches/rel. services (5-step)			−0.591
rs1_06_q	Belief: There are supernat. forces in the universe influencing human beings (5-step)	0.355		−0.560
rs1_02_q	Belief: God is to me just what is positive in human beings (5-step)			−0.506
r18_07q	Belief: Supernatural powers of deceased ancestors (4-step)	0.278	0.232	−0.424
r18_05q	Belief: Reincarnation (4-step)		0.235	−0.414

		Factor 1	Factor 2	Factor 3
rs3_04q	Belief: Horoscope can affect course of future (4-step)		0.254	−0.368
r18_06q	Belief: Nirvana (4-step)		0.304	−0.359
rs3_01q	Belief: Good luck charms sometimes bring good luck (4-step)		0.254	−0.340
r19_05q	Belief : Life only has meaning if you give it yourself			−0.335

The Creation of the Typology

The typology was created in an iterative way, going back and forth between the qualitative and quantitative datasets. The case-specific qualitative analysis as well as transversal coding of religious practices and beliefs already suggested four basic types. This intuition was then confirmed in a two-step cluster analysis (SPSS Inc. 2001). We tried a lot of different ways of setting up this cluster analysis (there are many possibilities concerning the number, types, and measurement levels of variables to include). These attempts resulted generally in three 'pure types' that could be interpreted as the 'institutional', 'alternative' and 'secular' type, and one or more 'distanced' types (that we normally combined into one 'distanced' type). However, the size of the types varied often quite considerably with different methods and setups.[12]

Finally we decided on a solution that: (a) used only standardized variables; (b) used only variables that loaded relatively high on the factor analysis that preceded the cluster analysis (those in Table A4 above); and (c) placed most qualitative respondents 'correctly' (according to our knowledge of the cases).

We ran the cluster analysis on the quantitative sample only, on the combined quantitative and qualitative sample and on the qualitative sample only. The cluster analysis on the quantitative sample only gave us five clusters: one 'institutional' (17.5 per cent), one 'alternative' (13.4 per cent), one 'secular' (11.7 per cent) and two less easily interpretable that were combined into a 'distanced' type (57.4 per cent). The cluster analysis on the qual sample gave a solution with 'institutional' (19.2 per cent), 'alternative' (16.4 per cent), 'distanced' (46.6 per cent) and secular (17.8 per cent). Table A5 gives the final cluster sizes for the quantitative and qualitative samples which are not significantly different.

---

[12]   Both the dependence of cluster size and number of clusters on the method and the parameters used are general problems found with cluster analyses. See for discussions Garson (2014), Burns/Burns (2008), Mooi/Sarstedt (2011).

Table A5   Cluster size in the quantitative and qualitative sample

	Quantitative sample		Qualitative sample		p
	N	%[1]	N	%[1]	n.s.
Institutional	195	17.5%	14	19.2%	
Alternative	149	13.4%	12	16.4%	
Distanced	640	57.4%	34	46.6%	
Secular	130	11.7%	13	17.8%	
Total	1114	100.0%	73	100.0%	

Notes: (1) We identify here valid percentages, i.e., we omit the 'missings' and 'others'.

We inspected the 'fit' of the typology one respondent by one, asking if the qualitative analysis would also have classified the respondent into the respective type. The (very few) cases that did not seem to 'fit' were inspected individually, comparing their qualitative and quantitative answers and trying to explain the differences. Finally, we decided to leave these individuals in the types assigned to them by the cluster analysis. Table A6 gives the cluster membership of individuals in the qualitative sample.

To obtain a 'second level', which the qualitative analyses also suggested, we differentiated again *within* the types: 1. within the *institutional* type, people belonging to an Evangelical church were combined into the evangelical subtype, while all others constituted the established subtype; 2. within the *alternative* type, we distinguished between those who are highly committed with regard to the alternative-spiritual factor (whom we called 'esotericists') and those who are less highly committed (whom we called 'Sheilaists and alternative customers'); 3. within the *secular* type, we created two groups through a repeated cluster analysis, one of which we called 'opponents of religion', and the other, 'indifferent'; 4. within the *distanced* type, we distinguished three subtypes through a repeated cluster analysis: 'distanced-institutional', 'distanced-alternative', 'distanced-secular'.

Table A6   Allocation of the interviewees (pseudonyms) to the four religious types

Institutional (19.2%)	Barbara, 58, Reformed	Dorothée, 32, Evangelical
	Barnabé, 56, Evangelical	François, 55, Reformed
	Beat, 18, Reformed	Gisèle, 63, Roman Catholic
	Béatrice, 44, Roman Catholic	Marc-Antoine, 63, Roman Catholic
	Bénédicte, 53, Evangelical	Nathalie, 41, Roman Catholic
	Berta-Lisa, 62, Roman Catholic	Stephan, 45, Roman Catholic
	Daniele, 46, Roman Catholic	Willi, 40, Evangelical
Alternative (16.4%)	Angela, 37, Roman Catholic	Klaus, 62, no religious affiliation
	David, 34, no religious affiliation	Lucia, 44, Roman Catholic
	Diane, 37, Roman Catholic	Maude, 50, Roman Catholic
	Eliot, 44, no religious affiliation	Michel, 63, no religious affiliation
	Emily, 62, Roman Catholic	Mona, 48, no religious affiliation
	Félicia, 55, Evangelical	Simon, 50, no religious affiliation
Distanced (46.6%)	Beryl, 64, Roman Catholic	Livia, 38, Reformed
	Bettina, 40, Roman Catholic	Maia, 19, Reformed
	Blandine, 63, Roman Catholic	Marcel, 64, Reformed
	Claude, 39, Reformed	Markus, 18, no religious affiliation
	Deborah, 41, Reformed	Mélanie, 33, Roman Catholic
	Elina, 25, Roman Catholic	Mima, 59, Roman Catholic
	Fabio, 57, Roman Catholic	Nadia, 37, Reformed
	Ferdinand, 25, Reformed	Niklaus, 47, Reformed
	Ingolf, 51, Reformed	Norbert, 70, Roman Catholic
	Jelena, 21, Roman Catholic	Olga, 38, Roman Catholic
	Juan, 65, Roman Catholic	Quentin, 50, Reformed
	Julie, 24, Roman Catholic	Rebecca, 45, Roman Catholic
	Kaitline, 63, Roman Catholic	Renate, 51, Roman Catholic
	Karol, 64, Roman Catholic	Renato, 41, Roman Catholic
	Katherine, 61, Roman Catholic	Vanessa, 41, Reformed
	Laurence, 40, Roman Catholic	Victor, 55, Roman Catholic

	Léa, 36, no religious affiliation	Wilma, 47, Reformed
Secular	Cécile, 38, Reformed	Nicolas, 36, no religious affiliation
(17.8%)	Daniela, 24, Reformed	Nils, 18, no religious affiliation
	Erich, 40, no religious affiliation	Peter, 65, no religious affiliation
	Ernesto, 68, no religious affiliation	Qasim, 38, Reformed
	Gregory, 70, no religious affiliation	Siegfried, 39, no religious affiliation
	Gustave, 30, no religious affiliation	Stan, 27, no religious affiliation
	Karine, 68, no religious affiliation	

The Creation of Three Dependent Variables

In a next step we created three summated rating scales for institutional religiosity (practices and beliefs combined), alternative practices and alternative beliefs on the basis of the selection presented in Table A4. These scales use the imputed values already mentioned and were used as dependent variables in some of our analyses. The reliability of these scales computed with Cronbach's Alpha was 0.910 for institutional religiosity, 0.705 for alternative practices and 0.705 for alternative beliefs.

A2 Short Profiles of the Respondents (Qualitative Sample)

- *Angela (37, Catholic, Western Switzerland).* Hailing from Italy, Angela was born in Switzerland and grew up there. As a midwife, the natural cycle of life represents for her an important reference point. She was brought up as a Catholic (baptism, communion, confirmation). Without having officially left the church, Angela sees herself as not religious; her attitude to religion is more indifferent than critical. She draws regularly on what alternative medicine offers (reiki, acupuncture, shiatsu, homeopathy, essential oils), and also draws on these in her work.
- *Barbara (58, Reformed, German-speaking Switzerland).* Barbara is an activity therapist in a nursing home. During an extended stay in the French part of Switzerland at the age of 18, she came into contact with an Evangelical church, whose way of celebrating religious services and the close friendships that arose fascinated her. At the time of the interview, Barbara was in the process of leaving a religious home circle, which she

perceives as being too close. She consciously maintains contact with the Reformed community, even though she regrets the fact that its members tend to comprise mostly the elderly. For Barbara, the fact that her whole life is shaped by religion is more important than going to church every Sunday.

- *Barnabé (56, Evangelical, Western Switzerland).* Barnabé is a farmer. Socialized in the Reformed faith, he converted at the age of 19 and joined an Evangelical church. His relationship with God is important, and he goes to religious service every week, and prays and reads the Bible every day. He is involved in the life of his religious community and sees the evidence of God's existence in nature.

- *Beat (18, Reformed, German-speaking Switzerland).* Beat is an apprentice and lives with his parents. He grew up in a Christian family. His relationships with his parents, siblings and other relatives are close. His baptism and confirmation were family celebrations. Beat is enthusiastic about the youth group that he belongs to and enjoys participating in religious services for young people. Alphalive courses offer him little because he himself has been religious since he was a small child.

- *Béatrice (44, Catholic, Western Switzerland).* Béatrice is a teacher, single and without children. She believes in God, in life after death, and prays in the morning and in the evening. She goes to mass, especially because she sings in the church choir. But she prefers having her conversations with God in the countryside. She criticizes the church in some respects and finds it too rigid.

- *Bénédicte (53, Evangelical, Western Switzerland).* Bénédicte works as a pharmaceutical assistant. She grew up in a very religious, Plymouth-Brethren family. After marrying a Moroccan who had converted to Protestantism, Bénédicte is now divorced. They had both been baptized in the Protestant faith prior to marriage, which, for Bénédicte, was a kind of preparation for marriage. After coming under pressure from her husband's family, who wanted her to convert to Islam, Bénédicte divorced her husband. Bénédicte is religious, prays every morning and evening, and goes at irregular intervals to the evangelical community to which her parents also belong.

- *Berta-Lisa (62, Catholic, German-speaking Switzerland).* Berta-Lisa is an office worker by profession. A mental and physical breakdown at the age of 34, the close deaths of both parents, and then her husband's long and serious illness led Berta-Lisa to distance herself from the traditionally Catholic religiosity with which she had grown up and which had previously had a strong impact on her life. Personal prayer is more important to her now than it used to be. She goes to church now not because of the priest, but when she feels the need to. Berta-Lisa's husband belonged to the Reformed Church. The denominational difference was never a problem for either of them, but her parents-in-law had great difficulty with it. Berta-Lisa has no contact with esoteric things.

- *Beryl (64, Catholic, German-speaking Switzerland)*. Beryl, a former primary-school teacher, was never a great churchgoer. She 'simply didn't find the way to it'. Her parents were Catholic, but not practising. In her childhood, her parents strictly observed that no meat would be eaten on Friday. Beryl's husband belongs to the Reformed Church. She is critical of the Catholic Church, but sees that it has importance, especially in the area of rituals (baptisms, weddings and funerals). Beryl has the gift of telepathy and can predict future events. She believes in guardian angels and in being able to contact the dead.
- *Bettina (40, Catholic, German-speaking Switzerland)*. Bettina is a housewife and farmer. She was brought up in a traditionally Catholic way: baptism, communion, confirmation, church marriage. Today, she sometimes goes to church, and prays every evening with her children and her husband. She believes in 'the God of the Bible' and in life after death, but finds it difficult to describe her beliefs more precisely.
- *Blandine (63, Catholic, Western Switzerland)*. Blandine used to be a housewife and is now retired. She is very close to nature, and feels drawn to alternative medicine; she practises magnetism and believes in reincarnation. She was brought up in a 'classic' Catholic way and had her son baptized 'because that's what you do'. Blandine is now very critical of the Catholic Church, though, and describes herself as having no religious affiliation, saying: 'I believe in my own thing'.
- *Cécile (38, Reformed, Western Switzerland)*. Cécile is a tax advisor and mother of a four-year-old girl. She was baptized as a member of the Reformed Church and remembers her religious upbringing as being boring and restrictive. She refused to be confirmed, which caused conflicts with her mother continuing to this day. Cécile is a rational person and sees a lack of coherence between what religious messages say – love thy neighbour as thyself, for example – and the tensions which they trigger. Nevertheless, Cécile had her daughter baptized, saying that any affiliation – even a religious one – contributes to personal development.
- *Claude (39, Reformed, German-speaking Switzerland)*. Claude was brought up in Germany, has a doctorate in biochemistry, and works in marketing for the pharmaceutical industry. Christianity has 'never really touched' him. Claude's mother is religious to a certain extent, but his father not at all. He himself 'could quite frankly not really get started with it'. Because of skin problems and allergies, he has tried alternative medicine and has come into contact with spiritual healers. Through this, he has been told that he has a special aura and capacity for empathy.

Fascinated by the idea of being able to influence everything himself, Claude studied mental training intensively for a period of time and practised sahaja yoga. In the meantime, though, the demands of everyday life mean that Claude is no longer active in this area.

- *Daniela (24, Reformed, German-speaking Switzerland)*. Daniela is studying physics. Although baptized in a Reformed church, she underwent no formative religious socialization. Her mother seems to be interested in certain 'esoteric' practices such as feng shui and tarot. Daniela describes herself as a scientific and rational being and as an agnostic.

- *Daniele (41, Catholic, Italian-speaking Switzerland)*. Daniele, a teacher of French as a foreign language, is currently unemployed. Up until he met his wife, religion had hardly played any role in his life, although he had been brought up as a Catholic. Today, though, he regularly goes to church and has recently had himself confirmed, which was an important event for him. Daniele often reads the Bible, but at the same time believes in guardian angels and listens to his inner voice. So, for example, his grandmother has appeared to him twice in a dream and given him advice – which proves to him that there is eternal life.

- *David (34, no religious affiliation, Western Switzerland)*. David is a photographer. He is married to a Romanian woman of the Orthodox faith, and situates himself somewhere between an 'I don't believe' and an 'I don't know'. David grew up in a family in which neither religion nor religious practice played a role. He was therefore also not baptized. He uses a wide variety of alternative medicine, from homeopathy, through various forms of Chinese medicine, to magnetism.

- *Deborah (41, Reformed, German-speaking Switzerland)*. Deborah, who by profession is a commercial clerk, sees herself as being neither religious nor spiritual. She has also never really concerned herself with the issue. In her childhood, going to church and praying were 'simply part of life'. In the meantime, though, she no longer practises – and does not do so with her daughter, either. Deborah believes in God in 'some shape or form', in life after death, and in 'the good in people'. As far as the power of stones is concerned, she says: 'doesn't do anything, so it can't do any harm'. Her partner attends esoteric courses, which Deborah judges neither positively nor negatively.

- *Diane (37, Catholic, Western Switzerland)*. Diane works part-time as a family helper. She is Catholic, describes herself as religious but not practising, although she does go every day to a small chapel near her house to pray. She believes in God, but above all in her guardian angel. Diane also practises and consumes certain forms of alternative medicine – sophrology, homeopathy, reiki, and healing through angels. She believes in life after death and imagines that she will then float on a small cloud and perhaps herself become a guardian angel.

- *Dorothée (32, Evangelical, Western Switzerland)*. Baptized as a member of the Reformed Church, Dorothée later turned to an Evangelical church. She is now married to a pastor from an Evangelical church and mother of three children. She often prays with her children and her husband, goes to church on Sundays, and reads the Bible. She believes in the healing power of prayer.

- *Elina (24, Catholic, Western Switzerland)*. Elina is studying economics. She grew up in a small Ticino village and was brought up as a Catholic; she was baptized and confirmed. She describes herself today as agnostic. When she goes to church to celebrate a life-cycle ritual of someone close to her or at Christmas time, she sees this more as a concession to family tradition than as a religious act. She takes a critical and somewhat amused look at the religious traditions of the village where she grew up.

- *Eliot (44, no religious affiliation, Western Switzerland)*. Eliot studied ethnology and has obtained a diploma from the European Institute for Qi Gong. Baptized and confirmed as a member of the Reformed Church, he acknowledges his Christian heritage, but describes himself as having no religious affiliation. He has a markedly holistic view of the world and practises qi gong every day.

- *Emily (62, Catholic, German-speaking Switzerland)*. Emily used to work as a dressmaker, but is now retired. She is a true family person who often talks with her husband, her two sons and her daughters-in-law about her religious and psychotherapeutic experiences. Emily is very interested in religious questions and spiritual issues. She had a positive experience of her own Catholic upbringing. She takes part in church life, but is critical of the Catholic Church. Emily attends numerous courses on polarity therapy, meditation and yoga, from which she draws a great deal of strength and self-knowledge.

- *Erich (40, no religious affiliation, German-speaking Switzerland)*. Erich is single and works as a model maker in a company. He is not religious and officially left the Catholic Church thirteen years ago. He would not support any institution that he does not believe in. Erich says that he believes in nature and evolution, and places great value on respect and honesty.

- *Ernesto (68, no religious affiliation, Italian-speaking Switzerland)*. Ernesto is a retired mathematics teacher. He had a 'classic' Catholic upbringing, and says: 'religion is forced upon you by your family and school'. He began to distance himself from religion when he was fourteen. In the 1960s, he became interested in 'liberation theology', which aims to improve life in 'the here and now'. For Ernesto, though, the official church restricts itself to making prohibitions and to promising an eternal life in the future. Ernesto now describes himself as being totally atheist.

- *Fabio (57, Catholic, German-speaking Switzerland).* Fabio works as an independent business consultant. Although he was socialized in the Catholic faith, religion now no longer plays any role in his life. Nevertheless, he can imagine that there is a higher power – of which he has no concrete idea. He vehemently criticizes the church and the Pope, and also the church's image of the human being as a 'poor sinner'; he does not believe in life after death, but thinks that, ultimately, we can know nothing about it. He neither goes to church nor prays, but he does sometimes visit the grave of his parents in the cemetery.

- *Félicia (55, Reformed, Western Switzerland).* Félicia is a housewife. As a child, she was baptized and confirmed as a member of the Reformed Church, went to catechism, and had religious lessons at school. Her parents were religious and went to church on Sundays, but did not practise their religion consistently. Félicia describes herself as a religious and spiritual person, even though she rarely goes to church and does not quite understand the beliefs that she learned in catechism. She lives her faith in God above all in her relationship with nature – for her, 'the forest is a cathedral'.

- *Ferdinand (25, Reformed, Western Switzerland).* Ferdinand is an engineer. Although he was baptized and confirmed as a member of the Reformed Church, he does not practise and believes not in God but rather in a form of 'collective unconscious, which spans the world'. He considers himself to be a Cartesian and scientific person, and sees the 'collective unconscious' as an explanation for everything that escapes rational thought. Ferdinand seems only to have good memories of religion, but the religious only appears in his memories in the context of anecdotes.

- *François (55, Reformed, Western Switzerland).* François is a male nurse and prefers to speak of religious culture rather than of religion. Although he does not practise, he sees his Reformed culture as belonging to his identity. He believes in God and sometimes goes to church with his (Catholic) wife, whom he calls 'his religious engine'. Solidarity and respect are cardinal virtues for him, and he has also been involved for several years in helping refugees.

- *Gisèle (63, Catholic, Italian-speaking Switzerland).* Gisèle was born in German-speaking Switzerland and then moved with her husband to Ticino. She has two children and works as a cashier in a supermarket. Gisèle's father was a non-practising Catholic, while her mother lived her Reformed faith in a very committed way. Born into a bi-denominational family, Gisèle was baptized as a Catholic. She refers to herself as a religious Catholic, but rarely goes to mass and lives her faith in her own way, detached from the church.

- *Gregory (70, no religious affiliation, Western Switzerland).* Gregory is an architect and is 'preparing for retirement'. As a frequent traveller, he has been especially impressed by the cultures of South America and Asia. Gregory was baptized as a member of the Reformed Church, but experienced no particular formative religious upbringing. He was never confirmed; he started three times, but a move and the departure of a pastor foiled these attempts. He supposes that his mother was not religious and describes himself as 'having no religious affiliation', even though he has not officially left the church. He thinks that religion is a 'moral hoax' and associates it with war and promises that cannot be fulfilled.

- *Gustave (30, no religious affiliation, Western Switzerland).* Gustave, who works as an electrical and sound engineer, is striving for a career change, and has begun a course at university to become a social worker. He had (in the canton of Neuchâtel) no religious socialization at all. Instead, he grew up in an anarchist milieu and he describes himself as non-religious. For him, solidarity is a fundamental value.

- *Jelena (21, Catholic, German-speaking Switzerland).* Jelena came to Switzerland from Croatia at the age of four. She was baptized and confirmed as a Catholic, and emphasizes the decisive influence that her geographical roots have had on her religion: 'Everyone there is Catholic'. During their first few years in Switzerland, Jelena and her family regularly went to Croatian religious services. Over time, though, she lost this habit, and she now no longer really goes to mass. During her adolescence, Jelena experimented with drugs and occult sciences. She ended this phase when she became pregnant at the age of 19. She would like to marry her boyfriend in church and have her daughter baptized, but difficulties with her immigration status have so far prevented her from doing so.

- *Juan (65, Catholic, Western Switzerland).* Juan, who was born in Spain, has had to emigrate twice for political reasons, the first time from Spain to Morocco (during the Franco dictatorship), and then from Morocco to Switzerland (during the struggles for independence). Juan is Catholic, but describes himself as being not particularly religious or practising. He says that he believes in God and prays occasionally – mainly from superstition and a sense of tradition. Juan's parents, and especially his mother, practise their religion and go to church regularly. Only in Switzerland have they distanced themselves from the institution. Juan stresses the value of work and says that he has always had to struggle his way through life.

- *Julie (24, Catholic, Western Switzerland).* Julie is studying geography and the sociology of migration at university. Of Portuguese nationality, she sees religion as being a natural part of life. She was baptized and confirmed, but has gone through several phases since then. During her youth, she was an atheist. Then followed a period in which she was attracted by esotericism and Buddhism. But when her father died suddenly as a result of an accident at work, she turned to Orthodox Christianity. She practises primarily on a personal level, such as when she reads particular literature. She does not pray and does not go to church regularly, either – mainly because she does not like the hierarchical structure of the institution.

- *Kaitline (63, Catholic, Western Switzerland)*. Kaitline was socialized as a Catholic. Baptized and confirmed, she attended a state school that was run by nuns. As a teenager, she was very interested in the church and considered joining a convent. She gave up this idea later on though, and married, had two children, and then divorced several years later. She was excommunicated as a result of the divorce, which she can only accept with difficulty. Since then, she has not entered a church, but maintains her faith and practises it in her own personal way.

- *Karine (68, no religious affiliation, Western Switzerland)*. Karine, a retired teacher (French, history and geography) believes in people and in the positive power that manifests itself during an illness. For her, a positive attitude has helped her to fight the breast cancer that she was recently diagnosed with. Karine stopped believing and practising at some point in her life. She nonetheless appreciates 'typical Christian' values such as 'charity' and respect for others. Being religious is for her a way to make life more bearable.

- *Karol (64, Catholic, German-speaking Switzerland)*. Karol, who was born in Czechoslovakia, came to Switzerland at the age of 24 (during the Prague Spring). He works as a technical engineer, is married and has two daughters. Although he grew up in a communist country where 'religion was not welcome', he was baptized a Catholic and then confirmed, and went to catechism. He describes himself as a Catholic 'in his own way'. He married in church and had his daughters baptized, but does not practise and does not believe in life after death.

- *Katherine (61, Catholic, Western Switzerland)*. Katherine comes from the French nobility and had a very Catholic upbringing. At the age of seven, she was placed in a boarding school run by nuns. What she experienced there still weighs heavily on her mind: she tells of numerous (physical and mental) abuses. Despite being excommunicated as a result of her divorce, she is still very religious. Today, she describes herself as Protestant, and explains that she lives her relationship with God in a direct way. She criticizes the church, citing its rules and the dubious decisions of its representatives.

- *Klaus (62, no religious affiliation, German-speaking Switzerland)*. Klaus plays a prominent role in his community. He had a very formative Catholic upbringing. Before distancing himself strongly from the church, he had toyed with the idea of becoming a Roman Catholic friar. Despite his break with the church, Klaus identifies the holy as being the main thread in his life. He maintains a very holistic and integrated view of life, does not believe in a single God, but in an immanent divine principle which resides everywhere and in everything. He also believes in reincarnation, practises breathing techniques, family constellation, and meditation.

- *Laurence (40, Catholic, Western Switzerland).* Laurence has completed training as an accountant and has two children. She was baptized as a Catholic and went to First Communion. Because she 'lost a bit of interest in religious instruction', she did not have herself confirmed. Although she does not practise, she does admit that religion is 'still there in the back of my head'. Today, Laurence wonders about the religious socialization of her children: had they better not be baptized and attend religious classes so as to 'belong to' the Catholic community?

- *Léa (36, no religious affiliation, Italian-speaking Switzerland).* Léa works as a clerk in the chemical industry. She was baptized as a Catholic and confirmed, but found catechism to be more of a constraint. As a teenager, Léa distanced herself from the church and its dogmas. Today, she is a committed environmentalist who believes in 'the All-One' and sees humanity as one animal species among others. She is interested in astrology and homeopathy, and believes in reincarnation and destiny.

- *Livia (38, Reformed, German-speaking Switzerland).* For Livia (housewife), religion is a life attitude, and she hates 'sectarian' positions. She is convinced of the existence of a higher power, likes the Biblical stories, but she thinks that it is important to remain open and to stand in life with both feet on the ground. She appreciates the fact that she can rely on her belief (and especially on her guardian angel). Livia prays every day with her children before going to bed. She occasionally goes to church, and especially at times of major celebrations, such as at Christmas.

- *Lucia (44, Catholic, Western Switzerland).* Lucia was born in Sicily, is a trained nurse, mother of three children, and experienced a 'traditional' Catholic socialization. She believes in God, in the power of the dead, and in eternal life. She goes to church almost every Sunday and prays regularly. This gives her strength. But Lucia has also been practising reiki for eight years, and she compares the cosmic reiki energy to God.

- *Maia (19, Reformed, German-speaking Switzerland).* Maia, a pupil at secondary school, does not believe in a personal God and struggles to define what she believes in. But she believes in a presence, everywhere and in heaven ('some kind of God or whatever, whether that now is Allah or Buddha or whatever'). She needs someone or something in which she can confide her worries, and thinks that it may be helpful to pray to a God in difficult situations. Maia argues for full religious freedom – everyone should believe in what they want to. For Maia, the world is populated by (guardian) angels and the spirits of the dead. She does not believe in hell, but in heaven, and in the fact that life somehow continues there after death. She never goes to church – unless to hear a gospel concert.

- *Marc-Antoine (63, Catholic, Western Switzerland)*. Marc-Antoine is a farmer, a market gardener, and also works as an insurance adviser for other farmers. He is strongly involved in village life. For some years, he was community organizer, and now holds office as president and treasurer in the parish council. As a committed Catholic, he goes to church every Sunday and prays every morning and evening. He shares his faith, which he places at the centre of his life, with his wife.
- *Marcel (64, Reformed, Western Switzerland)*. Marcel was trained as a commercial clerk and worked as an insurance consultant. When asked about his religious socialization, he first remembers his strict mother, a 'puritanical, very strict' Protestant who is partly responsible for his aversion to religion. Today, Marcel says of himself that he is practising, but he only goes to church when he sings there with the choir or for religious festivals. His faith was shaken recently by the death of a friend.
- *Markus (18, no religious affiliation, German-speaking Switzerland)*. At the time of the interview, Markus was doing an internship in a home for the disabled. He comes from a Reformed parental home, but was himself not baptized. He could have been confirmed, but rejected the opportunity. Markus himself sees rather a connection between spirituality and his drug experiences: 'LSD is spirituality'. Religion plays no role in his life, which is characterized by problems at school and in his relationships.
- *Maude (51, Catholic, Western Switzerland)*. Maude is a school head and teacher. Originally from Holland, she was brought up as a Catholic. She believes in God, whom she compares to a 'room' and a 'cushion' which she can rest on. She also believes in life after death and often prays for others. When she prays, she also likes to light candles, but prefers to speak of meditation rather than of prayer. She does not go to religious service, but likes going into the church – as long as she can be alone there.
- *Mélanie (33, Catholic, Western Switzerland)*. Mélanie works as a web editor. She was socialized in the Catholic faith, baptized and confirmed. She believes in God and thinks that this belief was given to her by her mother. She is somewhat distanced from the church, and describes herself as being religious but not practising. She prefers to live her spirituality while walking in the mountains.
- *Michel (63, no religious affiliation, Western Switzerland)*. Michel is director of a centre for alternative medicine (phosphenism, chromatotherapy, Chinese medicine, etc.). At the age of ten, he entered a church seminary,

but left four years later. He has bad memories of this time, when he was separated from his family and had to submit to rigid rules. He distanced himself from this – as he says – narrow-minded world marked by rigid principles. Today, he orientates his world view towards Christian hermetism and Eastern philosophies. Reincarnation is for him not a belief, but an 'inner security'.

- *Mima (59, Catholic, Italian-speaking Switzerland).* Mima is a retired teacher and sees religion as a conglomeration of values and rules of behaviour from her childhood. Religion is something personal for her and prayer is an opportunity to 'retreat'. Since her husband died, Mima no longer goes to church. She believes in God and the hereafter, and compares God to a door to another world.

- *Mona (48, Catholic, German-speaking Switzerland).* Mona has no school qualifications and was running a pub at the time of the interview. Mona believes vaguely in a personal God, but more important to her is the idea of rebirth and the (healing) power of certain plants. She knows something of the shamanic practices of North American Indians. Mona grew up in Canada. Her mother was an Indian, whose spiritual knowledge Mona has in the meantime passed on to her own daughter, who is an active member of a spiritual community. Mona is an important point of reference for this community because she knows about the meaning of rituals and practices, and can provide information about them.

- *Nadia (37, Reformed, German-speaking Switzerland).* Nadia is a trained pharmaceutical assistant but at the time of the interview, she was a wife and mother. She comes from a Reformed parental home without religious practice. As a young adult, she left the church together with her parents and sister. To be able to have a church marriage, though, she later rejoined the church. For Nadia, it was important 'to belong somewhere again'. Nadia and her husband therefore also had their two children baptized, but do not practise with them. Nadia thinks that one should 'simply maintain the tradition a little'. Nadia cannot imagine that there is life after death.

- *Nathalie (41, Catholic, Western Switzerland).* Nathalie works as a coordinator in the area of catechesis. Baptized and confirmed as a Catholic, she is still very religious and has always been very committed to religion: daily prayer, participation in church service, Catholic youth work, spiritual exercises and pilgrimages. Her family had given her, she says, the image of a terrible, punitive God, and it took some time for her to free herself of that image. Today, she is firmly convinced that God is love. She also believes in life after death. Nathalie has experienced many problems when working with priests, and speaks of frustration and dissatisfaction with regard to Catholic institutions.

- *Nicolas (36, no religious affiliation, Western Switzerland)*. Nicolas is a commercial clerk. He did not have any religious socialization. He has no memory of religious lessons at school. Nicolas therefore also refers to himself as agnostic. He believes neither in God nor in life after death, and shows no interest at all in religious questions. He only goes to church when a person close to him marries or is buried. For him, that is more a convention, if not an unwelcome duty.

- *Niklaus (47, Reformed, German-speaking Switzerland)*. Niklaus is by profession a manager in construction machinery, and is married to a Catholic. Niklaus does not go often to church. He feels observed and uncomfortable when he goes to the church service of the Catholic community to which most people in the village belong. He talks with God or also with his late father when he goes out on the pond with a boat that he has leased. 'That is then my religion'. The immediate experience of nature fulfills him. The only esoteric practice that Niklaus knows and practises personally is dowsing with a hazel twig. He feels that this is a gift that a person either does or does not possess, but Niklaus does not associate this gift with religion.

- *Nils (19, no religious affiliation, Western Switzerland)*. Nils is a pupil at school and is fascinated by science fiction. He wants to study physics. He hardly had any religious socialization. He thinks that he was baptized as a Catholic, but neither he nor his parents are religious. He is interested in ecology and animal protection, and admires environmental organizations.

- *Norbert (70, Catholic, German-speaking Switzerland)*. Norbert is a carpenter by profession, but is now retired. Despite his strict Catholic upbringing, he no longer has much to do with religion, even though as a child he once wanted to become a priest himself. His feelings of guilt with regard to his paedophile tendencies led him to get in touch with pastoral counsellors.

- *Olga (38, Catholic, German-speaking Switzerland)*. Olga, a housewife and former employee at Postal Telegraph and Telephone in Switzerland, had a church marriage because it is 'part of life'. Olga used to travel much, which brought her into contact with various forms of Islam and other Asian religions – therefore, she now sees these religions with 'more openness'. Religion is less important in her own life, but it nevertheless offers 'some support'. Religion plays no special role in the upbringing of her children, although having them baptized was still important to her. Olga does not go to church, but she prays every day in the evening. Olga believes in reincarnation, which gives her a 'feeling of reassurance'. Religion is not an issue in her relationship with her husband.

- *Qasim (38, Reformed, Western Switzerland)*. Qasim is a commercial clerk. He was baptized and confirmed as a member of the Reformed

Church, but describes himself today as an atheist. As a rationalist, he has developed an interest in Buddhism, which he describes as being more a lifestyle than a faith. Qasim believes in himself and in people, and he says that he would like to believe in reincarnation. He sees alternative medicine, which he is also interested in, pragmatically – as a learned skill and not as a gift belonging to chosen people.

- *Quentin (50, Reformed, Western Switzerland).* Quentin works as an employee in public administration. After a somewhat passive socialization in the Reformed Church, Quentin now asks himself many questions about the meaning and origin of life and of the universe. He says that he is not religious, but still thinks that there is something that transcends humans. He says that he does not practise, but also that he prays at difficult moments.

- *Rebecca (45, Catholic, German-speaking Switzerland).* Rebecca works as a secretary and photographer, but also helps out on the farm. She is generally interested in other religions, as long as they do not coerce their members or are 'extremist'. Since the first communion of her son, she has been very active in the parish, one reason for which is also the fact that the pastor is a kind person. In general, she does not have a close relationship to the Catholic Church. Rebecca cannot understand the reason for the split into different denominations (Catholic and Reformed). She and her husband enjoy ecumenical services. Rebecca believes in reincarnation.

- *Renate (51, Catholic, German-speaking Switzerland).* Renate is a nurse and specializes in pregnancy support and birth preparation. Her Catholic upbringing was very 'intensive', and she went to church with her family up to four times per week. Today, Renate goes to church because she can meet friends there and she likes to sing the hymns. She cultivates a holistic view of the world; she talks about a higher power that never leaves her on her own, but that neither works exhaustively nor intervenes in happenings in the world. She does not believe in life after death or in reincarnation.

- *Renato (41, Catholic, German-speaking Switzerland).* Renato is a Spanish citizen. He studied to be an electrical engineer at college, and now works in IT service management. He sees himself as an extremely rational person, but cannot explain and understand everything rationally. Religion plays a role for Renato in extreme emotional situations, be they positive (at the birth of his children, for example) or negative (during his parents' divorce or the death of his mother-in-law). Renato is critical of the church as an institution, but would never leave it. As a Spaniard, Renato was brought up a Catholic. His parents are much more Catholic than he is, although his parents' generation was not as extreme as in the times of Franco.

- *Siegfried (39, no religious affiliation, German-speaking Switzerland).* Siegfried is an engineer, is married and has three children. He has no religious affiliation. He and his wife left the church because they did not want to have their children baptized. He describes himself as a rational and technical person, but accepts that there is the unexplained and inexplicable. Siegfried neither believes in a higher power nor in a preordained destiny.

- *Simon (50, no religious affiliation, Western Switzerland).* Simon is currently working as a make-up artist. He had, he says, a strict Catholic upbringing and spent a year in a Catholic boarding school, an experience that explains his aversion to Catholicism now. While travelling, Simon came into contact with alternative spiritualities, and is fascinated above all by the power of the stars. He married as a result of his commitment to the stars, and not to the church. Simon believes in God and in the power of the stars, which he sees as God's hands. He prays daily to harmonize his consciousness.

- *Stan (27, no religious affiliation, Western Switzerland).* Stan trades in herbs, and works as a healing practitioner. In his youth, he spent eighteen months in a Jesuit boarding school, and participated in the religious life there. But little by little he gave up going to church on Sundays, distanced himself from religion, and sees himself today as an atheist through and through. His worldview is rational. He sees alternative medicine in a scientific context, and as having nothing to do with religion.

- *Stephan (45, Catholic, German-speaking Switzerland).* Stephan is a self-employed locksmith and is active in his community (as head of the local fire brigade) and in his parish (as parish president). Religion has always played an important role in his life. He goes regularly to church and prays with his family before eating. For Stephan, the community aspect of the church is particularly important. The community gives him strength.

- *Vanessa (41, Reformed, German-speaking Switzerland).* Vanessa is a nurse. As a child, she went to Sunday school, participated regularly in religious services with her parents, and belonged to a church youth group. Vanessa says that she believes in a higher being, without being sure that this being is 'God'. She prays by singing with her children in the evening, but does not go regularly to church.

- *Victor (55, Catholic, German-speaking Switzerland).* Victor is a lawyer and an active member of the Social Democratic Party. Although he does not believe in a theologically defined God, he does not reject the belief in something abstract. He does not believe in life after death and also does not go to church, except to Einsiedeln on feast days, when there is special spiritual music. For himself, he knows only one kind of religious ritual: he takes the time every Sunday to listen at home to a Bach cantata.

- *Willi (40, Evangelical, German-speaking Switzerland).* Willi runs a small business. As a child, he went with his mother to a evangelical community, and converted at the age of 16. Today, he is a member of a community in which he also has a position of responsibility. He reads the Bible every day, prays regularly, and goes to church with his family on Sunday mornings. Willi believes in Jesus Christ, in God and in the Holy Ghost. His faith plays an important role in his life.
- *Wilma (47, Reformed, German-speaking Switzerland).* Wilma is a nurse. She had a Reformed upbringing and appreciates the freedom and autonomy which, for her, are embodied by the Reformed Church. She goes regularly to religious service, but only when she feels like it. However, she is not integrated into a particular religious community. She thinks about religion and likes exchanging views about it with others. And so she also reads a lot of books and goes to lectures. She prays and believes in a higher power, but not in life after death.

A3 Tables

Chapter 3 (Four Forms of (Un)Belief)

Table A7   Selected beliefs and forms of practice of the four types (in per cent)

	Institutional	Alternative	Distanced	Secular	Total
God is interested in every person[1]	**89.7**	45.5	40.6	2.3	45.6
Life after death[1]	**63.4**	40.6	13.6	0	56.8
Goes to church at least once a month	**71.8**	6.0	6.9	0	23.8
Prays every day	**69.3**	23.5	20.8	0	27.2
Reincarnation[1]	29.1	**51.7**	31.5	9.5	31.2
There are people who can predict the future[1]	33.5	**57.4**	28.0	18.3	32.0
Has read an esoteric book[3]	9.4	**57.5**	14.4	10.0	18.7
Has had healing through hands[3]	25.3	**66.9**	33.6	31.3	36.3

	Institutional	Alternative	Distanced	Secular	Total
God is the positive in people (neither/nor)	20.0	26.9	**39.6**	20.0	31.7
God is a cosmic energy (neither/nor)	23.8	28.1	**39.3**	8.3	30.8
Christianity is the basis of Swiss society (neither/nor)	15.0	34.1	**39.4**	32.6	33.1
Goes to church approximately once or twice a year	5.2	19.0	**30.1**	15.7	27.2
Does not believe in God	3.6	8.1	5.2	**43.7**	9.7
Churches are not important for me personally[1]	4.6	47.8	32.8	**83.4**	35.9
Never goes to church	2.1	21.8	23.6	**73.2**	15.3
Religions lead more to conflict than to peace[2]	14.9	36.5	37.0	**49.6**	34.6

Notes: (1) Per cent agreeing fully or quite; (2) Per cent agreeing fully; (3) in the last year

Table A8   Denominational identity of the types and subtypes (in per cent)

		Feels belonging to a religion or denomination	Feels being a member of parish, congregation or religious community
Institutional	Established	98.9	81.4
	Evangelical	100.0	100.0
Alternative	Esoteric	65.6	40.7
	Sheilaists and alternative customers	58.1	25.0
Distanced	Distanced-institutional	87.9	48.9
	Distanced-alternative	72.8	26.7
	Distanced-secular	64.0	19.0
Secular	Indifferent	49.3	10.9
	Opponents of religion	11.1	0.0
Total		73.1	38.4

Table A9   Sociodemography of the four types

	Institutional	Alternative	Distanced	Secular	Total
Age					
18–30	5.6	15.3	15.3	26.2	14.9
31–40	14.8	19.3	17.7	22.3	17.9
41–50	22.4	32.0	18.6	15.4	20.7
51–60	18.4	18.7	18.3	15.4	18.0
61–70	9.7	8.7	16.4	11.5	13.6
71+	29.1	6.0	13.8	9.2	14.9
Gender					
Male	41.5	32.7	45.2	56.9	44.3
Female	58.5	67.3	54.8	43.1	55.7
Marital status					
Married	70.5	46.6	59.3	50.8	58.6
Widowed	11.9	5.4	7.9	1.5	7.5
Divorced	2.6	17.6	8.0	4.6	8.0
Separated	2.1	3.4	3.2	5.4	3.3
Never married	13.0	27.0	21.6	37.7	22.7
Level of education					
Obligatory schooling	37.6	20.7	23.0	11.5	23.9
Apprenticeship	32.5	30.7	44.7	42.0	40.4
School-leaving exam	11.9	15.3	9.5	15.3	11.4
Higher education	18.0	33.3	22.8	31.3	24.4
Occupational status					
Full-time	40.2	35.8	42.2	51.3	42.0
Part-time	18.4	35.8	24.4	20.4	24.4

	Institutional	Alternative	Distanced	Secular	Total
Housewife/ househusband	12.3	8.0	4.7	2.7	6.3
Unemployed	0.6	5.1	2.6	0.9	2.4
Retired	26.8	10.9	21.9	11.5	20.2
In education	1.7	4.4	4.1	13.3	4.7
Population of place of residence					
< 999	19.0	5.3	8.9	9.2	10.2
1,000–9,999	32.8	30.7	43.5	35.4	39.0
10,000–99,999	34.4	48.0	31.0	31.5	34.0
100,000+	13.8	16.0	16.5	23.8	16.8
Denomination					
Roman Catholic	52.0	28.7	34.5	11.5	34.1
Christian Catholic	3.6	2.0	2.3	0.0	2.2
Reformed	34.2	28.0	38.4	26.2	34.9
Evangelical	9.2	1.3	0.2	0.0	1.9
No religious affiliation	1.0	40.0	24.5	62.3	26.9
Connection to a political party					
Quite or very connected	30.1	18.8	15.7	15.7	18.6
Only rather sympathizing	33.3	40.3	28.4	33.6	31.4
Not close to any party	36.5	40.9	56.0	50.8	50.0
N	195	149	640	130	1115
%	100.0	100.0	100.0	100.0	100.0

Table A10   Sociodemography of the subtypes (in per cent)

	Institutional				Distanced			Secular	
	Established			Evangelical	Distanced institutional	Distanced-alternative	Distanced-secular	Indifferent	Opponents of religion
Age									
18–30	6.2			0	12.9	17.5	15.9	25.0	25.0
31–40	14.7			16.7	16.5	18.9	17.4	25.0	16.7
41–50	22.0			27.8	16.5	23.0	16.4	21.1	5.6
51–60	18.1			16.7	17.0	18.0	19.9	14.5	22.2
61–70	8.5			22.2	15.6	12.9	20.9	10.5	11.1
71+	30.5			16.7	21.4	9.7	9.5	3.9	19.4
Gender									
Male	40.7			50.0	40.6	39.4	56.7	48.0	69.4
Female	59.3			50.0	59.4	60.6	43.3	52.0	30.6
Marital status									
Married	68.6			88.2	65.2	52.1	60.6	50.0	50.0
Widowed	12.6	6.5	5.2	5.9	10.4	5.6	7.6	0	2.8
Divorced	2.3	12.9	19.0	5.9	10.0	8.8	4.5	2.6	11.1
Separated	2.3	3.2	3.4	0	2.3	5.1	2.5	5.3	5.6
Never married	14.3	16.1	29.3	0	12.2	28.4	24.7	42.1	30.6

	Institutional				Distanced			Secular	
	Established	Evangelical			Distanced institutional	Distanced-alternative	Distanced-secular	Indifferent	Opponents of religion
Level of education									
Obligatory schooling	40.4	5.6	18.8	21.4	31.8	19.0	17.4	10.5	19.4
Apprenticeship	32.0	38.9	28.1	30.8	45.3	34.3	55.2	42.1	52.8
School-leaving exam	10.1	33.3	15.6	15.4	8.1	13.4	6.5	15.8	5.6
Higher education	17.4	22.2	37.5	32.5	14.8	33.3	20.9	31.6	22.2
Occupational status									
Full-time	40.7	35.3	25.9	38.9	34.7	38.8	53.8	46.4	61.5
Part-time	19.1	11.8	48.1	32.4	23.3	31.1	18.3	29.0	3.8
Housewife/ househusband	11.1	23.5	7.4	8.3	6.4	2.9	5.4	2.9	0
Unemployed	.6	0	11.1	3.7	2.3	3.8	1.6	1.4	0
Retired	26.5	29.4	7.4	11.1	29.2	17.7	18.3	7.2	15.4
In education	1.9	0	0	5.6	4.1	5.7	2.7	13.0	19.2

Table A10 Sociodemography of the subtypes (in per cent, continued)

	Institutional		Alternative		Distanced			Secular	
	Established	Evangelical	Esoteric	Sheilaists / alt. custom.	Distanced institutional	Distanced-alternative	Distanced-secular	Indifferent	Opponents of religion
Population of place of residence									
< 999	19.1	16.7	0	6.8	12.1	4.6	9.5	6.7	13.5
1,000–9,999	30.9	50.0	37.5	28.8	47.5	44.4	38.5	37.3	40.5
10,000–99,999	35.4	27.8	53.1	46.6	26.9	33.3	33.0	34.7	29.7
100,000+	14.6	5.6	9.4	17.8	13.5	17.6	19.0	21.3	16.2
Denomination									
Roman Catholic	57.3	0	43.8	24.6	38.8	33.3	30.8	16.0	2.8
Christian Catholic	3.9	0	0	2.5	3.1	2.3	1.5	0	0
Reformed	37.6	0	21.9	29.7	45.5	37.0	31.8	33.3	8.3
Evangelical	0	100	0	1.7	.4	0	0	0	0
No religious affiliation	1.1	0	34.4	41.5	12.1	27.3	35.8	50.7	88.9

	Institutional		Alternative		Distanced			Secular	
	Established	Evangelical	Esoteric	Sheilaists / alt. custom.	Distanced institutional	Distanced-alternative	Distanced-secular	Indifferent	Opponents of religion
Connection to a political party									
Quite or very connected	31.2	17.7	27.2	16.9	11.2	20.5	15.6	14.9	20.0
Only rather sympathizing	31.8	47.1	45.5	38.1	25.6	31.2	28.3	39.2	22.9
Not close to any party	37.0	35.3	27.3	44.9	63.2	48.4	56.1	45.9	57.1
N	177	18	32	117	224	216	200	75	36
%	100%	100%	100%	100%	100%	100%	100%	100%	100%

Table A11 Selected beliefs of the four types concerning God (in per cent)

	Institutional	Alternative	Distanced	Secular	Total
There is something like a higher power.[1]	83.3	81.5	77.1	10.5	70.8
There is a God, who has revealed himself in Jesus Christ.[1]	97.8	44.7	46.7	7.2	51.8
There is a God, who takes care of every person.[1]	89.7	45.5	40.6	2.3	45.6
I know that God really exists, and have no doubts about it.	73.1	16.2	16.1	0	24.3
God – for me, that is nothing other than what is valuable in the human being.[1]	24.8	45.7	46.6	26.6	39.9
God – for me, that is a cosmic energy that influences our lives.[1]	18.1	50.6	44.8	6.0	35.3
The higher power – that is the eternal cycle of human, nature and cosmos.[1]	34.7	66.3	67.3	26.1	55.9

	Institutional	Alternative	Distanced	Secular	Total
There are transcendental powers in the universe that influence people's lives.[1]	43.2	59.1	48.7	4.8	43.7
I do not believe in a personal God, but I do believe that there is some higher spiritual power.	2.1	40.5	37.1	22.2	29.7
I do not know whether there is a God, and I also do not think that it is possible to find this out.	0.0	12.2	9.2	27.0	10.0
I do not believe in God.	3.6	8.1	5.2	43.7	9.7

Notes: (1) Per cent agreeing completely or quite

Table A12   Selected beliefs of the four types concerning life after death (in per cent)

Do you believe	Institutional	Alternative	Distanced	Secular	Total
... that there is life after death? [1]	93.0	72.1	50.4	16.0	56.8
... that there is a heaven? [1]	93.0	51.0	44.7	3.1	49.0
... that there is a hell? [1]	65.9	22.8	21.2	3.0	26.6
... in reincarnation, i.e., that people are always born again into this world? [1]	29.1	51.7	31.5	9.5	31.2
...in nirvana? [1]	17.3	33.6	18.4	1.6	18.1

Notes: (1) Per cent 'certainly' and 'probably'

Table A13   Selected forms of practice of the four types

	Institutional	Alternative	Distanced	Secular	Total
Going to church (once a month or more)	71.8	6.0	6.9	0.0	23.8
Other churchly activity (once a month or more)	34.9	4.0	4.2	0.0	9.1
Frequency of prayer (several times a week or more)	84.8	33.6	29.4	0.0	36.2
Altar or religious object at home (e.g., crucifix)	51.3	28.2	26.1	6.9	28.5
Personal sacrifice (e.g., fasting)	27.6	15.6	8.2	2.4	12.1
Visiting holy sites (several times a year or more)	48.7	30.9	17.1	3.1	0.0
Herbal remedies[1]	37.4	69.8	42.2	33.1	44.0
Reiki/acupressure/massage[1]	25.3	66.9	33.6	31.3	36.3
Breathing techniques/relaxation/body movement[1]	21.0	68.9	25.8	25.4	30.6
Esoteric books/magazines[1]	9.4	57.5	14.4	10.0	18.7
Stones/crystals/lucky charms[1]	8.7	44.3	13.6	3.8	15.7
Yoga[1]	7.7	32.9	11.7	11.5	13.8
Other alternative methods of healing[1]	3.1	27.5	8.9	5.3	10.0
Techniques of spiritual healing/services of a healer[1]	2.6	63.8	0.0	3.1	9.3
Far Eastern meditation[1]	3.6	26.8	4.1	3.8	7.0
Fortune teller/horoscope[1]	0.5	54.1	0.0	0.0	7.3
Esoteric rituals[1]	0.5	16.0	1.4	0.8	3.1
Donated money to church or religious relief fund	76.7	27.6	29.3	4.9	35.6
Donated money to denominationally neutral relief fund	64.1	58.5	55.0	41.2	55.3

	Institutional	Alternative	Distanced	Secular	Total
Baptized	97.1	93.6	93.8	80.2	92.8
Confirmed	92.7	91.5	87.4	62.8	86.3
Religious youth group	47.1	20.8	22.3	12.8	25.6
Did you have a church marriage? (only those married)	93.2	66.7	71.0	37.8	72.2
At least one child baptized	88.5	84.6	82.0	51.9	79.6

Notes: (1) Used in the last year

Chapter 6 (Values)

Table A14   Values of the four types

	Institutional	Alternative	Distanced	Secular
Religion as a value				
Importance of religious belief	52.9	4.1	4.6	0
Sexual and gender norms				
Sex before marriage bad[1]	25.9	1.4	3.9	6.2
Married people having an affair bad[1]	90.5	61.6	73.1	77.1
Homosexuality bad[1]	48.1	14.2	18.2	19.4
Abortion bad (due to disability of child)[1]	34.2	10.0	12.2	9.8
Abortion bad (due to low income of parents)[1]	70.4	37.4	41.7	31.1
Husband should work; wife should look after the children	42.2	23.4	21.4	10.7
Duty vs. self-development				
Maintenance of order (in Switzerland)	49.5	40.5	41.5	33.6
Obedience	22.9	3.1	11.1	5.3
Thriftiness regarding money and possessions	38.6	36.1	38.3	26.6
Imagination	11.4	27.8	21.5	24.5
Independence	44.7	56.1	58.6	52.6
Strengthening participation (in Switzerland)	10.8	22.3	22.2	20.6

Values of tolerance and respect				
Tolerance and respect for fellow human beings	65.2	68.4	68.7	60.6
Selflessness (generosity)	12.8	17.3	11.9	13.7
Sense of responsibility	67.1	70.1	66.3	63.2
Good manners	52.9	46.9	63.2	62.8
Work norms under difficult conditions				
Work hard to fulfil tasks	84.6	87.2	91.6	94.8
Do one's best	94.8	96.0	93.9	87.7
Maintain level of performance	81.8	89.3	91.9	90.7
Commitment to work	35.1	21.4	31.6	24.5
Determination, endurance	27.9	34.7	35.7	43.6

Note: (1) Always or almost always bad

Chapter 7 (Major Churches, Evangelical Churches and Alternative-Spiritual Suppliers)

Table A15   Attitude towards churches and alternative-spiritual suppliers (in per cent)

	Institutional		Alternative		Distanced	Secular
	Established	Evangelical	Esoteric	Sheilaists and alt. customers		
Feels a member of a parish, congregation or religious community	81.4	100.0	40.7	25.0	32.2	5.9
Large or total trust in churches	56.8	38.9	15.6	12.2	15.8	6.5
Churches and other religious organizations have too much power	8.2	33.3	53.3	21.5	17.9	49.6
Has own access to God, without church or religious service	35.8	27.8	78.8	87.3	40.2	30.2
Churches important:						
– for me personally	84.0	77.0	28.6	13.3	24.2	6.7
– for society	79.9	66.6	28.6	43.1	52.3	34.8
– for the dis-advantaged	86.2	75.0	68.0	63.8	70.8	63.1
Has thought about leaving the church	13.4	8.3	19.0	40.6	32.6	54.2
Has thought about joining the church	0.0	0.0	0.0	0.0	2.3	0.0
Some fortune tellers can predict the future	33.0	38.9	78.2	52.2	28.0	18.3
Some faith healers have supernatural powers	58.8	61.2	100.0	62.3	40.1	14.0

Chapter 8 (The Perception and Evaluation of Religion(s))

Table A16   Attitudes towards religion(s) (in per cent)

	Institutional		Alternative		Distanced	Secular	
	Established	Evangeli-cal	Esoteric	Sheilaists and alt. customers		Indifferent	Opponents of religion
Religions lead more to conflict than to peace							
… agree fully	14.1	22.2	43.8	34.8	37.0	37.8	75.0
… tend to agree	59.3	61.1	37.5	46.1	51.8	41.9	25.0
Strongly religious people are often too intolerant towards others							
… agree fully	15.5	17.6	43.8	36.8	32.0	41.3	63.9
…tend to agree	56.3	58.8	43.8	39.3	53.1	45.3	22.2

	Institutional		Alternative		Distanced		Secular
All religions in Switzerland should have the same rights							
... agree fully	10.7	27.8	15.6	13.9	16.2	24.3	16.7
... tend to agree	43.5	38.9	37.5	43.5	46.3	52.7	27.8
We must respect all religions							
... agree fully	32.6	29.4	21.9	31.6	25.7	37.3	42.9
... tend to agree	54.5	52.9	56.3	52.1	59.6	56.0	25.7
... The truth content of each religion is very low	2.3	13.3	9.4	34.3	12.9	14.7	97.2
... There are basic truths in many religions	83.2	66.7	90.6	64.8	84.1	82.7	2.8
... There is truth in only one religion	14.5	20.0	0.0	0.9	3.1	2.7	0

Table A17 What is your personal attitude towards members of the following religious groups? (in per cent)

	Institutional		Alternative		Distanced	Secular	
	Established	Evangelical	Esoteric	Sheilaists and alt. customers		Indifferent	Opponents of religion
Christians							
... very positive	47.5	50.0	25.0	17.1	20.8	10.7	2.8
... quite positive	47.5	38.9	59.4	37.6	46.9	41.3	8.3
... neither/nor	4.5	11.1	15.6	43.6	29.7	37.3	75.0
... quite negative	0.6	0.0	0.0	0.0	2.2	10.7	11.1
... very negative	0.0	0.0	0.0	0.9	0.3	0.0	2.8
Muslims							
... very/quite positive	32.7	22.2	43.8	25.9	29.2	21.1	2.8
... neither/nor	48.5	38.9	46.9	44.8	41.5	67.1	55.6
... very/quite negative	18.7	38.9	9.4	29.3	29.2	11.8	41.7
Hindus							
... very/quite positive	35.6	29.4	54.5	41.6	36.2	45.3	22.2

	Institutional		Alternative		Distanced	Secular	
… neither/nor	55.8	41.2	45.5	51.3	53.0	50.7	69.4
… very/quite negative	8.6	29.4	0.0	7.1	10.8	4.0	8.3
Buddhists							
… very/quite positive	38.0	11.8	74.2	58.0	46.8	58.7	27.8
… neither/nor	51.8	70.6	25.8	34.8	45.5	38.7	66.7
… very/quite negative	10.2	17.6	0.0	7.1	7.8	2.7	5.6
Jews							
… very/quite positive	43.0	64.7	43.8	33.3	31.8	44.0	5.6
… neither/nor	47.1	29.4	53.1	54.4	54.0	45.3	80.6
… very/quite negative	9.9	5.9	3.1	12.3	14.2	10.7	13.9
Atheists or the non-religious							
… very/quite positive	28.2	11.8	45.5	36.8	36.5	53.9	36.1
… neither/nor	51.2	70.6	51.5	58.1	56.5	40.8	61.1
… very/quite negative	20.6	17.6	3.0	5.1	7.1	5.3	2.8

Chapter 9 (The Change in Religiosity, Spirituality and Secularity)

Table A18   Frequency of churchgoing in Switzerland 1968–2009 in per cent
              (representative   surveys)

		year	weekly	1 – 2 times per month	max. 1 – 2 times per year
GP_68	Levy/Keller[1]	1968	30		
AP_75	Attitudes politiques 1975	1976	15	26	65.6
CES_88	Einstellungen und Praxis im Bereich der Religion in der Schweiz	1988	19	15.3	65.6
EVS_89	European Values Survey	1989	21.8	16.5	57.5
PI_91	Les Suisses et leur société: positionnements et images	1991	15.8	16.1	65.4
MZF_95	Familienzensus	1995	15.1		83.4
EVS_96	European Values Survey	1996	11.8	12.3	75.5
ISSP_98 RLS_98	International Social Survey Program	1999	10.8	12.2	75
SHP_99	Swiss Household Panel	1999	12.5	15.4	72.1
CID_00	Citizenship, Involvement, Democracy – CID	2000	12.1	12	75.7
ISSP_00	International Social Survey Program	2000	8.2	13.5	75
ISSP_01	International Social Survey Program	2002	8.6	12	75.5
ESS_02	European Social Survey	2002	10.9	12.4	76.6
EBCH_02	Eurobarometer	2003	8.7	12.5	78.5
EBCH_03	Eurobarometer	2003	8.8	13.4	77.7
ESS_04	European Social Survey	2004	13.1	13.1	73.6
SHP_04	Swiss Household Panel	2004	10.2	11.9	78
WVS_05	World Value Survey	2007	12	12.3	75.4
RM_07	Religionsmonitor	2007	11	12	76.3
ISSP/ RuM_09	International Social Survey Program 2009	2009	6.3	8.7	81.8

Notes: (1) Levy, René / Keller, Felix, *Les Suisses et leur société au début des années 1960 et 1990* (SIDOS Bericht 6418), 5

Source: Internal papers Englberger (2009) 'Forschungsbericht 1', 'Forschungsbericht 3'.

Table A19   Frequency of prayer in Switzerland 1988–2009 in per cent
(representative surveys)

		year	daily	less often than daily	never
CES_88	Einstellungen und Praxis im Bereich der Religion in der Schweiz	1988	41	41.4	17.6
RLS_98	Religion et lien social	1999	38.8	48.6	12.6[1]
ISSP_98	International Social Survey Program	1999	23.4	60.3	16.3
SHP_99	Swiss Household Panel	1999	33.1	38.5	28.4
ESS_02	European Social Survey	2002	28.5	45.6	25.9
ESS_04	European Social Survey	2004	29.3	41.9	28.9
RM_07	Religionsmonitor	2007	28.9	46.9	24.4
ISSP/ RuM_09	International Social Survey Program 2009	2009	27.9	47.3	24.8

Notes: (1) (never and no answer)

Source: Internal papers Englberger (2009) 'Forschungsbericht 1', 'Forschungsbericht 3'

Table A20 Change of belief in God and age (2009)

	Age										p
	18–30	31–40	Total N	41–50	51–60	61–70	71+	Total %	Total N		
I don't believe in God now and I never have	26.0	17.2	147	16.7	10.8	16.2	3.2	14.9	147		***
I don't believe in God now, but I used to	21.2	20.1	199	19.1	18.2	23.8	19.7	20.2	199		
I believe in God now, but I didn't use to	15.1	9.2	103	10.8	13.1	7.7	6.4	10.4	103		
I believe in God now and I always have	37.7	53.4	538	53.4	58.0	52.3	70.7	54.5	538		
Total	100	100	987	100	100	100	100	100	987		

Notes: p denotes the significance level of a nominal by nominal cross-tabulation. n.s. = not significant; * = significant on the 0.05 level; ** = significant on the 0.01 level; *** = significant on the 0.001 level.

Table A21   Change of belief in God and type (2009)

	Type				Total %	N	p
	Insti-tutional	Alter-native	Dis-tanced	Secular			
I don't believe in God now and I never have	0.0	13.0	13.0	46.8	14.7	145	***
I don't believe in God now, but I used to	0.5	19.8	21.9	44.4	20.3	200	
I believe in God now, but I didn't use to	9.9	14.5	11.3	3.2	10.5	103	
I believe in God now and I always have	89.5	52.7	53.8	5.6	54.5	537	
Total	100	100	100	100	100	985	

Notes: p denotes the significance level of a nominal by nominal cross-tabulation. n.s. = not significant; * = significant on the 0.05 level; ** = significant on the 0.01 level; *** = significant on the 0.001 level.

Table A22 Been thinking of leaving church / been thinking of joining a church, age and church membership (2009)

	Age								
	18–30	31–40	Total N	51–60	61–70	71+	Total %	Total N	p
Only church members: **I have been thinking of leaving the church**									
– yes	40.7	28.0	137	25.8	29.1	20.0	28.4	137	n.s.
– no	59.3	72.0	346	74.2	70.9	80.0	71.6	346	
Total	100	100	483	100	100	100	100	483	
Only church non-members **I have been thinking of joining a church**									
– yes	0.0	0.0	2	2.9	0.0	0.0	1.1	2	n.s.
– no	100.0	100.0	175	97.1	100.0	100.0	98.9	175	
Total	100	100	177	100	100	100	100	177	

Notes: p are based on simple correlation coefficients. n.s. = not significant; * = significant on the 0.05 level; ** = significant on the 0.01 level; *** = significant on the 0.001 level.

Table A23   Institutional religiosity beliefs 1988–1998–2009

	1988	1998	2009	Diff	p
There is a god who has made himself known in Jesus Christ[1]	76.8	65.1	51.9	−24.9	***
There is a god who is interested in every person individually		46.2	45.4	−0.8	n.s.
Importance of religion for me personally[2],[3]	50.4	44.2	35.1	−15.3	***
Importance of church for me personally[2],[3]		34.5	32.1	−2.3	n.s.
Self-description as religious		38.8	40.0	−1.2	n.s.
Feels as a member of the parish	53.7	41.5	38.4	−15.4	***

Notes: Difference denotes the difference between the last and the first percentage in the time series.

p denotes the significance level of a nominal by nominal cross-tabulation. n.s. = not significant; * = significant on the .05 level; ** = significant on the .01 level; *** = significant on the .001 level.

(1) completely agree and rather agree combined.

(2) categories 7,6,5 combined.

(3) Item wording has changed from importance for me personally of 1988: 'religion and churches'; 1998: 'churches'; 2009: 'churches'.

Sources: Data from CES_88, ISSP_98, RLS_98

Table A24   Alternative spirituality beliefs and practices 1988–1998–2009

	1988	1998	2009	Diff.	p
Alternative spirituality beliefs					
A person's star sign at birth, or horoscope, can affect the course of their future[1]		47.6	40.4	– 7.1	**
Some faith healers do have God-given healing powers[1]		47.3	44.0	– 3.3	n.s.
Good luck charms sometimes do bring good luck.[1]		41.1	40.3	– 0.8	n.s.
Some fortune tellers really can foresee the future[1]		41	33	– 14.9	***
The higher power is the eternal cycle of man, nature and cosmos[1]	53.8	64.2	54.5	0.7	***
Reincarnation [1],[3]	32.9	33.2	31.4	– 1.6	n.s.
Alternative spirituality practices					
Therapy using breathing technique, relaxation or movement[2]	24.1		30.9	6.8	***
Yoga[2]	18.4		13.6	– 4.6	**
Techniques of spiritual healing or using a healer[2]	15.8		9.3	– 6.4	***
Astrology, fortune telling[2]	15.4		7.3	– 8.1	***
Healing influence of stones or other objects[2]	6.9		15.7	8.8	***
Oriental type meditation, e.g. Zen	5.6	19.2	7.1	1.5	***

Notes: Difference denotes the difference between the last and the first percentage in the time series.

p denotes the significance level of a nominal by nominal cross-tabulation. n.s. = not significant; * = significant on the 0.05 level; ** = significant on the 0.01 level; *** = significant on the 0.001 level.

(1) Item responses 'Definitely true' and 'Probably true' combined.

(2) The 1988 item response is 'I use this regularly/I have already used this and there is something to it'; the 2009 item response is 'I have used this during the last year'.

(3) The wording is slightly different: in 1988: 'There is a reincarnation of the soul in a different life' and in 1998/2009: 'Reincarnation – being reborn in this life again and again'.

Sources: Data from CES_88, ISSP_98, RLS_98

Table A25   Correlates of importance of religion in various surveys in Switzerland

	Data set (year)						
Importance of religion	EVS (1989)	EVS (1996)	CID (2000)	EES (2002)	WVS (2005)	RM (2007	RuM (2009)
Gender	***	***	***	***	***	***	**
Age	***	***	**	**	***	**	***
Political orientation				**			**
Social status					*		***
Education	n.s.	***	**	**	n.s.		*
Nationality				n.s.			n.s.
Language region[1]	***	**			*	*	***
Urban-rural	***	*		***		*	**
Income	***	**	**	**	**		*

Notes: Results are based on simple correlation coefficients. n.s. = not significant; * = ($p <$ 0.05); ** = ($p < 0.01$); *** = ($p < 0.001$).

Results are stable across surveys: women, older people, right-wingers, people with lower social status, lower education, living in rural areas, and with lower income give on average more importance to religion.

(1) Results for language region are not consistent; sometimes the German-speaking, sometimes the French-speaking group appear to give more importance to religion.

Source: Internal papers Englberger (2009) 'Forschungsbericht 8'

Table A26   Correlates of self-description as religious in various surveys
in Switzerland

	Data set (year)								
Self-description as religious	AP 1975	WWO 1976	VS 1988	EVS 1989	ISSP 1998	ESS 2002	ESS 2004	WVS 2005	RuM 2009
Gender	***	***	***	***	**	***	***	**	**
Age	**	**	***	***	**	**	**	**	**
Political orientation	**				n.s.	**	n.s.		**
Social status	n.s.				n.s.			n.s.	**
Education	**	**	**	**	*	*	**		**
Nationality						n.s.	n.s.		n.s.
Language region[1]	***	*	***	***	***			*	n.s.
Urban-rural	**	**	*	*		***	*		**
Income	**		**	**	*	**	**	n.s.	**

Notes: Results are based on simple correlation coefficients. n.s. = not significant; * = (p < 0.05); ** = (p < 0.01); *** = (p < 0.001).

Results are stable across surveys: women, older people, right-wingers, people with lower social status, lower education, living in rural areas, and with lower income describe themselves as more religious.

(1) Results for language region are not consistent; sometimes the German-speaking, sometimes the French-speaking group appears to be more religious.

Source: Internal papers Englberger (2009) 'Forschungsbericht 8'

Table A27   The reproduction of the types and milieus in the qualitative and quantitative sample

Type parental background[1]	Type respondents						
Qualitative-sample	Institutional	Alternative	Distanced	Secular	Total %	N	p
institutional	31.6	21.1	42.1	5.3	100%	38	***
alternative	0.0	100.0	0.0	0.0	100%	1	
distanced	7.1	7.1	60.7	25.0	100%	28	
secular	0.0	16.7	16.7	66.7	100%	6	
Total	14	12	34	13	100%	73	
Quantitative-sample[2]	Institutional	Alternative	Distanced	Secular	Total %	N	p
institutional	28.3	14.1	52.2	5.1	100%	505	***
distanced	9.4	12.0	63.1	15.5	100%	393	
secular	5.6	16.1	57.2	21.1	100%	180	
Total	190	147	616	125	100%	1078	

Notes: (1) Parental background was operationalized: (a) in the qual sample on the basis of all information we had on the parents of respondents both from quan and qual answers; (b) in the quan sample on the basis of frequency of church-going of the mother when the respondent was 12 years old. If the mother went to church 2–3 times a month or more often -> institutional. If she went less often that 2–3 times a month, but more often than once a year -> distanced. If she went never or once a year -> secular. The operationalization of parental type for our quantitative sample is clearly less satisfactory than for our qualitative sample where we can judge the parental type on the basis of a much larger amount of indicators. The secular drift also shows up more clearly in our qualitative sample.

(2) There were no items that could have differentiated 'alternative' parents.

Table A28   Religiosity across the generations, 1989, 1999, 2009 (in per cent)

		Age						
		under 25	25–34	35–44	45–54	55–64	65+	p
Formal membership in a religion	1989	97.5	93.2	94.5	94.7	94.5	100.0	n.s.
	1999	88.0	93.8	89.4	88.4	91.6	94.7	*
	2009	57.1	70.8	68.2	75.5	71.7	82.8	***
Subjective membership in parish	1989	37.7	43.3	58.5	62.4	61.3	72.9	***
	1999	25.4	35.9	40.0	37.5	55.4	66.2	***
	2009	17.3	27.2	33.3	45.0	35.2	52.9	***
Frequency rel. service (monthly +)	1989	29.6	26.0	31.3	36.2	46.6	49.5	***
	1999	12.4	20.3	23.4	20.8	36.6	42.1	***
	2009	6.5	9.4	16.1	13.7	16.6	30.5	***
Subjective importance of religion[1]	1989	24.0	25.3	27.9	38.2	47.5	52.8	***
	1999	15.0	23.9	23.3	26.8	42.2	46.1	***
	2009	20.4	16.4	20.0	22.6	20.3	31.6	***

Notes: p are based on simple correlation coefficients. n.s. = not significant; * = significant on the 0.05 level; ** = significant on the 0.01 level; *** = significant on the 0.001 level.

(1) A seven-step scale was used. Here, we combine category 7 and 6 into a 'very important' percentage.

Table A29　Multiple linear regressions on frequency of church-going in 1989, 1999, 2009 (beta-coefficients)

	1989		1999		2009	
	Model 1	Model 2	Model 1	Model 2	Model 1	Model 2
Sex	0.084**	0.080**	0.40	0.050*	0.081**	0.085**
Age	0.188***	0.128***	0.191***	0.149***	0.166***	0.129***
Education	–0.044	–0.042	–0.019	–0.015	0.006	0.005
Urban-rural	–0.130***	–0.100***	–0.119***	–0.094***	–0.033	–0.020
Nationality:						
– Swiss	0.028	0.027	0.011	0.001	0.029	0.043
– Foreigner (refer.)	–	–	–	–	–	–
Language region:						
– German	0.059	0.066	0.033	–0.011	–0.040	–0.074
– French	0.048	0.079	0.014	–0.020	–0.055	–0.078
– Italian (refer.)	–	–	–	–	–	–
Confession:						
– Reformed	–0.184*	–0.074	–0.215**	–0.173**	–0.133*	–0.060
– Roman Catholic	0.096	0.074	–0.036	–0.104	0.030	–0.115
– Other Protestant	0.202***	0.209***	0.203	0.183***	0.131***	0.121***
– No religion	–0.203***	–0.162***	–0.276***	–0.250***	–0.438***	–0.409***

	1989		1999		2009	
- Other religion (refer.)	–			–	–	–
Church-going mother[1]		0.293***		0.253***		0.250***
R²	21.5%	28.8%	17.6%	22.6%	26.3%	32.0%
N	1279	1212	1555	1486	1200	1151

Notes: n.s. = not significant; * = significant on the 0.05 level; ** = significant on the 0.01 level; *** = significant on the 0.001 level.

(1) When respondent was 12 years old.

Table A30   Multiple linear regressions on importance of religion in 1989, 1999, 2009 (beta-coefficients)

	1989		1999		2009	
Sex	0.087***	0.101***	0.130***	0.140***	0.097**	0.098**
Age	0.218**	0.174***	0.186***	0.145***	0.094**	0.064*
Education	−0.103***	−0.111***	−0.083**	−0.080**	0.035	0.041
Urban-rural	−0.132***	−0.118***	−0.075**	−0.053*	−0.044	−0.038
Nationality:						
– Swiss	−0.015	−0.029	−0.094***	−0.099**	−0.028	−0.025
– Foreigner (reference)	–	–	–	–	–	–
Language region:						
– German	0.045	0.032	0.010	−0.031	−0.105	−0.111
– French	0.017	0.007	−0.061	−0.093**	−0.181**	−0.170**
– Italian (reference)	–	–	–	–	–	–
Confession:						
– Reformed	−0.100	−0.024	−0.163*	−0.115	−0.086	−0.057
– Roman Catholic	−0.008	−0.029	−0.041	−0.089	−0.046	−0.100
– Other Protestant	0.099**	0.101***	0.111***	0.094**	0.124**	0.124**
– No religion	−0.291***	−0.259***	−0.250***	−0.217***	−0.499***	−0.464***
– Other Religion (refer.)	–	–	–	–	–	
Church-going by mother when respondent was 12[1]		0.224***		0.232***		0.191***
R^2	19.3%	24.1%	15.5%	19.7%	28.5%	31.3%
N	1283	1216	1554	1485	763	736

Notes: n.s. = not significant; * = significant on the .05 level; ** = significant on the 0.01 level; *** = significant on the 0.001 level. (1) When respondent was 12 years old

Table A31   Multiple linear regressions on alternative beliefs and practices in 2009

	Alternative practices		Alternative beliefs	
	Model 1	Model 2	Model 1	Model 2
Sex	0.244***	0.247***	0.062*	0.064*
Age	−0.069*	−0.070*	0.096**	0.090**
Education	0.187***	0.185***	−0.060	−0.065*
Urban-rural	0.033	0.028	−0.031	−0.028
Nationality:				
– Swiss	0.041	0.041	−0.079*	−0.082
– Foreigner (reference)	–	–	–	–
Language region:				
– German	0.103	0.097	−0.043	−0.062
– French	0.134*	0.121	0.027	0.009
– Italian (reference)	–	–	–	–
Confession:				
– Reformed	−0.160	−0.144	−0.146	−0.136
– Roman Catholic	−0.156	−0.161	−0.167	−0.157
– Other Protestant	−0.046	−0.047	−0.171***	−0.171***
– No religion	−0.014	0.002	−0.147	−0.147
– Other Religion (ref.)	–	–	–	–
Church-going by mother when respondent was 12		0.030		−0.019
R²	12.3%	12.1%	3.7%	3.7%
N	1128	1083	1118	1075

Notes: n.s. = not significant; * = significant on the 0.05 level; ** = significant on the 0.01 level; *** = significant on the 0.001 level.

Table A32   A comparison of the typologies of 1988 and 2009

1988[1]		2008			
Exclusive Christians	7%	Institutional	17.5%	Evangelical	1.6%
Generally religious Christians	25%			Established	16.2%
New-religious	12%	Alternative	13.4%	Estoteric	2.9%
				Sheilaists/ alt. customers	10.7%
Religious Humanists	51%	Distanced	57.4%	Distanced-institutional	20.4%
				Distanced-alternative	19.7%
				Distanced-secular	18.3%
A-religious	4%	Secular	11.7%	Indifferent	6.8%
				Opponents of religion	3.3%

Notes: (1) The typology of 1988 can be found in Krüggeler (1993: 127)

References

Abbott, A. (1980). Religion, Psychiatry, and the Problems of Everyday Life. *Sociological Analysis, 41*, 164–71.

Abbott, A. (1988). *The System of Professions. An Essay on the Division of Expert Labor.* Chicago: The University of Chicago Press.

Adorno, T. W. et al. (1989). *Der Positivismusstreit in der deutschen Soziologie (13. Auflage).* Darmstadt: Luchterhand.

Aerne, P. (2006). *Religiöse Sozialisten, Jungreformierte und Feldprediger. Konfrontationen im Schweizer Protestantismus 1920–1950.* Zürich: Chronos.

Alba, R. (1999). Immigration and the American Realities of Assimilation and Multiculturalism. *Sociological Forum, 14*(1), 3–25.

Albert, H. (1984). Wertfreiheit als methodisches Prinzip. Zur Frage der Notwendigkeit einer normativen Sozialwissenschaft. In E. Topitsch (ed.), *Logik der Sozialwissenschaften* (pp. 196–228). Königstein: Athenäum.

Allen, C. (2001). Islamophobia in the Media since September 11th. Manuscript.

Altermatt, U. (1981). Schweizer Katholizismus von 1945 bis zur Gegenwart: Abschied vom 'katholischen Milieu'. *Politische Studien, 32*, 53–62.

Altermatt, U. (1988). Die Stimmungslage im politischen Katholizismus der Schweiz von 1945: 'Wir lassen uns nicht ausmanövrieren'. In V. Conzemius, M. Greschat & H. Kocher (eds), *Die Zeit nach 1945 als Thema kirchlicher Zeitgeschichte. Referate der internationalen Tagung in Hünigen/Bern (Schweiz) 1985* (pp. 72–96). Göttingen: Vandenhoeck & Ruprecht.

Altermatt, U. (1989). *Katholizismus und Moderne.* Zürich: Benziger Verlag.

Altermatt, U. (2009). *Konfession, Nation und Rom. Metamorphosen im schweizerischen und europäischen Katholizismus des 19. und 20. Jahrhunderts.* Frauenfeld: Huber.

Altglas V. (2011) The Challenges of Universalizing Religions. The Kabbalah Centre in France and Britain. *Nova Religio, 15*, 22–43.

Altglas V. (2014) *From Yoga to Kabbalah. Religious Exoticism and the Logics of Bricolage*, Oxford: Oxford University Press.

Barbagli, M., Dalla Zuanna, G., & Garelli, F. (2010). *La Sessualità Degli Italiani.* Bologna: Il Mulino.

Barro, R. J., & McCleary, R. M. (2003). International Determinants of Religiosity. *NBER Working Paper No. 10147.*

Barth, F. (1969). *Ethnic Groups and Boundaries. The Social Organization of Culture Difference. The Social Organization of Culture Difference*, Long Grove, IL: Waveland Press.

Barth, R. (1981). *Protestantismus, Soziale Frage und Sozialismus im Kanton Zürich 1830–1914.* Zürich: TVZ.

Basset, J.-C. (1996). *Le Dialogue Interreligieux. Histoire et Avenir.* Paris: Les Editions du Cerf.

Bastian, J.-P. (2007). The New Religious Economy of Latin America. In J. Stolz (ed.), *Salvation Goods and Religious Markets. Theory and Applications* (pp. 171–92). Bern: Peter Lang.

Baumann, M., & Behloul, S.-M. (2005). Religiöser Pluralismus. Empirische Studien und Analytische Perspektiven. Luzern: Transkript-Verlag.

Baumann, M., & Stolz, J. (2007a). Eine Schweiz – viele Religionen. Risiken und Chancen des Zusammenlebens. Bielefeld: Transcript.

Baumann, M., & Stolz, J. (2007b). Vielfalt der Religionen – Risiken und Chancen des Zusammenlebens. In M. Baumann & J. Stolz (eds), Eine Schweiz – viele Religionen. Risiken und Chancen des Zusammenlebens (pp. 344–78). Bielefeld: Transcript.

Becci, I. (2001). Entre pluralisation et régulation du champ religieux: Premiers pas vers une approche en termes de médiations pour la Suisse. *Social Compass,* *48*(1), 95–112.

Beck, U. (1983). Jenseits von Stand und Klasse? Soziale Ungleichheiten, gesellschaftliche Individualisierungsprozesse und die Entstehung neuer sozialer Formationen und Identitäten. In R. Kreckel (ed.), *Soziale Ungleichheiten. Soziale Welt, Sonderband 2* (pp. 35–74). Göttingen: Vandenhock & Ruprecht.

Beck, U. (1986). *Risikogesellschaft. Auf dem Weg in eine andere Moderne.* Frankfurt am Main: Suhrkamp Verlag.

Beckford, J. A. (2000). Start together and finish together: Shifts in the premises and paradigms underlying the scientific study of religion. *Journal for the Scientific Study of Religion, 39*(4), 481–95.

Beckford, J. A. (2010). The return of public religion? A critical assessment of a popular claim. *Nordic Journal of Religion and Society, 23*(2), 121–136.

Behloul, S.-M. (2007). The society is watching you! Islam-Diskurs in der schweiz und die konstruktion einer öffentlichen religion. *Theologische Berichte, 30*, 276–317.

Behloul, S.-M., & Lathion, S. (2007). Muslime und Islam in der Schweiz: viele Gesichter einer Weltreligion. In M. Baumann & J. Stolz (eds), *Eine Schweiz – viele Religionen. Risiken und Chancen des Zusammenlebens* (pp. 193–207). Bielefeld: Transcript.

Beitz, C. R. (2009). *The Idea of Human Rights.* Oxford: Oxford University Press.

Bellah, R. N. et al. (1985). *Habits of the Heart: Individualism and Commitment in American Life.* California: University of California Press.

Bellamy, J., Black, A., Castle, K., Hughes, P., & Kaldor, P. (2002). *Why People Don't Go To Church.* Adelaide: Openbook Publishers.

Benthaus-Apel, F. (1998). Religion und Lebensstil: zur Analyse pluraler Religionsformen aus soziologischer Sicht. In K. Fechtner, M. Haspel, K.-F. Daiber, S. Keil & U. Schwab (eds), *Religion in der Lebenswelt der Moderne* (pp. 102–22). Köln: Kohlhammer.

Benthaus-Apel, F. (2006). Lebensstilspezifische Zugänge zur Kirchenmitgliedschaft. In W. Huber, J. Friedrich & P. Steinacker (eds), *Kirche in der Vielfalt der Lebensbezüge. Die vierte EKD-Erhebung über Kirchenmitgliedschaft* (pp. 203–44). Gütersloh: Gütersloher Verlagshaus.

Berger, P. L. (1965). Ein Marktmodell zur Analyse Ökumenischer Prozesse. In J. Matthes (ed.), *Internationales Jahrbuch für Religionssoziologie* (pp. 235–49). Köln: Opladen.

Berger, P. L. (1980). *Der Zwang zur Häresie. Religion in der Pluralistischen Gesellschaft* (#, Trans.). Frankfurt am Main: S. Fischer Verlag GmbH.

Berger, P. L. (1982 (1980)). *Die Gesellschaftliche Konstruktion der Wirklichkeit. Eine Theorie der Wissenssoziologie*. Frankfurt am Main: Fischer Taschenbuch Verlag.

Berger, P. L. (1988 (1973)). *Zur Dialektik von Religion und Gesellschaft. Elemente einer soziologischen Theorie*. Frankfurt am Main: Fischer Taschenbuch Verlag.

Berger, P. L. (1990 (1967)). *The Sacred Canopy: Elements of a Sociological Theory of Religion* (#, Trans.). New York: Anchor Books.

Berger, P. L. (1999). The desecularization of the world: a global overview. In Weigel, G., Martin, D., Sacks, J., Davie, G., Tu Weiming, & An-Na'im A. A. (eds), *The Desecularization of the World. Resurgent Religion and World Politics* (pp. 1–18) Grand Rapids, MI: Eerdmans.

Bergman, M. M. (2008). The straw men of the qualitative-quantitative divide and their influence on mixed methods research. In M. M. Bergman (ed.), *Advances in Mixed Methods Research* (pp. 11–21). Los Angeles: Sage.

Beyer, P. (1994). *Religion and Globalization*. London: Sage.

Beyer, P. (1997) Religious vitality in Canada: the complementarity of religious market and secularization perspectives. *Journal for the Scientific Study of Religion, 36*: 272–88.

Beyer, P. (2013). Deprivileging religion in a post-Westphalian State: Shadow establishment, organization, spirituality and freedom in Canada. In W. F. Sullivan & L. G. Beaman (eds), *Ashgate AHRC/ESRC Religion and Society Series* (pp. 75–92). Williston: Ashgate.

Birkelbach, K. (1999). Die entscheidung zum kirchenaustritt zwischen kirchenbindung und kirchensteuer. Eine verlaufsdatenanalyse in einer kohorte ehemaliger gymnasiasten bis zum 43. Lebensjahr. *Zeitschrift für Soziologie, 28*(2), 136–53.

Bloch, J. P. (1997). Countercultural spiritualists' perceptions of the goddess. *Sociology of Religion, 58*(2), 181–90.

Bloch, J. P. (1998). *New Spirituality, Self, and Belonging. How New Agers and Neo-Pagans Talk about Themselves*. Westport: Praeger.

Bochinger, C. (1995). *'New Age' und Moderne Religion. Religionswissenschaftliche Analysen. 2. Aufl.* Gütersloh: Chr. Kaiser Gütersloher Verlagshaus.

Bochinger, C. (2012). *Religionen, Staat und Gesellschaft. Die Schweiz Zwischen Säkularisierung und Religiöser Vielfalt.* Zürich: Verlag Neue Zürcher Zeitung.

Bochinger, C., Engelbrecht, M., & Gebhart, W. (2009). *Die Unsichtbare Religion in der Sichtbaren Religion – Formen Spiritueller Orientierung in der Religiösen Gegenwartskultur.* Stuttgart: Kohlhammer.

Böckenförde, E.-W. (1991). Die Entstehung des Staates als Vorgang der Säkularisation. In ders. (ed.), *Recht, Staat, Freiheit. Studien zur Rechtsphilosophie, Staatstheorie und Verfassungsgeschichte* (pp. 92–114). Frankfurt am Main: Suhrkamp.

Bocking, B. (2005). Study of religions: the new queen of the sciences? In S. J. Sutcliffe (ed.), *Religion: Empirical Studies. A Collection* (pp. 107–22). Aldershot: Ashgate.

Boos-Nünning, U. (1972). *Dimensionen der Religiosität. Zur Operationalisierung und Messung religiöser Einstellungen* (#, Trans.). München: Chr. Kaiser Verlag.

Borowik, I. (2002). The Roman Catholic Church in the process of democratic transformation: the case of Poland. *Social Compass, 49*(2), 239–52.

Boudon, R. (1983). *La Logique du Social.* Paris: Hachette.

Boudon, R. (2003). Beyond rational choice theory. *Annual Review of Sociology, 29*, 1–21.

Bouma, G. D. (1997). *Many Religions, All Australian: Religious Settlement, Identity and Cultural Diversity.* Kew: The Christian Research Association.

Bourdieu, P. (1971). Genèse et structure du champ religieux. *Revue française de sociologie, XII*, 295–334.

Bourdieu, P. (1979). *La Distinction.* Paris: Minuit.

Bourdieu, P. (1983). Ökonomisches Kapital, kulturelles Kapital, soziales Kapital. In R. Kreckel (ed.), *Soziale Ungleichheiten. Sonderband 2* (pp. 183–198). Göttingen: Vandenhock & Ruprecht.

Bourdieu, P. (1987a). La dissolution du religieux. In ders. (ed.), *Choses Dites* (pp. 117–23). Paris: Editions de Minuit.

Bourdieu, P. (1987b). *Sozialer Sinn. Kritik der theoretischen Vernunft.* Frankfurt am Main: Suhrkamp.

Bovay, C. (2004). *Le paysage religieux en Suisse.* Neuchâtel: OFS.

Braybrooke, M. (1992). *Pilgrimage of Hope. One Hundred Years of Global Interfaith Dialogue.* London: SCM Press.

Bréchon, P., & Galland, O. (2010). *L'individualisation des valeurs.* Paris: Armand Colin.

Bréchon, P., Azria, R., Campiche, J. R., Javier, F., & Imaz, E. (1997). Identité religieuse des jeunes en Europe. Etat des lieux. In R. J. Campiche (ed.), *Cultures Jeunes et Religions en Europe* (pp. 44–96). Paris: CERF.

Brown, C. G. (2001). *The Death of Christian Britain. Understanding Secularisation 1800–2000*. London: Routledge.

Bruce, S. (1990). *A House Divided: Protestantism, Schism and Secularization*. London: Routledge.

Bruce, S. (1996). *Religion in the Modern World: From Cathedrals to Cults*. Oxford: Oxford University Press.

Bruce, S. (1999). *Choice and Religion. A Critique of Rational Choice Theory*. Oxford: University Press.

Bruce, S. (2002). *God is Dead: Secularization in the West*. Oxford: Blackwell.

Bruce, S. (2006). What the secularization paradigm really says. In M. Franzmann, C. Gärtner & N. Köck (eds), *Religiosität in der Säkularisierten Welt* (pp. 39–48). Wiesbaden: VS Verlag für Sozialwissenschaften.

Bruce, S., & Voas, D. (2010). Vicarious Religion: An Examination and Critique. *Journal of Contemporary Religion, 25*(2), 243–59.

Bruhn, M. et al. (1999). *Oekumenische Basler Kirchenstudie. Ergebnisse der Bevölkerungs- und Mitarbeiterbefragung*. Basel: Römisch-Katholische Kirche Basel-Stadt Evangelisch-Reformierte Kirche Basel-Stadt.

Bryant, J. M. (2000). Cost-Benefit Accounting and the Piety Business: Is Homo Religiosus, at bottom, a Homo Economicus? *Method & Theory in the Study of Religion, 12*(4), 520–48.

Bryman, A. (1988). *Quantity and Quality in Social Research*. London: Unwin Hyman.

Buchmann, M., & Eisner, M. (1997). The transition from the utilitarian to the expressive self: 1900–1992. *Poetics, 25*, 157–75.

Buomberger, T. (2012). Traumreisen und Alpträume. Wie Auto und Strassenbau in den 50er Jahren zu einer Selbstverständlichkeit wurden. In T. Buomberger & P. Pfrunder (eds), *Schöner leben, mehr haben. Die 50er Jahre in der Schweiz im Geiste des Konsums* (pp. 41–55). Zürich: Limmat Verlag.

Buomberger, T., & Pfrunder, P. (eds). (2012). *Schöner leben, mehr haben. Die 50er Jahre in der Schweiz im Geiste des Konsums*. Zürich: Limmat Verlag.

Burns, R., & Burns, R. (2008). Chapter 23. Cluster Analysis Business Research Methods and Statistics using SPSS (pp. 552–67). London: Sage.

Campbell, C. (1995 (1972)). The cult, the cultic milieu and secularization. In S. Bruce (ed.), *The Sociology of Religion. Volume II* (pp. 58–75). Aldershot: Edward Elgar Publishing Limited.

Campiche, J. R. (1996). Religion, statut social et identité féminine. *Archives de sciences sociales des religions, 95*(juillet-septembre), 69–94.

Campiche, J. R. (2008). La révolution religieuse de '68'. *Choisir, 581*, 15–18.

Campiche, J. R. (2010). *La religion visible. Pratiques et croyances en Suisse.* Lausanne: Presses polytechniques et universitaires romandes.

Caron, F. (2001). L'innovation. In H.-J. Gilomen, R. Jaun, M. Müller & B. Veyrassat (eds), *Innovationen. Voraussetzungen und Folgen – Antriebskräfte und Widerstände* (pp. 19–31). Zürich: Chronos.

Casanova, J. (1992). Private and public religions. *Social Research, 59*(1), 17–57.

Casanova, J. (1994). Religion und Öffentlichkeit. Ein Ost-/Westvergleich. *Transit – Europäische Revue, 8,* 21–41.

Casanova, J. (1996). Chancen und Gefahren öffentlicher Religion. In O. Kallscheuer (ed.), *Das Europa der Religionen. Ein Kontinent zwischen Säkularisierung und Fundamentalismus* (pp. 181–212). Frankfurt.

Cattacin, S., Gerber, B., Sardi, M., & Wegener, R. (2006). *Monitoring rightwing extremist attitudes, xenophobia and misanthropy in Switzerland.* An explorative study. Geneva.

Chaves, M. (1994). Secularization as declining religious authority. *Social Forces, 72*(3), 749–74.

Chaves, M. (2006). All creatures great and small: Megachurches in context. *Review of Religious Research, 47,* 329–46.

Chaves, M. (2011). *American Religion. Contemporary Trends.* Princeton: Princeton University Press.

Chaves, M., & Cann, D. E. (1992). Regulation, Pluralism, and Religious Market Structure. *Rationality and Society, 4*(3), 272–90.

Chaves, M., & Gorski, P. S. (2001). Religious pluralism and religion participation. *Annual Review of Sociology, 27,* 261–81.

Cimino, R., & Smith, C. (2007). Secular humanism and atheism beyond progressive secularism. *Sociology of Religion, 68*(4), 407–24.

Coleman, J. S. (1990). *Foundations of Social Theory.* Cambridge: The Belknap Press of Harvard University Press.

Comte, A. (1995 (1844)). *Discours sur l'esprit positif.* Paris: Hartmann.

Conze, W., & Kocka, J. (eds). (1985). *Bildungsbürgertum im 19. Jahrhundert. Teil I. Bildungssystem und Professionalisierung im internationalen Vergleichen.* Stuttgart: Klett-Cotta.

Cox, J. L. (2003). *Religion without God: Methodological Agnosticism and the Future of Religious Studies. The Hibbert Lecture.* Herriot-Watt University. 1–11.

Creswell, J. W., Plano Clark, V. L., Gutmann, M. L., & Hanson, W. E. (2003). Advanced mixed methods research designs. In A. Tashakkori & C. Teddlie (eds), *Handbook of Mixed Methods in Social and Behavioral Research* (pp. 209–40). Thousand Oaks, CA: Sage.

Dahinden, J., Duemmler, K., & Moret, J. (2010). Religion und Ethnizität: Welche Praktiken, Identitäten und Grenzziehungen? Eine Untersuchung mit jungen Erwachsenen. Schlussbericht.

Darwin, C. (1985 (1859)). *The Origin of Species.* London: Penguin Books.

Davie, G. (1990). Believing without belonging: Is this the future of religion in Britain? *Social Compass, 37*(4), 455–69.

Davie, G. (2006a). Vicarious religion: a methodological challenge. In N. T. Ammerman (ed.), *Everyday Religion: Observing Modern Religious Lives* (pp. 21–37). New York: Oxford University Press.

Davie, G. (2006b). Is Europe an Exceptional Case? *International Review of Mission, 95*(578/579), 247–58.

Davie, G. (2007). *The Sociology of Religion*. London: Sage.

Dawkins, R., & Vogel, S. (2008). *Der Gotteswahn*: Ullstein: Bantam Press.

Day, A. (2009). Believing in belonging: An ethnography of young people's constructions of belief. *Culture and Religion, 10*(3), 263–78.

De Graaf, N. D. (2012). Secularization: Theoretical controversies generating empirical research. In R. Wittek, V. Nee & T. A. B. Snijders (eds), *Handbook of Rational Choice Social Research* (pp. 322–54). Stanford: Stanford University Press.

Dijk van, T. A. (1993). *Elite discourse and racism*. Newbury Park: Sage Publications Ltd.

Dobbelaere, K. (1981). Secularization: a multi-dimensional concept. *Current Sociology, 29*(2 (Summer)), 3–153.

Dobbelaere, K. (2002). *Secularization: An Analysis at Three Levels*. Bruxelles: Peter Lang.

Dora, C. (1997). Die Zeit des katholischen Milieus: Vom ersten Weltkrieg bis zum Zweiten Vatikanischen Konzil. In F. X. Bischof & C. Dora (eds), *Ortskirche unterwegs. Das Bistum St. Gallen. Festschrift zum hundertfünfzigsten Jahr seines Bestehens* (pp. 91–223). St. Gallen: Verlag am Klosterhof.

Dubach, A. (2004). Unterschiedliche Mitgliedschaftstypen in den Volkskirchen. In J. R. Campiche (ed.), *Die zwei Gesichter der Religion. Faszination und Entzauberung* (pp. 129–78). Zürich: TVZ.

Dubach, A., & Campiche, R. (1993). *Jede/r ein Sonderfall? Religion in der Schweiz: Ergebnisse einer Repräsentativbefragung*. Zürich: NZN Buchverlag AG.

Dubach, A., & Fuchs, B. (2005). *Ein neues Modell von Religion. Zweite Schweizer Sonderfallstudie – Herausforderung für die Kirchen*. Zürich: TVZ.

Durkheim, E. (1985, 7e édition). *Les Formes Élémentaires de la Vie Religieuse. Le système totémique en Australie*. Paris: PUF.

Ebertz, M. N. (1993). Die Zivilisierung Gottes und die Deinstitutionalisierung der 'Gnadenanstalt'. In J. Bergmann, A. Hahn & T. Luckmann (eds), *Religion und Kultur* (pp. 92–125). Opladen: Westdeutscher Verlag GmbH.

Einstein, M. (2008). *Brands of Faith. Marketing religion in a commercial age*. London: Routledge.

Einstein, M. (2011). The evolution of religious branding. *Social Compass, 58*, 331–8.

Esser, H. (1996). Die Definition der Situation. *Kölner Zeitschrift für Soziologie und Sozialpsychologie, 48*(1), 1–34.

Esser, H. (1999). *Soziologie. Spezielle Grundlagen. Band 1: Situationslogik und Handeln.* Frankfurt: Campus.

Esser, H. (2000a). *Soziologie. Spezielle Grundlagen. Band 2: Die Konstruktion der Gesellschaft.* Frankfurt: Campus.

Esser, H. (2000b). *Soziologie. Spezielle Grundlagen. Band 3: Soziales Handeln.* Frankfurt: Campus.

Esser, H. (2000c). *Soziologie. Spezielle Grundlagen. Band 5: Institutionen.* Frankfurt: Campus.

Esser, H. (2000d). *Soziologie. Spezielle Grundlagen. Band 6: Sinn und Kultur.* Frankfurt: Campus.

Famos, C. R. (2007). Religiöse vielfalt und recht: Von göttlichen und menschlichen Regeln. In M. Baumann & J. Stolz (eds), *Eine Schweiz – viele Religionen. Risiken und Chancen des Zusammenlebens* (pp. 301–12). Bielefeld: Transcript.

Famos, C. R., & Kunz, R. (eds). (2006). *Kirche und Marketing. Beiträge zu einer Verhältnisbestimmung.* Zürich: TVZ.

Farr, R. M. (1990). Les représentations sociales. In S. Moscovici (ed.), *Psychologie sociale* (pp. 379–90). Paris: PUF.

Fath, S. (2008). *Dieu XXL. La Révolution des Megachurches.* Paris: Editions Autrement.

Favre, O. (2002). Les eglises évangéliques en Suisse: Identités en mutation. In R. J. Campiche (ed.), *Les Dynamiques Européennes de l'Évangélisme* (pp. 129–39). Lausanne: Observatoire des Religions en Suisse (ORS).

Favre, O., & Stolz, J. (2009). L'émergence des évangéliques en Suisse. Implantation, composition socioculturelle et reproduction des évangéliques à partir des données du recensement ٢···. *Schweizerische Zeitschrift für Soziologie, 2009*(3), 453–77.

Festinger, L. (1954). A theory of social comparison processes. *Human Relations, 7,* 117–40.

Field, A. (2000). *Discovering Statistics using SPSS for Windows.* London: Sage.

Finke, R., & Stark, R. (1992). *The Churching of America 1776–1990: Winners and Losers in Our Religious Economy.* New Brunswick, NJ: Rutgers University Press.

Flanagan, K., & Jupp, P. C. (eds). (2007). *A Sociology of Spirituality.* Aldershot: Ashgate.

Forclaz, B. (2007). Religiöse Vielfalt in der Schweiz seit der Reformation. In M. Baumann & J. Stolz (eds), *Eine Schweiz – viele Religionen. Risiken und Chancen des Zusammenlebens* (pp. 89–99). Bielefeld: Transcript.

Fox, J. (2008). *Applied Regression Analysis, Linear Models, and Related Methods.* Thousand Oaks: Sage.

Fox J. (2011) Separation of religion and state and secularism in theory and in practice. *Religion, State and Society*, *39*, 384–401.

Fox J. and Tabory E. (2008) Contemporary evidence regarding the impact of state regulation of religion on religious participation and belief. *Sociology of Religion*, *69*, 245–71.

Frank, K., & Jödicke, A. (2007). Öffentliche Schule und neue religiöse Vielfalt: Themen, Probleme, Entwicklungen. In M. Baumann & J. Stolz (eds), *Eine Schweiz – viele Religionen. Risiken und Chancen des Zusammenlebens* (pp. 273–84). Bielefeld: Transcript.

Franz, G., & Herbert, W. (1987a). Werte zwischen Stabilität und Veränderung: Die Bedeutung von Schichtzugehörigkeit und Lebenszyklus. In H. Klages, G. Franz & W. Herbert (eds), *Sozialpsychologie der Wohlfahrtsgesellschaft. Zur Dynamik von Wertorientierungen, Einstellungen und Ansprüchen* (pp. 55–101). Frankfurt/Main: Campus Verlag GmbH.

Franz, G., & Herbert, W. (1987b). Werttypen in der Bundesrepublik: Konventionalisten, Resignierte, Idealisten und Realisten. In H. Klages, G. Franz & W. Herbert (eds), *Sozialpsychologie der* Wohlfahrtsgesellschaft. Zur Dynamik von Wertorientierungen, Einstellungen und Ansprüchen (pp. 40–54). Frankfurt/Main: Campus Verlag GmbH.

Friese, S. (2014). *Qualitative Data Analysis with ATLAS.ti*. 2. ed. London: Sage.

Fritschi, A. (1990). *Schwesterntum. Zur Sozialgeschichte der weiblichen Berufskrankenpflege in der Schweiz 1850–1930*. Zürich: Chronos.

Gäbler, U. (1999). Schweiz. In G. e. a. Müller (ed.), Theologische Realenzyklopädie (pp. 682–712). Berlin: De Gruyter.

Gachet, C. (2013a). Etre évangélique dans une paroisse réformée. In J. Stolz, O. Favre, C. Gachet & E. Buchard (eds), *Le phénomène évangélique. Analyses d'un milieu compétitif* (pp. 233–56). Genève: Labor et Fides.

Gachet, C. (2013b). L'évolution du milieu: entre continuité et changements. In J. Stolz, O. Favre, C. Gachet & E. Buchard (eds), *Le phénomène évangélique. Analyses d'un milieu compétitif* (pp. 279–96). Genève: Labor et Fides.

Gachet, C., & Stolz, J. (2010). Lectures et légitimations. Les évangéliques et le récit biblique de la création. In P. Bornet, C. Clivaz, N. Durisch Gauthier, C. Fawer Caputo & F. Voegeli (eds), *Et Dieu créa Darwin. Théorie de l'évolution et créationnisme en Suisse aujourd'hui* (pp. 109–32). Genève: Labor et Fides.

Garson, G. D. (2014). *Cluster Analysis*. Statistical Associates Publishers.

Gauthier, F. (2011). Primat de l'authenticité et besoin de reconnaissance. La société de consommation et la nouvelle régulation du religieux. *Studies in Religion*. doi: 10.1177/0008429811429912

Gauthier, F., Martikainen, T., & Woodhead, L. (2011). Introduction: Religion in consumer society. *Social Compass*, *58*(3), 291–301.

Gebhart, W., Engelbrecht, M., & Bochinger, C. (2005). Die Selbstermächtigung des religiösen Subjekts. Der 'spirituelle Wanderer' als Idealtypus. *Zeitschrift für Religionswissenschaft*, *13*, 133–51.

Geertz, C. (1993a). Religion as a cultural system. In ders. (ed.), *The Interpretation of Cultures. Selected essays* (pp. 87–125). London: Fontana Press.

Geertz, C. (1993b). Thick description: Towards an interpretive theory of culture. In ders. (ed.), *The Interpretation of Cultures. Selected Essays* (pp. 3–33). London: Fontana Press.

Gergen, K. J., & Gergen, M. M. (1986). *Social Psychology*. 2. ed. New York, Berlin: Springer Verlag.

Gill, A., & Lundsgaarde, E. (2004). State welfare spending and religiosity: a cross-national analysis. *Rationality & Society*, *16*(4), 399–436.

Giordan, G. (2007). Spirituality: From a religious concept to a sociological theory. In K. Flanagan & P. Jupp (eds), *A Sociology of Spirituality* (pp. 161–80). Aldershot: Ashgate.

Giordan, G., & Pace, E. (2014). *From Religious Diversity to Religious Pluralism: What is at Stake?* Leiden: Brill.

Glock, C. Y. (1967). Über die Dimensionen der Religiosität (#, Trans.). In J. Matthes (ed.), *Religion und Gesellschaft. Einführung in die Religionssoziologie I* (pp. 150–68). Beinbek bei Hamburg: Rowohlt.

Goldthorpe, J. H. (2000). *Sociological Ethnography Today: Problems and Possibilities on Sociology. Numbers, Narratives, and the Integration of Research and Theory* (pp. 65–93). Oxford: Oxford University Press.

Gorski, P. S. (2000). Historicizing the secularization debate: Church, state, and society in late medieval and early modern Europe, ca. 1300 to 1700. *American Sociological Review*, *65*(1), 138–67.

Gruber, J., & Hungerman, D. M. (2008). The Church vs. the Mall: What happens when religion faces increased secular competition? *Quarterly Journal of Economics*, May, 831–62.

Grunder, H.-U. (2011). Primarschule. *Historisches Lexikon der Schweiz, 24.11.2011*.

Guggisberg, K. (1971). Die evangelisch-reformierten Kirchen. In E. Gruner (ed.), *Die Schweiz seit 1945. Beiträge zur Zeitgeschichte* (pp. 307–22). Bern.

Haack, S. (2006). Introduction: Pragmatism, old and new. In S. Haack (ed.), *Pragmatism, Old & New. Selected Writings* (pp. 15–68). Amherst: Prometheus Books.

Haenni, P. (2009). The economic politics of Muslim consumption. In J. Pink (ed.), *Muslim Societies in the Age of Mass Consumption: Politics, culture and identity between the local and the global* (pp. 327–42): Cambridge Scholars Publishing.

Haenni, P., & Lathion, S. (2011). *The Swiss Minaret Ban: Islam in Question. Translated by Tom Genrich*. Fribourg: Religioscope.

Halliday, F. (1999). 'Islamophobia' reconsidered. *Ethnic and Racial Studies, 22*(5 September), 892–902.

Hamilton, M. (2001). *The Sociology of Religion. Theoretical and comparative perspectives. Second edition.* London: Routledge.

Hammersley, M. (2008). Troubles with triangulation. In M. M. Bergman (ed.), *Advances in Mixed Methods Research* (pp. 22–36). Los Angeles: Sage.

Hanegraaff, W. J. (1998). *New Age Religion and Western Culture. Esotericism in the Mirror of Secular Thought.* New York: State University of New York Press.

Harris, S. (2004). *The End of Faith. Religion, Terror, and the Future of Reason.* New York: W.W. Norton & Company.

Harris, T. A. (2012). *Ich bin o.k., Du bist o.k.* Berlin: Rowohlt TB.

Hedström, P. (2005). *Dissecting the Social. On the Principles of Analytical Sociology.* Cambridge: Cambridge University Press.

Heelas, P., & Woodhead, L. (2004). *The Spiritual Revolution: Why Religion is Giving Way to Spirituality.* Maldon, MA: WileyBlackwell.

Helbling, M. (2010). Islamophobia in Switzerland: a new phenomenon or a new name for xenophobia. In H. Kriesi (ed.), *Value Change in Switzerland* (pp. 65–80). Lanham: Lexington Press.

Hero, M. (2010). *Die neuen Formen des religiösen Lebens. Eine institutionentheoretische Analyse neuer Religiosität.* Würzburg: Ergon Verlag.

Hirschle, J. (2010). From religious to consumption-related routine acetivities? Analyzing Ireland's economic boom and the decline in church attendance. *Journal for the Scientific Study of Religion, 49*(4), 673–87.

Hirschle, J. (2011). The affluent society and its religious consequences: an empirical investigation of 20 European countries. *Socio-Economic Review, 9*(2), 261–85.

Hirschle, J. (2012). Religiöser Wandel in der Konsumgesellschaft. *Soziale Welt, 63*(2), 141–62.

Hitchens, C. (2007). God is not great. How Religion Poisons Everything. New York: Warner Books.

Höhmann, P., & Krech, V. (2006). Das weite Feld der Kirchenmitgliedschaft. Vermessungsversuche nach Typen, sozialstruktureller Verortung, alltäglicher Lebensführung und religiöser Indifferenz. In W. Huber, J. Friedrich, & P. Steinacker (eds), *Kirche in der Vielfalt der Lebensbezüge.* Die vierte EKD-Erhebung über Kirchenmitgliedschaft (pp. 141–97). Gütersloh: Gütersloher Verlagshaus.

Höhn, H.-J. (2007). *Postsäkular. Gesellschaft im Umbruch – Religion im Wandel.* Paderborn: Schöningh Verlag.

Höllinger, F., & Tripold, T. (2012). *Ganzheitliches Leben. Das holistische Milieu zwischen neuer Spiritualität und postmoderner Wellness-Kultur.* Bielefeld: Transcript.

Hotz-Hart, B., Mäder, S., & Vock, P. (2001). *Volkswirtschaft der Schweiz. 3. Auflage*. Zürich: VDF Hochschulverlag AG an der ETH Zürich.

Huber, S. (2003). *Zentralität und Inhalt. Ein neues multidimensionales Messmodell der Religiosität. Aus der Reihe: Veröffentlichungen der Sektion Religionssoziologie der Deutschen Gesellschaft für Soziologie. Bd. 9*. Wiesbaden: VS Verlag.

Iannaccone, L. R. (1991). The Consequences of Religious Market Structure. Adam Smith and the Economics of Religion. *Rationality and Society*, 3(2), 156–77.

Iannaccone, L. R. (1992). Religious Markets and the Economics of Religion. *Social Compass*, 39(1), 123–31.

Iannaccone, L. R. (1994). Why strict churches are strong. *American Journal of Sociology*, 99(5), 1180–212.

Iannaccone, L. R. (1998). Introduction to the economics of religion. *Journal of Economic Literature*, 36(3), 1465–95.

Im Hof, U. (1997). *Geschichte der Schweiz* (6. Aufl. ed.). Stuttgart: Kohlhammer.

Imhof, K., & Ettinger, P. (2007). Religionen in der medienvermittelten Oeffentlichkeit der Schweiz. In M. Baumann & J. Stolz (eds), *Eine Schweiz – viele Religionen. Risiken und Chancen des Zusammenlebens* (pp. 285–300). Bielefeld: Transcript.

Inglehart, R. (1977). *The Silent Revolution: Changing Values and Political Styles Among Western Publics*. Princeton, New Jersey: Princeton University Press.

Inglehart, R. (1997). *Modernization and Postmodernization*: Princeton University Press.

Inglehart, R., & Baker, W. E. (2000). Modernization, cultural change, and the persistence of traditional values. *American Sociological Review*, 65, 19–51.

Inglehart, R., & Welzel, C. (2005). *Modernization, Cultural Change, and Democracy. The Human Development Sequence*. Cambridge: Cambridge University Press.

Jenny, M. (2008). *Guérisseurs, Rebouteux et Faiseurs de Secret en Suisse Romande. Avec repértoire d'adresses actualisé*. Lausanne: Favre.

Jordan W. R. (2002) Religion in the public square: a reconsideration of David Hume and religious establishment. *The Review of Politics*, 64, 687–713.

Kahneman, D. (2011). *Thinking, Fast and Slow*. London: Penguin Books.

Kalter, F., & Kroneberg, C. (2014). Between mechanism talk and mechanism cult: New emphases in explanatory sociology and empirical research. Kölner Zeitschrift für Soziologie und Sozialpsychologie, *Special Issue 54: Social Contexts and Social Mechanisms*, 91–115.

Kaufmann, F.-X. (1997). *Herausforderungen des Sozialstaates*. Frankfurt am Main: Suhrkamp.

Kecskes, R., & Wolf, C. (1995). Christliche Religiosität. Dimensionen, Messinstrumente, Ergebnisse. *Kölner Zeitschrift für Soziologie und Sozialpsychologie, 47*(3), 494–515.

Kelle U. (2001) Sociological explanations between micro and macro and the integration of qualitative and quantitative methods. *Qualitative Social Research* (On-line Journal). Available at: http://qualitative-research.net/fqs/fqs-eng.htm (Date of access: 10.04.2008).

Kelle, U. (2007). *Die Integration qualitativer und quantitativer Methoden in der empirischen Sozialforschung. Theoretische Grundlagen und methodologische Konzepte*. Wiesbaden: VS Verlag für Sozialwissenschaften.

Kelle, U., & Lüdemann, C. (1998). Bridge assumptions in rational choice theory: Methodological problems and possible solutions. In H.-P. Blossfeld & G. Prein (eds), *Rational Choice Theory and Large-Scale Data Analysis* (pp. 112–25). Colorado: Westview Press.

Kelley, D. M. (1986 (1972)). *Why Conservative Churches Are Growing. A Study in Sociology of Religion*. Macon, Georgia: Mercer University Press.

Keohane, R. O. (1982). The Demand for International Regimes. *International Organization, 36*(2), 325–55.

Kim, J.-O., & Mueller, C. W. (1978). Factor Analysis. Statistical Methods and Practical Issues. Newbury Park, CA: Sage.

King, G., Keohane, R. O., & Verba, S. (1994). *Designing Social Inquiry. Scientific Inference in Qualitative Research*. Princeton: Princeton University Press.

Klages, H. (1985). *Wertorientierungen im Wandel: Rückblick, Gegenwartsanalyse, Prognosen* (2. Aufl. ed.). Frankfurt/Main: Campus Verlag.

Klages, H. (1988). *Wertedynamik. Über die Wandelbarkeit des Selbstverständlichen*. Zürich: Edition Interfrom.

Klages, H. (1994). Werte und Wandel. *Soziologische Revue, 17*(2), 183–5.

Knoblauch, H. (1991). Die Verflüchtigung der Religion ins Religiöse. Thomas Luckmanns Unsichtbare Religion. In T. Luckmann (ed.), *Die unsichtbare Religion* (pp. 7–44). Frankfurt am Main: Suhrkamp.

Knoblauch, H. (2009). *Populäre Religion. Auf dem Weg in eine spirituelle Gesellschaft*. Frankfurt: Campus Verlag.

Kolping, A. (1952). *Der Gesellenverein und seine Aufgabe, zusammengestellt und herausgegeben von J. Nattermann*. Köln: Kolping-Verlag.

Krasner, S. D. (1982). Structural causes and regime consequences: regime as intervening variables. *International Organization, 36*(2), 185–205.

Krech, V. (2011). *Wo bleibt die Religion? Zur Ambivalenz des Religiösen in der Modernen Gesellschaft*. Bielefeld: Transcript.

Kroneberg, C. (2011). *Die Erklärung sozialen Handelns. Grundlagen und Anwendung einer integrativen Theorie*. Wiesbaden: VS Verlag.

Krüggeler, M. (1993). Inseln der Seligen: religiöse Orientierungen in der Schweiz (#, Trans.). In A. Dubach & R. Campiche (eds), *Jede/r ein*

Sonderfall? Religion in der Schweiz: Ergebnisse einer Repräsentativbefragung.
  (pp. 93–132). Zürich: NZN Buchverlag AG.

Kuckartz, U. (2014). *Mixed Methods. Methodologie, Forschungsdesigns und Analyseverfahren.* Wiesbaden: Springer.

Kuhn, T. K. (2007). *Religionsfreiheit – Beispiele aus dem Schweizerischen Diskurs des 18. und 19. Jahrhunderts* (pp. 13–36). Zürich: TVZ.

Lambert, Y. (2007 (1985)). *Dieu Change en Bretagne. La Religion à Limerzel de 1900 à nos Jours.* Paris: Les Editions du Cerf.

Lamine, A.-S. (2008). Croyances et transcendances: variations en mode mineurs. *Social Compass,* 55(2), 154–67.

Lamine, A.-S. (2010). Les croyances religieuses: entre raison, symbolisation et expérience. *Année Sociologique,* 60(1), 93–114.

Landert, C. (2001). Kasualien im Lichte der Statistik. *Reformierte Presse. Annex. Die Beilage der Reformierten Presse,* 44, 3–10.

Lechner, F. J. (1996). Secularization in the Netherlands? *Journal for the Scientific Study of Religion,* 35(3), 252–64.

LeVine, R. A., & Campbell, D. T. (1972). *Ethnocentrism: Theories of Conflict, Ethnic Attitudes, and Group Behavior.* New York: John Wiley & Sons, Inc.

Lincoln, Y. S., & Guba, E. G. (1985). *Naturalistic Inquiry.* Beverly Hills, CA: Sage.

Lindemann, A. (2012). *Italophobie et Islamophobie. Etude Comparative dans la Presse Suisse Romande de 1970 et 2004. Mémoire de Master.* Lausanne: Université de Lausanne.

Lindenberg, S. (1996). Die Relevanz theoriereicher Brückenannahmen. *Kölner Zeitschrift für Soziologie und Sozialpsychologie,* 48(1), 126–40.

Lindt, A. (1988). Der schweizerische Protestantismus – Entwicklungslinien nach 1945. In V. Conzemius, M. Greschat & H. Kocher (eds), *Die Zeit nach 1945 als Thema Kirchlicher Zeitgeschichte. Referate der internationalen Tagung in Hünigen/Bern (Schweiz) 1985* (pp. 61–71). Göttingen: Vandenhoeck & Ruprecht.

Loderer, B. (2012). Im Armeereformhaus. Das Sturmgewehr 57 als Fundament der Armee. In T. Buomberger & P. Pfrunder (eds), *Schöner Leben, Mehr Haben. Die 50er Jahre in der Schweiz im Geiste des Konsums* (pp. 201–15): Zürich: Limmat Verlag.

Long, T., & Hadden, J. K. (1983). Religious conversion and socialization. *Journal for the Scientific Study of Religion,* 22(1), 1–14.

Luckmann, T. (1967). *The Invisible Religion.* New York: MacMillan.

Luhmann, N. (1982). *Funktion der Religion* Frankfurt am Main: Suhrkamp.

Luhmann, N. (1987). *Soziale Systeme. Grundriss einer allgemeinen Theorie.* (#, Trans.). Frankfurt am Main: Suhrkamp, stw.666.

Luhmann, N. (1996). *Die Realität der Massenmedien.* Opladen: Westdeutscher Verlag.

Mader, L., & Schinzel, M. (2012). Religion in der Öffentlichkeit. In C. Bochinger (ed.), *Religion, Staat und Gesellschaft. Die Schweiz zwischen Säkularisierung und religiöser Vielfalt* (pp. 109–44). Zürich: Verlag Neue Zürcher Zeitung.

Mahoney, J., & Goertz, G. (2006). A tale of two cultures: Contrasting quantitative and qualitative research. *Political Analysis, 14,* 227–49.

Maissen, T. (2010). *Geschichte der Schweiz.* Baden: hier+jetzt.

Malinowski, B. (1984). Magic, Science and Religion. In B. Malinowski (ed.), *Magic, Science and Religion* (pp. 17–92). Westport: Greenwood Press.

Manzo, G. (2007). Variables, mechanisms, and simulations: Can the three methods be synthesized? A critical analysis of the literature. *Revue Française de Sociologie, 48*(5), 35–71.

Manzo, G. (2010). Analytical sociology and its critics. *European Journal of Sociology, 51*(1), 129–70.

Maxwell JA. (2005) *Qualitative Research Design. An Interactive Approach. Second Edition. Applied Social Research Methods Series. Vol. 41,* Thousand Oaks: Sage.

Mayer, J.-F. (1993). *Les Nouvelles Voies Spirituelles. Enquête sur la Religiosité Parallèle en Suisse.* Lausanne: Editions L'Age d'Homme.

Mayer, J.-F. (2007). Salvation Goods and the Religious Market in the Cultic Milieu. In J. Stolz (ed.), *Salvation Goods and Religious Markets. Theory and Applications* (pp. 257–74). Bern: Peter Lang.

Mayring, P. (2014). Qualitative Content Analysis. Theoretical Foundation and Basic Procedures. http://www.qualitative-content-analysis.aau.at/.

McLeod, H. (2000). *Secularisation in Western Europe, 1848–1914.* New York: St. Martin's Press.

McLeod, H. (2007). *The Religious Crisis of the 1960s.* Oxford: Oxford University Press.

Mead, G. H. (1967 (1934)). *Mind, Self & Society from the Standpoint of a Social Behaviorist.* Edited and with an Introduction by Charles W. Morris. Vol. 1. Chicago: University of Chicago Press.

Mesmer, B. (1988). Vom 'doppelten Gebrauchswert' der Frau – eine Einführung. In M.-L. Barben & E. Ryter (eds), *Verflixt und zugenäht! Frauenberufsbildung – Frauenerwerbsarbeit; 1888–1988* (pp. 15–22). Zürich: Chronos.

Miles, M. B., & Huberman, A. M. (1994). *Qualitative Data Analysis. An Expanded Sourcebook.* Thousand Oaks: Sage.

Miller, A. S., & Stark, R. (2002). Gender and religiousness: Can socialization explanations be saved? *American Journal of Sociology, 107,* 1399–423.

Monnot, C. (2013). Croire ensemble. Analyse institutionnelle du paysage religieux en Suisse. Zürich: Seismo.

Monnot, C., & Stolz, J. (2014). The diversity of religious diversity. Using census and NCS methodology in order to map and assess the religious diversity of a whole country. In G. Giordan & E. Pace (eds), *Religious Pluralism. Framing Religious Diversity in the Contemporary World* (pp. 73–91). Cham: Springer.

Mooi, E., & Sarstedt, M. (2011). *Chapter 9. Cluster Analysis A Concise Guide to Market Research. The Process, Data, and Methods Using IBM Statistics* (pp. 237–84). Berlin: Springer.

Moscovici, S. (1981). On social representations. In J. P. Forgas (ed.), *Social Cognition* (pp. 181–210). London: Academic Press.

Moser, M. (2004). *Frauen im Katholischen Milieu von Olten 1900–1950.* Fribourg: Academic Press Fribourg.

Mottner, S. (2007). Marketing and religion. In W. Wymer & A. Sargeant (eds), *The Routledge Companion to Nonprofit Marketing* (pp. 92–107). Abingdon, UK: Routledge.

Müller, M., & Veyrassat, B. (2001). Einleitung. Was sind Innovationen? In H.-J. Gilomen, R. Jaun, M. Müller & B. Veyrassat (eds), *Innovationen. Voraussetzungen und Folgen – Antriebskräfte und Widerstände* (pp. 9–13). Zürich: Chronos.

Need, A., & De Graaf, N. D. (1996). 'Losing my religion': a dynamic analysis of leaving the church in the Netherlands. *European Sociological Review, 12*(1), 87–99.

Norris, P., & Inglehart, R. (2004). *Sacred and Secular. Religion and Politics Worldwide.* Cambridge: Cambridge University Press.

Olson, D. V. A. (2005). Free and cheap riding in strict, conservative churches. *Journal for the Scientific Study of Religion, 44*(2), 123–42.

Onwuegbuzie, A. J., & Teddlie, C. (2003). A framework for analyzing data in mixed methods research. In A. Tashakkori & C. Teddlie (eds), *Handbook of Mixed Methods in Social & Behavioural Research* (pp. 351–83). Thousand Oakes: Sage.

Orsi, R. A. (2003). Is the study of lived religion irrelevant to the world we live in? Special presidential plenary address. *Journal for the Scientific Study of Religion, 42*(2), 169–74.

Pace E. (2008) Salvation goods, the gift economy and charismatic concern. In: Stolz J (ed.) *Salvation Goods and Religious Markets. Theory and Applications.* Bern: Peter Lang, 149–70.

Pahud de Mortanges, R. (2007). System und Entwicklungstendenzen des Religionsverfassungsrechts der Schweiz und des Fürstentums Liechtenstein. *Zeitschrift für evangelisches Kirchenrecht, 52*(3), 495–523.

Pahud de Mortanges, R. (2012). Die Auswirkung der religiösen Pluralisierung auf die staatliche Rechtsordnung. In C. Bochinger (ed.), *Religionen, Staat und Gesellschaft. Die Schweiz zwischen Säkularisierung und religiöser Vielfalt* (pp. 145–74). Zürich: Verlag Neue Zürcher Zeitung.

Parsons, T. (1975). *Gesellschaften. Evolutionäre und komparative Perspektiven.* Frankfurt am Main: Suhrkamp.

Parsons, T. (1999). Youth in the context of American society. In B. S. Turner (ed.), *The Talcott Parsons Reader* (pp. 271–91). Oxford: Blackwell.

Peirce, C. S. (2006). Some consequences of four incapacities. In S. Haack (ed.), *Pragmatism, Old & New. Selected Writings* (pp. 69–106). Amherst: Prometheus Books.

Pfister, R. (1974). *Kirchengeschichte der Schweiz. Von der Reformation bis zum zweiten Vollmerger Krieg*. Zürich: TVZ.

Pfister, R. (1984). *Kirchengeschichte der Schweiz. Dritter Band 1720–1950*. Zürich: TVZ.

Pickel, G. (2001). Moralische Vorstellungen und ihre religiöse Fundierung im europäischen Vergleich. In G. Pickel & M. Krüggeler (eds), *Religion und Moral. Entkoppelt oder verknüpft?* (pp. 105–34). Opladen: Leske + Budrich.

Pickel, G. (2011). *Religionssoziologie. Eine Einführung in zentrale Themenbereiche*. Wiesbaden: VS Verlag.

Piette, A. (1999). *La Religion de Près. L'activité Religieuse en Train de se Faire*: Paris: Editions Métailié.

Piette, A. (2006). Entre la sociologie et le Dieu chrétien: Résultats d'une enquête ethnographique dans des paroisses catholiques en France. *Information sur les sciences sociales, 41*(3), 359–83.

Plüss, D., & Portmann, A. (2011). Säkularisierte Christen und religiöse Vielfalt. Religiöses Selbstverständnis und Umgang mit Pluralität innerhalb des Christentums. Schlussbericht.

Pollack, D. (1995). Was ist Religion? Probleme der Definition. *Zeitschrift für Religionswissenschaft, 8,* 11–43.

Pollack, D. (2001). Kirchenaustritt *Religion in Geschichte und Gegenwart* (pp. 1053–6). Tübingen: J.C.B. Mohr Siebeck.

Pollack, D. (2003). *Säkularisierung – ein moderner Mythos? Studien zum religiösen Wandel in Deutschland*. Tübingen: Mohr Siebeck.

Pollack, D. (2006). Religious Individualization or Secularization: An Attempt to Evaluate the Thesis of Religious Individualization in Eastern and Western Germany.

Pollack, D. (2009). *Rückkehr des Religiösen?* Tübingen: Mohr Siebeck.

Pollack, D. (2011a). Historische Analyse statt Ideologiekritik: Eine historisch-kritische Diskussion der Gültigkeit der Säkularisierungstheorie. Geschichte und Gesellschaft. Zeitschrift für historische Sozialwissenschaft, *37*(4), 482–522.

Pollack, D. (2011b). Wahrnehmung und Akzeptanz religiöser Vielfalt. Bevölkerungsumfrage des Exzellenzclusters 'Religion und Politik' unter Leitung des Religionssoziologen Prof. Dr. Detlef Pollack.

Pollack, D., & Olson, D. V. A. (2008). *The Role of Religion in Modern Societies*. New York: Routledge.

Pollack, D., & Pickel, G. (1999). Individualisierung und religiöser Wandel in der Bundesrepublik Deutschland. *Zeitschrift für Soziologie, 28*(6), 465–83.

Polo, A. (2010). Quelles croissances pour les principales eglises évangéliques de Suisse? Gagnants et perdants de la période 1970–2008. Mémoire de master en sociologie des religions. Université de Lausanne.

Popper, K. R. (1960). *The Poverty of Historicism.* London: Routledge & Kegan Paul.

Porpora, D. V. (2006). Methodological atheism, methodological agnosticism and religious experience. *Journal for the Theory of Social Behaviour, 36*(1), 57–75.

Portier, P., Veuille, M., & Willaime, J.-P. (eds). (2011). *Théorie de l'*évolution et Religions. Paris: Riveneuve Éditions.

Portmann, A., & Plüss, D. (2011). Good religion or bad religion. Distanced church-members and their perception of religion and religious plurality. *Journal of Empirical Theology, 24*(2), 180–96.

Proust, M. (1896). *Les Plaisirs et les Jours.* Paris: Gallimard.

Putnam, R. D. (2000). *Bowling Alone. The Collapse and Revival of American Community.* New York: Simon & Schuster Paperbacks.

Putnam, R. D., & Campbell, D. E. (2010). *American Grace. How Religion Divides and Unites Us.* New York: Simon & Schuster.

Rademacher, S. (2009). Les spiritualités ésotériques et alternatives. diversité de la religiosité non organisée en Suisse. In M. Baumann & J. Stolz (eds), *La nouvelle Suisse religieuse. Risques et chances de sa diversité* (pp. 264–82). Genève: Labor et Fides.

Ramsel, C., Huber, S., & Stolz, J. (2013). Säkulare in der Schweiz. Wie verstehen sie sich? Welche Einstellungen haben sie zu religiösen Menschen oder Institutionen? In A. Heuser, C. Hoffmann & T. Walther (eds), *Erfassen – Deuten – Urteilen. Empirische Zugänge zur Religionsforschung* (pp. 85–96). Zürich: TVZ.

Reymond, B. (1999). *Le Protestantisme en Suisse Romande.* Genève: Labor et Fides.

Riesebrodt, M. (1990). *Fundamentalismus als patriarchalische Protestbewegung. amerikanische Protestanten (1910–28) und iranische Schiiten (1961–79) im Vergleich.* Tübingen: Mohr Siebeck.

Riesebrodt, M. (2007). *Cultus und Heilsversprechen. Eine Theorie der Religionen.* München: C. H. Beck.

Rodriguez, J.-D. (2005). Typologies des croyances fondées sur la méthode des clusters. Formulation d'une nouvelle classification basée sur la critique de trois typologies suisses concernant les croyances religieuses. Mémoire de licence en Sociologie. Genève.

Römer, T. (2004). *La Formation du Pentateuque: Histoire de la Recherche.* Genève: Labor et Fides.

Rose, S. (1998). An examination of the new age movement: Who is involved and what constitutes its spirituality. *Journal of Contemporary Religion*, *13*(1), 5–22.

Rose, S. (2001). Is the term 'spirituality' a word that everyone uses, but nobody knows what anyone means by it? *Journal of Contemporary Religion*, *16*(2), 193–207.

Ruff, M. E. (2005). *The Wayward Flock. Catholic Youth in Postwar West Germany, 1945–1965*. Chapel Hill: The University of North Carolina Press.

Russell, A. (1980). *The Clerical Profession*. London: SPCK.

Sacchi, S. (1992). Postmaterialismus in der Schweiz von 1972 bis 1990. *Schweizerische Zeitschrift für Soziologie, 18*(1), S. 87–117.

Sammet, K., & Bergelt, D. (2012). The modernisation of gender relations and religion: Comparative analysis of secularization processes. In G. Pickel & K. Sammet (eds), *Transformations of Religiosity. Religion and Religiosity in Eastern Europe 1989–2010* (pp. 51–68). Wiesbaden: Springer.

Sandikzi, O., & Ger, G. (2010). Veiling in style: how does a stigmatized practice become fashionable? *Journal of Consumer Research, 37*(1), 15–36.

Schelling, T. C. (2006 (1978)). *Micromotives and Macrobehavior*. New York: W.W. Norton.

Schmidt-Rost, R. (1988). *Seelsorge Zwischen Amt und Beruf. Studien zur Entwicklung einer Modernen Evangelischen Seelsorgelehre seit dem 19. Jahrhundert*. Göttingen: Vandenhoeck & Ruprecht.

Schnegg, B. (1988). Frauenerwerbsarbeit in der vorindustriellen Gesellschaft. In M.-L. Barben & E. Ryter (eds), *Verflixt und zugenäht!: Frauenberufsbildung – Frauenerwerbsarbeit; 1888–1988* (pp. 23–34). Zürich: Chronos.

Schneuwly Purdie, M., Gianni, M., & Magali, J. (2009). *Musulmans d'aujourd'hui. Identités plurielles en Suisse*. Genève: Labor et Fides.

Schranz, M., & Imhof, K. (2002). Muslime in der Schweiz – Muslime in der öffentlichen Kommunikation. Medienheft, Katholischer Mediendienst, Reformierte Medien.

Schulz von Thun, F. (1998). *Miteinander reden: 3. Das 'Innere Team' und situationsgerechte Kommunikation*. Reinbek bei Hamburg: Rowohlt.

Schulze, G. (1995). *Die Erlebnisgesellschaft. Kultursoziologie der Gegenwart*. Frankfurt: Campus Verlag.

Schumacher, B. (2012). Coolness (at) home. Der Kühlschrank und die eiskalte revolution am heimischen Herd. In T. Buomberger & P. Pfrunder (eds), *Schöner leben, mehr haben. Die 50er Jahre in der Schweiz im Geiste des Konsums* (pp. 69–83). Zürich: Limmat Verlag.

Schweitzer, A. (1966). *Geschichte der Leben-Jesu-Forschung. Band 1*. Tübingen: J.C.B. Mohr.

Schweizer, P. (1972). *Freisinnig – Positiv – Religiössozial*. Zürich: Theologischer Verlag Zürich.

Schweizerisches Pastoralsoziologisches Institut. (ed.). (1986). *Junge Eltern reden über Religion und Kirche. Ergebnisse einer mündlichen Befragung*. Zürich: NZN Buchverlag.

Schwinn, T., Kroneberg, C., & Greve, J. (2011). *Soziale Differenzierung. Handlungstheoretische Zugänge in der Diskussion*. Wiesbaden: VS Verlag für Sozialwissenschaften.

Sengers, E. (2009). Marketing in Dutch mainline congregations: What religious organizations offer and how they do it. *Journal of Contemporary Religion, 25*(1), 21–35.

Sharma, R., & Jenny, M. (2009). *Heilerinnen und Heiler in der Deutschschweiz. Magnetopathen, Gebetsheiler, Einrenker*. Lausanne: Favre.

Siegenthaler, H. (1987). Die Schweiz 1914–1984. In W. et al. Fischer (ed.), *Handbuch der Europäischen Wirtschafts- und Sozialgeschichte* (pp. 489–511). Stuttgart: Klett-Cotta.

Siegers, P. (2012). Alternative Spiritualitäten: neue Formen des Glaubens in Europa: eine empirische Analyse. Akteure und Strukturen. Studien zur vergleichenden empirischen Sozialforschung 1. Frankfurt/New York: Campus.

Simon, H. A. (1983). *Reason in Human Affairs*. Stanford, California: Stanford University Press.

Singh, S., & Ernst, E. (2008). *Trick or Treatment? Alternative Medicine on Trial*. London: Bantam Press.

Skenderovic, D., & Späti, C. (2012). *Les Années 68. Une Rupture Politique et Culturelle*. Lausanne: Editions Antipodes & Société d'Histoire de la Suisse romande.

Smart, N. (1973). *The Science of Religion and the Sociology of Knowledge*. Princeton: Princeton University Press.

Smith, C. (2003a). Introduction. Rethinking the secularization of American public life. In C. Smith (ed.), *The Secular Revolution. Power, Interests, and Conflict in the Secularization of American Public Life* (pp. 1–96). Berkeley: University of California Press.

Smith, C. (ed.). (2003b). *The Secular Revolution. Power, Interests, and Conflict in the Secularization of American Public Life*. Berkeley: University of California Press.

Späni, M. (2003). The Organization of Public Schools along Religous Lines and the End of the Swiss Confessional States. *Archives de sciences sociales des religions, 121*(janvier-mars), 101–114.

Spickard, J. V. (1995). Body, nature and culture in spiritual healing. In H. Johannessen (ed.), *Studies of Alternative Therapy 2: Bodies and Nature* (Vol. http://newton.uor.edu/FacultyFolder/Spickard/BodyNat.htm, pp. 65–81). Copenhagen: INRAT / Odense University Press.

Spickard, J. V. (2007). Micro qualitative approaches to the sociology of religion: Phenomenologies, interviews, narratives, and ethnographies. In J. Beckford & N. J. Demerath III (eds), *Handbook of the Sociology of Religion* (pp. 104–127): London: Sage.

SPSS Inc. (2001). The SPSS TwoStep Cluster Component. A scalable component enabling more efficient customer segmentation. White paper – technical report, TSCWP-01§01.

Stapferhaus Lenzburg (1997). *A Walk on the Wild Side: Jugendszenen der Schweiz von den 30er Jahren bis heute*. Zürich: Chronos.

Stark, R. (1999a). Atheism, faith, and the social scientific study of religion. *Journal of Contemporary Religion, 14*(1), 41–62.

Stark, R. (1999b). Secularization, R.I.P. *Sociology of Religion, 60*(3), 249–73.

Stark, R., & Bainbridge, W. S. (1985). *The future of religion*. Berkeley: University of California Press, Ltd.

Stark, R., & Bainbridge, W. S. (1989). *A Theory of Religion*. New York: Peter Lang.

Stark, R., & Iannaccone, L., R. (1994). A supply-side reinterpretation of the 'Secularization of Europe'. *Journal for the Scientific Study of Religion, 33*(3), 230–52.

Stolz, F. (2001). *Weltbilder der Religionen. Kultur und Natur; Diesseits und Jenseits; Kontrollierbares und Unkontrollierbares*. Zürich: Pano Verlag.

Stolz, J. (2000). *Soziologie der Fremdenfeindlichkeit. Theoretische und empirische Analysen*. Frankfurt/Main: Campus.

Stolz, J. (2006a). Explaining islamophobia. A test of four theories based on the case of a Swiss city. *Schweizerische Zeitschrift für Soziologie, 31*(3), 547–66.

Stolz, J. (2006b). Salvation goods and religious markets: Integrating rational choice and weberian perspectives. *Social Compass, 53*(1), 13–32.

Stolz J. (2007) *Salvation Goods and Religious Markets. Theory and Applications*, Bern, New York: Peter Lang.

Stolz, J. (2009). Wie kann man Religiosität erklären? Ein allgemeines Modell. In R. Schützeichel & C. Ludwig (eds), *Religion in der Moderne. Studienbrief der FernUniversität in Hagen* (Vol. Juillet). Hagen.

Stolz, J. (2009a). Explaining religiosity: Towards a unified theoretical model. *British Journal of Sociology, 60*(2), 345–76.

Stolz, J. (2009b). A silent battle. Theorizing the effects of competition between churches and secular institutions. *Review of Religious Research, 51*(3), 253–76.

Stolz, J. (2011). 'All things are possible'. Towards a sociological explanation of Pentecostal miracles and healings. *Sociology of Religion, 72*(4), 456–82.

Stolz, J. (2012). Religion und Individuum unter dem Vorzeichen religiöser Pluralisierung. In C. Bochinger (ed.), *Religionen, Staat und Gesellschaft. Die Schweiz zwischen Säkularisierung und Religiöser Vielfalt* (pp. 77–108). Zürich: NZZ.

Stolz, J. (2013). Entwurf einer Theorie religiös-säkularer Konkurrenz. *Kölner Zeitschrift für Soziologie und Sozialpsychologie, 65*(Sonderheft 1), 25–49. doi: 10.1007/s11577-013-0217-6

Stolz, J. (2015). Opening the black box. How the study of social mechanisms can benefit from the use of explanatory mixed methods. *Analyse & Kritik, 37* (1), forthcoming.

Stolz, J., & Ballif, E. (2010). *Die Zukunft der Reformierten. Gesellschaftliche Megatrends – kirchliche Reaktionen*. Zürich: TVZ.Stolz, J., & Baumann, M. (2007). Religiöse Vielfalt und moderne Gesellschaft. In dies. (ed.), *Eine Schweiz – viele Religionen. Risiken und Chancen des Zusammenlebens* (pp. 67–86). Bielefeld: Transcript.

Stolz, J., & Sanchez, J. (2000). from new age to alternative spirituality. Remarks on the Swiss case. In M. Moravcikova (ed.), New Age (pp. 530–45). Bratislava: Ústav pre vztahy státu a cirkví.

Stolz, J., & Usunier, J.-C. (2013). Religions as brands. New perspectives on the marketization of religion and spirituality. In J.-C. Usunier & J. Stolz (eds), *Religions as Brands. New Perspectives on the Marketization of Religion and Spirituality*. London: Ashgate.

Stolz, J., Chaves, M., Monnot, C., & Amiotte-Suchet, L. (2011). Die religiösen Gemeinschaften in der Schweiz: Eigenschaften, Aktivitäten, Entwicklung. *Schlussbericht. Collectivités religieuses, Etat et société. Programme national de recherche PNR 58.*

Stolz, J., Favre, O., Gachet, C., & Buchard, E. (2012). Le Phénomène Évangélique. A l'intérieur d'un Milieu Compétitif. Genève: Labor et Fides.

Stolz, J., Könemann, J., Schneuwly Purdie, M., & Englberger, T. (2011). Religiosität in der modernen Welt. Bedingungen, Konstruktionen und sozialer Wandel. *Schlussbericht. Collectivités religieuses, Etat et société. Programme national de recherche PNR 58.*

Strahm, R. (1987). *Wirtschaftsbuch Schweiz. Das moderne Grundwissen über Ökonomie und Ökologie in der Schweiz. Ein Arbeitsbuch mit 90 Schaubildern und Kommentaren. Zweite Auflage*. Zürich: Ex Libris Verlag.

Strauss, A. (2003(1987)). *Qualitative Analysis for Social Scientists*. Cambridge: Cambridge University Press.

Streib, H., & Hood, R. W. (2013). Modeling the Religious Field: Religion, Spirituality, Mysticism, and Related World Views. *Implicit Religion, 16*(2), 137–55. doi: 10.1558/imre.v16i2.137

Sullivan W. F and Beaman L. G. (2013) *Varieties of Religious Establishment*. Williston: Ashgate.

Suls, J., & Wheeler, L. (eds). (2000). *Handbook of Social Comparison: Theory and Research*. New York: Kluwer Academic.

Tajfel, H. (1978). *Gruppenkonflikt und Vorurteil: Entstehung u. Funktion sozialer Stereotypen*. Bern: Verlag Hans Huber Bern.

Tashakkori, A., & Teddlie, C. (1998). *Mixed Methodology. Combining Qualitative and Quantitative Approaches.* Thousand Oaks: Sage.

Taylor, C. (2007). *A Secular Age.* Cambridge, MA: The Belknap Press of Harvard University Press.

Theissen, G. (2001). *Der historische Jesus. Ein Lehrbuch. 3. Auflage.* Göttingen: Vandenhock & Ruprecht.

Tönnies, F. (1963 (1887)). *Gemeinschaft und Gesellschaft. Grundbegriffe der reinen Soziologie.* Darmstadt: Wissenschaftliche Buchgesellschaft.

Tschannen, O. (1991). The secularization paradigm: a systematization. *Journal for the Scientific Study of Religion, 30*(4), 395–415.

Van Hove, H. (1999). L'émergence d'un 'Marché Spirituel'. *Social Compass, 46*(2), 161–72.

Vischer, L., Schenker, L., Dellsperger, R., & Fatio, O. (eds). (1995). *Histoire du Christianisme en Suisse. Une Perspective Oecuménique.* Genève: Labor et Fides.

Voas, D. (2004). Religion in Europe – One Theme, Many Variations? *Paper presented at the conference of the Association for the Study of Religion, Economics, and Culture, Kansas City (October).*

Voas, D. (2009). The rise and fall of fuzzy fidelity in Europe. *European Sociological Review, 25*(2), 155–68..

Voas, D., & Bruce, S. (2007). The Spiritual Revolution: Another False Dawn for the Sacred. In K. Flanagan & P. C. Jupp (eds), *A Sociology of Spirituality*, (pp. 43–62): Ashgate.

Voas, D., & Chaves, M. (2014). Is the United States a Counterexample to the Secularization Thesis? Sponsored Talk by Sociology Department of Colloquium Committee and the Informal Seminar in Sociology of Religion.

Voas, D., & Crockett, A. (2005). Religion in Britain: Neither Believing nor Belonging. *Sociology, 39*(1), 11–28.

Voas, D., & Day, A. (2007). Secularity in Great Britain. In B. A. Kosmin & A. Keysar (eds), *Secularism and Secularity: Contemporary International Perspectives* (pp. 95–112). Hartford, CT: Institute for the Study of Secularism in Society and Culture.

Voas, D., & Doebler, S. (2011). Secularization in Europe: Religious change between and within birth cohorts. *Religion and Society in Central and Eastern Europe, 4*(1), 39–62.

Voas, D., Olson, D. V. A., & Crockett, A. (2002). Religious pluralism and participation: Why previous research is wrong. *American Sociological Review, 67*(2), 212–30.

Wallis, R. (1977). *The Road to Total Freedom. A Sociological Analysis of Scientology.* New York: Columbia University Press.

Wallis, R. (1995). Scientology: Therapeutic cult to religious sect. In S. Bruce (ed.), *The Sociology of Religion. Volume II* (pp. 46–57). Aldershot: Edward Elgar Publishing Limited.

Wallis, R., & Bruce, S. (1995). Secularization: The orthodox model. In S. Bruce (ed.), *The sociology of religion* (pp. 693–715). Aldershot: Edward Elgar Publishing Limited.

Warner, R. S. (1993). Work in progress toward a new paradigm for the sociological study of religion in the United States. *American Journal of Sociology, 98*(5), 1044–93.

Weber, M. (1984 (1920)). *Die protestantische Ethik I. Eine Aufsatzsammlung.* Gütersloh: Mohn.

Weber, M. (1985a (1922)). Religionssoziologie (Typen religiöser Vergemeinschaftung) (pp. 245–381). Tübingen: J.C.B. Mohr.

Weber, M. (1985b (1922)). *Wirtschaft und Gesellschaft.* Tübingen: J.C.B. Mohr.

Weber, M. (1988 (1920). Zwischenbetrachtung: Theorie der Stufen und Richtungen religiöser Weltablehnung. In ders. (ed.), *Gesammelte Aufsätze zur Religionssoziologie I* (pp. 536–73). Tübingen: Mohr Siebeck.

Weber, M. (1988 (1922)). Der Sinn der 'Wertfreiheit' der soziologischen und ökonomischen Wissenschaften. In ders. (ed.), *Gesammelte Aufsätze zur Wissenschaftslehre* (pp. 489–540). Tübingen: J.C.B. Mohr (Paul Siebeck).

Weger, K.-H. (1979). *Religionskritik von der Aufklärung bis zur Gegenwart. Autoren-Lexikon von* Adorno bis Wittgenstein. Freiburg im Breisgau: Herder.

Wenzel, U. J. (2007). *Was ist eine gute Religion? Zwanzig Antworten.* München: C. H. Beck.

Willaime, J.-P. (1996). L'accès des femmes au pastorat et la sécularisation du rôle du clerc dans le protestantisme. Archives de *Sciences Sociales des Religions, 95*(juillet-septembre), 29–45.

Willaime, J.-P. (2002). Les pasteures et les mutations contemporaines du rôle du clerc. *CLIO, Histoire, Femmes et Sociétés, 15*, 69–83.

Wilson, B. (1982). *Religion in Sociological Perspective.* Oxford: Oxford University Press.

Wilson, B. R. (1966). *Religion in Secular Society. A Sociological Comment.* London: C.A. Watts & Co.

Wimmer, A. (2008). The making and unmaking of ethnic boundaries: a multilevel process theory. *American Journal of Sociology, 113*(4), 970–1022.

Winzeler, C. (1998). *Strukturen von einer 'anderen Welt'. Bistumsverhältnisse im schweizerischen Bundesstaat 1848–1998, ihr historischer Wandel und ihre Inkulturation.* Freiburg: Universitätsverlag Freiburg.

Winzeler, C. (2005). *Einführung in das Religionsverfassungsrecht der Schweiz.* Freiburg: Schulthess.

Wohlrab-Sahr, M. (2011). Forcierte säkularität oder logiken der aneignung repressiver säkularisierung. In G. Pickel & K. Sammet (eds), *Religion und*

Religiosität im Vereinigten Deutschland. Zwanzig Jahre nach dem Umbruch (pp. 145–63). Wiesbaden: VS Verlag.

Wohlrab-Sahr, M., & Burchardt, M. (2012). Multiple secularities: Toward a cultural sociology of secular modernities. *Comparative Sociology*, *11*, 875–909.

Wohlrab-Sahr, M., & Krüggeler, M. (2000). Strukturelle Individualisierung vs. autonome Menschen oder: Wie individualisiert ist Religion? Replik zu Pollack/Pickel: Individualisierung und religiöser Wandel in der Bundesrepublik Deutschland. *Zeitschrift für Soziologie*, *29*(3), 240–44.

Wohlrab-Sahr, M., Schmidt-Lux, T., & Karstein, U. (2008). Secularization as Conflict. *Social Compass*, *55*(2), 127–39.

Wolf, C. (2008). How secularized is Germany? Cohort and comparative perspectives. *Social Compass*, *55*, 111–26.

Wonnacott, T. H., & Wonacott, R. J. (1990). *Introductory Statistics, 5th Edition*. New York: Wiley.

Woodhead, L. (2007). Why so many women in holistic spirituality? A puzzle revisited. In K. Flanagan & P. C. Jupp (eds), *A Sociology of Spirituality* (pp. 115–26). Aldershot: Ashgate.

Woodhead, L. (2008). Gendering Secularization Theory. *Social Compass*, *55*(2), 187–93.

Yamane, D. (1997). Secularization on trial: In defence of a neosecularization paradigm. *Journal for the Scientific Study of Religion*, *36*(1), 109–22.

Yin, R. K. (2002). *Case Study Research. Design and Methods. 3rd ed*. Newbury Park: Sage Publications.

Zick, A. (1997). *Vorurteile und Rassismus. Eine sozialpsychologische Analyse*. Münster: Waxmann.

Zürcher, B. (2010). Das Wachstum der Schweizer Volkswirtschaft seit 1920. *Die Volkswirtschaft. Das Magazin für Wirtschaftspolitik*, *1*(2), 9–13.

Index